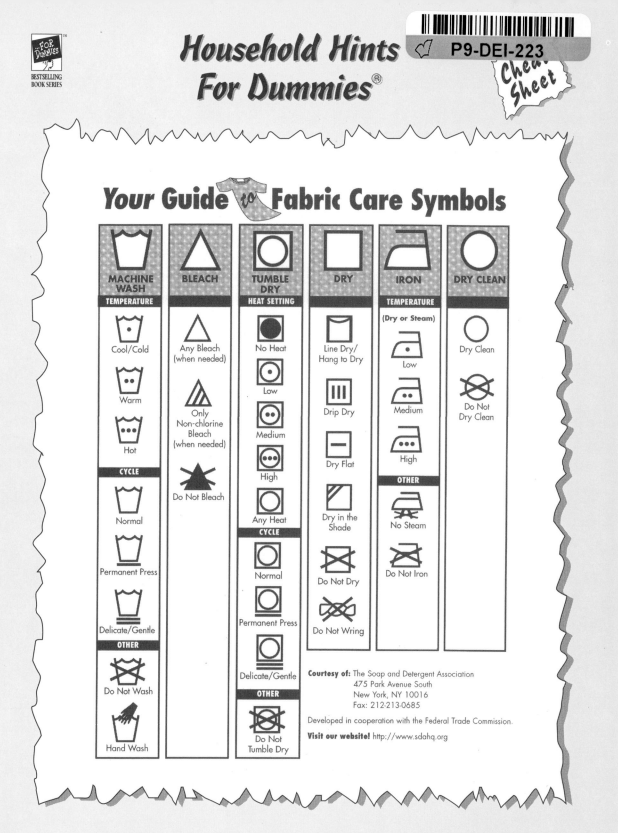

# Your Guide to Fabric Care Symbols

**MACHINE WASH**

TEMPERATURE
- Cool/Cold
- Warm
- Hot

CYCLE
- Normal
- Permanent Press
- Delicate/Gentle

OTHER
- Do Not Wash
- Hand Wash

**BLEACH**
- Any Bleach (when needed)
- Only Non-chlorine Bleach (when needed)
- Do Not Bleach

**TUMBLE DRY**

HEAT SETTING
- No Heat
- Low
- Medium
- High
- Any Heat

CYCLE
- Normal
- Permanent Press
- Delicate/Gentle

OTHER
- Do Not Tumble Dry

**DRY**
- Line Dry/ Hang to Dry
- Drip Dry
- Dry Flat
- Dry in the Shade
- Do Not Dry
- Do Not Wring

**IRON**

TEMPERATURE (Dry or Steam)
- Low
- Medium
- High

OTHER
- No Steam
- Do Not Iron

**DRY CLEAN**
- Dry Clean
- Do Not Dry Clean

**Courtesy of:** The Soap and Detergent Association
475 Park Avenue South
New York, NY 10016
Fax: 212-213-0685

Developed in cooperation with the Federal Trade Commission.

**Visit our website!** http://www.sdahq.org

*...For Dummies®: Bestselling Book Series for Beginners*

# Household Hints For Dummies®

## Casual Cleaning Calendar

No time to clean? Try to stay on top of basic tasks, and you can get your house company-clean in minutes. (You don't need to keep it company-clean if that's not your style; you just want to be able to get it there in a hurry when you need to.) Be rigorous about doing the following tasks on a timely basis:

### Daily

- If you cook: Wash dishes and wipe up counters and cooking areas.
- Sweep kitchen floor.
- Straighten out blankets and sheets on bed, whether or not you do a formal "make-up."
- Wipe down shower walls or sponge off the tub and bathroom sinks.
- Do a clutter check: remove, replace, or discard as appropriate.

### Weekly

- Vacuum carpets.
- Dust open surfaces.
- Change towels and bed linens.
- Clean toilets.
- Damp-mop floors.
- Discard or freeze leftovers from fridge.

### Monthly

- Use a duster with an extension to wipe around ceilings, air vents, curtain and window tops, and other cobweb-producing areas.
- Thoroughly clean one room.

### Quarterly

- Dust bookshelves and knickknacks.
- Wash windows on at least one side of the house, including tracks.
- Use crevice attachment where rugs meet walls, or remove dust and dirt from floor edges with a damp rag.
- Clean at least one closet.

### Semi-Annually

- Clean refrigerator coils.
- Change furnace filters.
- Change batteries in smoke detectors.
- Vacuum draperies.

### Annually

- Shampoo carpets.
- Clean out garage, basement, or junk room.

IDG
BOOKS
WORLDWIDE

## ...For Dummies®: Bestselling Book Series for Beginners

# Praise for Household Hints For Dummies

"Anyone who wants to make more time in their life for fun things should read Janet Sobesky's tips on getting both yourself and your house organized. They are logical, they are easy, and best of all, they work!"

— Pamela M. Abrahams, Senior Editor, Home Building and Architecture, *Country Living* magazine

"When you absolutely must clean up your act, *Household Hints For Dummies* will show you how to do it with style, humor, and common sense. From guides for the organizationally challenged to the lowdown on dirt, Janet Sobesky can help anyone become neater, cleaner, and better organized."

— Laura Green, coauthor of *Reinventing Home*

"On every page, there's some household hint or bit of advice that will have you saying, 'Why didn't I think of that?' Janet is an absolute master of tips, and this book shows her at her very best. A must!"

— Jane Chesnutt, Editor-in-Chief, *Woman's Day* magazine

"Help is here! Janet Sobesky's *Household Hints For Dummies* not only will make your life easier, but provides simple and practical ways to streamline *any* housework. If you would rather be doing something else, then this book is for you."

— Gale Steves, Editor-in-Chief, *HOME* magazine

"*Household Hints For Dummies* is packed with solid information. I found useful tips on every page. A 'must' for the home library of anyone who keeps house."

— Elaine Martin Petrowski, freelance writer and author of *Dream Kitchen*

# ...FOR DUMMIES™

# *References for the Rest of Us!*™

## BESTSELLING BOOK SERIES

Do you find that traditional reference books are overloaded with technical details and advice you'll never use? Do you postpone important life decisions because you just don't want to deal with them? Then our *...For Dummies®* business and general reference book series is for you.

*...For Dummies* business and general reference books are written for those frustrated and hard-working souls who know they aren't dumb, but find that the myriad of personal and business issues and the accompanying horror stories make them feel helpless. *...For Dummies* books use a lighthearted approach, a down-to-earth style, and even cartoons and humorous icons to dispel fears and build confidence. Lighthearted but not lightweight, these books are perfect survival guides to solve your everyday personal and business problems.

> *"More than a publishing phenomenon, 'Dummies' is a sign of the times."*
>
> — The New York Times

> *"...you won't go wrong buying them."*
>
> — Walter Mossberg, Wall Street Journal, on IDG Books' ...For Dummies books

> *"A world of detailed and authoritative information is packed into them..."*
>
> — U.S. News and World Report

Already, millions of satisfied readers agree. They have made *...For Dummies* the #1 introductory level computer book series and a best-selling business book series. They have written asking for more. So, if you're looking for the best and easiest way to learn about business and other general reference topics, look to *...For Dummies* to give you a helping hand.

**IDG BOOKS WORLDWIDE®**

1/99

# HOUSEHOLD HINTS FOR DUMMIES®

## by Janet Sobesky

*Home Design and Lifestyle Editor, Woman's Day*

**IDG**
**BOOKS**
WORLDWIDE

IDG Books Worldwide, Inc.
An International Data Group Company

Foster City, CA ◆ Chicago, IL ◆ Indianapolis, IN ◆ New York, NY

**Household Hints For Dummies**®

Published by
**IDG Books Worldwide, Inc.**
An International Data Group Company
919 E. Hillsdale Blvd.
Suite 400
Foster City, CA 94404
www.idgbooks.com (IDG Books Worldwide Web site)
www.dummies.com (Dummies Press Web site)

Library of Congress Catalog Card No.: 99-62840

ISBN: 0-7645-5141-8

Printed in the United States of America

10 9 8 7 6 5 4 3 2

1O/RS/QV/ZZ/IN

Distributed in the United States by IDG Books Worldwide, Inc.

Distributed by CDG Books Canada Inc. for Canada; by Transworld Publishers Limited in the United Kingdom; by IDG Norge Books for Norway; by IDG Sweden Books for Sweden; by IDG Books Australia Publishing Corporation Pty. Ltd. for Australia and New Zealand; by TransQuest Publishers Pte Ltd. for Singapore, Malaysia, Thailand, Indonesia, and Hong Kong; by Gotop Information Inc. for Taiwan; by ICG Muse, Inc. for Japan; by Norma Comunicaciones S.A. for Colombia; by Intersoft for South Africa; by Le Monde en Tique for France; by International Thomson Publishing for Germany, Austria and Switzerland; by Distribuidora Cuspide for Argentina; by Livraria Cultura for Brazil; by Ediciones ZETA S.C.R. Ltda. for Peru; by WS Computer Publishing Corporation, Inc., for the Philippines; by Contemporanea de Ediciones for Venezuela; by Express Computer Distributors for the Caribbean and West Indies; by Micronesia Media Distributor, Inc. for Micronesia; by Grupo Editorial Norma S.A. for Guatemala; by Chips Computadoras S.A. de C.V. for Mexico; by Editorial Norma de Panama S.A. for Panama; by American Bookshops for Finland. Authorized Sales Agent: Anthony Rudkin Associates for the Middle East and North Africa.

For general information on IDG Books Worldwide's books in the U.S., please call our Consumer Customer Service department at 800-762-2974. For reseller information, including discounts and premium sales, please call our Reseller Customer Service department at 800-434-3422.

For information on where to purchase IDG Books Worldwide's books outside the U.S., please contact our International Sales department at 317-596-5530 or fax 317-596-5692.

For consumer information on foreign language translations, please contact our Customer Service department at 1-800-434-3422, fax 317-596-5692, or e-mail rights@idgbooks.com.

For information on licensing foreign or domestic rights, please phone +1-650-655-3109.

For sales inquiries and special prices for bulk quantities, please contact our Sales department at 650-655-3200 or write to the address above.

For information on using IDG Books Worldwide's books in the classroom or for ordering examination copies, please contact our Educational Sales department at 800-434-2086 or fax 317-596-5499.

For press review copies, author interviews, or other publicity information, please contact our Public Relations department at 650-655-3000 or fax 650-655-3299.

For authorization to photocopy items for corporate, personal, or educational use, please contact Copyright Clearance Center, 222 Rosewood Drive, Danvers, MA 01923, or fax 978-750-4470.

# *About the Author*

**Janet Sobesky** is the Home Design and Lifestyle Editor for *Woman's Day* magazine, where she also edits the incredibly popular "Tip Talk" feature. She appears frequently on radio and television shows such as *Good Morning America* and the Discovery Channel's *Home Matters* as an expert on household maintenance, organization, and decorating.

# ABOUT IDG BOOKS WORLDWIDE

Welcome to the world of IDG Books Worldwide.

IDG Books Worldwide, Inc., is a subsidiary of International Data Group, the world's largest publisher of computer-related information and the leading global provider of information services on information technology. IDG was founded more than 30 years ago by Patrick J. McGovern and now employs more than 9,000 people worldwide. IDG publishes more than 290 computer publications in over 75 countries. More than 90 million people read one or more IDG publications each month.

Launched in 1990, IDG Books Worldwide is today the #1 publisher of best-selling computer books in the United States. We are proud to have received eight awards from the Computer Press Association in recognition of editorial excellence and three from Computer Currents' First Annual Readers' Choice Awards. Our best-selling ...For Dummies® series has more than 50 million copies in print with translations in 31 languages. IDG Books Worldwide, through a joint venture with IDG's Hi-Tech Beijing, became the first U.S. publisher to publish a computer book in the People's Republic of China. In record time, IDG Books Worldwide has become the first choice for millions of readers around the world who want to learn how to better manage their businesses.

Our mission is simple: Every one of our books is designed to bring extra value and skill-building instructions to the reader. Our books are written by experts who understand and care about our readers. The knowledge base of our editorial staff comes from years of experience in publishing, education, and journalism — experience we use to produce books to carry us into the new millennium. In short, we care about books, so we attract the best people. We devote special attention to details such as audience, interior design, use of icons, and illustrations. And because we use an efficient process of authoring, editing, and desktop publishing our books electronically, we can spend more time ensuring superior content and less time on the technicalities of making books.

You can count on our commitment to deliver high-quality books at competitive prices on topics you want to read about. At IDG Books Worldwide, we continue in the IDG tradition of delivering quality for more than 30 years. You'll find no better book on a subject than one from IDG Books Worldwide.

John Kilcullen
Chairman and CEO
IDG Books Worldwide, Inc.

Steven Berkowitz
President and Publisher
IDG Books Worldwide, Inc.

**Eighth Annual Computer Press Awards 1992**

**Ninth Annual Computer Press Awards 1993**

**Tenth Annual Computer Press Awards 1994**

**Eleventh Annual Computer Press Awards 1995**

IDG is the world's leading IT media, research and exposition company. Founded in 1964, IDG had 1997 revenues of $2.05 billion and has more than 9,000 employees worldwide. IDG offers the widest range of media options that reach IT buyers in 75 countries representing 95% of worldwide IT spending. IDG's diverse product and services portfolio spans six key areas including print publishing, online publishing, expositions and conferences, market research, education and training, and global marketing services. More than 90 million people read one or more of IDG's 290 magazines and newspapers, including IDG's leading global brands — Computerworld, PC World, Network World, Macworld and the Channel World family of publications. IDG Books Worldwide is one of the fastest-growing computer book publishers in the world, with more than 700 titles in 36 languages. The "...For Dummies®" series alone has more than 50 million copies in print. IDG offers online users the largest network of technology-specific Web sites around the world through IDG.net (http://www.idg.net), which comprises more than 225 targeted Web sites in 55 countries worldwide. International Data Corporation (IDC) is the world's largest provider of information technology data, analysis and consulting, with research centers in over 41 countries and more than 400 research analysts worldwide. IDG World Expo is a leading producer of more than 168 globally branded conferences and expositions in 35 countries including E3 (Electronic Entertainment Expo), Macworld Expo, ComNet, Windows World Expo, ICE (Internet Commerce Expo), Agenda, DEMO, and Spotlight. IDG's training subsidiary, ExecuTrain, is the world's largest computer training company, with more than 230 locations worldwide and 785 training courses. IDG Marketing Services helps industry-leading IT companies build international brand recognition by developing global integrated marketing programs via IDG's print, online and exposition products worldwide. Further information about the company can be found at www.idg.com.                                                                                     1/24/99

# Dedication

To my mother, who taught me how to clean, and my father, who taught me how to laugh about it, and to my family and friends who had the grace not to say "You're kidding" when they found out I was writing a book about cleaning. And to the many *Woman's Day* readers who've shared their household hints over the years.

# Acknowledgements

Special thanks to Brent Pallas, who provided inspiration, knowledge, and research, and whose drawings for this book added warmth as well as clarity. Thanks also to Martha Olandese for her superb research and writing assistance.

Thanks to the many people who helped with tips and technical advice: to my colleagues at *Woman's Day*, to Kerith McElroy, Alice Lee, and especially Mark Freidbeg for helping me figure out how to use my new computer; they were lifesavers.

The information from the following organizations and manufacturers was invaluable: National Kitchen and Bath Association, Diane Vann at the United States Department of Agriculture, Juvenile Products Manufacturers Association, Paint Quality Institute, International Fabricare Institute, Rowenta USA, The Maids International, The American Society of Home Inspectors, National Electrical Safety Foundation, AARP, Arthritis Foundation, ServiceMaster International, Hardwood Flooring Institute, Oak Flooring Institute, Electronic Industries Association, Jewelry Information Center, Silver Information Center, Leather Apparel Association, and other organizations who shared their wisdom with me.

Special thanks to The Carpet and Rug Institute, the Food Marketing Institute, and The Soap and Detergent Association for permission to reprint some of the information from their brochures.

## Publisher's Acknowledgments

We're proud of this book; please register your comments through our IDG Books Worldwide Online Registration Form located at http://my2cents.dummies.com.

Some of the people who helped bring this book to market include the following:

### Acquisitions and Editorial

**Project Editor:** Kathleen M. Cox

**Acquisitions Editor:** Holly McGuire

**Copy Editors:** Darren Meiss and Gwennette Gaddis

**Technical Editors:** Virginia Hixson and Sue Booker

**Editorial Manager:** Rev Mengle

**Editorial Coordinator:** Maureen Kelly

**Acquisitions Coordinator:** Jonathan Malysiak

**Editorial Assistant:** Jamila Pree

### Production

**Project Coordinators:** E. Shawn Aylsworth, Valery Bourke, Maridee Ennis

**Layout and Graphics:** Linda Boyer, Thomas R. Emrick, Chris Herner, Angela F. Hunckler, Dave McKelvey, Anna Rohrer, Jacque Schneider, Brent Savage, Janet Seib, Mike Sullivan, Brian Torwelle,

**Illustrator:** Brent Pallas, Ternion Design

**Proofreaders:** Jennifer Mahern, Nancy Price, Rebecca Senninger, Kathleen Sparrow, Ethel M. Winslow, Janet M. Withers

**Indexer:** Christine Spina

**Special Help**
Copy editors Rowena Rappaport and Jerelind Charles; senior project editor Pamela Mourouzis

### General and Administrative

**IDG Books Worldwide, Inc:** John Kilcullen, CEO; Steven Berkowitz, President and Publisher

**IDG Books Technology Publishing:** Brenda McLaughlin, Senior Vice President and Group Publisher

**Dummies Technology Press and Dummies Editorial:** Diane Graves Steele, Vice President and Associate Publisher; Mary Bednarek, Director of Acquisitions and Product Development; Kristin A. Cocks, Editorial Director

**Dummies Trade Press:** Kathleen A. Welton, Vice President and Publisher; Kevin Thornton, Acquisitions Manager

**IDG Books Production for Dummies Press:** Michael R. Britton, Vice President of Production and Creative Services; Cindy L. Phipps, Manager of Project Coordination, Production Proofreading, and Indexing; Shelley Lea, Supervisor of Graphics and Design; Debbie J. Gates, Production Systems Specialist; Robert Springer, Supervisor of Proofreading; Debbie Stailey, Production Control Manager; Tony Augsburger, Supervisor of Reprints and Bluelines

**Dummies Packaging and Book Design:** Patty Page, Manager, Promotions Marketing

◆

The publisher would like to give special thanks to Patrick J. McGovern, without whom this book would not have been possible.

◆

# Contents at a Glance

# Cartoons at a Glance

## By Rich Tennant

Fax: 978-546-7747 • E-mail: the5wave@tiac.net

# Table of Contents

## *Part IV: Home Troubleshooting* ...........................*221*

# Introduction

• • • • • • • • • • • • • • • • • • • • • • • • • • • • • • • • • • • • • • • • • •

*P*robably somewhere high on the list of life's unfortunate necessities is cleaning. There are people out there, I know, who relish it, just as I know there are others who vanish at the sight of a vacuum. But no matter what kind of house or apartment we live in and how many nifty appliances we own, dishes still get dirty, clothes still need to be cleaned, furniture still gets scratched, and dust and grime still collect. And whether we do it ourselves or hire someone, housekeeping chores just have to get done eventually.

## Housekeeping for the Millennium

Everybody has different standards of cleanliness. To some, it's clean as long as dirt is out of sight. Others won't rest until they have swept away every bit of dust under the refrigerator and on top of each door jamb. Most of us fall somewhere in between. But we all share an overabundance of tasks and underabundance of time to do them in. As we march into the millennium taking charge of our lives and expanding our horizons, we may find ourselves spending less time at home but wanting home to be more orderly and restful than it can possibly be without a little attention from us. And we want that attention to be minimal.

Most of us would really like a spic-and-span home but somehow can't seem to find the time, the tools, or the inclination to get it done. We think about it, read about it, and buy things that are supposed to make it easier. But the actual doing of it often gets put off until sheer necessity drives us into action: Your relatives are visiting, you're having a dinner party, your roommates are going to kick you out, or you can't get to the bed in your kid's room.

We too often see housekeeping as a chore rather than a vocation. And many of us forget to appreciate the beauty and serenity of a clean and orderly household. Housekeeping brings order out of chaos, an activity than gives relatively instant gratification. Who doesn't feel good when they look at a newly washed floor, put on a freshly ironed shirt, or sit in a nicely polished chair. Projects at the office can go on for weeks before we get any feedback, but a well-organized kitchen makes us feel good everytime we cook.

My goal in writing this book is to give you simple tools and techniques to keep your home in the shape you want it to be. You may never get to the point where you think that cleaning is fun ( I don't know that I ever will), but at least you'll get a kick out of finding the fastest, easiest, and cheapest ways to solving your nagging little household problems.

Just remember, I am not a clean-o-holic. Housekeeping doesn't come natural to me. I have to work at it like everyone else. In fact, when I was growing up my mother used to say that my room looked cleaner before I cleaned it than after. But keeping house is a topic that I never grow tired of. New and creative ways to solve pesky housekeeping problems are always cropping up. And nothing is more satisfying than finding the solution to a problem that's stumped you for a long time.

# Who Should Read This Book

Almost everyone knows something about cleaning. Whether we're aged 10, 25, or 50, we've all had to take care of our surroundings whether it's a small bedroom, an apartment, an office, or a 3,000 square foot home. Some of us may need more help in this area than others, and I wrote this book especially for those of you who do, such as the

- ✔ **Newly away from home:** So your mother took care of all this for you? Guess what, you have to do it yourself now. And maybe you weren't so interested in how it was done as long as it was done. It's time to solve your housekeeping problems yourself.

- ✔ **First-time homeowner or apartment dweller:** You've got a new place and you want to be proud of it. Whether you have new furniture or old hand-me downs, you want to keep it looking good. Even if your place is small, you still have the same kind of upkeep problems as any home-owner —floors to wash, sinks to clean, carpet to vacuum.

- ✔ **Housekeeping-challenged:** Okay, so cleaning the house isn't really your thing. You can't get it right no matter how hard you try. This book gives you surefire techniques to conquer any household problems.

- ✔ **Seeker of a better way:** You know how to take care of your house; you may have done it for years. But you're searching for quicker and easier methods so you can spend less time working and more time enjoying yourself.

# How to Use This Book

Believe me, I know the last thing you want to do is sit down and read a whole book about housekeeping. Beach reading this is not! Instead, leaf through the book and make yourself familiar with all the topics. If you find a something that interests you (or that you feel someone else in the family should know), put a marker on it. If you've got a problem that needs solving right now, go straight to the section.

Feel free to write on it or mark what works for you. And if you find a better way or if you get a good tip from a neighbor, put a note in the margin. Housekeeping and maintenance is a constant process of discovery and tweaking to make it fit your style and energy level.

# What's in This Book

This book is organized in six parts. If you've got a general area you're interested in, sit down with a cup of coffee and read the whole thing. If you're in the laundry room trying to figure out how to get the coffee stain out of your jeans, then head straight for the solutions in the clothes-washing chapter.

## Part I: Creating a Reduced-Stress Household

Getting your house in order usually involves putting some order in your life. Part I lays the foundation for setting up a household that runs smoothly and efficiently. Before you start to clean, you've got to clear out a path to do it. I offer specific ways to get your family organized, get rid of excess stuff, and sort the stuff you want to keep. Is your kitchen overloaded? Don't worry, there's space for it all. I show you where to put even the most awkward items.

## Part II: Keeping Your House and Stuff Clean

These are the nitty gritty basics in this part. Find out what tools and cleaning solutions are best and how to get family members to help you. We answer the age-old question: Do I clean from the top down or bottom up? You learn how to clean everything from windows to walls, floors to carpets, furniture and accessories. Plus it gives you speedy techniques to clean the rooms that always seem to need cleaning: the kitchen and the bathroom.

## Part III: Home Laundry and Clothing Care

You want to look as good as your house, right? Part III tells the best way to wash clothes so they come out sparkling clean. You'll get the facts on how to treat stains and different types fibers. Hate to iron? I show the basics for the novice and treatments for special care items like pleats and heavy fabric. Stumped by minor clothing repairs? This part gives you the answers to stuck zippers, loose buttons, and other simple sewing projects.

# Part IV: Home Troubleshooting

Okay, no matter how organized and clean our homes are, little accidents happen and things still go wrong. This part helps you solve some of those minor household problems that can drive you crazy. Squeaky doors? White rings on furniture? Pictures always tilted? Find the solutions here. If your appliances are giving you problems, I offer simple things to look for before calling the repair man. Even if you're an animal lover, bugs are always unwelcome visitors. I show you how to keep them out and how to get rid of them once they've walked through the door.

# Part V: Home Health and Safety

Keeping your family and home safe is everyone's concern. This part gives you simple techniques to make your home more secure, along with special tips on how to prevent break-ins while you're on vacation. I show how to childproof your home against accidents and give a list of child-friendly products. Are you sneezing or coughing more than usual? Your home and what's in it can make you sick. I give you ways to deal with pollutants, combat allergies, and dispose of toxic substances. Worried about how long to keep food? I provide a checklist that shows how long you can reasonably keep foods in the freezer or on the shelf.

# Part VI: The Part of Tens

Here's a special treat for you. Find out about 10 things you can do around your home quicker than you thought possible and 10 things your kids can do for you around the home. Also, perform a great cleanup if you've got only 10 minutes.

# Let These Icons Guide You

Sprinkled throughout this book are cute little pictures called icons that highlight important information. Here's the decoder key:

This icon points out time-tested ways to get stuff clean with a minimum of muss and fuss.

 This bomb steers you away from strategies that could damage your furnishings or threaten your safety.

 When you want to save money, look for the dollar sign. Some things cost little but work big.

 Sometimes we need time more than money. Watch the clock for tips that help you get back to the good life fast.

 Sometimes you want to know the technology behind the tip — why and how stuff gets clean. Read this when you want to know more than what to do.

This icon marks alternatives to harsh chemicals; look for this when you want to be kind to yourself and your planet.

# Out, Darned Spot! Where to Go from Here

You bought this book to get a handle on your household, to create a haven of order from the chaos in your life. See what you need to tackle first — the task that most frustrates you, the one you never understood, the cleaning task you've always wanted to master (or just get by with). Set small, realistic goals and work toward them steadily and with humor. The dirt is always with you, but you don't need to let it run your life. By developing a few simple habits, you can make a clean sweep. Start now!

# Part I

# Creating a Reduced-Stress Household

If I could just get him to wipe his feet before entering the house, it would cut my cleaning day in half.

# In this part . . .

**G**etting your house in order usually involves putting some order in your life. Part one lays the foundation for setting up a household that runs smoothly and efficiently. Before you start to clean, you've got to clear out a path to do it. Here are the basics of a clean house, specific ways to get yourself and your family organized, and counsel on setting up the most critical room in the house: your kitchen.

# Chapter 1

# The Basics for a Clean House

*I* grew up in a house that was always clean. It wasn't until I lived on my own that I realized how much work it was to keep a house tidy, day in and day out. I always assumed that you cleaned once and it stayed that way for months. I was shocked the first time I washed a floor, and it got dirty a couple hours later when someone stepped on it with muddy shoes.

Cleaning, I'm told, comes naturally to some people. They're the ones who dust the tops of doorways and never have dirty dishes "resting in the sink." But, for most of us, cleaning is an ongoing process of trial and error, mixed with the occasional "lick and a promise." Just like parenting, we're thrust into a situation without any background knowledge. We often go from making our daily bed to being responsible for a whole household full of dirty kitchen floors and grimy bathroom grout. And because most of us didn't follow our mothers around on Saturday morning studying her cleaning techniques, we rely on television commercials and the back of packaged cleaners for instructions.

You'd think that cleaning would be simple. After all, people have been tidying up for centuries without all the cleaning products that we have at our fingertips. Pounding the clothes clean on a rock in the river used to be an all-day task.

The problem today is that, even though the wonders of modern chemistry and technology make cleaning less time-consuming than it used to be, we still don't have the time to wait for the laundry to line dry or to iron handkerchiefs. We're too busy shuttling kids to soccer, or writing reports for work, or freeing our inner child. We still want the pleasures of a clean house, but we want to get it clean quickly, with minimal effort. Well, you can have your house and clean it too, but you need to acquire a few simple techniques and find some practical cleaning products so you'll spend less time cleaning the place and more time having fun in it.

# Keeping Messes at Bay

Preventing problems before they start is smart, no matter what we're doing. If only we watched what we ate or exercised regularly, we wouldn't have to worry about those extra pounds, but that's another book. As far as cleaning is concerned, stopping messes before they start will save you both time and money. A spotless house may be only a dream for many of us, but you can at least get a head start on the mess. This section gives you some ideas on ways to keep messes from starting:

- Put wastebaskets in every room for easy disposal of messes when they happen.
- Install a kitchen fan over the stove and dispose of almost 200 pounds of grease annually. Be sure to clean the filter regularly.
- Put a rubber mat under your pet's food to keep the dishes from moving and stop messes from soiling the floor.
- Use coasters on furniture to prevent water marks and other stains.
- Put self-stick felt bottoms on the legs of chairs, sofas, tables, or other objects that could scratch floors or tables.
- Put mats inside and outside of all doors that lead into the house.
- Wipe up spills immediately to prevent stains and the need for excessive scrubbing.
- Put saucers under all plants so that no water or dirt falls to the floor.
- Spray fabric protector on household linens and upholstery. (Read the label and test on a small portion of fabric in a hidden area first.)
- Put liners in drawers and shelves.

# Cleaning the Right Way

Do you feel as if you clean and clean, but never get the results you want? Are you spending too much time cleaning for too little reward?

You may be doing all the right things but you may not be doing them in the smartest, most efficient way. You need to become your own cleaning professional. Cleaning professionals use some incredible methods to whip through a house. Out of necessity, they've developed lots of clever, time-saving techniques. After all, if you had to clean all day, every day, you'd find the best ways to get it done right *and* get it done fast. Take a look at some of the methods that the professionals use.

## Declutter before you clean

Not only do all those papers and shoes on the floor look messy, but they are separating you from the real dirt. Vacuuming the rug is impossible if it's covered with other stuff. Do this first: Make a quick circle around the room and pick up the magazines, stray shoes, toys, purses, and so on. Put them in a box to deal with later. Then go for the dust rag and the vacuum. The job will be much easier to accomplish.

## Organize your cleaning supplies

Save steps and find a way to carry your brushes, rags, whisks, and cleaning solutions with you all at once. Try a bucket, an apron full of pockets, a child's wagon, a plastic caddy, whatever works best for you. Just don't waste time running to the kitchen to get the soap while you're cleaning the bathroom. If you have the room, you may want to leave a set of cleaning supplies in the rooms that you clean often, like the kitchen and bathroom, so you'll have them at your fingertips.

## Dos and don'ts for getting things clean

Before you drag out your high school chemistry book to attack spots and spills, remember that all chemicals, even those used in household cleaners, can be harmful if not used properly. Always read all labels and follow the manufacturer's instructions. Use these precautions when using any cleaning solutions around your home:

- ✔ **Don't** mix a chlorine bleach product with any cleanser containing ammonia. Many tub and tile cleaners, all-purpose cleaners, powdered cleansers, and automatic dishwasher detergents contain chlorine bleach. Liquid dishwashing detergents and window and floor cleaners often contain ammonia. Mixed together, even in small amounts, bleach and ammonia can emit dangerous gases. A bleach product used *after* an ammonia product can also emit fumes unless the ammonia is thoroughly rinsed off first. Products that are safe when used alone can be dangerous when mixed with other products.

- ✔ **Don't** save old cleaning product bottles and reuse them for any other purpose. Reactions can occur between the product left in the bottle and the chemicals in the new mixture. Instructions that are printed on the bottle for the old product can be misleading or even dangerous for the new mixture.

- ✔ **Do** always open the windows or doors and make sure the room is well ventilated when working with chemical cleaners. Some fumes are merely unpleasant, but others can cause injury to lungs and nasal passages.

## For the obsessively organized or the totally unorganized

Need a new system? If you can't quite seem to get all your chores finished or you just want to keep better track of what you need to do, try this trick. Make up a cleaning schedule with times for each chore and write each task on an index card. Cards may read: "Monday: wash kitchen, 20 minutes," "Tuesday: dust knickknacks, 15 minutes," and so on. Or write the schedule on a calendar so that you can look at a week's worth or a month's worth of cleaning duties. If you don't want to do a certain chore as scheduled on one day or if you don't have time, exchange it for something else. This helps you remember what needs to be done and helps you to plan your chores in advance.

✔ **Don't** buy a different cleaning product for every single job in the house. An all-purpose liquid cleaner mixed with water can be used for countertops, faucets, appliances, cooktops, tile, window blinds, small plastic appliances, resilient flooring, but can damage TVs or electronic equipment. Ammonia can also be used on floors, windows, painted woodwork, faucets but not on plastic windows, aluminum storm door windows or electronic equipment. Be sure to read the label on the bottle to see what the manufacturer recommends. Always test in an inconspicuous place before using a new cleaner.

✔ **Do** give the cleaning solution a chance to work. It's human nature to spray something with cleaner and attack it immediately with a sponge or scrubber, but modern cleaning solutions are designed to give better results when they're given time to soak into the dirt and grime.

Perform this little test: Spray some cleaner on a burnt bit of grime on the stove. Don't try to wipe it immediately, or you'll have to scrub hard. Instead, let the solution sit for a few minutes. The dirt will soften up and wipe away with little effort. Be patient and do something else while the cleaner does the work. Just be sure to get back to it before the liquid dries up.

✔ **Don't** drench the spot. Read product labels and use the amount recommended on the bottle. Using double the amount of liquid recommended won't give you double the amount of cleaning power. You'll just spend more time rinsing and wiping.

✔ **Don't** clean *everything* every time you clean. Look for what's dirty and work on that. What's the point in washing every kitchen cabinet if only the door handles are smudged? Your house will still look clean and you can cut several minutes (and maybe hours) off your cleaning time.

# A Cabinet Full of Cleaners

Walk down the aisles of any grocery or discount store, and your eyes can glaze over at the number of different types of cleaners. You can spend hours just reading the labels. But don't worry. You need only a few to help you clean just about everything around the house. Keep these basics (and a few not-so-basics) stocked in your cleaning cabinet.

## Chemical cleaners

Here are the basic cleaners you should have. Your grocery store carries many different brands. Ask your friends what they use and read the label carefully to see exactly what each contains. Experiment and see which works best for your cleaning style.

- **All-purpose liquid cleaner:** Use on large surfaces such as the floor, countertops, shower stalls, laminated cabinets, tile, appliances, and woodwork. These products usually come in a spray bottle or in a concentrated liquid form that you can mix with water for bigger jobs.

- **Ammonia:** This heavy-duty cleaning product is effective for cleaning a multitude of items around the home. It comes in both plain (without color or fragrance) and sudsy formulas. Plain ammonia mixed with water in small amounts is good for cleaning glass and mirrors because it rinses off completely. In stronger solutions, it can get rid of grease and stains on range burners, ovens, and windows, and can strip wax from floors. The sudsy ammonia, with soap added, works well on garbage pails, kitchen burners, and sinks.

  Ammonia is poisonous and the odor and fumes can be irritating, so use it in mild amounts in a well-ventilated area, and wear rubber gloves. Rinse thoroughly and as quickly as possible.

- **Bleach:** Familiar for laundry use, bleach is also good for removing stains on hard surfaces such as grout or porcelain and as a disinfectant to kill bacteria and fungi, including mold and mildew. See "Dos and don'ts for getting things clean," earlier in this chapter, before you mix any bleach solution.

- **Borax:** This is a water-soluble, salt-type product that works as a household deodorizer and cleaner. Used in the laundry, it can help to loosen stains and soil.

- **Disinfectant cleaner:** This type of cleaner removes soil and contains antimicrobial agents. (Pine oil is one that you may be familiar with.) Use these to kill bacteria and germs on countertops, cutting boards, toilets, and so on.

- **Glass cleaner:** These cleaners are light-duty liquids designed to clean without streaking. Use on glass, kitchen countertops, appliances, mirrors, and so on.

✔ **WD-40:** Yes, WD-40. Don't ask me why, but it works like magic to remove crayon from a variety of surfaces, cleans sticky surfaces, removes soap scum from bathtubs and showers, takes off stickers and adhesives from glass, and performs a host of other tasks. It is flammable, so be sure to use it away from any heat sorce and in a well-ventilated area.

Like my mother before me, I always use rubber gloves when I'm using any chemical or harsh cleaner. Buy a sturdy pair that you'll be comfortable using. Be sure to get them slightly larger than your hands so that they won't stick to your hands when wet.

## Natural cleaners

As Dorothy said, sometimes what we need is right in our own backyard. Look in your kitchen cabinets for some very effective cleaners.

✔ **Baking soda:** Besides absorbing odors in refrigerators and freezers, baking soda makes a good scouring powder (because of its mild abrasiveness) to remove light soil and stains on sinks, counters, and stovetops. Mixed with water, it makes an all-around, light-duty cleaner, and used full strength, it can keep drains clear.

✔ **White vinegar:** A mild acid, vinegar is a good all-purpose cleaner and deodorizer. Mixed with water, it cuts grease and dissolves film on glassware and windows. A little salt and vinegar can remove tarnish from copper and rust stains from sinks.

✔ **Lemon juice:** Also a mild acid, lemon juice can remove tarnish and mineral stains, and cut grease.

✔ **Club soda:** Many people swear by club soda to remove wine stains, shine tile, and clean windows.

✔ **Salt:** A mild abrasive, salt can be used to absorb grease or wine stains. Mixed with vinegar or lemon juice, it cleans copper and brass.

## Homemade cleaners

Plenty of good cleaners on the market can attack a myriad of stains and dirt, but you can make cheaper and more eco-friendly cleaners at home. Make sure that you clearly label your homemade cleaners. Don't put them in a recognizable food containers where folks could mistake the cleaner for food. List the names and amounts of ingredients and directions for use and use a skull and crossbones or some other symblo to warn users. You want to make sure that the rest of the family knows that it's a chemical cleaner and not water or lemonade.

- **All-purpose cleaner:** Mix ½ cup ammonia, ½ cup white vinegar, ¼ cup baking soda, and 1 gallon water.

    Or mix ½ cup baking soda and 2 quarts water.

- **Mirror cleaner:** Mix 2 cups isopropyl rubbing alcohol, 2 tablespoons liquid dishwashing detergent, and 2 cups water. Pour into a spray bottle.

- **Toilet bowl cleaner:** Pour ½ cup chlorine bleach into bowl and let stand for 10 minutes. Scrub with toilet brush and flush.

- **Oven cleaner:** Put 1 cup ammonia in a glass or ceramic bowl. Put the bowl on the bottom of a cold oven and leave it in the closed oven overnight. The next morning, pour the ammonia into a pail of warm water and use this solution and a sponge to wipe away the loosened grime. Wear rubber gloves. Be careful of the fumes. They are very strong when you first open the oven.

- **Bathtub and tile cleaner:** Mix 1 cup vinegar in 1 gallon warm water. Spray a small area. Leave spray on for 1 minute, and then wipe off with clear water.

    Or mix ½ cup vinegar, 1 cup clear ammonia, ¼ cup baking soda, and 1 gallon water.

- **Plastic laminate and appliance scrubber:** Sprinkle baking soda on a damp sponge, rub the stain, and wipe off the surface with a damp cloth.

- **Floor cleaner:** Mix ½ cup vinegar, and 1 gallon warm water. Wear rubber gloves.

# Arming Yourself with the Right Tools

A workman may blame his tools for a job poorly done, but it really does help to have the right equipment at hand when you're doing any job. The tools for cleaning are nothing high tech, but good quality, sturdy supplies will make the job easier. And more fun too! Buying a new piece of equipment can even inspire you to clean.

## Brooms, brushes, and buckets

I've bought many bristle brooms in the past because I assumed that natural was better. But after seeing the trail of straw that many of these brooms leave on the floor, I now opt for an angled synthetic model. They can reach easily into small corners, and their bristles are slightly flared on the bottom to pick up dirt and dust easily.

A small hand-held whisk broom is a good daily tool for quick pick-ups of dirt on chairs, upholstered furniture, floors, and the edges of rugs.

Sometimes you have to scrub, and a good brush is your best friend. I carry three brushes while cleaning.

- For spot cleaning floors and flat surfaces, I use an oval synthetic bristle model with a comfortable handle.

- In the bathroom, a grout brush can't be beat for scrubbing mildew and dirt in grout and cleaning behind the faucet and drain in the bathtub. A grout brush is a stiff synthetic brush that looks like a large toothbrush.

- For getting into small spaces, the ever-present toothbrush is a necessary tool. Use it where you want a soft bristle — behind stove knobs or under the handles on kitchen cabinets.

My favorite brand brushes are from OXO GOOD GRIPS. They have rubber ergonomically styled handles that cushion your hands no matter how hard you scrub and are easy to grip no matter how wet your hands are. They're great for people who have arthritis or other problems gripping.

To hold your cleaning solutions, get a heavy-duty plastic bucket with a sturdy handle. Many professional cleaners recommend using two buckets for cleaning jobs. One holds the cleaning solution. The second bucket is used for rinsing the sponge. This method keeps the cleaning fluid fresher. You might want to get each one in a different color so you know at a glance which is the rinse and which is the cleaner.

If you've got a broom, you also need a dustpan. Get one with a slightly sloping edge and flexible vinyl lip so it's easy to sweep dirt into it. A nice luxury: a long handle so you don't have to bend over.

## Cleaning cloths and sponges

If you want to see proof of the great hereafter, look inside someone's rag bag. All manner of old clothes and socks lie there. They can be reincarnated into wonderful cleaning cloths at any minute, but remember that some work better than others. High on the list are 100 percent cotton, soft, lintless cloths. Cloth diapers are among my favorites. (My sister gives me a couple dozen as a Christmas present every year.) I like socks too because they're easy to hold onto—just slip them over your hands. Old T-shirts or cotton flannel pajamas are good candidates. Best are white or light colored fabrics that won't bleed color when they get wet.

I use sponges for most cleaning jobs because they absorb more cleaning fluid than cloths, yet they drip less and are much neater to wring out. A few different kinds will cover most cleaning jobs.

- Get a regular cellulose sponge for working on large surfaces such as walls or kitchen cabinets.

- ✔ For scrubbing, get a sponge with an abrasive nylon backing.
- ✔ For most surfaces that have a tendency to scratch, the least abrasive white backing will be sufficient.

Use different colored sponges for different jobs: yellow for dishes, green for floors, blue for the bathroom, and so on.

Be sure to clean your sponges after each use. They can absorb and spread around more germs than you want to think about. Squeeze them in some warm water and liquid dishwasher detergent after each use and let dry. Or pop them into the dishwasher every time you do a load. Anchor your sponges on the top shelf between some glasses. The hot water will help to sterilize them. Toss out your sponges if they have a strong odor or if they're falling apart.

## Rubber gloves

Like my mother before me, I always use rubber gloves when I'm using any chemical or harsh cleaner. Buy a sturdy pair that you'll be comfortable using. Be sure to get them slightly larger than your hands so that they won't stick to your hands when wet. Shake a little baby powder inside before you put them on, and they'll be easy to remove. If you are allergic to latex, several companies now make gloves that are as durable as latex but are made out of allergy free materials. (Magla is one brand.)

## Sponge mop

A mop with a replaceable head is good for most everyday cleaning. Before you go shopping for one, measure the width of your bucket and get a sponge head that will fit it easily. Move the wringer up and down to make sure that it operates smoothly. When you purchase a sponge mop, buy a couple of extra replacement heads to eliminate a rush trip to the store when you need a new one.

After you use the mop, wash the head in hot, soapy water and rinse it thoroughly. Hang it by the handle or turn it upside down to prevent any distortion in the sponge from laying it on the floor.

## Vacuum cleaner

A vacuum cleaner is an indispensable item for modern housekeeping. Not only does it keep the rug clean, but with the right attachments, it dusts and cleans from the ceiling to the floor, from the sofa to the shutters.

When you go to purchase a vacuum cleaner, take a test model for a dry run. See how noisy it is and how easy it is to push. Make sure that it has an upholstery brush, a crevice tool, and a round dusting brush. Look for an extra long cord so you can pull it easily from room to room. Buy a machine that other family members will feel comfortable using. Remember that vacuuming is one job the whole family can do. Look for these features when shopping:

✔ **Uprights are the most popular type.** They're great if you have a lot of carpeting because they gently beat and stir up the dirt in carpet fibers so that their powerful motors can suck it up. Most come with hoses and attachments to clean wood floors, furniture, and other household items (see Figure 1-1).

✔ **Canister vacuums work best on hard surface floors and stairs.** They're smaller and easy to maneuver into snug spaces. They're easier to store, an advantage if you live in an apartment and have a small amount of storage space. One note: some people find it awkward pulling the body of the machine around after them. Look for one with a beater bar in the power nozzle for more effective carpet cleaning.

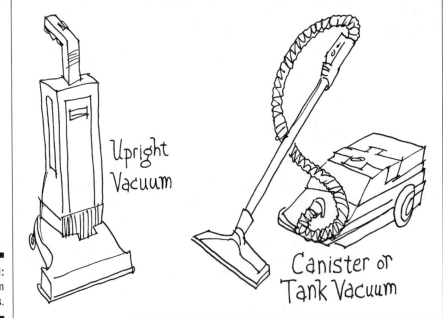

**Figure 1-1:**
Vacuum
cleaners.

✔ **Hand-held cordless vacuums are indispensable for quick spot cleaning and hard-to-reach areas.** I know some people who use nothing but a cordless vacuum and don't seem to mind cleaning the floor on their hands and knees. New models have higher wattage motors for more suction power and some have long handles so you don't have to bend over at all. Even kids find them fun to use. Just make sure you keep them charged up.

# Getting Help from the Troops

When I was young, my father always said that we didn't need an automatic dishwasher because we already had four in the house (my three siblings and me). I didn't think it was very funny at the time, but it was somewhat true. Kids should help with chores, but you can make it more palatable for them. This section gives you some ideas for getting your kids involved in cleaning.

✔ **Make a list:** Write down all the jobs that need to be done and post the list in a prominent place. That visual aid eliminates any pleas of ignorance from family members and cuts down on the need to nag and explain. The list can be as simple or as complicated as you like, depending on your energy level and artistic skill. Describe the task and the amount of time that performing it should take. If the job is a general category, such as "clean the family room," list all the tasks that are involved: vacuum the floor, dust the furniture, pick up the magazines off the floor, polish the clock, and so on. This leaves no room for guesswork as to exactly what needs to be done.

✔ **Assign the tasks:** Cleaning isn't one of those just-can't-wait-to-do activities. Someone has to get the ball rolling and figure out who's going to do what. Otherwise, you can discuss and argue about it forever while the house keeps getting dirtier. You have a couple of choices: If you have a democratic household, you can ask people what they want to do. Or have a mini lottery: List all the jobs and their skill level (1, 2, or 3) on small pieces of paper and let everyone pick two or three jobs each week. If they don't like what they got, they can trade back and forth. Or just be old-fashioned and assign them tasks according to their skill level. Be sure to rotate the jobs frequently. Your family will be more challenged if they're trying something new.

✔ **Show kids the ropes:** Most children don't have a clue how to clean things — or care for that matter. It's important that you spend some time teaching them exactly what you want done for each task. Be really specific: what sponge to use, which things to dust, how to load the dishwasher, and so on. Not only will you spend some time together, but your child will have a positive experience when he does the chore.

✔ **Assess your kids' skills:** Don't expect your child to do something that may frustrate him and end up being more work for you in the end. Every child is different and you've got to tune in to which jobs each will feel comfortable doing.

✔ **Praise your kids:** Everyone likes to hear that her work is worthwhile and appreciated. Look over the job after it's done, and give your kids lots of praise. Be specific and enthusiastic: "I really like the way you made the bed. I couldn't do it that well myself." They'll be more likely to want to do it again if they received positive feedback the first time.

✔ **Start a job incentive program:** Most kids don't have any natural motivation to keep their rooms clean. Aside from praise or the threat that they can't play outside until it's clean, most children would never even notice that the bathroom faucet is dirty, much less get motivated about cleaning it. It helps to offer little rewards for a job well done. (How often do we complain at work if we don't get a good raise?) You can set up pre-arranged awards — maybe $1 for cleaning the basement or 50 cents for sweeping the driveway. Or make a list of things the kids want (video games, more TV privileges, sports activities, sleepovers) and offer coupons that are redeemable for the good stuff. Set up a program for "the worst chore of the week" and give double coupons for performing it well.

If you don't want to give them rewards for a task that you consider their duty, such as cleaning their room, at least give them a bonus for something that's above and beyond their normal activity, such as polishing the car. Make sure that all the jobs are performed to your satisfaction before they get the reward. The point is to set up a system that works for you.

✔ **Have fun:** You should be able to enjoy yourself no matter what you're doing. Let your kids put on their headphones and work their way around the house listening to their favorite music. Or make it a game by giving a prize to the one who cleans the fastest or who picks up the most shoes off the floor. And always save some of the fun jobs around the house for the kids — picking flowers, making placecards for the table, or baking bread.

# Chapter 2

# Getting Organized

. . . . . . . . . . . . . . . . . . . . . . . . . . . . . . . . . . . . . . . . . . . . . . . . .

*In This Chapter*

▶ Getting yourself organized

▶ Getting your family organized

▶ Managing your time

. . . . . . . . . . . . . . . . . . . . . . . . . . . . . . . . . . . . . . . . . . . . . . . . .

You've seen them — people who are incredibly organized. They have that unmistakable look of calm on their faces. In their houses, bills get paid on time, presents arrive on the birthday date, tools are in the toolbox, reading glasses can always be found, and a month's supply of toilet paper is always in the bathroom. It's that state of living that we all yearn for — where everything is under control.

Of course, it's impossible to control everything all the time. But it is possible for even the slobs among us to develop habits that can keep our world from spinning out of control. Past due notices, spaceless tabletops, and paperless toilets are not the keys to a happy life. And the more you let these daily annoyances rob you of the serenity and precious time, the more overwhelmed you will feel and the less you'll be able to accomplish.

Why does it seem easier for some people to get organized than for others? After years of talking to professional organizers and people who are really organized themselves, I've noticed that they all follow the same basic principles. This chapter outlines those principles for you.

## A Place for Everything: Setting the Ground Rules for Organization

I'm sure that your mother told you this time and again: *Have a place for everything and put everything in its place.*

But this maxim really is one you can live by. How can you put something away if you don't know where it goes? Establishing a designated spot for everything is a time saver and a stress saver. You never have to think "Where should I put this so I can find it again?" And your family will find it much easier to neaten up because they know that the soccer balls go in a blue basket in the garage, and the remote control belongs in a basket next to the couch.

## Select a logical place

Where *do* you put everything? Most people have standard places for things: tools and lawn mower in the garage, dinnerware in the kitchen, makeup and nail file in the bathroom. Seems logical.

But what good does having your nail file in the bathroom do if you're always breaking your nails when you wash dishes? How about keeping an extra nail file in a cabinet drawer next to the sink? You can save yourself the aggravation of running to the bathroom when you break a nail.

The point is: Keep things near where you are likely to use them, and you'll not only save time and aggravation looking for them, but you actually might clean up that mess when you make it rather than waiting until you find the right equipment.

Before you can store things near where you'll use them, you have to determine where that is. Most of us put things where our mothers or fathers always kept them, whether that's the best place for us to store them or not. If you always have to travel through the house to get the appliance you need, consider finding another, more convenient storage place. That may call for some creativity. I have a friend who keeps her vacuum cleaner out in her family room, dressed in a maid's costume. That may be extreme, but you get the picture.

## Use it or lose it

Get rid of things that you don't use.

Most of us have developed a million excuses for why we're saving something — "It might be worth something someday," or "My grandmother gave me that." But the truth is this: All that stuff is taking up space and costing you time and money. See Chapter 4 for hints on how to lose it when you don't use it.

## Make a list

Keep lists.

Santa would never make it through the holiday if he didn't make a list and check it at least twice. He has to be organized.

List-making is the hallmark of really organized people. Good lists remind you of errands that you need to run, jobs that you must do, purchases that you need to make, messages that you should deliver, and important dates to remember. But don't get bogged down with too many lists. Two is enough, a Long Term List and a Daily List. The Long Term List is your life story in list form. It contains everything you want to do, have to do, take care of, or buy in the future, along with dates it needs to be done and suggestions of how to go about it. Carry it with you and anytime you think of something you need to do, write it down.

Your Daily List is your immediate-action list. Make it up every morning or the night before if that's more convenient. It should consist of things you want to accomplish that day. Choose items from the Long Term List and immediate deadlines, chores, or appointments. If there's something you automatically do every day like jogging, making your bed, or brushing your teeth, you don't need to write it down. This list is to remind you to do things, not a blow-by-blow diary of your day. Limit the list to what's realistic to accomplish — about 8 to 10 things for most people.

Set priorities and give each task a number. But don't get too bogged down by the numbers. If it's more convenient to do #3 at a certain time before #1, go for it. Just be sure to try to get #1 done by the end of the day. After you've finished something, cross it off your list. Not only will your prioritized list tell you what still needs to be done, but it will give you a boost of satisfaction when you finish a job well done. Transfer anything not accomplished to the Daily List for the next day.

When I moved from my parents' house, my mother gave me a month-by-month list of birthdays for our family and friends. For more than 20 years, I have kept that list, adding names and dates as they came along. It's a bit wrinkled around the edges, but it still holds an important spot on my bulletin board. Mom's list has helped me to remember more things than I can ever count.

Some people say they can't find the time to make a list. Believe me, if you start out devoting even five minutes to thinking through your day and setting goals, you'll end up with time you didn't know you had. Try it.

## Include the family

Make it a family affair.

You can be the most organized person, but if no one else in the family follows your system, your system can't work. Have a family meeting and try to come up with a plan that works for everyone. Ask for your family's advice and see what's important to them. Lack of interest? Then work up the simplest plan possible. If your plan isn't easy for everyone to follow, no one will stick to it.

You may also need a system for encouraging compliance the first weeks or so while everyone's getting used to the new plan. I know a family that fines people 50 cents for each misplaced item.

## Do a little, but get it done

Do a little every day.

For those of you who are organizationally challenged, getting and staying organized is an ongoing process. Don't expect it to happen overnight. Remember that it probably took years to get to the state you're in. Set aside a few minutes each day to file some papers, put tools back in place, or put organizers in your drawers. Don't get distracted while you're organizing. Don't stop to answer the phone, read a letter, or sew on a button. That's for another time. If you have a big project you need to get done, like organizing your closet or kitchen, break it down into smaller segments that won't take more than 30 minutes or an hour. For example, break cleaning your closet into tasks such as going through your shoes and other accessories, getting stuff off the floor, giving away clothes that don't fit, storing out-of-season clothes, hanging all the jackets, pants, and skirts together. Doing this keeps the task from becoming overwhelming. If you have a short attention span for this type of thing (and most of us casual cleaners do), set a definite time and stop when the alarm goes off. Make these organizational breaks part of your daily or weekly routine. This keeps the task from becoming overwhelming.

Even the most organized among you can stand to take a look at your priorities and rethink what you MUST do each day. You may find that you have more time to spend on more pleasurable activities if you, too, are content to do a little each day and break the big tasks into smaller, less stressful units.

# Making It Easy on Yourself and Others

Remember that none of the previous "rules" is written in stone. The way to keep your incentive to get and stay organized is to give yourself a break sometimes. Let the dishes go one day so you can play with your kids. Luxuriate in bed and forget to make it. Be flexible, be sensible, and you'll succeed.

## Try it — if you don't like it, change it

Okay, so you thought the system you worked out was the answer to all your problems. It sounded so good, but it doesn't seem to be working for you. If things aren't working the way you think they should, just do something different.

For example, I got really excited a couple of years ago when an organizer suggested that I use the "tickler system" to file all the papers in my office. That involved creating file folders for every day of the month (that's 30) and one for every month in the year (12 more), and filing things according to when I would initiate action on each paper. This system, although it works great for others, was a disaster for me. I filed things and couldn't remember what day I had put them in. So I cut back to seven "active" folders for each day of the week and one "future" folder. For me, handling more than eight folders at a time was too much.

***Moral of the story:*** Don't worry about backtracking on what you thought was a brilliant solution to your problems. You'll find another brilliant solution. See more tips on handling papers in Chapter 4.

## Invest in some new, fun equipment

Buying new tools is great for jumpstarting your interest in organizing. Hundreds of different kinds of hooks, containers, notebooks, bags, boxes, clips, baskets, hangers, shelves, and other stuff are available, all of which can inspire you to look at organizing your stuff in a new way. Go to stores and look through catalogs and select what's good for you. But don't just buy willy-nilly — a useless storage item creates more clutter. Look at your problem carefully, measure your space, and try the item out before buying a dozen.

After staring at a lump of shoes on the floor of my closet, I bought several plastic shoe storage boxes. I labeled each one: blue flats, black suede heels, and so on. These boxes have given me the impetus to keep my shoes neat. I stack them and get great pleasure out of looking at them. Whatever it takes to inspire you or to give you a fresh outlook on a problem is well worth the investment.

Often, coming up with your own organizational solutions is even more fun than buying new: It matches the solution to your personal organizational style, recycles useful items to spare environmental clutter, and gives added impetus to using the solution rather than living with the problem.

***Remember:*** All the fun, new equipment in the world will only be more clutter if you don't train yourself in the first basic rule: Have a place for everything and put everything in its place. And I do mean train yourself. If you don't already do this naturally, you need to persist in reminding yourself to put things away until it becomes a habit.

## What you see is what you get

I use labels and other visual reminders to help me see immediately how I've organized things. For my shoeboxes, I created little white tags with shoe type and color written on them. My bookcase has shelf labels for different categories, and my craft supplies are in see-through bins with labels listing the contents. Sound a little obsessed? Not really. My system makes things easy for me to find.

Making your own labels is fun. Use your computer to print a batch for each member of the family in different colors and typefaces. Or buy a label maker (available at office and variety stores) that punches out letters manually. Give the kids a box of crayons and some craft paper and let them whip up colorful labels. And kids love stickers. Let them use a variety of colors and characters to label their stuff. Giving everything a nametag will help everyone in the family to find things and put them back where they belong.

# Using Simple Tools to Keep You on Track

Show me a modern family, and I'll show you a schedule that NASA would have a hard time keeping straight. You have timetables to follow, dates to keep, games to attend, lessons to take, and appointments to meet. You really need to develop a simple system that keeps all the need-to-know information in one place. You have many options. Whichever you choose, make sure that everyone in the family can use it and keep the information up-to-date.

## Designate a family message center

Are you and your kids suffering from mixed and confused messages? Does "Oh yeah, I thought I told you that" sound familiar? Try this: Hang a bulletin board near the phone (see Figure 2-1) in a central location. Tie a pen or pencil to the board with a long string and attach a pad of self-stick notes. When someone takes a message, that person is responsible for listing it on the board.

*One caveat:* Everyone has to remove the notes for his messages when he sees them so that the board doesn't get overrun with pieces of paper. Assign a family member to remove outdated messages a couple of times each week.

## Keep a family calendar

Your calendar should be Command Central. Hang it in a central spot in the house — the kitchen, the front hallway, any place where people pass by every day. All planned activities, carpooling dates, game times, and appointments should be written on it.

Be sure to include corresponding phone numbers, addresses, and driving directions. Doing so will save you from searching for the information when the date arrives.

**Figure 2-1:**
A family
calendar
and
message
center can
help you
track dos
and dates.

The family calendar is also a good spot to list each family member's chores. Write down the date that the job should be completed and make sure to mark it after it's finished.

Choose whatever kind of calendar you like — a reusable wipe-off kind, a chalk board, a preprinted one from the office supply store, or a home computer-generated one with dates and deadlines printed on it. Or you could attach it to a bulletin board with extra space for messages, invitations, or photos. Just make sure it's large enough for everyone to write on easily and something that your family will use.

## *Set up a household file*

A household file is a good place to keep all the stuff that helps you run your home. Some things to include in this file are:

- ✔ Telephone numbers for the painter, plumber, and other service people

- ✔ Operating information for household electronics (TV, computer, and VCR)

- ✔ Household maintenance information, such as when the washing machine was last serviced and who did it

✔ Decorating information such as paint colors that were used for certain rooms; phone numbers of upholsterers, drapery makers, and seamstresses; and instruction manuals and warranties for appliances

✔ Medical information such as phone numbers for your doctors and the hospital

✔ School information such as teachers' and coaches' names and phone numbers, important letters, and announcements

Put the file in a drawer in a central convenient location like a desk, the kitchen, the family room, your home office.

## Install a key holder

Stop the sometimes endless search for keys by installing a small key rack near the message center or some other central location. Each family member can have a labeled hook onto which to slip his keys when he enters the house. Other keys that aren't used daily, such as keys for the basement, the back door, or bike locks, also belong here. Before you hang your key rack, sort through all your keys and throw away any that can't be identified or are old and outdated.

## Check out color coding

A less tangible tool, but an equally great idea, is to use color to highlight what's important, to whom things belong, and where things should go. This list gives you an idea of where to start colorizing your household:

✔ The family calendar (mentioned earlier in this chapter) can be further streamlined by writing dates or activities in a different color for each person. This makes it easy for each person to spot her comings and goings.

✔ Prioritize your daily to-do calendar by noting top priority items in red, or put morning tasks in green and afternoon tasks in blue.

✔ Towels, toothbrushes, and cups in personal shades will help to keep things straight in the bathroom.

✔ If you put colored labels on the items in your freezer, you'll be able to tell whether it's fish, meat, or chicken at a quick peek.

✔ Put a red highlight under any tax-related item in your checkbook. At tax time, you can easily spot those expenses without having to pore endlessly over each page.

# Where Has All the Time Gone?

Next to money, time is probably the most desired commodity, yet we can't beg, borrow, or steal it, and no one seems to have enough. But if you analyze your life, you can probably find ways to get back some of the time you lose because of haphazard activity. Try at least some of the suggestions that follow.

## Delegate, delegate, delegate

Stop trying to do everything yourself.

Many people use the excuse that it's faster to do something themselves than to explain to someone else how the task should be done. That excuse may work for certain highly specialized jobs, but often you get stuck in the trap of doing everything.

- ✔ If someone else can do it, let him do it (even if it means letting him do it his way; give him this book if you're worried).
- ✔ If guests ask to bring something to a party and you're frantically getting ready, give them a choice of salad or appetizer or dessert.
- ✔ If you can't stand to do a particular job, hire someone to do it or trade tasks with a friend who doesn't mind that job but has another that you can do.
- ✔ Seek out businesses that pick up and deliver — the time you gain will be well worth the money.
- ✔ Make sure that family members share chores.

Set some standards, but if someone doesn't do the job just the way you would, don't worry. Just sit back and enjoy the extra time you have.

## Create your own "time out" time

Train yourself to filter out distractions when you want to get something done. Let the answering machine take all the telephone calls. Tell other family members that you need 30 minutes to yourself. Get to the office an hour early to enjoy some uninterrupted time to work on projects.

If you can grab only 30 minutes each day, that adds up to an extra 14 hours per month. You practically gain an extra day!

## Start each day with a plan

Before you start your day, sit down and develop the most efficient plan of action. For example:

- ✔ If you have errands to run, map them out so that you do several in the same area and don't waste time backtracking across town.

- ✔ Try to arrange doctor, dentist, or hair appointments so that two or three family members can go at once.

- ✔ When you're shopping for a specific item, always let your fingers do the walking by calling first. Don't rush off to a store only to find that the item is sold out.

Just make sure that your plan has enough flexibility to accommodate the inevitable "emergencies" that pepper your days. It's your plan, and you can change it if you want to. The idea is to manage your stress, not add to it.

## Do two things at once

You can find many opportunities to get double the benefit from your time. Consider such do-able duets as

- ✔ Washing the dishes while you talk on the phone
- ✔ Making to-do lists while waiting in the doctor's office

Of course, these are just suggestions. You can come up with your own. The point is to look for activities that are a natural fit and thus fill otherwise "dead" time (such as the time you spend walking upstairs) with purposeful activity.

## Just say "no"

You probably don't have time to do everything *you* want to do, much less what everyone else wants you to do. If your natural tendency is to say "yes" to everything, only to regret it later, try saying five simple words: "Let me check my schedule." That will give you time to stand back, without pressure, and analyze whether you have the time or energy to drive kids to the soccer game, make 100 cupcakes for the school play, or staff a booth at the church bazaar. Your excuse doesn't have to be elaborate. It can be as simple as "I have other commitments." Go over your to-do list each day, rank your priorities, and see if you have time for anything else. Then ask yourself if the activity you're being asked to do is worthwhile to you. If it's not, just say no.

# Chapter 3

# Setting Up Your Kitchen

· · · · · · · · · · · · · · · · · · · · · · · · · · · · · · · · · · · · · · · · · · ·

### In This Chapter

▶ Starting a storage system

▶ Finding new space

▶ Creating work centers

▶ Storing odd-sized items

· · · · · · · · · · · · · · · · · · · · · · · · · · · · · · · · · · · · · · · · · · ·

*H*ave you ever looked around your kitchen and thought you had *too much space?* I'll bet that's never happened. You probably thought you had *too much stuff!* Well, just look at these statistics: According to the National Kitchen & Bath Association, the average kitchen is the storage place for 95 pieces of china and glassware, 105 utensils and gadgets, and 175 packages, bottles, boxes, and jars of food. That's over 450 items stuffed into drawers and under cabinets and who knows where else.

The challenge lies in finding space for everything and organizing it so you can get to it fast. Nothing is more frustrating than searching through drawers for measuring spoons or teetering on a step ladder to hunt for pots and pans. Yet, most of us do it every day. The good news is that with careful planning you *can* find space for storing things and make every inch of space count.

## Desperately Seeking Space

The kitchen is probably the busiest room in the home. Even if it's small, it's a place not only to cook, but to relax, read, watch TV, do homework, socialize, and even entertain. Because your family spends so much time there, you notice even more when it doesn't function efficiently. The kitchen usually suffers from the "if only" syndrome: "If only I had more space, if only I had one more shelf, if only I had a pantry." The list can go on and on, but because most kitchens are far from ideal, you have to be creative with what you've got. To do this, you need to analyze what's in your kitchen and what you want and need from it. Ask yourself a few questions:

# The right spot

Before you start rearranging things in your kitchen, stand in front of the cabinets and lift your arms. Where can they reach comfortably? In general, it's best to store all the things that you use most often in the cabinets and countertop area between your knees and about a foot above your head. Select your most-used pots and pans, everyday dishes, spices, gadgets, appliances, condiments, and canned and packaged foods, and put them in that space. Put your least-used items on the very top or bottom cabinets or at the back of deep shelves. Heavy items that are used frequently should be stored on the bottom shelves or in drawers. Avoid putting heavy pots and pans on high shelves. Unless you're really into pumping iron, you don't want to be moving several pounds of metal and steel above your head on a daily basis. Not only is it uncomfortable, but it can be dangerous for you and your family. Use that space to store large, lightweight things that can be lifted with ease.

Don't pile several items on top of each other, even if they are lightweight. Limit your stacks to a couple of items. Moving several things out of the way just to get to the one you need is annoying and a waste of time. The kitchen isn't the place to play shuffleboard.

✔ **What's wrong with it now?**

And don't answer "Everything!" While you're working in the kitchen, note its most annoying features. Where would you like more room? Where does the storage come up short? Do you need more pantry space for your groceries? Can you reach your pots and pans easily? Isolate what the problems are and write them down. It's easier to come up with good solutions when you know exactly what's bothering you.

✔ **How do you use your kitchen?**

Do you bake often? Do your children make snacks in the microwave? Do you use mostly prepared food? Is your kitchen a gathering place or a gourmet retreat? Your lifestyle should determine how you organize your space. For example, if you bake regularly, it's a good idea to set up an area with all the baking supplies stored together. But if your pie pan is rarely used, banish it to an out-of-the-way place. If the kids use the kitchen to do homework, you'll want to leave some empty space where they can spread out everything to work. If you assess your habits, you'll be able to organize your kitchen in the most efficient way.

✔ **Which things do you really use?**

You probably have bought lots of gadgets and appliances over the years that seemed as if they would help in the kitchen. Remember that microwave butter melter or the automatic potato chip maker? Some of them really do help and some of them don't. Buying them is fine — they keep the economy going and they sometimes make cooking more fun. The problem is that they may not fit into your cooking patterns now. Take a look at how many pots, pans, dishes, and silverware you actually use day after day. Chances are that all you need to make an average dinner is a couple of pots and pans. The same goes for dishes and silverware. If only four people are eating dinner every night, you don't need to keep a service for ten handy. And do you want to know the scary truth about glasses? The more glasses you have in the kitchen, the more glasses people will use. More glasses means more washing and more work. Weed out what you don't use often.

# Developing a Smart Storage System

Kitchen storage should be logical. Whether you love or loathe to cook, things will go more smoothly if you can find something fast. Schedule some time to go through the kitchen and begin reorganizing following the basic principles listed in this section.

Before you rush to a housewares store to buy storage products, measure the area that you want to reorganize, and make a drawing of the area to help you estimate how many units you need to purchase. Take your measurements with you to save unnecessary trips back to the store to purchase more items or to return items.

## Sort food by category

Make up food groups according to your cooking and eating patterns. Arrange them together on shelves, in the pantry, or in drawers. When you cook, you'll go to one spot for supplies.

Some categories that you may consider grouping together are

- ✔ Vinegars and oils
- ✔ Hot sauces and salsas
- ✔ Snack foods such as potato chips, popcorn, and cheese whiz
- ✔ Foreign food ingredients
- ✔ Pasta, rice, and dried beans
- ✔ Extra spices that you don't use often

✔ Flour, sugar, baking powder, baking soda, cake mixes, and other baking supplies

✔ Cereals

## *Store items near where you use them*

Kitchens are organized around areas where most of the work takes place. Kitchen designers see the space between the refrigerator, sink, and stove — the kitchen triangle — as most important (see Figure 3-1). You do most of the preparation, cooking, and cleaning in this work triangle, so the items should be close together and accessible.

You can create other work centers in your kitchen by storing food and appliances that are used together in the same area. This saves steps because everything is in one spot. It also saves time when you clean up because you have dirtied only one section of the kitchen. It's more convenient for the rest of the family, too. Because things are stored in a logical spot, it's easier to return them to their proper place.

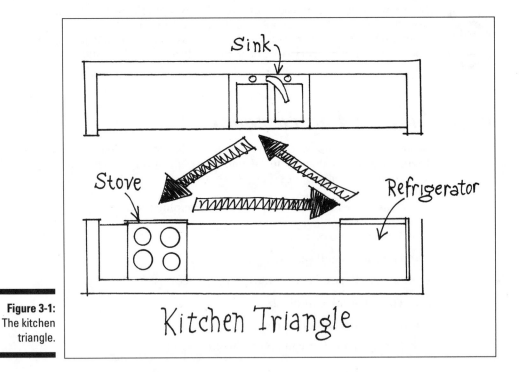

**Figure 3-1:**
The kitchen
triangle.

But be flexible. Well-used items can be stored in more than one place if you have the space. For example, a set of measuring cups or spoons could be stationed in the baking area inside the flour container and also near the stove where you prepare the rest of the food.

Use the following suggested work areas or develop some that fit your specific cooking habits:

- **Baking center:** Mixer, bread machine, measuring cups and spoons, rolling pin, pie and cake pans, cookie sheets, and all baking ingredients (flours, baking powder, sugar, and so on)

- **Breakfast center:** Toaster, breadbox, cereals, marmalade, tea, tea-pot, coffee, coffeemaker, spoons, sugar bowl

- **Cleaning center:** Dish soap, sponge, scrubber, countertop cleaner, and towels

- **Beverage center:** Cocoa, sodas, dry mixed drinks such as iced tea, glasses, spoons

- **Communications center:** Telephone, bulletin board, shelves for cookbooks, pens, paper, and so on

- **Snack center:** Popcorn maker, microwave, paper plates and cups, and snack supplies (popcorn, potato chips, pretzels, and so on)

## Keep items handy

Think of the things you use every day. Are they stored so that you can grab them when you need them? Analyze what you use the most, and then find a space for them on the countertop or the shelves directly nearby. Use these ways to keep things at your fingertips:

- Hang coffee mugs on cup hooks underneath the top cabinets.

- Store dishes and flatware near the dishwasher.

- Put wooden spoons and spatulas in a pitcher near the stove.

- Mount the microwave on a shelf above the stove. Make sure it's properly vented — check you instruction manual for details.

- Put a ring holder or coffee mug near the sink to store your watch and rings while doing dishes.

# Store it far away if you don't use it often

Which items do you dig out of hiding only once or twice a year? Think fish poacher, Thanksgiving platter, or fondue pot. If they aren't used often, store them out of the way but easily accessible, such as in the basement or garage. Put things that are used together in the same box. For example, group the Thanksgiving platter, napkins, placemats, and napkin rings. Or the fondue pot, skewers, and cookbook. Be sure to put a big label on the box. If you're worried about finding these items again, make a list of all the stuff you banished and their location. Store the list in a kitchen drawer or home file.

# Search high and low for extra space

You probably have more space in your kitchen than you realize. I know that all your shelf and pantry space may be crammed to the gills, but look around. Try to think about your space in a new way.

Most kitchens use horizontal shelving, but there's more in them-thar rooms. Unusual storage spots can sometimes be more convenient because they're closer to the task at hand. Search the following places for extra space.

### On the wall

Walls can be the last frontier of storage. Everything else may be full, but you usually have a bare spot that you can grab for storage on the wall. Use some of these ideas to find some new places to put things.

- ✔ **Pegboard:** Cheap and easy to find, pegboard can easily hold kitchen gadgets or pots and pans of many different sizes and shapes. Paint the pegboard to match your cabinets or the kitchen surfaces.

  To keep the pegboard organized, trace the outline of the spoon, whisk, bowl, or any other gadget on the board, and write the name underneath. A cooking school I attended used this method to make it easy for every student to put things back in their proper place.

- ✔ **Grid storage systems:** Made of criss-crossed metal or plastic, grids are a clean look that come in many different sizes and configurations for wall-mounting. Cookware and gadgets hang from S-hooks. Be sure to get hooks with one end that fits snugly on the grid. Otherwise, the hooks have the tendency to fall off when you remove items.

- ✔ **Homemade storage racks:** You can make a storage rack from something as simple as a 2-inch by 4-inch piece of lumber. Hang it either vertically or horizontally and attach it securely to the wall studs. Paint or stain, and then screw in hooks the length of the board. Because this is so narrow, it can fit into tight spots in a corner or above a shelf.

If your cutting board or wooden spoons don't have an opening to insert a hook, just drill a hole in the handle of the spoon or the corner of the board.

✔ **Wooden shaker peg racks:** Available by the foot in home centers or through catalogs, most shaker peg racks are unfinished and can be painted or stained any color. Use them to hold aprons, towels, oven mitts, and so on.

✔ **Magnetic steel bars:** Get knives out of a drawer (which isn't good for knives anyway) and display them where you can reach them easily. Magnetic bars can also be used for hanging metal utensils such as spatulas or scissors.

If you have small children in the house, hang knives and such out of their reach.

### On the ceiling

Stand in your kitchen and look up. See anything? If not, you've got some storage space. Hang things high or within arm's reach, depending on how often you use them. Make sure that you have adequate clearance for cabinet doors and the head of the tallest person in the family. You don't want any six-footers butting heads with pots and pans.

✔ Sturdy metal racks come in all sizes and shapes to hold pots and pans. They make an attractive display as well.

✔ Convert a small ladder into a ceiling rack. Attach it to the studs with lengths of chain, and hang items from S-hooks looped around the rungs.

✔ Hang a collection of baskets from the rafters for a rustic look. They give the kitchen ceiling a rich texture while acting as hidden storage bins for items that you don't use often.

Before you hang the baskets, make a list of what's inside each one and store the list in a nearby drawer. That will eliminate guesswork when you go to search for something.

### Inside or on doors

All those flat vertical surfaces inside the cabinet doors present a wealth of storage space. Attach hooks or clips to hold placemats, napkins, or utensils. Or tack up a small bulletin board as a handy catch-all for kids' artwork or school messages. Hang a clipboard to hold grocery lists or recipes while you're cooking. Narrow shelves and wire racks are available to mount inside the cabinet doors.

Measure the space before you install anything to be sure that you have enough room to shut the door without interfering with the contents on the shelves inside.

### On top of the cabinets

The space between the top cabinet and the ceiling often goes unused. Make a shelf by nailing a board that's sized to fit on top of the cabinets. You'll have a great place to store cookbooks or platters that you want out of the way but still within sight. Or make an attractive arrangement of baskets, boxes, or pieces of pottery, and store things you rarely use inside such as turkey laces or cake decorating tips. It looks much neater than storing a large group of smaller items.

### Inside cabinets

Most upper cabinets have 12 inches of vertical space between shelves. That usually makes for wasted space because it's hard to stack anything that high. You risk accidents and breakage.

I solved that problem in my own kitchen by putting in some plastic-coated wire racks with legs on each shelf. They're easy to install — no hammers or screws necessary. Just place them on the shelf. The wire racks create a new storage area about 5 inches high, literally doubling the available space in cabinets. Dishes, cups, cans, and bottles can be stacked to a reasonable height on these racks.

For the lower cabinets, pull-out drawers or racks are available in many sizes. They're installed on a set of rollers for easy retrieval of items stored below.

### Between the cabinets

Many manufacturers have noticed that the area between the top cabinets and the countertop is often underutilized and have created all sorts of nifty products to take advantage of that space. Baskets, cookbook racks, towel holders, radios, microwaves, clocks, and even TV sets can be mounted in this space.

Why not screw in some cup hooks to get mugs off the countertop? Another possibility: Stacked cubes in front of the backsplash provide extra space to store spices, cups, saucers, or condiments. Just remember to leave plenty of space on the countertop.

## Find still more extra space

We've gone up the walls, and inside, under, and on top of the cabinets. But you can still find room for storage. Just keep looking.

- Fill empty space over a window with a narrow shelf to hold trays or platters that you rarely use.
- Install a narrow shelf under the top cabinets to hold spices and small jars. Make it about 3 inches wide and about 6 inches from the bottom of the top cabinets.

✔ Add a piece of furniture from another part of your house. A bookcase or a dresser painted to match the color of the walls or cabinets can add lots of extra storage. You can store canisters, cookbooks, hand mixers, even pots and pans that you want to hide, in a drawer.

✔ A wheeled cabinet creates an extra counter space or work area. One with doors looks neater because everything is hidden inside. But if you're a visual person, consider a rolling metal rack so you can see everything at a glance. A friend of mine even used one of those big automobile tool storage cabinets in a high-tech kitchen. It's already on wheels, and he added a butcher-block top.

✔ Tiered plastic shelves can house lots of little bottles and jars that are assorted sizes. The shelves look like a long stairway, are about 2 inches wide, and adjust to different lengths. They don't eliminate the clutter, but they make seeing things much easier. Store the taller and larger objects, such as Worcestershire sauce and vinegar bottles, in the back and keep the smaller spice bottles in front.

✔ Use a couple of file cabinets as a base for a kitchen desk. Use a hollow core door, cut to fit, as a desktop. Paint the cabinets to match the decor. The drawers give plenty of space for recipes, home files, and even storage for kitchen gadgets.

✔ Buy an expandable cutting board that fits over the sink. It adds several more inches of valuable work area, and clean-up is easy because you can scrape garbage right into the sink.

## *Store odd-sized items creatively*

Your kitchen is full of odd-sized items that just don't want to conform to that staid network of shelves. But with a little creativity, you can find a place for almost everything.

✔ **Large platters:** Store these vertically in a cabinet. Dish racks or even office file folder racks can hold them upright in a small space. I found space in a nearby linen closet and nailed a narrow piece of wood on the side and edge of the shelf to prevent them from falling and then stacked them vertically one next to the other. You can create a narrow display shelf with strip molding and lean the platters against the wall. Put a piece of putty behind the platters to keep them from slipping.

✔ **Pan lids:** Depending on the number and size of lids, several workable options are available. If you have a large number of lids or are the "piler not filer" kind of person, buy a plastic dishpan to throw them in. They'll be contained and, if you need one, you can just yank out the whole container and look inside. Or they can also be stored vertically in a dish rack.

You can also make a simple wall rack by nailing two 1-inch square blocks to either end of a narrow strip of wood and mounting it on the wall. The lids slip behind the strip and their handles keep them from falling down.

- ✔ **Cookie sheets:** Slip them inside a large plastic bag and slide them into the space between the refrigerator and the lower cabinet.

- ✔ **Sponges and scrubbers:** Install a plastic or metal tilt-out tray in the cabinet panel in front of the sink. (The panel looks like a drawer but actually nothing is behind it.) The tilt-out trays come in various lengths and are available at home centers.

- ✔ **Plastic grocery bags:** Stuff them inside an empty paper towel tube or tissue box. The tube fits neatly in a drawer. You'd be surprised how many fit inside.

- ✔ **Spices:** I store the bottles by category in those little plastic see-through berry boxes that you get at the grocery store. Herbs (rosemary, thyme, oregano, and so on) go in one, peppers (black, white, and red) go in another.

- ✔ **Glasses, stemware:** Glasses can take up a lot of room in a cupboard. Make the most of your present space by positioning every other glass upside down. If you have enough room between the top and bottom cabinets, put up a rack on the underside of the cabinet that holds glasses from their stems.

- ✔ **Soft bags of soap, beans, and drinks:** Use clean, empty shoeboxes to stack envelopes or bags of food and store them in the cupboard. If bugs are a problem, place the envelopes in plastic shoeboxes and snap on the lid.

- ✔ **Garbage bags:** Store the full roll in the bottom of the trash basket. When you throw the top one out, just reach into the bottom for the replacement. They'll be easy to find underneath.

- ✔ **Cookie cutters:** Tie them together with a ribbon and hang them on a hook. They'll be decorative and organized.

## Use decorative storage

Kitchen storage conjures up the idea of some ugly mess because much of what's available doesn't exactly qualify for the Museum of Modern Art. Don't hesitate to use your decorating savvy to bring some attractive accessories into the kitchen. Unusual accessories give your kitchen character and are just as effective at containing the mess. Look for possible storage items at garage sales and flea markets, and don't hesitate to use accessories that you may not normally envision in the kitchen.

Here's a potpourri of things you can use for storage that don't have to be tucked inside a drawer:

✔ Antique tins can store spices or dry mixes.

✔ Colored glass jars store pasta.

✔ Ceramic flower pots hold sponges, brushes, and rubber gloves.

✔ Beautiful wicker baskets store onions or potatoes where they can breathe.

✔ Metal mailboxes, painted or stenciled, can hold small appliances.

✔ Chinese bamboo vegetable steamers hold tea bags and accessories.

✔ Old wooden milk cartons keep rolled napkins or silverware handy.

✔ Metal lunch boxes are whimsical containers for small gadgets or spices.

✔ Brightly colored shopping bags hide over-sized items.

✔ Simple, open baskets make a collection of coffee mugs look inviting.

## Keep things well contained

If you just organize what's already inside cabinets and drawers, you'll have more space. Use these quick ideas to keep your cabinets in order.

✔ Put lazy susans in corners of cabinets to give better access to the stuff stored in hidden corners.

✔ Install pull-out shelves or a simple dishpan to hold bottles of detergent and cleaning products. Or store them in a bin with a handle that you can take with you when you're cleaning.

✔ Divide up drawers with a two-tiered plastic cutlery tray. You can bring it with you to set the table. Position all the handles towards the back so you can tell at a glance what everything is.

✔ Use small boxes or plastic drawer dividers to create your own individualized storage system. You can customize almost any drawer. If you have odd-sized tools that you use often, such as an ice cream scoop, garlic press, or can opener, having a separate space for them helps maintain order.

✔ Place a jar or pitcher on the countertop to hold odd-sized or over-sized spoons, utensils, or spatulas that take up room in drawers.

✔ When shelf space is limited, roll up towels and other linens instead of folding them. More than twice the number of items will fit in the same amount of space.

## Free up freezer space

If you have a new freezer with lots of shelves and an ice machine, consider yourself lucky. My freezer harkens back to the days when they called it the "ice box." It's one big box and, believe me, it has lots of ice in it (on the walls and the door — but that's another problem). With all the things that are stuffed inside, it's imperative that you have an easy way to get to them or you can end up missing items just like lost explorers at the North Pole. They look like unidentifiable chunks of glacial ice.

A few well-placed organizers will help get the mess in order and turn your freezer into much more usable space.

- **Plastic-coated wire racks:** The same ones that are great for cabinet shelves do double duty in your freezer. They make it much easier to neatly stack frozen food boxes or ice cube trays. They're lightweight and easy to see through.

- **Clear plastic bins:** Store meat, chicken, and vegetables in lidded bins that are designed to hold clothing (I use a sweater box). Because they're clear, what's inside won't be put out of sight and out of mind. And the lids not only protect what's inside, but they let you stack one on top of the other.

Put color-coded labels on the front of the boxes so you can tell at a glance which food category it is. For example, store meat in a box with a blue label, vegetables with a green label, and leftovers with a red label.

When adding items to your freezer collection, put the newer items in the back and move the older foods to the front so you use them up first.

When you put anything in the freezer, be sure to stick on a special freezer label listing exactly what it is and the date that you put it in the freezer.

See Chapter 9 for more about caring for your kitchen.

# Part II
# Keeping Your House and Stuff Clean

The 5th Wave                    By Rich Tennant

"Oh yeah, this was a neat job, Lieutenant—definitely the work of organized crime. Very organized. Look how neatly everything's labeled. And we're pretty sure they vacuumed the carpet before leaving."

# In this part . . .

*T*his part gets down to the real nitty-gritty, hurty-gertie dirt. Win the war against dust (though you may lose a battle) Find the answer to that age-old question: Top down or bottom up? In this part, you get rid of the clutter and progress to cleaning everything from windows to walls, from floors to furnishings, collectibles, and miscellaneous stuff. And you get tips for cleaning those rooms that never stop needing cleaning: the kitchen and the bathroom.

# Chapter 4

# Decluttering and Basic Storage

• • • • • • • • • • • • • • • • • • • • • • • • • • • • • • • • • • • • • • • • • • • • • •

• • • • • • • • • • • • • • • • • • • • • • • • • • • • • • • • • • • • • • • • • • • • • •

*O*kay, I have a problem with clutter. Although I prefer to call it a collection of things ranging from pig cookie jars to, believe it or not, ceramic snakes. Pile that on top of various hobbies, drawers of doodads to complete every task, and the troublesome habit of clipping something out of every newspaper and magazine that I read, and you begin to get the picture. What to do?

Because my first instinct is to clutter rather than declutter, I've had to learn from the ground floor up how to think like a "neat" person. After talking to many professional organizers and reading several of their books, I've learned how to get rid of things and still feel happy. In this chapter, I share with you those things that I have found most helpful. If you attract clutter, decluttering will be difficult but not impossible. The first step is to define for yourself what is and is not clutter. Then get rid of the clutter and organize the rest. Read on.

## What Is Clutter, Anyway?

Clutter can be different things to different people. To some, it's all the things in the house that are out of place. To many, it's the mountain of paper that comes into the house, some wanted and some unwanted: bills, magazines, invoices, invitations. To others, it's things that are not being used, haven't been used, and won't ever be used, that are just taking up space. Whatever your clutter problem is, you can overcome it if you're determined to throw useless things away and find creative places to stash your "treasures."

You may not realize it, but clutter is robbing you of three things that are probably in short supply in your life: money, space, and time. How can all your precious things be stealing from you? Read on.

## Clutter robs you of space

The fact that clutter robs you of space is pretty obvious. Practically every household has precious space taken up by things that just sit there and are never even used. The more extraneous and useless stuff you have, the harder it is to store the things you really need and want in a place where you can get to them easily.

For example, one woman I know has two shelves in her kitchen filled with old pots and pans. Some are hand-me-downs, others are garage sale pick-ups, and she even has one that she used in college. But she doesn't use them. Whenever she goes to reach for a pot or pan, she has to dig through this pile of pots to get to the three good ones that she always uses. She's wasting her most convenient space (as well as her limited time) with piles of items she never needs.

## Clutter robs you of money

Here's a thought that should really hit home: Storage space for your clutter costs you big bucks.

Stephanie Culp, a professional organizer and author of *Streamlining Your Life* (published by Writer's Digest Books), suggests that you do a cost-per-square-foot estimate of your living space. Divide your mortgage or rent by the square footage of your home. For example, if you pay $1,000 a month mortgage for a 1,000 square foot house, that works out to $1 a square foot. Then, figure out how many square feet of your home is devoted to storage.

If a 100-square-foot basement room is unusable because it's filled with junk, you're paying $100 a month for storage. And that's probably the tip of the iceberg — what about closets filled with out-of-date clothes, bookshelves stuffed with books you don't read, and drawers crammed with clothes that need mending. That's all space you're paying for. If you heard someone was spending half their mortgage on storage space, you'd think they were crazy. And yet many of us do it all the time.

In addition, clutter often prevents you from finding what you're looking for, which often results in money spent buying duplicate items of something you already have but you need but can't find. I once cleaned out my kitchen drawers and found four potato peelers! I knew I had one peeler, but I couldn't find it when I needed it, so I bought another one. This is how clutter begets clutter.

## Clutter robs you of time

Try adding up all the time you spend picking up clutter, looking for misplaced items, asking others to move their things, or figuring out just where to put something. I'll bet it adds up to an extra day or two a month. That's time you can spend doing something fun or just relaxing.

# Your Decluttering Plan: One Step at a Time

You know *why* you should get rid of your clutter, but *how* should you go about doing it? Hire a bulldozer, get rid of everything, and make a new start? (Believe me, I've thought of that myself.) You don't have to be that drastic. The best way is to do it one step at a time. Don't expect to do it all in one day — it probably took you and your family years to accumulate all that stuff. It needn't take you years to get rid of it, but you've got to start somewhere and keep at it. The suggestions in the following sections should help.

## Start with what you can finish

Okay. You're ready to start. If you're a clutter-bug, avoid thinking that you can declutter everything in an hour, a day, or even a week. You'll overwhelm yourself and sink beneath your stuff. Start with small but visible areas so you can see and benefit from your progress. Loosely schedule your time and don't tackle more than you can finish in the time you've allotted.

Start with one small area, a chest of drawers, the floor in the living room, or the garage walls, and work until you finish that. Or try decluttering by category: Go through the kids' toys, all the magazines over five years old, or just the craft supplies. Set small realistic goals that you can accomplish easily. Make sure that you can finish what you start, or have a definite (but flexible) plan for finishing. The plan is what keeps you from feeling overwhelmed.

## Box it up

Arm yourself with *at least* six cardboard boxes and write these labels on the front of each:

- ✔ **Put back:** Use this box for things that belong in another area of the house.

- ✔ **Put away:** Use this box for things you'll put in long-term storage.

- ✔ **Give away:** Use this box for things you intend to sell at a garage sale or give to friends. If you're giving things to friends, write down what goes to whom while you're going through the boxes. Tape the note to the side of the box so you won't have to spend time digging through it again.

- ✔ **Give to charity:** Use this box for items you want to donate to charity. Make a list of what you're giving, what it's worth, and the charity it's going to. Store the list in your household file (see Chapter 2) in case you want to claim a tax deduction.

- ✔ **Get rid of:** Use this box for things that will go in the trash.

- ✔ **Can't decide:** Use this box for things you don't use a lot but can't bring yourself to throw away. This box speeds up the decluttering process because you can postpone some painful decisions.

    Put a date on the "can't decide" box and store it in an out of the way place. Take it out in six months or a year. You'll probably wonder why you saved it.

Go through the area that you want to declutter and throw things in the appropriate boxes. If it helps you to pretend you're on a TV game show and the faster you fill up the boxes, the more you win — go for it.

## Decide what to keep or throw out

This is the hard part: Deciding what to keep and what to toss. But the process for deciding is simple: Look at each item and ask yourself, "Do I really use this?" Or, "Would I have a hard time getting a new one if I needed it?" If the answer is: "No," get rid of it. If you're afraid you won't have the willpower to throw anything out, invite a hard-nosed friend to come over while you're decluttering. A second opinion from a certified nonclutterer confirming your decisions is helpful when you're on the fence.

Certain discards should be no-brainers, but sometimes you need to see things on paper. So here goes. Don't spend a second debating whether you should get rid of these items:

- **Keys you can't identify** (You moved out of that apartment 10 years ago.)

- **Clothes and shoes that don't fit** (You may never be that size again.)

- **Pens with dried-up ink** (You'll never get them to work again.)

- **Duplicate utensils, pots, or baking pans** (Do you need five pizza cutters?)

- **Unfinished sewing or craft projects** (They're probably out of fashion anyway, assuming you have all the pieces.)

- **Junk mail** (Believe me, they'll send more.)

- **Old and unused household cleaning supplies** (How many old jars of furniture polish do you need and why hold on to the brands you tried out that don't work as well as your old favorites? Just be sure to follow community regulations when disposing of them.)

- **Containers from take out food** (You only need a couple — get rid of the rest.)

- **Old paint in cans** (Save a small amount for touch-ups and dispose of the rest according to community regulations.)

- **Text books from high school or college** (Sure, they cost a lot back then, but the world has changed since your high school geography class.)

- **Parts for appliances you no longer own** (They won't fit on another one.)

- **Old toys that haven't been played with for a year** (Motivate kids with the one in, one out rule — to get a new toy, they must get rid of an old one.)

- **Makeup that's more than one year old** (It gets spoiled and can act as a host for bacteria.)

- **Restaurant guides more than two years old** (The restaurants or their menus may no longer exist.)

- **Expired coupons** (Maybe you're not a coupon person; save time and clutter by not clipping them in the first place.)

If you feel bad about throwing something away, make yourself feel better by taking these halfway options:

- **Lend the item to someone who needs it.** At least the item's being recycled, and you can always get it back when you need it. (You probably never will — need it, or get it back.)

- **Have an exchange party with friends who wear similar sizes or have similar tastes.** You can exchange things for something that you *will* want to wear or to use. If you don't find anything you want, you're better off because you'll be down one more thing.

✔ **Give it away:** If you have clothing that still fits, but that you haven't worn in a while, tie a dated label onto the hanger and put it in the back of the closet. Look at it again in six months; if you haven't worn it in that time, give it away. Same for other items you've never used and may not need.

✔ **Keep doors closed:** If other members of the family can't bring themselves to declutter, at least make them keep their stuff in their own rooms with the doors closed so that no one else has to look at it.

✔ **Get it repaired:** If you don't want to throw something away because it needs fixing, take it to the repair shop right away so you can use it again. Consider tossing it if the cost of the repair is more than the cost of a replacement. Don't let it sit around broken for years. If you haven't been motivated to fix it, chances are you don't need it.

## Finish your task

Once you finish cleaning out a small area, see how you feel. If you're invigorated by how good it feels to get rid of things, keep going on to another area. If you're exhausted or your schedule demands that you do something else, put away the boxes until the next session. Just be sure to schedule a next session.

When you've finished cleaning out an area, put the contents of the "get rid of" box in a trash bag and throw it out immediately before you backtrack on your decisions. Put the "give away or give to charity" box in the car so that you can take it with you on your next trip. (If you take it to the garage, unfortunately, you risk never taking it out again.) If you can't sort through the "can't decide" box right then, set a definite date to do it later, and then *decide*.

---

## Doing good with discards

If what's stopping you from decluttering is the thought that you can't stand to waste things (for example, by just throwing out items you no longer want), find a group that will put them to good use.

Many national organizations, such as the Salvation Army and Goodwill Industries, are looking for clothing and furniture in good condition. Every community has homeless shelters in need of clothing. Hospices for abused families or children's homes can use unwanted toys or kid's clothing. You can give books to libraries and nursing homes. Donate magazines to clinics or schools for reading and craft projects. Some animal shelters use old rugs and towels to make the cages more comfortable.

Look in your phone book or ask your friends for other civic or religious organizations that might need your castoffs. Be sure to call the group first to find out exactly what it can use and what condition the donated item should be in. If you're so inclined, you can often get a tax-deduction letter for the items you donated.

# Storage Basics

Just finding someplace to shove something in your house can be a relief, but stuffing stuff doesn't necessarily solve your storage problems. It may solve the problem for the time being because the item is not in view, but the same search for storage space will eventually happen again.

Think before you put something away. Use the guidelines in the following sections for the most efficient long-term storage.

## Store things where you use them

The prime rule of sensible storage: Before you put something away, you should ask, "where do I *use* this?" rather than "where should I *store* this?" It doesn't make sense to store scissors and tape in the bathroom or your tools in the bedroom if you routinely use these items in the kitchen or garage. Sure you might occasionally need tape in the bedroom or tools in the bathroom. But the real goal is to store items where you use them most often; that way, you can find them fast when you need them and return them quickly when you're done.

Sometimes, the best storage space may not seem the most logical, but good storage can be anywhere that your activity patterns determine is most useful. For example,

- ✔ If kids like to hang out in the kitchen with you, fill a kitchen drawer with paper and crayons or toys.
- ✔ If you like to read in the bathroom, keep a small basket or magazine stand there to hold everything neatly.
- ✔ If you iron your clothes before you go to work each day, consider storing a small ironing board in the bedroom for touch-ups.

The goal is to make the item's location most convenient for everyone.

### Make things accessible

The more frequently you use an item, the more accessible it should be. Things you use often, like coffee cups, spice bottles, the telephone book, or stuff you have to get to quickly, such as bandages or medicine, should be in easy-to-reach shelves, cabinets, or drawers at a height from about mid-thigh to shoulder. Things that you only need to get to occasionally, like extra toilet tissue or guest towels, you can place above the shoulder. Of course, if you have small children, store hazardous or breakable things where they can't get them — *so they're only accessible to you.*

### Group like things together

Put categories of related things together, like broom and dustpan, hammer and nails, and scissors with buttons and thread. Create mini activity centers: Everything you need for a certain task should be stored in one place.

## Put it away, but not forever

Store stuff that you use only once or twice a year, such as the holiday dishes or ornaments, seasonal sporting equipment, electric blankets, or floor fans, in an out-of-the-way place. If you have the room, put all these items in the same location: the basement, the attic, shelves in the garage, or under the stairs. That way, you automatically know where to look for something that you don't use that often.

If you store items in boxes, make sure that you put a large, readable label on each box listing its contents, such as, Christmas: dishes, ornaments; Halloween: costumes, decorations; summer: outdoor toys, beach towels; winter clothes: hats, gloves, scarves.

If your storage area is small and you have to stack several boxes on top of each other, make a diagram showing the location of each box and store the diagram in your household file (see Chapter 2). When you go to look for something, you'll know exactly where it is. Using this little trick will keep your back in shape for a few more years: You won't have to lift a million boxes to find something. Store items that you use more often towards the front, less-used boxes towards the back.

## Rotate: For collectors only

If you're a collector, it's a good idea to pare down your collection periodically and put some of it in long-term storage. The unexpected benefits of this strategy are:

✔ You can see each individual item better because your display is less cluttered.

✔ When you retrieve stored items for display, they will seem like new to you.

I have a ceramic pig collection that was overtaking three shelves. I tearfully said good-bye to several porcines, wrapped them up, and placed them in boxes. My collection on display looked and felt new because I had room to rearrange it. Now I pack and unpack some a couple of times a year, which makes the collection more fun.

## Obey the one-in, one-out rule

Set a limit on how much room you're going to allow for storage. After you've reached that limit, make a rule that for every new thing you want to store, you've got to get rid of something to make room for it. Not only will this rule give you an incentive to throw things away, but what you save will be in better shape because it's less crowded.

# Finding Extra Storage Space

Except for people who are genetically inclined to rid their house of every unnecessary item, it's a rare and unusual person who feels they have enough storage space. Even if you have many closets, you can never have enough. The following sections describe other places and containers in which you can find more space to put things.

## The entryway

Place some of the following items in your entryway to store things you need on your way in or out:

- **Pegs and hooks:** If you don't have a front closet, put up a shaker-type peg rack or install hooks on the wall to hold coats, scarves, and hats. Install hooks low enough so that kids can reach them.

- **Wooden hat stand:** Get one from a flea market, antique store, or office supply store to help organize your outside clothing if you need storage by a door, but don't want to put holes in the wall.

- **Tray for wet boots:** Put a plastic or metal tray on the floor to corral wet shoes or boots in inclement weather.

- **Umbrella stand:** Keep umbrellas handy by storing them in a wicker basket or ceramic crock. Line the bottom with plastic to catch any drips.

## The bedroom

Here are some tips for getting extra storage in your bedroom:

- **Use your mattress:** Put extra blankets or sheets that you don't use very often between the mattress and the box spring.

- **Make roll-out storage:** Put wheels on the corners of an old drawer or storage bin (see Figure 4-1). Check to make sure that the wheeled item fits under your bed with the wheels on. It can hold toys, blankets, out-of-season clothes, or wrapping paper. You can pull it out easily to see what's inside.

✔ **Add hooks:** Install several small hooks or a plastic-coated grid on the inside of your closet door to hang purses, belts, or necklaces. Or attach a curtain rod or towel bar to the inside of the closet door to lay pants over or to hold belts or ties.

✔ **Use dividers:** Divide up drawers with shoe boxes or self-closing plastic bags labeled for separate colors and types of pantyhose, tights, and socks. Fold or roll socks to avoid stretching them. Keep a small bag in the drawer to hold socks that have no partners. Throw solo socks away after six months if the mate has not shown up.

✔ **Use utensil trays:** Keep costume jewelry in a top drawer. Use a sectional utensil tray or an ice cube tray to keep small items separated. Store valuable jewelry in a padded box or jewelry bag.

✔ **Create a knick-knack bowl:** Put a pretty dish or bowl on your dresser top to hold watches, rings, necklaces, and spare change.

✔ **Store linen sets together:** Fold up both sheets and pillowcases and store them inside a matching pillowcase.

✔ **Add a skirt:** Put a skirt on a round table next to your bed and hide anything underneath — magazines, knitting supplies, or the telephone book. The table looks pretty and no one will pick up the skirt to look.

✔ **Use a hamper:** Store out-of-season clothes in an old wicker hamper.

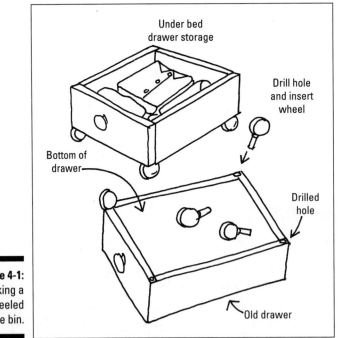

**Figure 4-1:**
Making a
wheeled
storage bin.

## Shoe-bagging your stuff

My favorite all-purpose, ready-made multiple storage unit is the shoe bag. They come in different sizes, containing from 4 to 16 pockets.

People who like their messes covered up will go for the kind made of opaque canvas material; those who like to see what's inside will like the clear vinyl. In either case, put labels on the outside of each pocket so you can easily tell what's inside. You can hang them over a door or nail them to a wall in every room of the house:

✔ **In the bathroom:** Cosmetics, hair dryers, nontoxic medicines, combs, brushes, hair curlers, scrunchies, brushes

✔ **In the front closet:** Hats, gloves, keys, school messages, small items you take out the door each day

✔ **In the kitchen:** Utensils such as peelers, zesters, garlic presses, wooden spoons, packets of dry soup or salad dressing, meat thermometers, small bags of spices you don't use often

✔ **In the workshop:** Screwdrivers, sandpaper, nails, nuts, bolts, bottles of glue, tape measures, duct or electrical tape

✔ **In the craft or sewing room:** Needles, thread, scissors, buttons, soft tape measures, yarn, knitting needles, bobbins, bottles of glue, sewing machine accessories

✔ **In the kids' room:** Small toys, socks, hair ribbons, rolled T-shirts, books, crayons, pens and pencils, rulers

✔ **In the bedroom:** Pantyhose, underpants, lingerie, necklaces, bracelets, rings, earrings, bulky socks

✔ **In the home office:** Envelopes, stamps, scissors, bills, tape, staplers, push pins

Back of closet

Shoe bag storage

# *The workshop/basement/garage*

You can get lots of extra space in the workshop or basement area by following these tips:

✔ Build shelves in the space under the stairs for extra storage.

✔ Mount empty coffee cans or jars to a board on the wall to store nails, small tools, glues, and polishes.

✔ Put up a pegboard to hang tools. To keep it organized, outline each tool with a magic marker. You can then tell what goes where.

✔ Get everything up off the floor. Hang bikes on hooks from the wall rafters and garden tools on walls.

✔ Store sports equipment, such as hockey sticks, soccer balls, and footballs, in a large garbage can.

✔ Use a plastic cutlery tray to organize miscellaneous tools, such as screwdrivers, pliers, screws, nails, and so on, in a drawer.

✔ Use old file cabinets from yard sales or junk stores to hold tools, outdated household files, and old games.

✔ Get a portable hose caddie that you can roll outside in the summer and inside in the winter. Or nail an old tire on the wall and wind the hose around it.

## Around the house

Here are some other tips useful for wherever you can carve out some space:

✔ If you can't find space in any one area, get a table on wheels and roll it out to where you use it most often.

✔ Use buckets or plastic caddies as portable totes for stored items that you need to use together, such as tools or cleaning supplies.

✔ Install wire half-shelves onto regular wood shelves to create more levels.

✔ Make a side table next to the sofa in the living or family room by throwing a piece of fabric or a throw over a small file cabinet.

✔ Slit a cardboard tube (from a paper towel) lengthwise and slip it over a hanger to store tablecloths without wrinkles.

✔ Look for small gaps to store flat items. I store a folding stepladder between a cabinet and the wall in my kitchen. I also found the perfect place for flat, unfolded boxes between the sofa and the wall, and now I station the ironing board in a gap between some shelves and the wall.

✔ Use lazy susan movable discs to keep things organized but visible under the sink in the bathroom.

✔ No room for a shelf? You can buy shelves as narrow as six inches that go from the floor to the ceiling.

## Triple Crown containers

The number of containers available in which to store things is almost limitless, but I use the following three over and over again. They're great for drawers, closets, and on shelves in just about any room of the house. When in doubt, use one of these:

- **Baskets, baskets, baskets** are the clutterer's best friend. You can put them in any room. They look good and hide a myriad of homeless items: household tools, knitting supplies, magazines, paper, board games, extra silverware, or napkins (see Figure 4-2). Put anything you want to keep organized, but hidden, inside them.

- **Clear, plastic storage boxes** rate #1 for storage. Since you can see what's inside, they save you hours of digging to find things.

- **Zip-top plastic bags** are the best for containing loads of small things around the house. Use them to hold socks, screws, cookie cutters, hair rollers, markers, cake decorating tips, combs, passports, batteries, buttons, paper clips, patterns — well, you get the picture.

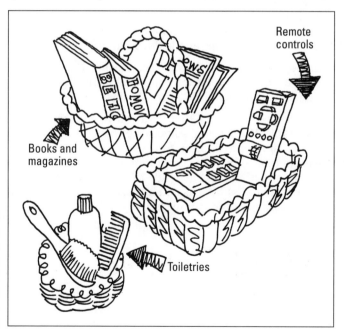

Remote controls

Books and magazines

Toiletries

**Figure 4-2:** Baskets are pretty and practical for extra storage.

# Storing Stuff, Apartment Style

Storing things in a small apartment with limited space can be a real challenge. I know this from experience.

The good news: The lack of space will inspire you to get rid of clutter. The bad news: It's necessary to get rid of this clutter or you won't have any space in which to live.

The principles of smart storage that I discuss earlier in this chapter are even more important in an apartment than in a house because you have fewer options. So remember to put your things in accessible, convenient places, close to where you use them, and store what you do not use often. Don't give up! You have many ways to find more space:

- ✔ **Go up as high as you can.** Don't be afraid to mount shelves that go practically up to the ceiling or put up a set of cabinets close to the upper molding. Use this area for long term storage. Keep a small stool handy to use as a ladder.

- ✔ **Get double-duty furniture.** A bench with a seat that lifts up, a coffee table with drawers, a wall unit with doors, or an ottoman with removable cushions can contain lots of clutter. Look for space under platform beds, side tables, and inside footstools.

- ✔ **Partition it off.** A painless solution that doesn't have to be nailed into a wall: Station a pretty screen or a row of tall plants in front of a pile of stuff. This technique follows the old principle: If you can't see it, it doesn't exist.

- ✔ **Decorate creatively.** Skirt a table and you've got a great storage area under the table. Use stacked suitcases or baskets as a table next to a bed. Put a hollow core door on top of some file cabinets to create a dining room table or work area. I've known people who piled up coffee table books and used them as a side table. Use wooden wine cases from the liquor store to hold books and magazines. Look at everything in your house as a possible storage helper.

# Storing Hard-to-Store Items

I don't know about you, but I've stood bewildered many times while holding onto something, wondering, "Where should I put this?"

Some things pose a problem — they're too little, too big, they wrinkle, or they just get messy. Here's a list of some of those problem items with tips for how to solve those storage dilemmas:

- ✔ **Place mats:** Put each set of mats in cardboard file folders or hang them from office clips on the inside of pantry doors.

- **Buttons, needles, or other small craft supplies:** Place these in empty film canisters or prescription bottles.

- **Tablecloths:** Install a curtain rod in the back of the closet, behind the clothes, and hang tablecloths without wrinkles or fold marks.

- **Extension cords:** Fold these lengthwise, then stuff them *inside* a cardboard tube from a paper towel.

- **Holiday lights:** Wrap these around the *outside* of a cardboard tube from a paper towel.

- **Large items such as skis or surfboards:** Place these under beds if you don't have a spare closet or basement.

- **Bicycles:** Use racks attached to the ceiling or wall to store bicycles off the floor. If you live in an apartment, get a bike rack pole that extends from the floor to the ceiling and doesn't need to be permanently mounted.

- **Plastic grocery bags:** Stuff these inside an empty tissue box or a cardboard tube from a paper towel. Or make a holder by cutting off a sleeve from an old sweatshirt or shirt. Put elastic tape around the shoulder seam end. If you like, sew a loop on the top so it can hang from a hook. Stuff the bags in the top opening and pull them out from the cuff end, as shown in Figure 4-2.

- **Gift wrap:** Store gift wrap, tape, and scissors together in one large cardboard box. Keep rolls of gift wrap from unrolling by wrapping it around a tube and putting a rubber band over the tube; or cut off one leg of an old pair of pantyhose and slip it over the whole tube. You can also buy long, multilayered plastic boxes to store all your wrapping supplies together.

- **CDs (compact discs):** Taking the CDs out of their plastic cases greatly reduces the amount of storage area they take up. I like to put mine in special notebooks for CDs that hold the CD and the case booklet. If you can't bear to take them out of the original case, you can get specially made storage towers or shelves. For the low-tech music lover: Cover a cardboard shoe box with fabric and store them inside.

- **Keepsakes:** If you're the kind of person who has to save baby's first tooth, the necklace you caught at MardiGras, the dried bouquet from your first prom, or the matches from your cruise, at least keep them organized. If you like to look at them often, buy a deep shadow box picture frame and mount several items inside, dated and labeled. Otherwise, get a large storage box with a lid and keep everything inside. Try to limit yourself to one box. You might want to organize your keepsakes by category or event — wedding, baby stuff, vacations, and the like — so you have one box for each. When stuff starts getting up to the rim, follow the "one in, one out" rule that I discuss in Chapter 1. Give something away before you put in a new item.

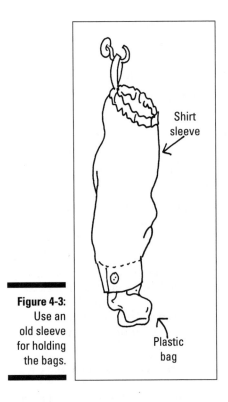

**Figure 4-3:**
Use an old sleeve for holding the bags.

Shirt sleeve

Plastic bag

# Safe Storage Dos and Don'ts

Finding a place to store things doesn't do you much good if the space isn't safe for the items you're storing or for you and your family members. Accidents happen, and prevention is the best policy — even for storage spaces. The following sections present the basics of storage safety.

## Dos

Remember the following list to avoid accidents when storing things:

✔ **Do clean any item made out of fabric before you store it.** (See Chapter 11 for more information about cleaning fabrics.) Bugs love to eat any kind of food stain, even those you can't see.

✔ **Do protect clothes, records, books, or anything of value from moisture damage in a moist climate.** If you have to store items in the basement or garage, protect them from moisture by placing them in large plastic trash cans or storage boxes with tight-fitting lids. Friends of mine have lost books and records because they were stored unprotected in a basement that flooded. Keep anything of value off the floor if possible. If you have room, install metal shelves available from home centers. They're cheap, sturdy, and easy to assemble.

✔ **Do store breakable items on sturdy shelves in a low traffic area.** Vibrations from walking and other movements could precipitate a fall if you use a frequently entered area. Avoid using a busy area in the basement or garage where family members could bump into shelves.

✔ **Do keep anything that could be dangerous to children out of their reach.** Store household chemicals, weapons, knives, plant supplies, and cosmetics up high or in a locked cabinet. For extra protection, wrap sharp objects in a cloth or push corks onto the sharp points. See Chapter 22 for more tips to childproof your home.

✔ **Do keep a list of everything you store.** For insurance purposes, describe what each item is and how much it's worth. This accounting should really be done for everything in your home, room by room. Store this list and any other important papers in a fireproof lockbox or in a safety deposit box.

## Don'ts

Follow these don'ts to keep you and your stored items in good shape:

✔ **Don't store clothes in plastic bags.** Garments can't breathe properly in them. In a moist climate, this can promote mildew.

✔ **Don't cram things into closets or drawers.** Cramming causes clothes to wrinkle, and delicate items will break in cramped space if they are jostled around too much.

✔ **Don't store heavyweight items high or on precarious shelves.** You can lose your balance easily if you're standing on a ladder to get these items, increasing the chances of an accident.

✔ **Don't store things in a very damp room.** They can rust or become mildewed.

✔ **Don't store anything near the source of direct heat.** Many items like vinyl records, compact discs, computer equipment, and film can be warped and permanently damaged. Avoid any extremes of temperature.

# Fighting the Paper Pile-Up

To me, paper is one of the biggest storage problems we face. Reams come into our homes every day through the mail, from schools, and in magazines and newspapers. Add to that the coupons, bills, ATM receipts, and magazine clippings that we want to save and the amount gets enormous. To keep it under control, you've got to establish a daily routine to deal with it. Set up a work area to go through paperwork. It could be a desk, a countertop, or a board on top of two file cabinets; just make sure that you have some place for storage. Keep your supplies, paper, pens, tape and labels, and files within arm's reach. Then use the following tips to help keep your paper under control:

- **Take a few minutes every day to go through incoming papers and act on them immediately.** Try to go by the organizing principle of handling every piece of paper only once. Stand by a wastebasket as you go through the mail and immediately dump anything you don't want into the trash. Put any other papers in different folders as you go through them. Label them according to what action you're going to take: Pay, File, Read, Answer, Call. Have a "hold" file for things you're going to use soon, such as invitations, tickets, and announcements. If you do it every day, it will be a lot easier than trying to muddle through a month-long pile of papers.

- **Keep all your bills in one place so that none get lost.** A friend of mine stores bills to be paid in a pretty basket hanging on the wall by the door. Because she looks at them every day as she goes in and out, she never forgets to pay them on time. If looking at your bills every day doesn't appeal to you, keep them together in a file, a box, or drawer with some stamps and pens nearby. Schedule times to pay them.

- **Set up a permanent filing system.** Use a small metal file, a deep drawer, or a cardboard box to hold everything. I like to use hanging file folders because they're easier to leaf through, and they don't fall over when you move them. Label the permanent files clearly or color code them by category if that's easier for you — for example: blue folders for mortgage, pink folders for kids' sports information, yellow folders for repair bills. Go through these files periodically and clean them out. Anything over a year should either be thrown away or labeled and stored in a permanent file in an out-of-the-way storage place.

The real problem with paper overload is not only getting it, but wanting to save it. I have such an urge to clip and save that I've often thought the perfect job would be working for a clipping service. I could read all day, clip lots of stuff, and then give it to someone else. The following sections provide some suggestions for what to do with those papers that tend to become permanent residents after entering your house.

## Newspapers and magazines

Store your newspapers as you go through them in a "recycle-ready" paper grocery bag. At the end of the week, you can just carry the bag, papers and all, out to the recycling bin.

Before you cut out another clipping from the newspaper, ask yourself "Can I find this somewhere else?" Chances are, most of the stuff you're saving can be found in a library or on the Internet. Many daily newspapers are online now, so you can keep up on the news on your computer without dealing with stacks of paper.

Magazines are another pile-up problem. It's easy to sign up for a lot of magazines before you realize how many are stacking up in your house. Set yourself a limit. Once a year, look at all the subscriptions you have and cancel any that you don't read regularly. Remember, you can always buy them at the newsstand if you see an article you want to read. Or get together with some friends and share subscriptions.

Organize the magazines you receive by storing them in a central place in a large basket or magazine rack.

Clipping fever hits many people who subscribe to magazines. If you're the kind of person who clips now to read later, just be sure to file as you go. Put the clipping in the proper file: to read, to call, travel information, and so on, so that you can find the article when you need it. Try to follow the one-in, one-out rule: Every time you put something in, look through the file and see if there's an item you can get rid of. If you don't need the information for something specific, throw it out.

# Recipes

I hate to admit it, but I am a recipe junkie. I have clipped hundreds of pieces of paper thinking that one will be the ultimate recipe. Recipe clippings can definitely get out of hand and, of course, as with anything else you clip, the recipes are no good to you if you can't find them in a snap.

Talk to 10 different people and you'll find 10 different ways of keeping recipes. I store mine in a loose-leaf binder with vinyl sleeves and dividers for different food categories. The clippings stay put when you slip them in the sleeves, but they can be moved or removed easily. When I'm cooking, I can take out a page, carry it to anywhere I need, lay it down on the counter, and the vinyl coating protects it from spills. I like binders better than recipe boxes because you don't have to recopy the recipe onto small index cards, and you have more room for longer recipes.

A woman I work with, who has a lot of cookbooks, likes to write the names and pages of her favorite recipes from each book on the book's front inside page. When she opens the cookbook, she can tell at a glance what her favorites are from that book.

To cut down on the amount of clippings you save, specify a certain day each week to try a new recipe. Throw out the ones you don't like. Or stop clipping altogether and use your computer to store your favorite recipes or research new ones on the Internet. I know some great Web sites that offer thousands of recipes along with nutritional information and cooking tips. Among my favorites is www.food.epicurious.com.

## Memorabilia

Memorabilia are the sentimental stuff that you don't really "use" but can't bear to throw away. What are they? Holiday or birthday cards, special dinner menus, the picture of the winning soccer team, your kid's artwork, a postcard from last year's summer cruise, personal letters, graduations programs.

Don't feel guilty about saving it, but don't be overly sentimental either. Go through this pile of stuff like Scrooge and ask yourself if it really has any special meaning. Try to throw at least half of it away. Then store your memorabilia in a sturdy box with a cover. If you have several family members, give each a box with a label. When stuff gets to the top of the box, go through it again and see what you can discard.

If you have the time, arrange your memorabilia by year in a scrapbook, an album, or a three-ring notebook. You'll be more apt to look at it and enjoy it that way.

To protect valuable mementos and records from fire or flood, store them in a fireproof, metal strong box in a safe place in your house or in a safety deposit box in the bank.

## Craft stuff

Anyone who does any craft or building projects has plenty of paper lying around. Not finding a piece of a pattern when you need it can be very annoying. Following a few simple guidelines will help avoid this frustration:

- ✔ Don't try to stuff patterns back into their original envelopes. Instead, get some plain 8 ½ x 11-inch business envelopes and put all the pieces inside. Tape the original pattern envelope to the outside so you can identify it at a glance. File the envelopes together in a cabinet or a heavy-duty expanding file.

- ✔ Go through your patterns periodically and get rid of the ones that are out of style or no longer fit.

- ✔ If you want to save craft projects from a magazine, cut out all the instructions along with the photograph of the finished project, staple them together, and file them in an envelope.

# Photographs

The ideal way to organize photographs is to go through each set, identify and date them, and put them in a photo album. Avoid common magnetic albums. After a few years, they can stain and damage photographs. If the negatives are valuable to you, purchase special storage sleeves from a photo shop that fit into a three-ring binder.

The casual way to organize photos is to file them in a special photo box for long-term storage, or a shoe box if you're not worried about preserving them for posterity. Separate them with index cards that have information about the pictures and the date written on it. If, like most of us, you probably won't use the negatives again in this century, either throw them out or file them together in another box in their original envelopes.

To keep photos in top condition, don't store them in a room with temperature extremes or in a moist basement or garage.

Cut down on the number of pictures you're saving by throwing away any that aren't flattering, have unknown people in them, or aren't perfect technically. Just save the good ones. Remember, for every good photograph you see in a magazine, dozens are taken and are laying unused in envelopes somewhere.

# Warranties and instruction manuals

Save warranties and instruction manuals in case of operation questions or repairs. Store these booklets together in an expanding file folder with labeled sections: dishwasher, water, microwave, tools, small appliances, and so on. Staple the store receipt to the back of the manual. If you need proof of purchase for a warranty, you'll be able to find it easily.

# Chapter 5

# Dust-Busting

* * * * * * * * * * * * * * * * * * * * * * * * * * * * * * * * * * * * * * * * * * *

* * * * * * * * * * * * * * * * * * * * * * * * * * * * * * * * * * * * * * * * * * *

*1* know, you hate to dust. So what else is new? Dusting can be frustrating, time-consuming, and, well, just plain dusty. You clean one day, and then, seemingly from nowhere, dust reappears.

But, like failing to floss your teeth, dust can wreak havoc if it's ignored. Something that might have taken a few minutes can turn into a full-scale attack with scrub brushes, heavy duty cleaners, and hours of hard labor. Take mini blinds, for instance. They're a pain to dust, but basically it's a quick swipe with your weapon of choice and they're done. If ignored (believe me, I know from experience), airborne grease and dirt cling to them like glue. To get them clean, you're facing a day-long task of removing them from the window, hosing them down outside, drying them in the sun, and then rein-stalling them. (It makes me shudder to just think about it.)

Aside from just good looks, getting rid of the dust is good for you and your family's health. I can tell how long dusting has been ignored by the number of sneezes I make when I enter a room. Five or six sneezes tells me it's time to dust. With all the unknown allergens in your life (see Chapter 21 for an almost-complete rundown), this allergen is simple to deal with.

## *The Dust-Busters: Dusting Tools*

Clean cloths are the number one dust-busting tool. The best dust cloths are lint free and 100 percent cotton. (There's no point in using dust cloths that will just leave a trail of some other substance in their path.) Recycle those unwearable light-colored T-shits, cotton flannel pajamas, and old linen napkins by turning them into dust cloths. Just cut them into a size that's large enough to fold a couple of times and hold comfortably in your hand. That way you can dust on one side and then turn to the other side and refold when one side gets dirty. Other good sources of dust cloths are cloth diapers (unused and washed, of course), fabric scraps, and cheesecloth.

When cutting up old clothes, make sure you take off any buttons, zippers, or other objects that could scratch your furniture.

Treat your own dustcloths: Dip cloths in a solution of 2 cups water and 2 tablespoons lemon oil and air dry before using. Do not machine dry.

## *Lambswool duster*

A long fluffy tube of lambswool on a stick is a favorite of professional cleaners because it attracts and holds dust. Try to get one that has a handle that can be extended to ceiling height so you can clean chandeliers and ceiling corners without having to get up on a ladder (see Figure 5-1). After you're finished using the duster, take it outside and shake it or bang it against the bottom of your shoe until the dust comes off. In my opinion, lambswool works much better than a feather duster, which has a tendency to just move the dust around rather than picking it up.

**Figure 5-1:**
Use an extension on your lambswool duster for ceilings and such.

## The versatile vacuum cleaner

The vacuum is an under-appreciated cleaning tool. You may think of it as something to use just to clean the carpet, but with just a few attachments (see Figure 5-2), your vacuum can help you speed-clean the whole house. The most commonly used attachments include the

- ✔ **Crevice tool:** Picks up dirt from wicker furniture, wall heaters, windows and window sills, heating ducts, air conditioner filters, and furniture crevices.

- ✔ **Dusting brush:** Also cleans along baseboards, shelves, top of door frames, window sills, piano keys, carved furniture and picture frames, door moldings.

- ✔ **Upholstery tool:** Sucks out dust from upholstery and can also be used for draperies, mattresses, carpet stairs.

- ✔ **Wall/Floor brush:** Gets surface dirt off walls, non-carpeted floors, and ceilings.

Your vacuum is one of the best tools you can use for dusting because it actually picks up the dust and holds it inside the machine until the bag can be emptied. All canister and most upright vacuum have crevice and brush attachments that clip onto the hose, enabling you to pick up from just about anywhere with ease.

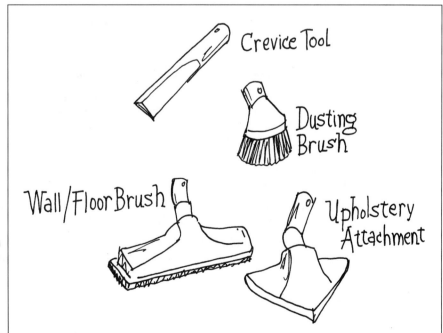

**Figure 5-2:**
Some useful vacuum cleaner attachments.

# Keeping dust in check

Follow these tips to ward off dust before it can take hold:

**Use a doormat by all entrances.** Most professional cleaners claim that the biggest cause of household dirt and dust is carried in through the front door. And not in bags, but on the soles of our feet. Stopping short of trying to get your family and guests to take off their shoes (a losing task as far as I'm concerned), the problem can be kept in check by putting mats in front of all the exterior entrances. Not just any mat either. Forget about the crocheted mat your Aunt Doris gave you. It's got to have a solid rubber backing that prevents slippage when you're rubbing shoes back and forth on it. And it should be stiff enough to scrape off the dirt.

**Do a filter check.** Change or clean the filters in your air conditioners and furnace every month or two depending on how serious your dust problems are. Don't forget to vacuum the dust and lint from the heating vents and registers often. They are the main source of air to your home and if they are dusty, they're just transmitting dust to the rest of the room.

**Be a dirt detective.** Look for hidden dust in forgotten places that you can't see at first glance like beneath your refrigerator, behind the sofa, the floor of your closet, window sills, and moldings.

**Make your house airtight.** Keep your windows closed. Check caulking and weather stripping around your home. If windows and doors aren't sealed tightly enough, dust will seep in continuously and your dusting won't be able to keep up with it.

**Remove the dust catchers.** Sift through plants, knickknacks, loads of shelves, silk flowers, for starters. I know you don't want to give them up, but if you're really concerned about dust, these are some of the major places where dust collects and sits. If you can't bear to part with your collections, keep them in cabinets with glass front doors and cleaning will be much easier.

## *Unconventional dusting products*

Have you noticed that many people take sheer joy in making do with what they have? With that in mind, I've included some more unconventional products that many friends have adapted to suit their own particular dusting style:

- **Hair dryer:** Okay, I know it blows the dust around, but set on cool, it's a fast and quick solution to get dust out of delicate areas like around silk flowers or on knickknacks.

- **Old socks:** I especially like these because I can't feel the dirt but still have the flexibility to clean carved furniture or table legs.

- **Soft paintbrush:** A new soft bristle brush is great for getting into narrow areas like door jambs, around window moldings, and into corners.

- **Dryer softener sheets:** A favorite of many friends who cringe at the thought of wasting anything. They swear that used softener sheets actually prevent dust from collecting. It is logical after all — static electricity is what attracts dust to things like TV sets and glass topped tables. If those little sheets keep static electricity off clothes, they should work to keep it off other possessions as well.

- **Cotton gloves:** You may have worn them in the fifties (don't tell anyone if you did) or you've seen them in vintage clothes stores or tag sales. Pick some up and use them to clean. They're soft and flexible so you can manipulate your hands into and around small items like mini-blind slats.

- **Wedge-shaped foam paint brush:** The narrow end of this brush makes it a natural to get into small areas like the tracks of the sliding doors or the corner of windows.

Some people like to use the two-fisted method and put a sock or a glove on each hand. They get double the cleaning with half the effort, covering twice as much surface in half the time.

# Dusting 101 . . . How Do You Dust

In case I haven't said it in plain English yet, the basic idea of dusting is to pick up the dust and remove it — not just move it around or fling it into the air. The simplest method is to spray a very light spritz of water on a cloth, and dirt will cling to the cloth like magic. Spray-dusting products like Endust are helpful too, especially when you're dusting furniture. Just make sure you spray liquid on the cloth, not the item you're cleaning.

Table 5-1 presents some common dust collectors you may have in your house and methods of cleaning them:

| Table 5-1 | Daily Dusting How-To's | |
|---|---|---|
| *Item* | *By Hand* | *By Machine (Vacuum Cleaner Attachment)* |
| Blinds (mini or venetian) | Lambswool dusting tool or cotton gloves | Dusting brush |
| Computer screen | Wipe with soft cloth | Soft dusting brush or tiny minivacs designed for the purpose |
| Computer keys | Wipe with a soft cloth from the center out | Dusting brush |

*(continued)*

**Table 5-1 (continued)**

| Item | By Hand | By Machine (Vacuum Cleaner Attachment) |
|------|---------|----------------------------------------|
| Dresser drawers | Move everything to one side, wipe with cloth | Crevice attachment |
| Books | Lambswool dusting wand or socks | Dusting brush |
| Framed posters, pictures | Soft cloth very lightly misted with glass cleaner | Soft dusting brush |
| Leather furniture | Wipe with a soft cloth or old socks | Dusting brush |
| Pleated lampshade | Paintbrush or hair dryer | Dusting brush |
| Radiator | Old sock on the end of a yardstick | Crevice tool |
| Shutters | Foam brush or old socks | Dusting brush |
| Sofa | Whisk broom | Upholstery attachment |
| Telephone | Soft cloth misted with all purpose cleaner | Dusting brush |
| Wood surfaces | Soft cloth sprayed with dust control spray (like Endust) | Dusting brush |

## Start at the top: The natural order of dusting

Everything in life has a natural order, and this applies to dusting as well. The rule is: Dust from the top down. The reason is simple — gravity.

Dirt falls down to the floor when you dust. So why would you want to make double work for yourself by cleaning the tabletop first and then have to back-track when the cobwebs from the ceiling gently fall on top of it? Your goal here is to clean once, not twice.

## Dust first, then vacuum

This is another logical order, but one worth repeating. Since dirt will fall onto the floor when you're dusting, it makes sense to vacuum after you're finished. It makes it even easier because you don't have to worry about where the dust is falling. Save your vacuuming for the final pickup.

Dust and vacuum on rainy or humid days. The dampness keeps the dust from rising and floating.

## Solve your special dusting problems

I cover the most common dusting problems earlier in this chapter, but some items in the home can make you scratch your head and put off dusting for another week or two — not the way to go. Stop scratching and read on for solutions to some of your dusting dilemmas:

- **Under appliances:** Secure a leg of old pantyhose or a sock around the end of a yardstick with a rubberband or thumbtack and slide under the appliance.

- **Cobwebs on ceiling:** Wrap an old T-shirt or towel around the end of a broom. Hold in place with the twist tie from garbage bags or a rubber band.

- **Chandelier:** Get in and around the bulbs and arms of your light fixture with a soft lambswool duster on an extension rod.

- **Silk flowers:** Set the hair dryer on low and move it in a back and forth motion over the flowers. The dust will blow right off.

If you're sweeping dust into a dustpan, moisten the pan slightly to keep the dust from floating out of the dustpan and into the air.

# Chapter 6

# Vertical Cleaning: Windows and Walls

Cleaning windows and walls is time well spent. If either is dingy, the whole room takes on an unkempt look. No matter how much you clean and polish the other items in the room, it will never feel really clean. It's like dressing to the nines without combing your hair or polishing your shoes. You may look okay, but something is marring the finish.

Then, why does everyone cringe at the thought of cleaning walls and windows? It's a big job but not a really tough one. All it takes is water, cleaning solution, and a little elbow grease. And the benefits are obvious. Without even changing a light bulb, rooms instantly look brighter. And everything else looks cleaner by comparison.

## Ya Say Ya Don't Do Windows?

Gazing out a sparkling clean window does wonders to improve your outlook on the world. A dirty window makes everything look gray and depressing. But through a clean one, the world looks sharp and promising. Depending on your weather and general environment, the job needs to be done only once or twice a year. You'll instinctively know that it's time to clean when you see a gentle haze covering your view.

The job goes a lot faster if you have some able-bodied help. A good candidate is someone who really wants something (a video game or new shoes) or someone who owes you a big favor (they stayed out too late or forgot your birthday). Get the troops assembled! Sponges! Squeegees! Water! Speed is of the essence. The faster you work, the fewer streaks you'll have and the sooner it will be done.

## Putting together a window-cleaning kit

You've probably got most of the items needed for a basic window-cleaning kit around the house. But one thing that you may need to invest in is a squeegee. If you've got large expanses of window surfaces, a squeegee really helps speed up the job.

- **Good sponge:** Used to apply the cleaning solution onto the glass. It should be a size that fits comfortably into your hand and a couple of inches thick. You can use a rag, but it's messier. Don't use any rags of a brightly colored fabric that could bleed onto the panes, the wall, or your clothing.

- **Large plastic bucket:** Get one with a sturdy bottom and handle so it won't tip over. If you have two buckets, use them for this job. One holds the cleaning solution, and the other holds either the dirty water or clean rinse water.

- **Old towels or sheets:** Lay them on the floor to protect your flooring from any drips or spills.

- **Squeegee:** This is one tool that all cleaning professionals agree is a must. It makes wiping the solution off windows much easier. Look for one with a soft and pliable rubber blade (see Figure 6-1). It should adhere firmly to the window so that the water comes off evenly. Adding an extension rod will help you reach those high windows.

- **Water-resistant apron:** This is a job where you really need an apron. Unless you are one of the neatest people on the face of the earth, your clothes will get messy. Either wear something that you want to mess up so you'll have an excuse to throw it out, or dress in a water-resistant poncho or apron.

  Make a disposable apron from a large garbage bag. Cut holes for your head and arms, and slip it over your clothes. You may look a little strange, but it will definitely protect you from dirty water.

## Washing windows from start to finish

Okay, you've got a squeegee and, if you're wearing a waterproof apron, you look like a geek, but following these tips will make your window washing a success:

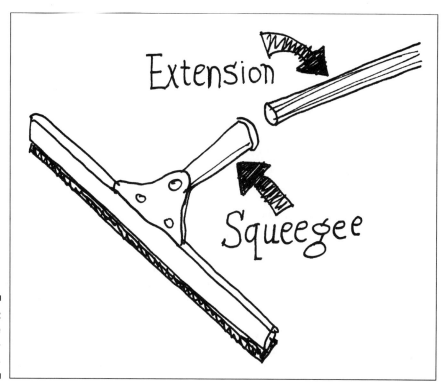

**Figure 6-1:**
A squeegee and extension rod.

✔ **Remove window screens:** Take the window screens out before beginning your cleaning.

✔ **Stay out of the sun:** Don't wash windows on a bright, sunny day. I'm not worried about the UV rays, although this can be a problem if you are outside washing windows all day. The fact is that if you work in direct sun, the dirty water dries on the windows before you can wipe it off. That practically guarantees streaking. A warm, dry day is the optimum condition. Obviously, avoid window washing when you see a huge snow cloud or thunderstorm overhead.

✔ **Clean from top to bottom:** Like many cleaning jobs, windows should be washed starting at the top and working your way down. This trick keeps the part that you've already cleaned free from drips.

✔ **Consider water as your best friend:** If you've been a consistent cleaner and your windows aren't covered by a thick layer of grime, you can use the simplest ingredient ever — water. That's just fine for rinsing off a thin coat of dirt.

✔ **Use soap sparingly:** If you haven't been good and the dirt is a little thicker on those panes, don't make a common mistake and think that a thick mixture of detergent and water will clean your windows faster. Too much soap is a near disaster because it causes streaks and leaves a thin film that's difficult to rinse off. As with any cleaning job, use detergents sparingly to avoid spending unnecessary time rinsing off the cleaning solution.

✔ **Mix some solutions at home:** Commercial window cleaners are cheap and easy to use. For heavy-duty dirt, you can make your own cleaner from 4 tablespoons of either non-sudsy ammonia or vinegar (don't mix them together) and 1 gallon of water.

To give windows extra shine, use this old-fashioned mixture ¼ cup cornstarch in ½ gallon of warm water. It gets rid of dirt quickly and makes windows sparkle.

✔ **Don't let the solution drip off the windows:** Dunk your sponge into the cleaning solution and wring it out so that it isn't dripping wet. The fewer drips you have going down the window, the faster the cleaning will go. Move the sponge over the window, and cover it with the solution.

✔ **Squeegee away:** It's time to put that squeegee to use. After the window is wet, start at the top corner and pull the squeegee across from side to side. This stops the cleaning solution from dripping down. Use overlapping vertical strokes to clean off the rest of the window.

Between each swipe of the squeegee, wipe the dirty water off the blade with a damp cloth. It's important to use a damp wiping cloth to lubricate the blade so that it glides easily across the glass. Always use overlapping strokes, whether you're wiping vertically or horizontally, to reduce the chance of streaking.

✔ **Take pains with the small panes:** Soak a sponge in cleaning solution, wring it out, and wipe the pane in a circular motion. Dry with a clean cloth.

✔ **Use a blackboard eraser for last-minute shine:** Do you still see some streaks or feel that your windows look dull? After the windows are dry, rub the glass with an ordinary blackboard eraser. It eliminates marks and makes the glass shine.

## Newspaper to clean windows?

Although many people swear by newspaper to wipe down windows, an equal number of people say that it's not the best way to dry them. Proponents of the newspaper method say the ink on the newspaper gives windows extra shine. Nonbelievers point to the mess created by mounds of wet newspapers. After the newspaper gets wet, the ink can bleed on your hands and anything else nearby. Any kind of paper (including some types of paper towels) has the tendency to just move the cleaner around on the window. My favorite solution is the squeegee. It's less messy and works more efficiently because it actually lifts and removes dirty water.

## Which side are the streaks on?

If you're washing both the inside and outside of your windows on the same day, use a side-to-side stroke on the outside and an up-and-down stroke on the inside. If a streak appears, you'll know quickly where the problem is.

## *Solving special problems*

Washing windows doesn't just involve panes of glass. Other parts of the window need consideration. Here's how to deal with some of them.

- ✔ **Wood windowsills and window frames:** Clean the sills before you wash the windows themselves. Why? Dirty water is going to drip on something whenever you wash. Cleaning a few drips on the sills is a lot better than rewashing a whole window. First, give the sills and frames a quick swipe with the brush attachment of a vacuum cleaner to remove surface dirt. Wash with a mild solution of 1 teaspoon of liquid dish detergent and 1 gallon of warm water, but use the same caution as you would when dealing with any wood surface. Don't saturate the wood with water. Wring the sponge out thoroughly and wipe quickly. Rinse and dry thoroughly.

    To clean hard-to-get-at dirt in the corners of windows, use an old toothbrush or a cotton swab.

- ✔ **Aluminum frames:** Avoid using strong ammonia cleaner on unpainted aluminum windows. It can cause pitting and damage the finish. Give aluminum frames a good shine with a cream polish meant for cleaning your silver.

    *Weather alert:* The temperature of aluminum windows is affected by the weather outside. On a really hot day, the aluminum may be too hot to touch comfortably.

- ✔ **Paint on window glass:** Remove paint drips left from your last paint job by first soaking the area with a sponge dipped in warm vinegar to soften the paint and then gently scraping away the spot with a plastic spatula or credit card. If that doesn't work, try using a flat razor or paint scraper and working in one direction, gently lifting off the paint. Be careful not to scratch the glass.

- ✔ **Stubborn stains:** Rub stains with a rag dipped into a strong solution of ammonia and water. If the stains persist, work on them with a plastic scrubber or a soft brush. (Test on a small area first to make sure that it doesn't scratch the glass.) Rinse off thoroughly with water. Hard water sprinkler spots can be removed by rubbing with a cloth dipped in white vinegar and then rinsing.

✔ **Fiberglass:** Wash with a solution of ½ teaspoon dishwashing liquid to ½ gallon water. Rinse; then dry with a clean cloth. Don't use anything abrasive.

✔ **Stained glass:** Spray with a glass cleaner and wipe dry with a clean cloth. Don't use any abrasive sponges, cleaners, or cleanser; they can scratch glass.

## Scouring those screens

Unless you have casement windows, you've got to remove the screens before you wash the windows outside, so why not dive in and clean them too? Before you take the screens off, write a number on a hidden corner of the window and write the corresponding number on the screen. When you put the screens back on, match the numbers on the windows, and the screens will be back in the right places.

While the screens are still on the window, vacuum them with the brush attachment. This step saves time because it gets rid of a substantial amount of dirt quickly. Then remove the screens, carry them outside, and lay them down on an old sheet or dropcloth. Scrub the screens with a brush and a mixture of all-purpose cleaning solution and warm water. Rinse them off with the hose. Shake the screens to get rid of excess water, and let them dry in the sun.

# Cleaning Window Treatments

When selecting window coverings, take heed: Elaborate window treatments with yards and yards of pleated fabric are real dust catchers, and long billowy curtains puddled on the floor are just waiting for stains to happen. Simpler is better, as far as cleaning is concerned. Before you buy any window treatment, check to see whether it's washable or can only be dry cleaned. At least you'll know what you're in for when the inevitable happens. Certain windows in your house may get more use or may be subject to dust. In those areas, you should get window fabrics or blinds that are washable.

## Roller shades

If you dust roller shades regularly with a soft cloth or the brush attachment of the vacuum, you won't need to go crazy cleaning the whole shade. Most of the dirt will be near the bottom of the shade, where fingers leave telltale marks when you pull the shade up or down. If the shade is washable, clean the smudges by wiping the shade with a soft cloth dipped in a mild detergent solution. If the shade isn't washable, or you just can't face cleaning the whole thing with soap and water, rub marks off with an art gum eraser available in art stores.

---

# Loosening a stuck window

If your window just won't budge, try these ideas.

✔ Position a small block of wood against the sash and tap the block lightly with a hammer. Repeat this action all the way around the sash.

✔ Slide the dull blade of a kitchen knife or spatula gently between the sash and the window frame. Work it back and forth across the bottom and up and down along the sides of the sash.

---

A shade that's been hanging up for a long time and needs a thorough cleaning can be washed with a soft cloth and a mild detergent solution. Take the shade down and unroll it on a flat surface for the easiest cleaning job. Put an old (but clean) plastic shower curtain underneath. Keep the ends flat by holding them down with a brick or a bottle filled with beans or rocks. If the shade has a rough finish, use a soft brush in a gentle scrubbing motion. Otherwise, a cloth is fine. Wash in sections and rinse as you go. Shake off the water and hang the shade unrolled on the window to dry. Put a protective cloth on the floor underneath.

## Mini-blinds

You can save yourself lots of work if you remember to dust your blinds often, as I talk about in Chapter 5. The dust eventually turns into a sticky coating that is hard to remove. If your blinds are just a little dirty, wash them in place.

First, lay a plastic cloth underneath to catch drips. Slip your hands into a pair of old cotton tube socks (or cotton gloves) from your rag bag and dip them into a solution of all-purpose cleaner and water. Wring them out well. (This is a situation where wringing your hands actually does some good.) Start at the top of the blinds and wrap your hands around one slat at a time, moving from side to side. Rinse with a damp sponge or cloth and towel dry each slat.

If your blinds are really dirty, more serious methods are in order. Remove them from the windows. Take them outside (not on your neighbor's front lawn) and lay them down, fully extended, on a plastic dropcloth. Wash with a solution of your favorite all-purpose household cleaner and water. Let them dry on the cloth or hang them on a clothesline.

If outdoors is not an option, give your blinds a good bath. To guard against your tub getting scratched, cover the bottom with a clean, plastic shower curtain. Fill the tub about halfway with an all-purpose cleaner and water. Open the blinds and spread them out in the tub. Let them soak for several minutes; then wash both sides with a sponge. Drain the water and refill the tub with clear water to rinse the blinds. Drain again and wipe off as much water as you can with a dry cloth. Hang them back up on their brackets, but be sure to protect the floor with a couple of old towels or a shower curtain.

## Curtains and drapes

Regular dusting of window treatments with a vacuum is the most effective way to keep them clean. Gently grip the fabric and pull it tight, then vacuum gently from the top to the bottom with the dusting attachment of your vacuum.

You can also "dust" them by tossing them in the clothes dryer on the "air only" setting. Of course, that involves taking them down and putting them back up. Be sure to remove any rings or hooks before putting them in the dryer.

Before attempting to wash curtains or drapes, check the manufacturer's care label. If you can't find one, it's best to have them dry cleaned.

Many curtains today are safe for the washer and dryer. If you wash and dry them at home, remove them from the dryer immediately and hang them over the shower curtain rod. This lessens wrinkling and can practically eliminate ironing in many cases, especially if they are made from a polyester fiber.

If your draperies are washable, check the care label for the lining fabric. It's often a different type of fabric than the drape itself. If the lining is more fragile than the drape, follow those instructions for washing. Avoid washing any drapery treatments that are very full and heavy. The weight of wet fabric could wreak havoc with your washer. Be safe and have them dry cleaned.

## Getting Rid of Dirt on Your Walls

Unfortunately, a dirty wall can make a whole room look shabby even if everything else is in relatively good condition. Spots on walls seem to appear mysteriously like they do on your clothes. Oh sure, kids may occasionally decide to do artwork on the wall, but marks that appear out of nowhere look so noticeable — they almost seem to glow in the dark. If you're bothered by a dirty wall, you may think "Why wash? I'll just wait and paint." In reality, washing the wall is much cheaper, faster, and less painful — in terms of disruption to your life — than painting. But, don't get too worried yet. In most rooms, all you need is some judicious spot cleaning and dusting to keep the walls looking good.

Keep in mind that some paint finishes don't wash well. Flat paints don't tolerate washing well, while gloss and semigloss finishes usually wash wonderfully. Always test on a hidden area first.

## Washing walls, step by step

Two widely divided schools of thought exist when it comes to washing walls. The classic method says to wash from the bottom up because drip marks are easier to remove from clean walls than dirty ones. The other method says that you're going to have drips anyway, so why drip on newly cleaned walls. Whichever method you choose, the most important thing is to keep drips under control by wringing out your sponge or cloth judiciously and washing a small area at a time. Follow this simple step-by-step method:

1. **Dust the walls to remove any surface dirt.**

   Use a vacuum cleaner or a broom that's covered with a T-shirt or pantyhose pick up dirt.

2. **Mix up a cleaning solution.**

   Use a solution of all-purpose cleaner and water or a light squirt of liquid dish detergent and water in a bucket.

3. **Dunk a 1½-inch-thick sponge about halfway into the solution.**

   Doing so keeps the sponge from getting so saturated that it causes excessive dripping. Wring it out slightly, but leave enough solution to get the wall wet.

4. **Wash a small area at a time.**

   Don't make broad, sweeping strokes trying to cover the whole wall at once. Stick to an arm's reach, about a 3-foot-by-3-foot section, overlapping with the preceding area as you go. If you try to do a large area, the wall dries before you have a chance to rinse it off. That practically guarantees streaking. Squeeze the dirty water out of the sponge as you go. Rinse the wall well, and then move to the next area. If your walls are particularly dirty, you may have to make several changes of water.

5. **After you've covered several sections, wipe the area dry with a clean, absorbent cloth, such as a cloth diaper or towel.**

6. **Don't forget your baseboards.**

   They often get dirtier than walls because of shoe scuffs or bumps from the vacuum cleaner. After you've washed the wall, wipe down the baseboard with the same solution and dry it with a cloth.

## Making your wallpaper pretty again

The good news is that most wallpaper sold today is vinyl coated, so it's easy to wash. The bad news is that eventually it gets dirty, and if you leave dirt on for too long, it will be even harder to get off.

Sometimes you can avoid washing altogether if you give the wallpaper a good dusting. Vacuum the wallpaper in an upward motion with the brush attachment of your vacuum cleaner. This works great on untreated or flocked paper and fabric-covered walls. If your vacuum won't reach the ceiling, use the old-fashioned method of tying a T-shirt or pantyhose around a broom and giving the walls a once-over.

If you still think you've got to wash, check beforehand to make sure that the paper is either water-resistant or vinyl-coated and can stand up to washing. Look on the back of your roll of wallpaper or check with the store where you purchased it. Don't wash any untreated wallpaper.

Test the cleaning solution on a hidden section of wall before you start. If the paper isn't damaged, keep going. Wash in the same way as described previously for walls, using as little water as possible. Too much water near the seams can cause the paper to pull away from the wall.

Clean nonwashable wallpaper with a special dough-type cleaner available at paint stores (see Figure 6-2). Rub the paper with the dough in overlapping strokes, folding as you go to keep exposing clean surfaces of the dough. Always test on a hidden portion of the wall first.

## Cleaning wood paneling

The reason people get wood paneling in the first place is that it's easy to take care of. Most real and fake (hardboard) paneling has a protective finish that, if dusted regularly with the brush attachment of your vacuum, will remain in pretty good shape.

For a more thorough cleaning, wipe with a soft cloth, lightly moistened with a mild solution of water and a vegetable-based detergent, such as Murphy's Oil Soap. Don't soak the paneling with liquid or leave it wet for a long time. To dry, wipe it down with a towel, following the grain of the wood as you go.

## Doing doors

Most doors need only spot cleaning around the knob, edges, and bottom. If the door is wood, wipe off the smudges with a mild solution of Murphy's Oil Soap and water. If the door is painted or is made of another material, spritz on some mild household cleaner, let it sit for a minute or two, and then wipe it dry.

Wallpaper Dough

Scuff marks from shoes on the bottom of a door can be removed with a pencil eraser or a spray of cleaning solution and a light scrub with plastic scrubber. Test on an out-of-the-way section to make sure that this doesn't remove the finish.

# Attacking Stains on Walls

If you keep up with spot cleaning, your walls will stay clean and sparkling for years. By the time you think you should wash the walls, you'll want to change the color anyway. But in case some unforeseen glitches occur, use these methods to get common stains off.

## Stain solving on washable walls

The kind of paint on your walls will affect your ability to get stains out. A flat paint is porous and absorbs dirt and grime, making stain removal difficult. Use flat paint in areas with less traffic, such as bedrooms or living rooms. Paint with some sheen — gloss, semi-gloss, eggshell, or satin — is more stain- and dirt-resistant. Use this kind of paint in hallways and kitchens.

When treating stains on either finish, wash the stain first with a detergent solution. If the stain remains and you want to use an abrasive cleaner, be aware that it may affect the finish. Lots of scrubbing on a wall with an abrasive cleanser will take off some of the paint finish. It's especially noticeable on semi-gloss paint because the sheen will appear flat. You may get the stain off, but you'll also have a big dull spot. Flat paint is more accepting of an abrasive cleaner, but if you scrub too hard, you may expose any other painted surface underneath.

Ammonia-based cleaners can cause discoloration in oil-based paints. They have a tendency to turn yellow. Check the label on your cleaner. If it has ammonia in it, be sure to dilute it with plenty of water.

This list gives you cleaning tips for some troublesome messes that you may encounter:

- **Tape:** Masking tape that's been left on walls is hard, but not impossible, to get off. Lift off the end of the tape by moistening with a dab of oil-free nail polish remover to soften the glue. Pick up the end and start peeling the tape back slowly and evenly. Then set your hair dryer on low, and move it back and forth across the tape as you pull it. The heat from the dryer will soften the glue and make it easy to pull. After the tape is gone, wash with a detergent and water solution.

- **Crayon:** Many kids look at a big blank wall as a canvas waiting to be filled up. I know I did once — but only once. Crayon marks can be the bane of a parent's existence, but the problem is easily solved. Spray the area with a multipurpose spray such as WD-40 and let it stand for a few minutes. Wipe clean with a soft cloth or paper towel. Then wash the area with a mild solution of liquid dish detergent and water. Rinse off with a damp sponge.

  Test this on a small hidden area first. Do not use on a wall with flat paint. Use in a well ventilated area away from heat.

- **Grease:** This can be a tough one to tackle. First, try wiping it off with a paper towel, and then spraying with a heavy-duty household cleaning detergent. Let the detergent sit for a few seconds, and then rinse and dry. If that doesn't work, try applying a paste of cornstarch and water. Let it dry to a powder, and then vacuum it off.

- **Scuff marks:** You usually have scuff marks along baseboards or at the bottom of doors. Try rubbing them off with an art gum eraser. Or spritz lightly with an all-purpose cleaning solution and rub gently with a plastic scrubber until the stain comes off.

# Stain solving on wallpaper

Before you start treating any stain, be sure to test the cleaning method on a hidden part of the wall. Even if a paper is vinyl or waterproof, don't take a chance. Fixing damaged wallpaper is a big job. This list gives you hints for cleaning some of the most common messes on wallpaper.

✔ **Grease:** Blot the grease with a paper towel. Then place several white paper towels or thick blotting paper over the stain and press the paper with an iron set on low heat. The idea is to make the grease dissolve into the paper. Depending on how much grease is in the paper — and for your sake, I hope it isn't much — keep repeating this technique with a clean section of paper until the grease is absorbed. You may have to make several tries. If it's only a small stain, try rubbing the spot with a piece of rye bread. Work the bread into a ball and rub the area gently. Or, you can try to make an absorbent paste out of cornstarch and water, apply it to the spot, and let it dry.

✔ **Crayon:** Use the same technique as for washable wallpaper or try the WD-40 solution in the wall section. Spot test on a section first. It may be impossible to remove crayon from non-washable paper.

✔ **Fingerprints:** Dirt and grime on fingers can often be a problem especially around light switches. Rub gently with an art gum eraser or a piece of rye bread wadded into a ball.

✔ **Felt-tip pen:** If you're lucky and the pen contains washable ink, wipe the spot with some mild detergent and water. Or spritz with laundry prewash spray, rinse, and wipe dry. If that doesn't work, blot the area with a cloth moistened with rubbing alcohol, but test on a hidden area first. Just remember that spots from these pens can spread like crazy, so when you're treating them, blot up the stain very carefully.

# Chapter 7

# Dirt Underfoot: Cleaning Floors and Carpets

. . . . . . . . . . . . . . . . . . . . . . . . . . . . . . . . . . . . . . . . . . . . .

*In This Chapter*

▶ Taking care of wood floors

▶ Keeping carpets clean

▶ Getting rid of stains and spots

. . . . . . . . . . . . . . . . . . . . . . . . . . . . . . . . . . . . . . . . . . . . .

*O*h, the beatings a floor can take! Season after season, dirt is continually carried into your home from streets, lawns, sidewalks, and dirt paths on the soles of every person who walks in the door. Along with the dirt come the scratches, spills, and scrapes from shoes, furniture, skates, bikes, and other two-legged and four-legged things.

Keeping your floors clean is not only crucial to the good look of your home but is actually necessary for the longevity of the floor. Hard pieces of dirt left on floors can cause nicks and scratches. Stains and spills can be difficult, if not impossible, to clean if left unchecked. Vacuuming, sweeping, and dust-mopping regularly are the best defense.

# Get a Handle on Dirt

Unless you live in a plastic bubble, dirt will find its way into your home. You can minimize its effect by using some common-sense methods that bear repeating.

✔ **Mat it down:** Put thick mats inside and outside of all entrances and exits to your house. Cleaning professional Don Aslett says that 80 percent of the dirt in a home comes in through the doors. Door mats remove dirt, mud, and grime from the soles of shoes before the dirt can be scattered throughout the house.

✓ **Cover it up:** Before starting any kind of messy project — washing the windows, painting the walls, dyeing your hair, feeding your two-year-old — cover the surrounding area with some kind of protection. If you like to load up on professional gear, buy a couple of inexpensive plastic tarps at a hardware store or other store that sells home improvement items. They're like big sheets of plastic wrap. Otherwise, grab some newspaper, old shower curtains that aren't too grungy, or your tent's tarp. Then, when the drips start to fall (and you know they will), you have something protecting the surface.

✓ **Blot it off:** Whether a spill happens on a wood floor, linoleum, or nice fluffy carpet, get a paper towel or rag to wipe it up immediately. I learned this unfortunate life lesson long ago: The longer you procrastinate, the more the spill will seep into the carpet or the floor's finish and possibly become a permanent stain.

# Be Kind to Your Flooring

Floors are tough, but they aren't impervious to everything. They can be hurt, too. Before using any floor care product, read the label and be sure that it's the right product for your floor. Many products may be good for one surface but can ruin another. If you're moving into a new house or an apartment, ask the owner or builder to give you information about the type of flooring that's installed: what material it is, how it's been treated, and any written product or warranty information.

## Caring for wood floors

Wood floors are beautiful and long lasting, but they usually require more care than other surfaces. After all, good looks don't always come easy. You should vacuum and dust-mop at least once a week to remove dust and debris from the seams between the boards and to prevent dirt from being ground into the floor.

Use the brush attachment on your vacuum cleaner that's meant specifically for hard floors. Some attachments and the heads of most upright vacuums have beater bars that fluff the fibers of carpet but can damage the surface of a wood floor. A canister vacuum with special bare floor attachments is a good investment if you have lots of wood flooring.

### Finishing school for your floors

The type of finish on your wood floor determines what kind of care you give it. Two basic types of finishes exist:

✔ **Surface finish:** If your floor has been installed recently, it probably has what's called a *hard coat finish* — a protective coating that looks like clear plastic on top of the wood. The most popular hard coat finish is polyurethane, but several other treatments look and act the same. All are relatively carefree and never need waxing. This type of finish can scratch, however, so be careful when moving furniture.

To test whether you have a urethane-finished floor, dab a few drops of paint remover on a hidden area of the floor like a corner or a closet as the finish will be permanently altered. If the finish bubbles in a few minutes, it's a hard coat finish.

To clean a hard-coat-finished floor, first sweep or vacuum with the bare floor attachment; then give it a quick damp-mopping with a mixture of ½ cup white vinegar and 1 gallon water. Dip a sponge mop into the solution, wring it out very thoroughly — it should be about half dry — and then mop a section of the floor. Mop up any drips or puddles. Dry the floor with a clean cloth as you go along.

Or use a cleaner made specifically for the finish on your floor. Check with the manufacturer of your floor for recommendations.

Never use wax or any oil-based cleaners on a surface finish. If you find a dull spot on the floor, rub it with a clean, soft cloth until the shine comes back.

✔ **Penetrating wax finish:** This type of finish applied as a wax on the surface is absorbed into the wood fibers, which protects the floor from within against dirt, stains, chips, and scratches. It usually has a matte or satin appearance. A new floor with this type of finish should be waxed before the floor is used as an added protection against dirt.

If you aren't sure whether your floor has a penetrating finish, move your hand across the floor's surface. If you can feel the wood grain, your floor probably has a penetrating finish.

If the finish looks dull, buff it with a clean, soft rag. If that doesn't work, use a one-step cleaner/polisher made specifically for this type of floor. Apply a thin coat over a small area and spread it evenly with a wax applicator, rubbing in the direction of the grain. Wipe off any excess liquid. Let the cleaner dry for about 20 minutes and then buff with a clean cloth. You probably won't need to wax more than once or twice a year, but pay special attention to high-traffic areas. They may need additional vacuuming or waxing to keep their shiny finish. (Use mats or throw rugs to cut down on your cleaning time.)

In addition, painted or faux (fake) finished wood floors are popular today. They can be a stop-gap cure for a floor that's not in great condition. You don't have to spend the time or money to refinish the floor. Clean with a mixture of 1 gallon of water and 2 tablespoons of mild soap (such as Murphy's Oil Soap), wringing out the mop so that it's almost dry before you apply the cleaning solution. Wipe dry with a clean cloth.

Never soak a wood floor with any liquid.

### Protecting the finish

Wood floors, like wood furniture, are strong — some have been around for centuries. But because they are porous, wood floors don't react well to excess moisture, extremes of weather, or poor treatment. Take these minor precautions to help keep your wood floors in good shape:

✔ Never saturate a wood floor with water. Water can cause the planks to warp and buckle, raise the grain, and stain the finish.

✔ Avoid scratches by putting some kind of covering on the bottoms of chair legs. Try these treatments:

• Coat chair legs with a layer of clear nail polish, rub them with floor wax, or glue on felt floor protectors (the kind that are sold at home centers, discount stores, or catalogs).

• When moving a piece of furniture, slip tube socks over the legs or lay old towels underneath them. You can then pull or push the sofa or chair wherever you want and not have to worry about scratches or scuffs on the floor.

✔ Because hiking boots with lug soles and cowboy boots with stiff wooden heels can wreak havoc with some finishes, put your foot down and insist that heavy-soled people leave their boots outside with the wild animals.

✔ To prevent fading or other discoloration due to sunlight, close the curtains or blinds during periods of intense sun or install sheer curtains to block ultraviolet (UV) rays.

Floors with a penetrating wax finish need to be waxed with a liquid or paste wax at least once a year. The easiest method is to apply a liquid wax, but paste waxes are more durable. Be sure to read the label and buy one that's made for your floor. Using waxes made for resilient or tile floors can damage the finish. And don't try to use furniture polish on your floor. My friend Ingrid did this and, not only did it make the floor dangerously slippery, it also took forever to get off.

### Providing disaster relief for waxed floors

Accidents will happen, and most can be treated effectively if you hop to it and take immediate action. Table 7-1 addresses some common problems and solutions for waxed floors only. Don't use these methods on any floor treated with polyurethane or other surface treatments.

| Table 7-1 | Wood Floor Stains and Common Solutions |
|---|---|
| *Stain* | *Solution* |
| Alcohol | Rub the spot with liquid or paste wax. |
| Burns | Rub with extra fine steel wool dipped in floor cleaner. Wipe dry. Rewax. |
| Chewing gum, crayon, wax | Harden the area with an ice cube until the gunk is brittle and scrapes off with a dull knife. If debris remains, apply some solvent-based wax around it (but not on it) and allow to soak under the stain to loosen. |
| Heel marks, scratches | Rub with fine steel wool dipped in floor cleaner. Wipe dry. Rewax. |
| Oil, grease | Soak cotton with hydrogen peroxide and apply to the stain. Soak a second piece of cotton with plain ammonia and put it on top of the first layer of cotton. Repeat until the stain is absorbed. |
| Water | Rub the stain with very fine steel wool and rewax. For large stains, lightly sand with fine sandpaper, and then clean with a very fine steel wool and mineral spirits or floor cleaner. Refinish and rewax. |

## Maintaining resilient floors

Most of us have some kind of resilient floor — vinyl, no-wax vinyl, asphalt tile, linoleum — somewhere in our homes. They are the unglamorous work-horses that seem to look good no matter what you do to them. But they, too, need regular cleaning to keep them in top shape. Doesn't everything? You can find a wide selection of good commercial cleaners at most grocery stores, discount stores, and home centers. Be sure to read the label carefully so that you buy the right kind of cleaner for your particular floor.

To clean a resilient floor, first vacuum the floor before washing it so that you can remove any surface dirt. If the floor is only slightly dirty, damp-mop by going over it with a mixture of all-purpose cleaner and water. Be sure to read the cleaner's label to make sure that it works on your type of floor. To damp mop, follow these steps:

1. **Dip the mop into the cleaning solution and wring it out well so that it isn't dripping wet.**

   This is the *damp mop* part.

# Buyer, be smart

When you're trying to decide what type of flooring to buy, stop and do a reality check before you make a purchase. Certain types of flooring require more care than others. If you're a low-maintenance person (like I am), shop smart and consider the following before you take out your credit card and commit yourself to a life of continuous cleaning:

✔ **Avoid light or dark solid colors.** Practically every bit of dust, dirt, and grime will show up in a big way. We all know that light colors show dirt more — just look at all your white shirts with stains on them. But most people think that dark colors will hide the dirt. Not so! Dust, dirt, and sand are lighter in color than you think. They show up more on a dark surface than on a light one.

✔ **Look for multi-colored patterns.** A variety of different colors and textures can camouflage dirt and scratches much better than solid color surfaces.

✔ **Avoid floors with deep grooves in the pattern.** As you'd expect, dirt just sinks into the indentations below the surface, making it and hard to clean. Slightly textured floors are good for hiding scuffs, dirt, and scratches. But avoid a deeply patterned texture. Like the floor with grooves, a textured floor tends to hold the soil and look dirty.

✔ **Avoid floors with a matte (dull) finish.** Floors with a matte finish look great and are fashionable, but you notice stains and spills more than on a shiny surface. Matte floors need more care than other finishes to look their best.

2. **Mop a small area at a time (about 3 or 4 feet).**

3. **Rinse and wring the mop frequently.**

   Have two buckets handy — one for your cleaning solution and one for clean water.

4. **Check the cleaning solution, and change it when it becomes too dirty.**

5. **Rinse the floor with clean water, and wipe it dry with a clean rag.**

   Wiping dry rather than air-dryings may sound like an unnecessary step, but you get more dirt up in the extra wiping process than you can imagine. The more dirt that comes up now, the longer you can wait until your next cleaning.

Always test a new cleaner on an inconspicuous corner to make sure that it doesn't damage a floor. Never flood a resilient floor with water. It can seep into the seams and cause the floor to buckle.

Table 7-2 is a useful day-to-day cleaning chart for common floor surfaces in your home. You may also have problems with grungy grout between the tiles. Stop grout-cleaning problems by sealing new grout on a tile floor with silicone sealer. Clean old, dirty grout with a heavy-duty household cleaner and a grout brush. For heavily stained grout, scrub with a solution of 2 tablespoons liquid chlorine bleach to 4 cups of water.

**Table 7-2     Cleaning Chart for Various Non-Wood Hard Floor Surfaces**

| Surface | To Clean | To Polish | To Fix Scuffs and Heel Marks | Avoid |
|---------|----------|-----------|------------------------------|-------|
| Ceramic tile, glazed | Vacuum and damp-mop with an all-purpose cleaner; dry with a soft cloth. | Doesn't need polishing. | Rub with a plastic scouring pad and non-abrasive cleaner. | Abrasive cleaners. |
| Ceramic tile, unglazed | Vacuum and damp-mop with an all-purpose cleaner. | Once a year, strip the finish and reseal with a commercial sealer and water-based wax or acrylic self-polishing wax. | Rub with a plastic scouring pad and non-abrasive cleaner. | Abrasive cleaners, strong soaps, or acids. |
| Linoleum | Vacuum and damp-mop with a mild all-purpose cleaner. | Apply two thin coats of self-polishing, water-based floor wax; let dry between coats. | Rub gently with fine grade steel wool dipped in liquid floor wax; wipe off with a damp cloth. | Solvent-based products, hot water, and strong soaps. |
| Vinyl | Vacuum and damp-mop with an all-purpose cleaner dissolved in water. | Apply two thin coats of self-polishing, water-based floor wax; let dry between coats. | Scrub lightly with a synthetic scouring pad dipped in liquid floor wax; wipe with a damp towel. | Abrasive cleaners. |
| Vinyl, no-wax | Vacuum and damp-mop with an all-purpose cleaner recommended for no-wax floors | Surface should have a permanent shine, but if it becomes dull in high-traffic areas, apply a commercial gloss-renewing product. | | Solvent-based products or cleaners with pine oil, strong soap, hot water, or abrasives. |

# Keep Your Carpet Clean

Keeping your carpet clean not only pleases your mother but actually extends the life of the carpet. If you don't remove the surface dirt and grime, they get ground into and imbedded in the carpet fibers, eventually causing the fibers to break down. When the fibers break down, the carpet can lose its finish and resilience. In addition, the deeper the dirt gets into the fibers, the harder the dirt is to remove. Regular weekly cleaning (more often in high-traffic areas) is the optimum way to keep your carpet clean and healthy.

## Vacuuming 101

Before you start to vacuum, declutter the area so you don't have to start and stop while working. Go around the room and pick up toys, coins, paper clips, safety pins, rubber bands, and other small objects that can clog the vacuum. (This is a good job for kids to do.)

If you're working on a large room, don't try to vacuum the whole width and length at once. Break the room into small sections so that you can easily keep track of what you've done. Getting your rug really clean takes time, so put on your Walkman, start meditating on the millennium, and go slowly over each section.

Move the vacuum back and forth in overlapping strokes. You really need to go over each section several times to suck up all the dirt. A quick once-over won't do it!

High-traffic areas such as hallways, entrances, and exits need ever more coverage — the National Carpet and Rug Institute suggests going over them seven times.

Remember this time-saving tip: You can cut down on vacuuming and save wear and tear on your carpet by putting throw rugs in high traffic areas. Popping a throw rug into the washing machine is much easier than vacuuming a whole room.

Other areas besides hallways get a lot of heavy use: the carpet in front of chairs and sofas, under desks, near the phone, and so on. When you sit down, you unknowingly deposit lots of dirt when you rub your shoes over the carpet. To make sure that you get all the grime when vacuuming, move the chair a couple of inches or lift the leg of the chair or table and vacuum underneath.

Every few weeks, move all the furniture to one side of the room and use the attachments to give all the hidden areas a deep cleaning.

### Avoiding problems

Although, vacuuming is relatively simple, a few problems can arise. Follow these tips for a handle on these special cases:

- ✔ **Static electricity:** If your carpet makes sparks when you walk across the room, mist it very lightly with a mixture of ½ cup fabric softener and 2½ cups water. Don't walk on it until it dries thoroughly.

- ✔ **Area (or throw) rugs:** Vacuum both the top and underneath of an area rug to get rid of dirt particles that wear down the rug. Stand on one end of the rug to hold it down and keep it from being sucked into the vacuum. Sisal should be wiped down with a damp cloth after vacuuming.

   To fluff up the fibers on a small throw rug, shake it out well and then throw it into the dryer on air fluff with a damp towel. If the rug needs to be cleaned, follow the manufacturer's instructions. If it's washable, put it in the washing machine with warm — not hot — water. If the rug has a rubber backing, dry it on the lowest setting. Intense heat from either the washer or dryer can make the backing disintegrate.

- ✔ **Fringe:** To prevent fringe from being caught in the agitator, set your canister vacuum on low and use the upholstery tool, if you have one. If you have an upright vacuum, tilt it back on its wheels and push it *over,* but *not on,* the fringe.

### Keeping your vacuum in good health

Check periodically to make sure that the brushes on the head of your vacuum are clean and that the hoses are free from obstacles that could restrict air passages.

If you think the hose is blocked, turn off the machine and unplug it. Disconnect and straighten out the hose. Gently move a broomstick or a straightened hanger into the hose to dislodge anything that may be stuck inside. Remove any threads that are twisted around the brushes by cutting and gently unraveling them after the machine is turned off.

If you feel the machine is lacking suction power, check the soil bag. The problem may be that the bag's too full. The vacuum runs more efficiently when the soil bag is less full. Check the bag frequently, and change it when it's about half full.

## Staying on top of spots and spills

Stains and spills are going to happen. That's a fact of life.

You can forbid everyone to eat in the living room, and you can make family and friends take off their shoes, but eventually, someone or something is going to slip and splat. And then you've got a spot.

But don't panic. If you're prepared, you can do lots of things before you start calling in the disaster squad. The key is to tackle the spot quickly, before it sets, using clean white cloths or paper towels.

In your anxiety to treat the spill quickly, however, you need to avoid the following don'ts:

- **Don't use colored cloths or towels to wipe up a spot.** The liquid in the spill can make any colored dyes in the cloth bleed onto the carpet and cause a new stain, which could be a worse problem than the spill. Talk about double trouble!

- **Don't rub or scrub the spot.** Thinking that the more you rub, the better you clean is a natural reaction. But it's not true! In this case, rubbing and scrubbing can force the spill further into the fibers of the carpet and make it more difficult to clean.

- **Don't pour cleaning fluid on the spot:** Flooding a spot with too much cleaning fluid (even if it is The Good Stuff) can spread the stain and damage the backing of the carpet. Use a spray bottle or blot it with a clean cloth.

- **Don't remove the cleaning solution immediately:** Let it sit on the spot for 5 to 10 minutes. Then start blotting.

Instead, be prepared. Put together a few necessary supplies in a carryall tray or basket. The following section describes what's needed in a quick-'n'-easy spot and stain removal kit. And when disaster strikes:

- **Act fast.** Your chances of removing a spot skyrocket if you act immediately. You don't have to clear out the room and stop traffic. Just do something to work on the stain right away.

- **If it's solid, scrape it up.** That piece of chocolate, or mound of mud should be removed with a spoon while it's still intact. If it's dry, vacuum it up. Many times, the majority of the spill can be eliminated before you attack it with any cleaning liquid.

- **Blot up liquid spills.** Use a white absorbent cloth or several white paper towels. Don't rub or scrub, which can spread the mess. Just keep pressing with the towels until all the liquid is absorbed. Sometimes just a light spray of plain water will lift a spot. Blot gently afterward.

Stockpile these essentials in a carryall tray or basket for the day when disaster strikes, and you'll be able to bound into action faster than a speeding bullet:

- Several thick, absorbent, white cloths, such as towels, washcloths, or cloth diapers (my favorite!)

- Liquid dishwashing detergent

- Dry-cleaning solvent available at hardware or department stores.

✔ Spray bottle filled with a mixture of ¼ teaspoon liquid dishwashing liquid and 1 cup water

✔ Spray bottle of clear water for rinsing

✔ White vinegar

✔ Plain ammonia

✔ Nail polish remover — nonacetone

✔ Spoon or old credit card to scrape up solid spills

### Following basic spot-removal techniques

You can be successful at cleaning up spills if you have patience and some stick-to-itiveness. Just remember that spots don't always come up easily. You may have to repeat a spot removal technique several times until you achieve success. Rinse off each cleaning solution before applying another one. Don't be lulled into complacency because you have a stain-resistant treatment on your carpet — it's a good defense against stains but even with that protection, certain spills can leave permanent marks if left untreated.

Table 7-3 lists common spots and suggested removal strategies. Follow the strategies in order, starting with the first suggested spot removal solution and continue as long as there is improvement. If that doesn't work, go on to the next step. Remember, keep trying. If the stain remains, call a professional.

| Table 7-3 | Spot Removal Chart for Carpets | | | | |
|---|---|---|---|---|---|
| *Spill* | | | *Solutions* | | |
| | *Step 1* | *Step 2* | *Step 3* | *Step 4* | *Step 5* |
| Alcohol | Detergent | Ammonia | White vinegar | Warm water rinse | Call a pro |
| Candy | Detergent | Ammonia | White vinegar | Warm water rinse | Call a pro |
| Chocolate | Dry-cleaning fluid | Detergent | Ammonia | White vinegar | Warm water rinse |
| Coffee with cream and sugar | Dry-cleaning fluid | Detergent | White vinegar | Warm water rinse | Spot removal kit |
| Crayon | Dry-cleaning fluid | Detergent | Call a pro | | |
| Egg | Detergent | Ammonia | White vinegar | Warm water rinse | Call a pro |

*(continued)*

**Table 7-3** *(continued)*

| Spill | Step 1 | Step 2 | Solutions Step 3 | Step 4 | Step 5 |
|-------|--------|--------|------------------|--------|--------|
| Glue, household | Detergent | White vinegar | Warm water rinse | Spot removal kit | Call a pro |
| Grape juice | Detergent | White vinegar | Warm water rinse | Spot removal kit | Call a pro |
| Greasy food | Dry-cleaning fluid | Detergent | Warm water rinse | Call a pro | |
| Markers, felt tip | Detergent | Warm water rinse | Call a pro | | |
| Salad dressing | Dry-cleaning fluid | Detergent | Spot removal kit | Warm water rinse | Call a pro |
| Spaghetti sauce | Detergent | Ammonia | Warm water rinse | Call a pro | |
| Wine | Detergent | White vinegar | Ammonia | Warm water rinse | Spot removal kit |

The Carpet and Rug Institute suggests taking the following steps for getting rid of most spots. Remember to act fast, scraping up solids and blotting up liquids.

1. **Pretest any spot removal solution on a hidden portion of the carpet to see whether it damages the fibers or dye.**

   To pretest the solution:

   - Put a few drops of cleaner on each color of the carpet, and hold a clean cloth or towel on the area for 10 seconds.

   - Check whether any dyes from the carpet bled onto the cloth or whether the carpet appears changed in any way.

   - If you see any change, try another cleaning solution or call a professional.

2. **Apply a few drops of the first suggested cleaning solution from Table 7-3, let sit 5 to 10 minutes, and blot gently.**

   Work from the edges of the spill to the center to prevent the spill from spreading. Keep blotting and applying the cleaning solution until no more of the spill transfers to the cloth. This may require several tries.

3. **If you no longer see any improvement, rinse with warm water, blot, and then go to the next solution listed in the table and repeat these steps.**

After you've removed the spill, rinse the spot and cleaning solution thoroughly with a spray bottle or a dab of water on a clean cloth. Don't pour on water when rinsing; you don't want moisture in the floor or padding. Press down on the area with an absorbent cloth to soak up all the cleaning solution.

To absorb the liquid, cover the area with several white paper towels and weight them down with a heavy, flat object (books or magazines may fade into the carpet). Replace the paper towels and continue this process until all the moisture is absorbed.

### Making your own spot-removal solutions

Follow these concentrations recommended by the Carpet and Rug Institute when mixing the cleaning solutions used in Table 7-3. Anything stronger may damage the carpet. If you need to try two or three different cleaning solutions on the same spot, use in the order suggested in Table 7-3 and be sure to rinse between each step.

- ✔ **Detergent solution:** Mix ¼ teaspoon dishwashing liquid (clear, non-bleach, non-lanolin) with 1 cup warm water. After you apply the solution, let it sit on the stain for 8 to 10 minutes and then rinse thoroughly until all the detergent disappears.

  Never use automatic dishwashing detergent or laundry detergent — each of these products contains chemicals that may change or even destroy the color of the carpet.

- ✔ **White vinegar solution:** Mix 1 cup white vinegar with 2 cups water.

- ✔ **Ammonia solution:** Mix 2 tablespoons household ammonia with 1 cup water.

- ✔ **Dry-cleaning fluid:** Use a nonflammable spot removal solution, such as Carbona Stain Devils or K2R. Put the cleaning fluid on a cloth or sponge — not directly on the carpet, which could destroy the backing.

- ✔ **Nail polish remover:** Use one that contains acetone (read the label) and treat in the same manner as dry-cleaning solvent. Those containing amyl acetate can be used, but they leave a residue that can cause rapid soiling.

- ✔ **Spot-removal kit:** Available at carpet and department stores, they contain a stain-resistant solution that's applied after the detergent solution that's also in the kit. Be careful not to apply the stain-resistant solution before the spot is completely removed or the stain could become permanent. Also available for most common household spots are dry extraction cleaning compound kits. Follow the directions carefully on both kits.

If you've tried all the suggested solutions and nothing works, throw in the towel and call a professional rug cleaner. For other carpeting questions, call the Carpet and Rug Institute at 800-882-8846 or go to its Web site at www.carpet-rug.com.

### Handling pet stains, burns, smells, and other special carpet problems

These three stains are really tough (but not impossible) to remove:

- **Animal messes:** Blot liquid messes with a towel, and scrape off solids with a spoon. Flush with lukewarm water, and then apply a mixture of equal parts white vinegar and water. Again, blot the liquid until it's dry. If the spot remains, apply a solution of ¼ teaspoon dishwashing liquid and 1 cup water. Blot again. Reapply the vinegar solution and let it sit for 5 minutes. Then blot the excess liquid with several towels, replacing the towels until all the moisture is removed. For several pet messes, use an enzymatic cleaner from a pet store. Follow the label instructions and test on a hidden area first.

- **Chewing gum:** Put an ice cube in a plastic bag and hold it on top of the gum to harden it. Pick at the gum and pull off as much as you can very carefully so that you don't pull up any carpet fibers. Dot with methyl salicylate (Extra-Strength Ben-Gay) and gently pull the rest off. After the gum is removed, clean the area with a detergent solution, followed by a warm water rinse.

- **Ink:** Pour a small amount of rubbing alcohol (90 percent isopropyl) on a cloth. Dot the stain carefully, following the previously mentioned basic stain removal techniques, and then blot. Don't pour alcohol directly on the stain or rub the stain — that can cause ink to spread. And believe me, when ink spreads, there's no stopping it.

In addition, your carpet can be marred by other types of accidents and events. Even just having your furniture sit still on the carpet for long periods of time can cause problems. The following list provides solutions to the most common concerns:

- **Burns:** For a small burn from a cigarette or a match, carefully clip off any blackened tufts in the rug, using small, sharp scissors. Trim the fibers around the immediate area very slightly so the indentation won't show so much. If you have a small area that's burned down to the backing, you can try repairing it, as shown in Figure 7-1.

    Using a utility knife guided and a metal ruler, cut a square patch of carpeting slightly larger than the burned area from a carpet remnant or hidden area like a closet floor. Center the patch over the burned area and cut a piece of the area the same size as the patch. Be careful not to cut through the pad. Remove the damaged piece and check to make sure the new patch fits. Line the outside of the hole with double-stick carpet tape. Lightly apply fabric glue to the edges of the patch and the patch into the hole. After the glue sets, fluff up the fibers between the patch and the surrounding carpet to blend them in.

If the burn is large, call a professional to replace that area of carpet.

✔ **Dents:** Dents occur when furniture stays in one place for a long time. Prevent this problem by periodically repositioning your furniture around the room. Moving it slightly will do the trick. To fix a dent, brush the area with your fingertips to loosen and gently pull up the tufts. Wait a couple of days, and if the depression still exists, mist the area with warm water. Hold a hair dryer set at low over the area and lift the pile with your fingertips while you move the dryer back and forth over the spot.

Cutting Carpet patch to fit

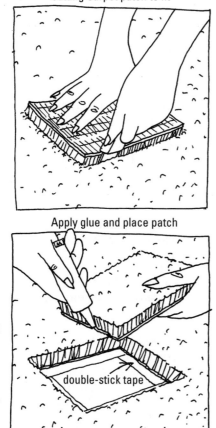

Apply glue and place patch

double-stick tape

**Figure 7-1:**
You can repair small burns with tufts of carpet.

- **Fading:** The color of a carpet or rug can fade if the carpet is continually exposed to strong sunlight. Your best defense is to draw the curtains during the day when the sun is at its brightest. (Dyed nylon or olefin carpets resist fading better than other fabrics.)

- **Carpet odors:** Sprinkle a dry carpet with baking soda, wait 15 minutes, and then vacuum. (Test on a hidden corner first.) Or use a commercial oder remover.

- **Snags:** A loose carpet thread that has pulled away from the carpet is known as a snag. Clip it off carefully with small scissors so that it's level with the rest of the carpet. As an extra precaution, knot before clipping. Don't pull on it — you could unravel the carpet. What a long thread that would be!

## Doing "The Big Clean"

Every 12 to 18 months, you should have your carpet deep-cleaned before it looks dirty. This is just what you think it is — a big job. You have three basic methods to choose from (use the method recommended by the carpet manufacturer to maintain the warranty if it's still valid):

- **Dry extraction:** A dry compound is brushed on the rug, the soil is absorbed into the compound, and the carpet is vacuumed.

- **Rotary shampoo:** A neutral detergent, made just for carpet, is applied to the carpet. Br sure to rinse and extract all the moisture.

- **Water extraction:** A cleaning solution is injected into the pile and then extracted. The extraction of all the moisture is inportant.

The easiest to do yourself is the dry extraction method. But you can rent equipment and do the rotary shampoo or water extraction methods yourself. Just be sure to follow the manufacturer's directions for the equipment and apply the solutions carefully. Don't use more than the suggested amount of shampoo solution and minimize the amount of water used. Residue left on carpet can cause faster resoiling. As I said, it's a big job, and that means you can make a big mess if you aren't careful.

If you choose to have your carpet professionally cleaned, do a little research before you pick a service. Ask your friends for recommendations, or the store where you purchased your carpet. Have the service come to your home to make an estimate. Get everything in writing. After you decide on a company, check with the Better Business Bureau to see if any complaints have been filed against it. Be wary of anyone who offers an excessively low price or who adds on a lot of *extras* to the price. Like everything else, if it sounds too good to be true, it is.

# Chapter 8

# Cleaning Furniture and Other Objects d'House

. . . . . . . . . . . . . . . . . . . . . . . . . . . . . . . . . . . . . . . . . . . . . .

## In This Chapter

▶ Cleaning wood furniture

▶ Taking care of upholstered pieces

▶ Caring for other furniture types, such as leather and wicker

▶ Cleaning electronics and other miscellaneous stuff

. . . . . . . . . . . . . . . . . . . . . . . . . . . . . . . . . . . . . . . . . . . . . .

Since I started going to flea markets and watching a TV program called *The Antiques Road Show,* I've had this recurring dream: Twenty years ago, I bought a little table for twenty bucks. Then I go on this TV show and they tell me that there are only two tables like it in the entire universe, but unfortunately, mine is only worth one-half a gazillion bucks because I've been using the wrong polish all these years. The finish just ain't what it used to be.

Fortunately, this is only a dream. The maintenance, care, and cleaning of your furniture need not be a nightmare. The three basic enemies of furniture are dust, sunlight, and liquid — all the elements of the primordial soup that gave birth to the universe. Dust, sun, and moisture can also put an end to your fine furniture if you let them have their way with it. In this chapter, I give you the weapons you need to foil these invaders.

Remember that, unlike clothing, furniture doesn't always come with a care label. Always inquire about care and cleaning when you purchase a piece from an antique dealer, furniture store, or craftsman.

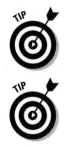
If you purchase a fine antique, write down any special cleaning and care information on the dealer's business card. Store this with any other relevant information, such as the receipt of purchase, in a home file.

Dry winter air, direct sunlight, and heat are bad for furniture because they dry out the wood. To combat the problem, use a humidifier in the winter, hang curtains to reduce sunlight, and keep furniture away from direct heat sources such as radiators or heating vents.

# Taking Care of Wood Furniture

Traditionally, only two types of finishes were used on wood furniture. The first is an oil finish, sometimes referred to as a *soft finish* because of its porous nature and feel. This type of finish is most often found on older and finer pieces. The second, and by far the most common, is a shellac, lacquer, polyurethane, or varnished finish that is sometimes referred to as a *hard finish*. Recently, however, some manufacturers of mass-produced furniture have been applying a third type of finish — a plastic laminate finish similar to a no-wax floor in its ease of care and upkeep. Knowing the finish on your furniture is key to giving it proper care.

The easiest way to determine if your furniture has an oil finish is to apply a dab of boiled linseed oil to a cloth and rub it on. If the oil disappears and is absorbed into the finish, you have an oiled (or soft) finish. If it's not absorbed and instead beads up like drops of water on glass, you have a hard (or lacquered) finish. Wipe off the oil. Don't panic if the finish momentarily darkens. The oil will eventually be absorbed into the wood.

Boiled linseed oil is available in hardware stores, already labeled as "boiled." Never boil or heat it up at home.

## Polishing different finishes

After you determine what type of finish your furniture has, select a polish or wax made specifically for that type of finish and test it on a hidden area. Read all the product information on the bottle. After you find a product that you like, stick with it. Applying one polish on top of another brand can sometimes dull the finish. Never apply wax to a soft (or oiled) finish because doing so can damage the surface.

Whether your finish is oiled or lacquered, never apply polish or wax directly to the wood. Always apply it first to a soft, lint-free cloth and then use the cloth on the wood. Also, never apply polish or wax without dusting first to avoid grinding in the dust and embedding it in the finish.

### Caring for oiled finishes

Many polishes for oil finishes are available commercially. Clean furniture with oiled finishes regularly with a lightly dampened cloth to remove dust. Once a year, apply boiled linseed oil or some comparable product in a well-ventilated area to replenish the natural sheen of the finish and to prevent the wood from drying out. Never apply wax to a soft (oiled) finish as it can damage the surface.

---

# The first line of defense

Dust is everywhere. You can see it in the sunlight. You can't avoid it, but you can stop it from damaging your furniture (and creating a sneeze-field in your home) by regular dusting.

Dusting is the first line of defense in the care and cleaning of furniture. To prevent any unsightly and damaging build-up of dirt, you should dust from once to several times a week, depending on your personal standards of cleanliness. Remember these two important things: Never "dry-dust," and always move in the direction of the wood's grain.

Dry-dusting is just what it sounds like: You dust with a dry, untreated cloth. Dry dusting can scratch your furniture, and it doesn't really do a good job of getting rid of the dust. Always use a soft cloth to dust, and always treat the cloth with some kind of dusting spray, which not only has an antistatic agent but also helps reduce the abrasive effects of dusting. Remember: You want to pick up the dust in your dust cloth, not spread it around or throw it off the furniture into the room.

Always dust in the direction of the wood's grain. Failure to do so over a period of time can cause scratches and stress in the wood's finish — sort of like swimming against a current. For more about the proper way to dust, see Chapter 5.

---

You can also clean and revive an oil finish every six months with lemon oil, which is actually mineral oil scented with lemon. Apply the oil to a clean cloth, and rub it in. If you spray or apply the oil directly onto a piece of furniture, you run the risk of saturating the oil in one particular spot or allowing it to build up around hardware, cracks, crevices, and decorative moldings.

### Polishing and cleaning varnished and lacquered finishes

With varnished and lacquered finishes, dust about once a week with a soft cloth slightly dampened with a dust spray. Every eight weeks or so, apply a wax polish appropriate for your type of finish. Polish in the direction of the grain and buff with a clean cloth to avoid build-up.

Don't over-polish furniture. Over-polishing creates a dust trap and build-up of wax.

Hand wash and air-dry any cloths used for polishing and waxing furniture. Never put them in the washer and dryer. They can leave a harmful residue in the washer and are flammable in the heat of the dryer.

You can add a certain degree of gloss by buffing, but a truly shiny surface is best obtained in the original finish. In other words, buy your furniture with a high-gloss finish, if that's your cup of tea.

Protect surfaces that get a lot of wear, such as the arms of chairs and rockers, by polishing them more frequently.

Lightly dust fine antique furniture or exotic woods often. Use a paste wax or an old-fashioned furniture cream for the best results — many modern aerosol polishes contain too many solvents and silicones. Apply any polish sparingly to avoid build-up and do this only once or twice a year.

To restore the original finish on some flea market finds, try cleaning quickly with water and a non-alkaline soap. Get the soap sudsy, and dip a sponge or rag into the suds. Apply only the suds to the furniture. Wipe off. Test this procedure on an inconspicuous part of the item to make sure that it doesn't damage the finish. Dry with a soft cloth and buff lightly following the wood's grain. Never wash any veneer pieces. Veneer is a thin layer of grained wood glued on to more common woods as a decorative finish. If you wash a veneer piece, moisture may seep under the veneer and cause it to buckle or come loose. If you have any particular concerns, consult a furniture repair professional or perhaps the dealer where you purchased the piece.

## Fixing spots and stains on wood finishes

Coasters, hot plates, trivets, tablecloths, and ashtrays are your best friends in the battle against furniture stains and spots. Anything that prevents an accident means that you have one less problem to deal with. Try to get your family in the habit of putting coasters under sweating glasses and trivets under hot casseroles at the dinner table.

This may seem too obvious to mention, but I mention it anyway: Wipe up all spills immediately. Just as too much dryness and heat is bad for wood, so is too much moisture. But if an ounce of prevention isn't worth a pound of cure, use the solutions in this section to take care of problems.

- **Burn marks:** One of my childhood memories is attending a party and looking up at all the adults walking around in a gentle haze of cigarette smoke. Today, most gatherings have at least a half-mile of visibility. Still, a *few* smokers are out there. Keep an ashtray on hand, preferably a hand-held model that can catch burning ashes.

  But if an ash should slip through the gauntlet and land on an edge somewhere, leaving a light burn, try mixing a paste of finely powdered pumice (available at most hardware stores) with boiled linseed oil. Use a soft cloth and gently rub it on in the same direction as the wood's grain. Repeat this procedure as necessary.

  Deeper burns may require semi-professional help and involve filling in the hole with wood filler and then coloring in the spot to match the original surface. For the uninitiated, this may be something akin to programming the VCR.

- **Candle wax:** This is tough to prevent unless you put large plates beneath every candle. Be especially wary and vigilant, though, of brightly colored holiday candles. These may contain dyes that can seep into the grain and permanently stain your furniture. Most wax, however, can be removed by lifting it up carefully. (You don't want to remove the wax but leave a scratch.) Use something stiff but soft to pry the wax up from the furniture. A piece of cardboard, a credit card, or (my personal favorite) a plastic pastry scraper works great, but be sure to use it gently. If the wax still doesn't budge, try waving a hair dryer set on low over the spot to soften it, but don't let the dryer get hot enough or close enough to melt the wax. If a mark remains, rub the area with extra-fine steel wool dipped in mineral spirits, and then wipe dry.

✔ **Odors:** Smells of smoke, summer-house mildew, or attic stuffiness can linger on furniture for what seems like an unbearably long time. Put furniture in a well-ventilated room or outside to air out and rub it down with a cloth slightly dampened with a mixture of 2 parts vanilla to 4 parts water.

✔ **Scratches and cracks:** Most scratches can be wiped away with a good polishing or can be buffed out with wax. For deeper scratches, try that old favorite — crayon. Use one that matches the color of the finish, rub it in gently, and then buff with a clean cloth. You can also purchase specially made wax fill-in sticks at a hardware store or home improvement center for this purpose.

This may sound *nuts,* but you can also try rubbing a light scratch with the meat from Brazil nuts, pecans, or walnuts to disguise a scratch. Buy sticky-backed sheets of felt to put on the bottom of lamps, vases, and other tabletop items to prevent scratches in the future.

✔ **Stuck-on paper:** How a piece of damp paper can stick to the top of a table or chair is amazing. You'd think it was applied with cement. But don't fret. You *can* get it off. Just pour some salad oil onto a cloth and dampen the paper thoroughly. Wait about five minutes and rub along with the grain with a cloth, or try extra-fine (0000) steel wool. Wipe dry.

✔ **Water spots and crayon marks:** These have something in common besides the kids who sometimes are responsible for them. That common ingredient, believe it or not, is mayonnaise. It's not just for sandwiches anymore. Wipe a small amount of mayonnaise on either kind of stain, let it sit a couple of minutes, and then remove it with a clean cloth. Or try leaving a small dab of petroleum jelly on a water spot overnight. Wipe it away in the morning.

Some water spots disappear on their own if you wait a day. If, however, the water spot seems especially stubborn, it may not be water, but some other type of spill. Try rubbing the stain with a small amount of denatured alcohol on a clean cloth. For milk-product stains, rub the spot with a damp cloth dipped in ammonia, and then wipe dry.

✔ **White heat marks:** If you forget to put down a trivet beneath a bowl of steaming hot mashed potatoes on Thanksgiving, you may be looking at more than football games in the morning. What you have is a white heat mark. Again, a little mayonnaise should do the trick. Salad oil or denatured alcohol should also work on these spots. Don't forget to let the area dry and then polish it again.

# Caring for Upholstered Furniture

Run your finger atop any undusted tabletop and you immediately see the problem. Run your fingers on top of an upholstered sofa and what do you see? That's right, you see an upholstered sofa. The point is upholstery needs dusting. Even if you don't see it, the dust is there, building up day after day.

An undusted cushion isn't as innocent as it may seem. Besides the obvious dirt piling up inside the cushion, allergy sufferers may react to the dust particles and dust mites that live in upholstered furniture. Lowering the humidity in your house with a dehumidifier helps, because mites need humidity to live (see Chapter 18 for more information on getting rid of mites). But you really need to clean upholstered furniture with the upholstery attachment of your vacuum, cleaner at least once a week, more often if someone in your house suffers from allergies. Use the crevice tool, a long and thinly tapered attachment, to vacuum along seams and into crevices and hidden corners.

Never use a vacuum with extra power suction on upholstery because it can damage your fabric or pull off fringes and seams.

Rotate your sofa cushions, just as you do your tires, so that they wear evenly.

If you spill something on your fabric, blot it up immediately. Even if your upholstered furniture has been treated with fabric protector, you must still clean up mishaps promptly. Fabric-protecting treatments are stain-resistant, not stainproof. They're harder to stain, and easier to clean, but they can and do stain. When cleaning up a spill, don't use a wiping motion, which can spread the stain around. A blotting motion is the proper way to soak up the stain — simply press a cloth or paper towel against the stain and let it blot up the moisture. Replace the blotting cloth when it gets too wet. Keep blotting until you can no longer see the stain on your blotter.

The furniture industry has developed a "cleanability" code that is helpful when you're trying to figure out how to clean your upholstered furniture. Check on the underside of cushions or the back of your furniture for these codes. They suggest what type of cleaner to use for the fabric you have. See Table 8-1 to break the code:

| Table 8-1 | Upholstery Cleaning Codes |
|-----------|---------------------------|
| **Code** | **What It Means** |
| W | Use a water-based cleaner |
| S | Use a water-free dry-cleaning solvent |
| WS | Use either a water-based or solvent-based cleaner |
| X | None of the above can be used. Clean fabric only by vacuuming or light brushing, or have it professionally cleaned. |

## When cleaning just won't do it

Do you remember your grandmother's doilies draped over armchairs? They could be removed easily and cleaned. You can create modern slip-cover or tie-on versions with something as simple as a napkin, an old sheet, or a canvas dropcloth.

Got a tough stain on a cushion that you can't remove? When no one is in the room, just turn the cushion over.

Before you attempt to use an upholstery cleaner to clean any upholstered furniture, spot clean in an unseen area to test the cleaner's reliability. Many spot cleaners are available commercially for upholstery. If you use one, be sure to read all the instructions and watch out for a cleaner that may remove not only the stain but also some of the dye in your fabric — in essence, replacing a stain with a lighter spot. Always check for colorfastness.

- ✔ **For lipstick or grease-based stains:** Use a dry-cleaning solvent but (and I can't say this enough) always read the label first and follow the instructions carefully. In many cases, if used improperly, solvents may damage your foam cushions and padding.

- ✔ **For lighter, non-greasy stains:** Use a foam or spray upholstery cleaner. Always test for colorfastness first. Or mix together ½ teaspoon mild liquid dishwashing detergent and 1 quart water. Shake the mixture or whip it up with a wire whisk to get some good suds. Lightly sponge on the suds and then blot dry with a towel. To prevent any chance of mildew, be extra careful not to get the fabric on a cushion soaking wet. Whenever possible, remove the fabric cover from the cushion for spot cleaning.

- ✔ **For dried-on food stains:** Remove by scraping gently with an old credit card or blunt knife, and applying an appropriate stain remover, if needed. After any upholstery treatment, remember to vacuum the furniture thoroughly to remove any detergent or cleaner residue that could attract more dirt.

For a really deep and thorough cleaning, rent a professional steam extraction machine. This machine actually forces the cleaner into the fabric, while sucking it back out again — very similar to a steam carpet cleaner.

# Cleaning Non-Wood, Wicker, and Outdoor Furniture

I'm a big fan of leather furniture because of its easy-care characteristics. I like my living casual. Lots of other people do, too, as you can tell by the number of people who turn the outdoors into their living space in the summer. When the weather cools off (and in some areas of the country it never does), they often bring the outdoor furniture inside to be used in informal settings in a breakfast nook, family room, or indoor porch. Whether you live outdoors or indoors most of the time, you still need to clean this casual furniture to maintain its life and keep yourself and your guests from the inevitable grime that attaches to outdoor furniture. This section tells you how to keep casual furniture clean.

## Leather furniture

A long time ago, I spent several hours in a furniture store trying to pick out the perfect sofa. My original foam model had deteriorated into a pitiful version of its former self. I chose a neutral fabric-covered piece with a sturdy frame and was about to give the clerk my credit card when my hand touched the sofa I was sitting on while waiting to make my purchase. That sofa was leather, and granted, it was a wee bit more money, but I changed my mind instantly and purchased it. I've never regretted it. You see, I'm a bit of a spiller, and I like to stretch out and relax occasionally with lemonade, a pillow, and a book. And the toughness of leather was meant for a slightly messy housekeeper like me.

Although leather is relatively carefree, you should dust and vacuum your leather furniture regularly with the upholstery attachment of your vacuum. If it needs a deeper cleaning, wipe it off with saddle soap, but be sure to check the leather manufacturer's care label first. Use as little water as possible.

If the leather starts to feel and look dry, rub it with some white petroleum jelly or castor oil. Never wax it. Leather won't absorb wax. Wipe off any excess jelly or oil with a clean cloth.

## Wicker, bamboo, and cane furniture

Wicker furniture also needs to be dusted and vacuumed regularly, using the soft brush attachment of your vacuum. Be careful that you don't pull up any splintering edges.

Wash wicker with a mild, sudsy detergent, such as Murphy's Oil Soap. Use as little water as possible to get it clean. Use a soft brush to really get into the edges. Rinse with clean water and dry thoroughly.

You can use the same procedure on bamboo furniture. Unlike wood furniture, bamboo, wicker, rush, and sea grass furnishings actually benefit from a little moisture, so give them a damp wipe with a clean cloth now and again.

To lighten an unfinished, discolored wicker chair, mix ½ cup bleach with 2 quarts of water, and apply with a sponge. Be sure to wear rubber gloves when applying this mixture. After the chair has lightened sufficiently, rinse off with clean water and let dry.

Wash cane seats with a mild detergent and water, but be careful not to get the detergent on the chair frame. Don't forget to clean underneath the seat, too. Fix stretched seats by sponging them with hot water and allowing them to dry.

## Outdoor furniture

Many people are stymied by how to treat furniture that lives outdoors, subject to far more moisture and dirt than indoor furniture. Here are tips for handling the most common outdoor furniture materials:

- **Wood:** Redwood furniture is great for the outdoors because it fares well in the elements. It's often stained and treated at the factory and only needs to be sponged down with a mixture of mild suds and water to clean. If the furniture has no factory-applied finish, coat it with a wood preservative before using it for the first time. Follow the directions on the can of sealer. Before applying the preservative, scrub the furniture with a mixture of detergent and water, rinse, and let dry. Then apply one or two coats of sealer as needed. Periodically, scrub and reapply the finish as needed.

- **Aluminum:** Almost everyone has had a piece of outdoor aluminum furniture at one time or another. Aluminum furniture is inexpensive, lightweight, and relatively easy to care for. Sometimes the finish can become oxidized or pitted from extremes of weather. To clean up, apply a specially formulated aluminum cleaner/polisher. Afterwards, wash down with detergent and water. Hose it down to rinse it and let it dry thoroughly. If the finish is really damaged, rub with a soapy steel wood pad, rinse, and let dry. Protect the finish by giving it a quick coat of automobile wax.

- **Wrought iron:** Scrub painted wrought iron furniture with a brush dipped in detergent and water, rinse, and let dry. Check the finish periodically for scratches. If scratches reach the bare metal, the metal can rust and the rust can spread. Immediately touch up scratches with a rust-inhibiting primer and paint.

# Tackling Telephones and Household Electronics

Well-used phones are a magnet for germs. Wipe phones clean often, using a cloth sprayed with household cleaner — don't spray the cleaner directly on the phone. Wipe the phone and dry it with a clean cloth. To clean the pad of the phone, use a dab of cleaner or detergent on a cotton swab and go in and around the buttons.

Following is a list of other communications items likely to be in your home and how to care for them:

- **Camcorders:** Blow off any dust with a blower brush. If any smudges or fingerprints remain, wipe the lens gently with lens cleaning paper or a clean, lint-free cotton cloth dampened with a drop or two of lens-cleaning fluid. You can get this fluid at camera stores. Wipe the lens in a gentle spiral motion from the center outward.

- **Compact discs (CDs):** Always handle CD's by holding them on their edges or with your finger through the hole. Clean off any dust with a soft, lint-free cloth, wiping in straight strokes outward from the center hole of the disc to the edge. Wiping in a circular motion can leave a residue on the disc which can cause scratches. If the CD needs more cleaning, use a disc-cleaning kit sold at audio stores. Never use a household cleaner or an abrasive substance — they can scratch the grooves or damage the coating.

  The laser pickup on the CD player can get dusty when the drawer is opened and closed. To solve this problem, periodically insert a CD lens cleaner available from the audio store; this cleaner is a CD with a brush mounted on the surface that cleans off the laser pickup.

- **Computer:** Prevent the computer from getting dirty in the first place by putting a dust cover over the monitor, keyboard, printer, and disk drive when not in use. Read your instruction manual to see whether your computer has any special cleaning needs.

  - **Computer keyboards:** Dust regularly with the soft brush attachment of your vacuum or a computer vacuum cleaner with a tiny nozzle and brush. To get rid of any lingering dirt, give it a shot of compressed air (available from computer stores). Every now and then, unplug the keyboard and clean the keys with a lint-free cloth dipped in special computer cleaning fluid or a presaturated pad.

  - **Computer monitor:** You can clean the screen with a cloth dipped in the same computer-cleaning fluid. Spray the fluid on the cloth, not the screen.

Don't use household or window cleaners. They create a film which attracts dust and can yellow the screen. Don't use household ammonia or powders to clean the outside cover, they can scratch the finish.

✔ **Smoke detector:** Vacuum the cover with the soft brush attachment a few times a year. If you have a removable cover, gently vacuum the sensor chambers.

✔ **TV set:** Dust regularly with a soft, lint-free cloth. If a smudge gets on it, wipe off with a cloth slightly dampened with water. Never use any alcohol or ammonia based cleaners as they can damage the screen. To protect large screens, buy a Super Shield, an acrylic covering that you slip on top of the screen to protect it from dirt and damage.

✔ **Videocassette recorder (VCR):** The heads on a VCR attract dirt and dust particles and need to be cleaned after every 20 hours of use, more if you rent or borrow tapes frequently. It's easy to do: You just pop a cleaning tape cartridge, available in audio stores, in the machine and push "play." Three different cleaning systems — wet, dry, and magnetic — are available. Check the instruction manual to see if the manufacturer of your machine has specific recommendations. The magnetic method, thought to be the safest, has on-screen audio and video signals that tell you when the heads are clean. The dry method is believed to wear down the heads. The wet method uses a cartridge with moistened tapes that cleans as it plays. If any streaks or lines show up after cleaning, take the VCR to a professional.

# Cleaning Chandeliers, Candlesticks, Books, and Other Stuff

Every household has a variety of things that need to be cleaned. Some are delicate, like chandeliers. Others just seem to live to catch dust, like baskets or books. Still others are well-used and can take a pounding. The following list includes some of the most common miscellaneous cleaning tasks.

✔ **Baskets:** For day to day cleaning, brush out dust with a stiff paintbrush or clean with the brush attachment of your vacuum cleaner. It's okay to wash baskets, just be sure to dry them off thoroughly or they can mildew and rot. Clean with warm water and a mild soapy solution like Murphy's oil soap and a soft cloth. Rinse thoroughly, dry off with a terry cloth towel, then air dry before putting it away.

✔ **Books:** Dust with the soft brush attachment of the vacuum or use a feather duster. Any smudges on the hard covers of books can be cleaned off with a lightly dampened cloth.

✔ **Candlesticks:** Wax drippings will be easier to remove if you place the candlestick in the freezer for an hour to shrink the wax and then peel it off. Or soak the area in hot water (except wood) and rub lightly, then rinse in hot water. To keep candlestubs from sticking, put a couple drops of water in the bottom of the candleholder.

✔ **Chandeliers:** Dust periodically with a feather duster or blow off the dust with a hair dryer set on low heat. Before you go to clean the chandelier, turn it off and let the bulbs cool. Cover the floor underneath with several thicknesses of newspaper or towels to catch any drips and to cushion any prisms that might fall. Spray the prisms with window cleaner or with a homemade solution of 2 teaspoons rubbing alcohol and a pint of distilled water. Put on a pair of soft white cotton gloves and gently rub each prism dry.

✔ **Coolers:** Shake some baking soda on the surface of the inside of the cooler and scrub with a damp sponge. Rinse off with water and dry with a soft towel. Prop the lid open for a couple days to dry thoroughly. Clean off the outside with a mild, soapy solution. Avoid using bleach or abrasive cleaners on the outside as the color could change.

✔ **Cut glass:** Sprinkle baking soda on a damp cloth and wipe glass. Rinse off with clean water and polish with a soft cloth.

✔ **Eyeglasses:** Dip glasses in a solution of mild dishwashing detergent and water and wipe with a soft cloth. Rinse off in clear water and blot dry with a soft cloth. Avoid wiping the glass dry, there may be small particles of dirt that can scratch the glass.

✔ **Fans:** Unplug any fans before cleaning. Spray the blades of ceiling fans with all-purpose household cleaner and wipe off with a damp cloth. Use a long handled duster to dust off the blades regularly. Vacuum the dust off the grilles on portable fans with the brush attachment. Dust the blades inside by blowing the dust off with a hair dryer set on low. If you can take off the grille, clean the blades off with household cleaner and a damp cloth.

✔ **Fireplace glass doors:** Spray the cool glass with a commercial glass cleaner or a mixture of ¼ cup vinegar, 1 tablespoon ammonia, and 1 quart water. Wipe off with a soft lint-free cloth.

✔ **Picture frames:** The glass on the frame can be cleaned by wiping with a cloth dampened with window cleaner. Never spray the glass itself. It could seep behind the frame and damage the artwork. Clean wood frames by rubbing with a cloth dampened with a couple of drops of wood oil.

✔ **Vases:** These can be one of the most frustrating things to clean because it's hard to get down inside it. Don't put your finger in there. Fill it half full with a solution of dishwashing liquid and water or a teaspoon of ammonia and water, then add some uncooked rice or beans and shake. The rice will scrape the dirt off. You can also try a teaspoon of automatic dishwasher detergent and water or a denture tablet and water. Rinse out thoroughly after these treatments.

# Chapter 9

# Caring for Your Kitchen

. . . . . . . . . . . . . . . . . . . . . . . . . . . . . . . . . . . . . . . . .

### In This Chapter

▶ Cleaning while you work

▶ Cleaning the stove, refrigerator, and other appliances

▶ Keeping drains flowing smoothly

▶ Minimizing odors

▶ Washing dishes and other cookware

. . . . . . . . . . . . . . . . . . . . . . . . . . . . . . . . . . . . . . . . .

*T*he kitchen may be the heart of the home, but it can also be the headache. Even with the most modern appliances and care-free surfaces, the kitchen still isn't self-cleaning. All the dust and dirt that afflicts other rooms gathers here, along with the dishes from everyone's meals and the debris of daily cooking. You can get away with not cleaning the living room and bedroom for days, maybe even for weeks, but if you don't clean the kitchen on a daily basis, it's chaos. Luckily, manufacturers have developed cabinets, appliances, floors, and utensils that need a lot less elbow grease to keep clean than in your mother's day. And most of us have the luxury of being able to slip the dishes into the dishwasher and forget them for at least a few hours. But like everything else, if you're smart about the way you cook and clean, the kitchen will sparkle without much effort.

## Keeping the Kitchen Clean While You Work

Cooking is a messy task. You can't avoid spilling or dropping food on your clothes, the counter, or the floor at some time or another. But if you're careful while you cook and adopt some cook-'n'-clean policies, you can keep the mess in check and eliminate a nightmare clean up after each meal. Here are some simple tips:

✔ Water causes grease to bubble up and spray on walls and the back of the stove while you fry foods. Make sure all food is as dry as possible before putting it in the frying pan. Wipe off foods that you've rinsed. And let all frozen foods defrost thoroughly and pat them dry before frying them. If oil starts to bubble up, invert a colander over the pan to stop the spatters.

✔ Choose the right size pan for the job. If you're baking food with lots of liquid, make sure the sides of the pan are high enough to prevent spills when you lift it out of the oven. When you put food in a pan, make sure you have enough room for any ingredients that you add during cooking or any food that might expand or bubble up.

✔ Prevent pots from boiling over by putting a thin layer of cooking oil around the top inside of your pot.

✔ Slip your cookbook into a clean plastic bag while you cook to prevent it from getting covered with spills and spots.

✔ Keep a couple of plastic sandwich bags nearby while you're doing messy jobs such as mixing meat loaf or kneading bread. If you get a phone call while you're cooking, you can slip your hands into the bag and avoid dirtying the phone.

✔ Cover your work area with a piece of waxed paper or pastry paper to keep the countertop clean while prepping food or mixing pastry. Before you put the paper down, lightly wet the counter underneath so the paper will stay in place.

✔ Put a washable floor mat in the area where you have the most spills. Cleaning the mat is easier than cleaning the whole floor.

✔ Be conservative with the heat when you cook. Cooking on too high a heat causes scorching and boil-overs that are hard to clean.

✔ Use a large pan when cooking foods such as pasta, rice, milk, and dried beans, which have a tendency to boil over easily. Always keep an eye on the stove so you can immediately take care of any mishaps.

✔ Put the plastic top from a coffee can under bottles that tend to drip, such as honey, olive oil, and salad oil bottles. The plastic top will catch drips that you don't.

A few minutes spent preparing your work surface to prevent and avoid clean-up problems can save you hours of heavy clean-up time later and keep your kitchen looking nice while you cook.

# Cleaning Cabinets, Counters, Floors, and Faucets

Even though most of the surfaces in the kitchen are designed to stand up to daily use, they still need diligent care to keep them clean and looking good. Some are more delicate than others. If you have any doubt about how to clean a surface, test the cleaning fluid or brush or pad on a hidden area first. If it leaves any unwanted mark, switch to something else. You can clean most kitchen items with a few cleaning agents that you already have in your kitchen cabinets.

## Butcher blocks

Avoid saturating the surface of your butcher block with water. As with any other wood product, too much water can cause warping. Wipe stains and daily spills with lukewarm water and mild suds and then rinse off.

To deep clean, rub in a solution of ½ cup baking soda and 1 quart water with a synthetic scouring pad. Rinse well and dry off with paper towels or a clean cloth. When completely dry, renew the finish by rubbing in boiled linseed oil or mineral oil with fine grade steel wool. Apply a second coat after 24 hours.

To disinfect the surface, wipe with a mild bleach and water solution; then rinse and dry off.

## Cabinets: Start with the handles

Most of the cabinet cleaning you'll have to do is around the handles, where dirty hands reach out and touch everyday. If you keep the handle areas clean, you can go for quite a while without doing a major wash down of the whole cabinet. Wipe up any smudges or spots with a household cleaner and a sponge as soon as they occur. Use a cotton swab or a toothbrush dipped in cleaning solution in the narrow areas around the handle.

Keep kitchen cabinet shelves clean by lining them with washable paper. For little spills, you simply wash off the paper. If the shelf gets really dirty, you just change the paper. Voilà — they're clean!

## Countertops: Kitchen workhorses

Keeping the kitchen countertops clean is important not only for good looks but also for sanitary reasons. Most kitchen work is done on the countertops — boy, do they take a lot of abuse. Knife scratches, spills, and burns from pots and pans can all cause damage. And bacteria from uncooked food are available to contaminate other surfaces and other foods if you're not careful.

Always use cutting boards when doing any kind of kitchen task. Not only do cutting boards keep the countertop free from cuts and scratches, but spills and stains are easier to clean off of the cutting board than the countertop. And you can use separate cutting boards for different foods. Plastic or acrylic cutting boards are more sanitary than wooden ones, as they don't absorb meat and other juices.

Never prepare vegetables on a cutting board used for chicken.

Clean most spills with an all-purpose household cleaner. Stubborn spots can be removed with a paste of baking soda and water. If you're using oven or drain cleaner in the area, don't put it on the countertop or you may mar its finish. In addition, never put a hot pan on the countertop unless you put a trivet underneath the pan.

### Acrylic

Nonporous surfaces with names such as Corian or Nevamar are made of acrylic and can withstand a lot of punishment. For daily cleaning, use a two-sided scrubbing pad with a sponge on one side and fiber scouring pad on the other. Wipe up spills with soap and water. Use the scouring pad side with powdered cleanser to get rid of stains, burn marks, or greasy spots.

### Formica or plastic laminate counters

Formica or plastic laminate is a waterproof material that is easy to keep clean, which is why so many people choose it for their kitchens. It's not indestructible, however; it can be burned and scratched — so treat it with care.

For everyday cleaning, use a sanitizing household cleaner. Most common kitchen stains — mustard, ketchup, coffee, or ink from price stickers — can be rubbed out with a damp sponge sprinkled with baking soda. If the stain persists, make a paste of baking soda and water and a couple of drops of lemon juice. Let dry, and then wipe off with a sponge dipped in clean water.

Don't clean with abrasive cleaners or steel wool, which can leave scratches that not only make the countertop look unattractive, but also catch dirt and breed germs.

## Floors

See Chapter 7 for how to clean your specific type of floor. Just be sure to wipe up spills as soon as they occur. And don't be afraid to use your vacuum on the kitchen floor. With the right attachments, it's faster and removes dirt better than sweeping. Use the crevice tool to reach under the range, around the baseboards, and behind the refrigerator.

If you want to give your floor a quick clean and don't have a commercial product handy, mix ½ cup vinegar and 1 gallon warm water. Dip a mop into this solution, wring out throughly, and use it on asphalt, linoleum, vinyl, rubber tile, and no-wax floors.

## Sinks and faucets

Use the following tips to keep your sinks shiny and your faucets sparkling:

- ✔ **Stainless steel sinks:** Clean with a sponge dipped in hot, sudsy water or wipe off with a soft cloth and window cleaner. To polish, rub with a cut lemon or a cloth dampened with lemon juice.

- ✔ **Porcelain sinks:** Clean regularly with a nonabrasive household cleaner or with baking soda sprinkled on a damp sponge. If your white sink is stained, fill with a solution of 3 tablespoons of bleach per gallon of water. Let sit for an hour, remove, and rinse off.

- ✔ **Faucets:** Spray glass cleaner on a dry cloth and give the faucets a quick swipe. Or rub with a little baking soda on a slightly damp cloth. Don't use steel wool or any abrasive cleaner — either could scratch the finish. Remove lime deposits caused by hard water by wiping with a white vinegar and water solution.

## Keeping drains flowing

Drains often get sluggish because we pour things down them that we shouldn't. Never pour oil or grease down the drain. Both can clog the pipes. Instead, put oil and grease in an old coffee can or a jar with a lid and throw it in the rubbish.

If your drain appears slow, flush it out with a teakettle of boiling water or the hottest water possible from the faucet. Afterwards, put 4 tablespoons of baking soda and ½ cup white distilled vinegar into the drain. Wait 15 minutes. The soda and vinegar will foam up and agitate whatever is slowing things up. Run some hot tap water again to rinse it out.

# Cleaning Stoves and Ovens — Nobody's Favorite Tasks

The key to keeping the stove clean is to wipe up spills as they happen. After all, an appliance that gets hot enough to bake food will logically also turn spilled food and grease spatters into something akin to cement. Keep a bottle of light-duty household cleanser so you can clean up as accidents happen. A spill that's still hot is usually soft and easily wiped up.

A surefire stain maker is the mixing spoon that we all lay down on the stovetop while we're cooking. If you don't have a spoon rest, lay your spoons on a damp sponge on the cooktop. After you're finished, just clean off the sponge in sudsy water or throw it in the dishwasher.

Most gas stoves or cooktops are made of porcelain enamel, stainless steel, or a glass/ceramic combination. They're relatively easy to take care of and will take a lot of heavy-duty use. Read your owner's manual for specific details on how to clean your particular range.

### Ranges and cooktops

For a thorough cleanup, remove the grates and control knobs and soak them in the sink in warm soapsuds. If the pans under the grates (called *drip pans*) are removable, put them in the same solution to soak. By the time you get finished cleaning the rest of the stove, the dirt should be falling off. Rinse them and dry thoroughly before you put them back in place. You don't want any water dripping underneath or behind the inside of the stove.

Now you're ready to tackle the rest. Stovetops and backsplashes (the wall area behind your sink and counters) are subject to the stains from boiled-over pots, spilled gravy, and spattering grease, day in and day out. Most porcelain enamel models can be cleaned with a heavy-duty household cleaner. If dirt or stains are caked-on, spray some cleaner on the spot, let sit for a few minutes, then rub off with a plastic scrubber. Rinse with clean water.

Never use harsh scrubbing pads or steel wool on any cooktop, no matter how nasty the spill. They can scratch the surface.

### Stainless steel stoves

Stainless steel stoves are becoming more popular than ever. They look so high tech and shiny that any speck of dirt seems glaringly out of place. Clean off spots with a baking soda and water paste. Rinse and wipe with a paper towel. Give it extra shine with a cloth dampened with vinegar. Or wipe with a cloth slightly dampened with mineral oil, rinse, and dry with a soft cloth.

### Glass ceramic cooktops

Clean when cool with mild dishwashing liquid and water or a cleaner made especially for this type of cooktop. Rinse well and buff with a dry cloth. Treat a burned-on spill with a baking soda and water paste or a nonabrasive powder. Remove stuck-on food with a nonabrasive scrubber.

For spots that just won't budge, cover with a baking soda paste and a damp cloth for 30 minutes. If anything's still stuck, remove it by carefully shaving it off with a single edge razor, making sure that you don't scratch the surface.

Although glass surfaces are relatively easy to care for, special attention must be taken because of their sensitivity to dirt. Bottoms of pots and pans should be clean when you place them on a cooktop. Make sure the rag or sponge you use to wipe them off has no dirt or grease on it left over from cleaning the rest of the kitchen. Any residue on the cloth can leave a film on the stove that often doesn't appear until the stove is heated up the next time.

### Gas burners

Clean gas burners occasionally to make sure that no burned-on food is clogging the holes. Clogs prevent the proper amount of air reaching the gas. (A yellow flame can be one sign of this.) Wipe off a spill as soon as the stove is cool enough to touch. Clean the top of the burner by lightly rubbing with a cloth dipped in detergent and water. Clean the holes by poking them with a straightened paper clip or safety pin. Don't use a toothpick; it can break off and clog the hole.

### Coils

Coils on electric stoves are basically self-cleaning. Just turn on high to burn off any spill. Because solid heating elements are sealed to the cooktop, spills stay on the surface rather than going into drip pans. To clean, wait until the heating element cools and wipe with hot-sudsy water. Dry off by putting the element on medium setting for a couple of minutes. Be careful with your coils; they can break if you hit them or drop heavy objects on them.

## Cleaning the oven

Who likes to do this? I know I put it off as long as possible, sometimes even resorting to looking the other way when I put something into the oven. It must be the feeling of crawling into a dark, greasy hole that gives most people the creeps. After all, oven-cleaning has been rated as one of the most hated chores. Many new ranges have self-cleaning features that do much of the cleaning for you. Lucky you, if you have one — they only require minimal care. The rest of us have to use a little more energy and elbow grease to keep ours clean.

The following lists some items in every oven that need special attention:

- ✔ **Oven racks:** First remove the racks and set them to soak in a solution of hot soapy water. Extra greasy racks should be put in a stronger solution of ½ cup ammonia to ½ gallon hot water. After they've soaked, get rid of burned on dirt with a plastic scrubber. Wear rubber gloves when working with heavy ammonia solutions.

- ✔ **Broiler pan:** Remove the pan and grilltop while still slightly warm (but not hot) and pour off any grease or accumulated debris. Rinse in very hot water. Put a squirt of dishwashing detergent into the pan, add some water and cover the whole mess with a wet rag or paper towels and let sit for 30 minutes. Scrub with a nylon scrub pad and hot soapy water. Rinse, then dry.

- ✔ **Glass doors and windows:** Wipe off with a cloth dipped in ammonia. Let the solution soak into the surface and then clean it off with a sponge and hot water. Scrub any remaining spots with a plastic scrubber. Never use a steel wool pad, which will scratch the glass.

Out of scrubbers? Use the plastic mesh bag that onions and shallots come in, fold into several thicknesses and scour away. Unfold it to rinse it off.

### Conventional oven

You may cringe at the thought of cleaning the oven, but unless you're cooking lots of fatty roasts or extremely juicy pies, the job doesn't have to be done more than a few times a year.

If you notice something dripping while you're cooking, sprinkle some salt on it immediately after the oven is turned off but still warm. Then, when the oven is cool, wipe off all the salt and the stain.

Conserve your cleaning energy and don't clean the whole oven if it only has a few spots on it. Just cover the stains for 30 minutes with a cloth soaked in ammonia. Lift the stains off with a plastic scraper and wipe with detergent and water. Rinse with a sponge dipped in clean water.

A relatively painless way to clean the oven, and avoid spraying a whole lot of chemicals inside, is to place a cup of ammonia in a cold oven. Shut the door and leave it overnight. When you open the oven door the next day, stand back and turn your face away. The fumes are strong but dissipate rapidly. Wear rubber gloves and wipe off the loosened food and grease with paper towels or an old rag. Rub any stubborn spots with a plastic scrubber and a mixture of liquid dishwashing detergent and soapy water. Rinse the oven, first with a vinegar and water solution and then with clean water. There, that wasn't so bad, was it?

Now the bad news: If you've let the oven go for along time, the ammonia trick may not be strong enough. You may need to use a commercial oven cleaner. Because commercial oven cleaners are extremely caustic, you should follow the instructions on the can carefully. Never spray oven cleaner in a hot oven. Put strips of aluminum foil over the heating elements, oven wiring, and thermostat to protect them. Cover everything that could come in contact with the cleaner. Put paper on the floor and nearby countertops, put on rubber gloves, and wear an apron or an old shirt. I've never done this job without black, messy goo dripping on something I didn't want it to. Make sure that you rinse the oven carefully according to the instructions on the can and remove every speck of cleaner before you turn the oven on again.

### Self-cleaning ovens

This type of oven uses high heat to burn off soil and reduce the grime to a light coating of ash at the bottom. You just adjust the oven to the right setting, and it does the dirty work for you. But even this method needs a little care:

✔ Before you start the cleaning process, give the oven a fast wipe with a damp cloth to get rid of anything that could cause smoke during the cleaning process. Then clean the frame around the exterior of the oven and the door liner outside of the gasket with a sponge dipped in hot, soapy water. Use a scouring pad and baking soda to clean up any tough spots. Rinse well.

Never clean the gasket itself; cleaning fluids, even water, can damage it.

✔ Wipe off the ash residue after the cycle with a damp cloth.

Always follow the manufacturer's directions for cleaning the oven and never use commercial oven cleaner for this type of surface.

### Continuous cleaning ovens

Continuous cleaning ovens have a porous porcelain enamel finish on the oven liner that absorbs and spreads spills that burn off while the oven is hot. The longer the cooking time and higher the temperature, the more the oven cleans. Be sure to read your instruction manual for more details on cleaning. Occasionally, clean out the oven with a nylon pad dipped in cold water. Wipe dry.

Large spills can burn and harm the surface so they need to be wiped up as soon as possible. While they're still warm, blot stains with paper towels. After the oven cools, scrub with all-purpose cleaner and a nylon net pad. Let the solution sit on the stain for 30 minutes; then wipe off the softened soil and sponge down with clean water, making sure no water drips into the base of the oven.

Again, never use soap or commercial oven cleaners on this type of oven because they can harm the surface.

## Foiled again

Good old aluminum foil can be your first line of defense in the kitchen to cut down on stains:

✔ When you're making a large roast, chicken, or turkey, form a foil tent over the pan to prevent splattering of the oven roof and sides. Crimp the foil all around the sides of the pan to form a tight seal and hold it in place.

✔ If you're baking a pie or casserole, lay a sheet of foil on the bottom rack of the oven to catch any drips that might leak from the pan. Don't cover the whole rack — lay down a piece that's about one inch larger than the pan to allow for proper air circulation.

## Cleaning the exhaust fan

Cooking odor and grease go hand in hand with cooking. That's why vent hoods and exhaust fans are so handy in helping get rid of these kitchen pollutants. Unfortunately the fan often become grease-laden itself, which is why you should clean it frequently to keep it running efficiently.

Read the owner's manual first. Turn off the fan and make sure it's cool to the touch before cleaning.

Soak all the removable parts and the filter in dishwashing liquid and hot water. Rinse and let dry. Clean the hood, fan blades, and knobs with a cloth sprayed with degreaser. Wipe off with a clean cloth or paper towels.

Don't spray liquid directly onto the fan itself.

## Cleaning the Refrigerator

My friend Jane likes to clean her refrigerator right before she goes on a major shopping trip. Sounds crazy, but there is method to this madness: The food supply is at its lowest, so she has less stuff in the refrigerator to remove. And while she's removing stuff from the refrigerator to clean it, she can see what looks good and what looks like it needs to be replenished or replaced. She adds to her grocery list right there on the spot.

A thorough, big-time cleaning takes a little work, but you don't have to do it that often. Here's how:

1. First, TURN OFF the refrigerator.

2. Remove all the shelves and drawers and let them come to room temperature.

3. Wash shelves and drawers in warm, sudsy water; rinse off and dry.

   Don't put them in extremely hot water. It can cause plastic or glass shelves to warp or crack.

4. In a small bucket, mix a solution of 2 tablespoons baking soda and 1 quart warm water. Dip a sponge in the solution and wash down the walls. Rinse with clean water and dry with a soft towel or paper towels.

5. Wash the gasket with the baking soda solution and use a toothbrush to clean off any dirt in the folds. Rinse and dry.

To spot-clean, use the same baking soda solution you made in Step 4 to wipe off any stains or spills. You don't have to remove the shelves — just move the food out of the way.

## Defrosting and cleaning the freezer

If you have a manual-defrost freezer, you need to defrost it when the ice gets to be about ¼ inch thick. If the frost gets too thick, the freezer won't operate properly.

Depending on how you use your freezer and how old your refrigerator is, defrosting may need to be done anywhere from a couple times a year to once a month in the summer. Unfortunately in my case, it needs to be done several times a year. Every time I open the freezer, I look for the tell-tale signs of frost forming — signs that I'll have to do this unpleasant task again. But, I try to look in the bright side: I have more opportunity than most people to really inspect what's in the freezer.

Unplug the refrigerator to avoid any possibility of electrical shock. Then start your defrosting:

1. Take out all the frozen food and store it in a cooler or wrap it in several layers of newspaper.

   This whole job gets really cold — you're in the freezer after all. I always put on rubber gloves to protect my hands when I pick up those nasty chunks of ice.

2. Empty the ice cube trays and wash them in sudsy water.

3. **To speed up the defrosting process, I like to put a couple of pans of hot water in the freezer. Leave the door ajar slightly and keep checking the progress of the meltdown. Sop up the water as the ice melts and replace the pans of hot water when they get cool.**

   Resist the urge to poke or scrape with a sharp knife or spatula — that can damage the lining of the freezer.

4. **When the freezer is clear of frost, wipe it down using a solution of 2 tablespoons baking soda and 1 quart warm water. Rinse and dry.**

Turn the freezer back on and allow it to come back up to temperature. This whole process shouldn't take more than about 30 minutes. Check the food and make sure it's still frozen. If any feels warm or soft to the touch, throw it away. Replace the food, wiping off any moisture that might have collected as the food started to defrost.

## *Attacking the exterior*

Remove all your magnets, picture frames, notes, lottery tickets, and sticky notes. Wash down the door with warm sudsy water or a spray household cleaner. Remove the panel at the bottom of the refrigerator and wash. Slide out the defrost pans and wash with sudsy water. (This pan can be the cause of mystery odors if not cleaned periodically.) In some models, the condenser coils for the refrigerator are located on the bottom, behind the grille. They should be cleaned a couple of times a year so the refrigerator can properly vent heat into the room. (Check the manual that came with your refrigerator for specific cleaning instructions.) Unplug the refrigerator and dust the coils with something long and skinny, such as the crevice tool of your vacuum, an automobile windshield brush, or a yardstick covered with pantyhose. Don't forget to wipe off any crud that falls on the floor underneath the fridge. Put back the defrost pan and grille.

If your coils aren't located underneath the refrigerator, they're in the back or at the top. Check your instruction manual. If they're at the top, pull off the grille and vacuum. If they're in the back, you have to pull the refrigerator away from the wall and vacuum.

Clean off the top of the refrigerator with heavy-duty household cleaner if it's really scummy. If the top of the refrigerator gets neglected because you're too short to see up there, cover the top with some paper towels or waxed paper. When it comes time to clean, all you have to do is remove the paper and replace it.

# Cleaning Small Appliances

Most of us keep a battery of small appliances on our countertops. They may reduce our work load, but they also create some of their own. They, too, must be cleaned after every use and also have the unfortunate habit of accumulating dirt and grime just sitting on the countertop. Because most are made of heavy-duty plastic, they only need a quick wipe-down when you're cleaning the countertop.

Always unplug appliances before you start cleaning them. Read your manual carefully. Parts of some appliances can be put in the dishwasher, others must be positioned on the top shelf, and a few should be washed by hand. Always take care to avoid getting the electrical connections, coils, cord, or plug wet.

## Blender

Cleaning the blender by hand is simple and fun. Just fill it halfway with water and squirt ½ teaspoon liquid dishwashing detergent into it. Put the lid back on and turn the blender on low for about 30 seconds. Rinse and dry. Sponge down the base with a warm sudsy solution or use a spray household cleaner. The narrow areas around the edges of the buttons can be cleaned with a cotton swab dipped in cleaning solution.

## Food processor

I often shy away from using the food processor just because I feel it's easier to wash one knife than all the parts of the processor. For some jobs, however, it's a lifesaver. Cleanup is much easier if you rinse off the blades and bowls as you go. Either wash by hand or put on the top shelf of the dishwasher, depending on the recommendations in your instruction manual.

Wash the blade carefully by hand to avoid the possibility of scraping your hand against it while removing stuff from the dishwasher shelves.

Avoid using scouring pads or abrasive cleansers to clean the bowl or blades because they can scratch the surface. Clean off the base with a quick wipe with household cleaner and a paper towel.

Lightly coat the blades with non-stick cooking spray before using. Doing so makes food debris come off much easier.

# Coffeemaker

The removable parts of a drip coffeemaker — the pot, lid, and basket — can be washed by hand in a sudsy solution or on the top rack of the dishwasher, depending on the recommendations from the manufacturer. Periodically, you need to clean the insides to get rid of mineral deposits from water. How often you need to do this depends on the hardness of your water supply and how often you use the coffeemaker.

If you detect a bitter taste in your coffee, you know it's time for a thorough cleaning. Once a month is usually a good guideline.

Pour 4 cups of white distilled vinegar into the coffeepot and add enough water to make 10 cups. Pour this solution into the coffeemaker. Put a filter in the basket and press the *On* button just like you would to make a cup of coffee. (Some coffeemakers have special clean cycles, so check your manual first before cleaning.) When about half of this mixture has dripped into the pot, turn off the machine and let it sit for about 30 minutes. Pour the mixture back into the machine, turn it on and let the full solution run through. Run a couple of decanters of plain water through the machine to rinse out all the vinegar.

# Toaster

Always unplug the toaster before you start cleaning it. Let it cool, then open the crumb tray and empty it or turn the toaster upside down over a trash can and shake it. Clean out the corners and dislodge any remaining crumbs with a soft brush. Wipe the tray with a damp cloth. Dry off thoroughly.

If the outside of your toaster is chrome, spray window cleaner on a damp cloth and wipe. Buff with a dry cloth. Stubborn spots can be treated by wiping with a damp plastic scrubber and baking soda. Plastic exteriors should be wiped down with a sponge dipped in a sudsy solution. Never immerse the toaster in water or drip anything inside.

To remove stuck toast, unplug the toaster and let cool. Press the handle down; then turn the toaster upside down over the trash can and shake the contents free. Resist the urge to put any forks or knives into the toaster to remove stuck food. They can damage the interior.

# Toaster oven

Cleaning your toaster oven is important because excess crumb buildup can cause a fire. Empty out the tray after the oven cools down and periodically turn the toaster on its side and give it a shake to remove anything else lodged inside. Try to remove any spills as soon as possible with a nylon mesh scrubber dipped in hot soapy water. Letting food spills sit and bake on will result in something akin to cement. Remove the rack and metal tray and soak them in sudsy water or put in the dishwasher according to your instruction manual. Scrub off any stains with hot soapy water and a nylon or polyester scrubbing pad.

Clean the oven exterior after it cools down with a soft cloth and window cleaner if it's stainless steel or a sponge dipped in sudsy water if it's plastic.

## Cleaning odds and ends

Nothing beats a kitchen for sheer volume of variety of stuff that needs to be cleaned. The following list provides tips for cleaning the most commonly used odds and ends:

- ✔ **Electric can opener:** Remove the cutting assembly, if possible, and soak in warm water with liquid dishwashing detergent or place in the dishwasher according to the manufacturer's directions. If you can't take off the assembly, use a soft toothbrush to scrub away any dirt on the cutter.

- ✔ **Grater:** Remove soft cheeses and other things that stick to the grater by rubbing with a toothbrush or a cut potato or lemon. Cut down on sticking next time by spraying with non-stick cooking spray before you grate.

- ✔ **Rolling pin:** Wipe off any residue with a damp sponge dipped in soapy water immediately after using. Don't immerse or soak in water, which could warp the wood.

- ✔ **Sponge:** Put in the top shelf in the dishwasher to deep clean every couple of washes. Or soak in a solution of 1 tablespoon bleach to 1 quart of water. Sponges can harbor lots of bacteria so clean them religiously after each use in warm, soapy water and allow to dry out completely. Throw it away if it develops an off-odor. Try to get a new sponge about every 30 days. Because they harbor germs, don't use sponges to wipe up messes from raw meat, fish, or chicken.

- ✔ **Tea kettle:** Get rid of lime deposits from hard water by boiling a mixture of 2 cups water and 2 cups vinegar. Let sit for several hours. Pour off the liquid and the lime should go with it. Rinse with clean water.

- ✔ **Thermos (vacuum) bottles:** Put 1 tablespoon baking soda inside and fill with warm water. Shake to mix the solution. Let sit for about ½ hour and rinse out.

- ✔ **Wooden cutting boards:** Wash with a hot sudsy water and a plastic scrubber or brush. To sanitize after cutting meats and poultry, wash with soap first, then apply a solution of 3 tablespoons bleach mixed with 1 gallon of water. Let sit with solution on it for a couple of minutes, rinse well, and dry.

## Where to store your cleaning products

Under the sink may seem like the most convenient place to store your cleaning products, but *don't* store cleaning products there. First of all, they're within the reach of the exploring hands of small children. In addition, the moist environment doesn't do good things to powdered dishwasher detergent. It can cause it to get lumpy so that it won't dissolve when you put it in the dishwasher. A cool dry spot works better; store your cleaning supplies within arm's reach in an upper cabinet or in a nearby closet.

# Minimizing Mystery Odors

I don't know about you, but there's been many a time I've stood in my kitchen with my nose up in the air trying to figure out the source of some unidentified odor. I wiggle my nose into every nook and cranny in the kitchen, but the source still eludes me. Then after playing what-dun-it for hours, I realize the cause is a neglected garbage pail or a dirty refrigerator drip pan. The next time you're on the trail of an unwanted, pungent aroma, use the tips in Table 9-1 to find the source and solve the problem.

| Table 9-1 | Finding and Fixing Foul Odors |
|---|---|
| *Where to Look* | *What to Do* |
| Freezer | Clean the interior with a solution of equal parts vinegar and water or wipe down with a cloth dampened with pure vanilla extract. Wipe off with a clean cloth. |
| Microwave oven | Dip a damp cloth in baking soda and wipe the inside of the oven. Rinse and dry. Or put 1 tablespoon of lemon juice in a bowl of water and heat on full power for one minute. Allow the oven to cool and wipe down the oven walls with paper towels. |
| Vegetable bin | Clean out with a mixture of 1 teaspoon of baking soda to 1 quart water. Rinse and dry off. Line the bottom of the vegetable bin with paper towels to absorb any moisture in the future and make it easy to clean. |
| Disposal | Run hot tap water after each use and periodically put several lemon rinds and some ice cubes through the grinder. |
| Trash can | Wash out with a baking soda and water solution or use a heavy-duty household cleaner with ammonia in it. To keep it sweet smelling in the future, put a fabric softener sheet at the bottom. |
| Whole room | Simmer a cup of vinegar on top of the stove. |

## Dealing with odors on your hands

There are as many different methods for getting smells off your hands as there are smells. Many chefs prefer rubbing hands with cut lemon. Others swear by a paste of baking soda and water. One of the latest and most unusual methods is to rub your hands against stainless steel, such as the kitchen faucet. For some reason, the chemical reaction between the metal and your hands removes the smell.

## Fixing funky fridge fragrances

Be diligent about getting rid of spoiled foods. The plastic material that forms the walls and bins of the fridge can absorb nasty food odors. If you've ever had a power outage that resulted in a week of spoiled food in the fridge, you know that the smell is from the netherworld. It gives you new respect for anyone who would become a pathologist.

You can get rid of awful smells with just a little effort. First, take everything out of the refrigerator. Then try one of these methods:

- ✔ **Charcoal:** Set the refrigerator on low. Spread activated charcoal (available at pet stores or drug stores) in two or three shallow pans and lay them on the shelves in the refrigerator and the freezer. Don't forget to put a pan with several pieces in the crisper drawers, too. Leave them in the refrigerator for several days. The charcoal is specially treated to remove odor molecules from the air.

- ✔ **Coffee:** Pour about a cup of dry coffee grounds on a couple of paper plates and place them on different shelves in the refrigerator. Let the refrigerator run on low for a couple of days. After the bad smell is removed, some coffee odor may linger, but you can remove it by wiping down the walls with a baking soda and water solution.

- ✔ **Cat litter:** Spread cat litter in a shallow pan and place it on a shelf. Leave the fridge on low for several days. Recheck to see if any odor lingers. If most of the smell is gone but there's still some lingering odor, repeat again with a new batch of kitty litter.

- ✔ **Newspaper:** Set the refrigerator on low. Pack all the shelves in both the refrigerator and freezer with wadded up newspaper. Spritz them lightly with water or put a couple bowls of water in the refrigerator. Leave for 5 or 6 days. When the odor is gone, remove the newspaper and wash down the walls to remove any ink residue.

Even if you're a clean-o-holic, a stray onion or rotten lime may be lurking in your refrigerator somewhere, secretly hiding behind a bottle of salad dressing or a can of capers. This breech of refrigerator etiquette may be the cause of an annoying odor, but not one that can't be solved quite easily. Wrap or package vegetables in plastic containers with lids. If it's something that's really strong-smelling, such as an onion, store it in a glass container with a screw top lid. The onion odor won't penetrate the glass, and the onion will stay fresh for a week. Throw away any food that's rotten.

To make the fridge sweet-smelling again, spread some baking soda on a tray and leave in the refrigerator until the odor is gone. Or soak some cotton balls in imitation vanilla extract and place them in bowls on shelves in the refrigerator. Let sit until the odor goes away.

# Doing Dishes without Doing Them In

You'd probably be shocked (or maybe not) if you added up the number of hours you've spent in your life washing dishes. It's one of those inevitable tasks that must be performed day in and day out. But whether you're lucky enough to have an automatic dishwasher or you have to do it by hand, you can definitely make the process easier and more efficient.

## Using the automatic dishwasher

I'd be willing to wager that there aren't two people on the face of the earth who load the dishwasher the same way. While I prefer to line up everything in parallel rows, my mate insists on laying everything on an angle. Some people like to alternate sizes of items or put all the silverware of the same type in each bin. When you get your dishwasher, be sure to read the manufacturer's instructions for loading. Every model has different features and is designed differently, so what may work for one model, may not be efficient for another.

Here's a list of some general principles recommended by manufacturers on how to get the most from your dishwasher.

- ✔ Scrape off food and lightly rinse the dishes before putting them in. I know that many manufacturers claim that you can skip this step but most dishwashers can actually dispose of soft food. Leaving large pieces of food on dishes only invites problems such as clogging the dishwasher or depositing small particles of food on dishes during the washing period. In addition, flatware can be tarnished if acidic and salty food is left on it for too long.

- ✔ Load unlike pieces of silverware together. Don't nest all the spoons and forks together in one compartment. They may cradle inside one another and prevent water from hitting all the sides of each piece. Don't wash stainless steel flatware and silverware together because an electrolytic action between the two metals can cause them to pit.

✔ Place all the dishes and pans so the soiled areas are facing the center where the hot water spray comes from. Don't overload the dishwasher. If dishes are too close together, the water and detergent can't get in between them to clean everything.

✔ Load glasses and cups face down if possible, nested in the cushioned prongs of the top rack. Allow enough space between them so that any stems or handles don't touch other items and cause chipping. Glasses with recessed bottoms should be angled so the water drains off.

✔ Wash any plastic, heat-sensitive items on the top rack as far away from any heat sources as possible.

✔ Put sharp items in the silverware basket with the points down to prevent any cuts when reaching in the dishwasher.

✔ Long-handled utensils such as kitchen spatulas should be laid flat in the top rack so they don't fall through to block the wash arms. Small and lightweight items should also be placed so that they don't fall through the racks.

✔ If you're washing delicate glasses, use the china crystal setting on the dishwasher or the light wash cycle. Turn off the dishwasher before the heat dry cycle and let them air dry. If you have a problem with spotty glasses, take them out after the rinse cycle and hand dry.

### Determining dishwasher detergent

The amount of automatic dishwasher detergent you should use depends on the hardness of your water. You can find out how hard your water is from the city water department or the county extension agent. Read your dishwasher manual carefully for the manufacturer's recommendations. In general, an average load with medium hard water can be cleaned with about 2 tablespoons of dishwasher detergent. Hard water can require 3 or more tablespoons.

Use only automatic dishwasher detergent specifically meant for automatic dishwashers. Any other type of detergent or soap, including liquid dishwashing detergent meant for washing dishes by hand, can cause too many suds and hinder the water action necessary for cleaning in the dishwasher. Other types of detergents produce too many suds and can cause an overflow.

Start out with a minimum amount of detergent and experiment to see whether your dishes get clean. If your water is very hard, try adding a liquid rinse agent to the dishwasher. Don't use a rinse agent if your water is soft or if you have a water softener.

## What NOT to put in the dishwasher

The dishwasher is great for many things — in fact, people use it in all kinds of strange ways. A friend told me she used it to poach a whole fish (something I don't recommend). But, some things are definitely best cleaned the old-fashioned way — by hand. Those things include

✔ Antique or hand painted china

✔ Good crystal glasses or milk glass

✔ Pewter or sterling silver

✔ Cast iron, copper, or tin pans

✔ Good knives, especially with hollow or wooden handles

✔ Plastic containers or appliances

✔ Wooden dishes

Before you buy powdered automatic dishwasher detergent, shake the box. If it's fresh, it will sound loose and powdery. If it's hard and lumpy, it's probably old and won't be as effective a cleaning agent. Add the detergent right before loading the machine. Otherwise, the detergent may become sticky from moisture in the air and cake in the cup. Gel type detergents are preferred by some, but powders have been reported to outperform gels in getting off dried-on foods and preventing spottings.

## Washing dishes by hand

When I was growing up, we didn't have an automatic dishwasher. My father said we never needed to buy one — we already had four (meaning me and my three siblings). Ever since those days, I have always cringed at the thought of washing dishes and I was wildly happy when I moved into an apartment with an automatic dishwasher. I swore I would never wash another dish by hand. But sometimes, even the most dyed-in-the-wool dishwasher haters must pick up a sponge and do the nasty deed by hand. If I had known then what I know now, it wouldn't have seemed like such an onerous task.

### Getting ready

While you're cooking, fill the sink with soapy water and put the mixing bowls, measuring spoons and other utensils in it to soak as you use them. This will loosen most of the grime before you actually get ready to wash. Try to do the dishes right after the meal. If you can't, at least wipe off any food with a scraper, stack the dishes and soak the pans in hot water.

Use *hot* water to soak pans that are greasy or were used to cook sugary foods. Use *cold* water to soak pans with milk, eggs, or starchy food residue on them. Hot water will set dairy food residue and make it harder to get off.

### Washing in the right order

Fill up the sink or dishpan with the hottest water your hands can stand. Hot water is really needed to get the dishes clean. Of course, put a couple of squirts of dishwashing liquid in the pan and swish around the water to create some suds and dissolve the liquid.

Before putting the dishes in the water, wipe off any grease from dishes, pots, and pans with a paper towel. Then put the dishes in the sink or pan. The dishwater will stay cleaner longer if you wash the least soiled items first and move on to the more heavily soiled.

Follow this order when washing:

1. **Glasses**
2. **Silverware**
3. **Eating dishes**
4. **Serving dishes**
5. **Cooking utensils**
6. **Pots and pans**

Change the water when it becomes dirty or greasy. Rinse the dishes in hot water, either under the faucet or by dipping in a half-full pan of hot water. Change the water as it becomes sudsy.

### Washing sterling silver

Many manufacturers of sterling silver and silver plate say it can be washed in the dishwasher. If you are anti-dishpan, check the care instructions for your silverware before putting it in the dishwasher. Just be sure not to pile it on top of other dishes or pans that could scratch the surface. To be safe, take your silver out of the machine before the drying cycle starts and hand dry. Just remember to wash silver promptly after using it; don't let it sit with other dishes in the dishwasher for a long time.

Keep silver away from any stainless steel flatware or cookware; silver has a reaction to stainless steel that can cause pitting.

If your silver is very costly, an antique, or a family heirloom, I'd play it safe and wash it by hand. Use warm, sudsy water and be sure to keep it away from anything rubber when washing. Rubber gloves, rubber bands, and even a rubber draining mat can cause it to tarnish. Dry off with a soft cloth immediately to avoid water spotting.

---

# What's stuck can be unstuck

**Glasses and pans:** If two glasses or pans are stuck together, put cold water in the top glass and dunk the bottom glass in hot water. The cold water will make the top contract and the hot water will make the bottom expand so it will come off easily.

**Contact paper:** To remove shelf paper that's stuck, move a hair dryer — set on medium heat — over the paper. The heat from the hair dryer will loosen the glue so you can pull it off.

**Stuck jar top:** If you can't remove the top (or lid) of a screw-top jar, wrap a rubber band around the top and use it to grasp onto. Or put on a pair of rubber gloves and use them to get a grip. Tops won't stick in the future if you coat them inside with a little bit of cooking oil.

---

Certain substances — olives, vinegar, salt, eggs, and flowers, among others, can have an adverse effect on silver. You're better off serving these foods in other containers or using a liner in your silver dish.

To clean off tarnish, you can use any of several good commercial polishes on the market. Follow the directions on the package. Use a soft cloth or a damp sponge to apply the polish, rinse with warm water, and polish with a soft, dry, clean cloth. Keep turning the cloth over to expose a clean surface until all the tarnish is removed. Use a cotton swab to get into crevices.

Never use all-purpose metal polishes to clean silver — their chemical formulas are too harsh.

Store silver carefully. Don't pile pieces on top of each other. If possible, store your silver in a special tarnish-resistant cloth.

### Handling special problems

Some items don't seem to fit the normal rules for dishwashing; they're too fragile, made of special-care materials, or present abnormal risks. The following lists the most common problem pieces and how to care for them:

- ✔ **China and delicate glassware:** When you're washing delicate china or glassware, line the sink with a thick towel. As an extra precaution, cushion the faucet by tying on a hand towel with a string or rubber band. Not only does this keep you from chipping or breaking china if you happen to bump it against the sides, but it also keeps dishes from slipping around on the bottom of the sink. Put the dishes in one at a time instead of piling them one on top of another. And make sure glasses and dishes are at room temperature. Putting cold dishes into very hot water can cause them to crack. Use a soft brush to get dirt out of indentations in cut glass.

✔ **Knives:** Don't put sharp knives in the dishpan with other dishes. You can cut yourself when you reach in and the knives' sharp edges may dull when they come in contact with other dishes.

✔ **Wooden bowls and plates:** Don't soak. Just put in suds long enough to wash quickly. Rinse and then dry off well before putting them away.

## Misusing cleansers

Cleansers are scouring agents that contain abrasives, detergent, and bleach. They are highly effective for many tough cleaning jobs but should not be used on any delicate surface that could be easily scratched. In the kitchen, some of the things they should *not* be used on are

✔ Sterling silver or silverplate

✔ China

✔ Highly polished finishes on appliances

✔ Acrylic or baked enamel

✔ Glass tableware or oven glass

✔ Soft plastics

# Keeping Cookware Cooking: Pots, Pans, and Serving Dishes

If you buy good pots and pans and treat them with care, you can expect them to last for decades. Many of my favorite pots and pans have been with me for more than 25 years, carried from kitchen to kitchen, stove to stove. They have been my good friends, lasting longer than boyfriends, apartment leases, cooking trends, and jobs. If you want your pots to last a long time, follow these basic tips to avoid problems:

✔ Don't run cold water into a hot pan. It can cause metal to warp and can even crack glass or earthenware.

✔ Don't use excessive heat on pans. Keep flames on gas stoves low enough so that they only touch the bottom of the pan. Check the care instructions before you put a pan in a hot oven or under the broiler.

✔ Always scour pans with plastic scrubbers first. If a stain still won't come off, try to soak the stain off the pan. If you feel you need a metal scraper to get it clean, test it on the side or bottom of the pan first. Metal scrubbers can remove the finish on some pans.

The following sections contain cleaning tips for specific pots and pans to keep your cookware cooking for a long time.

## Cleaning aluminum

Aluminum pans are excellent heat conductors, but you must treat them with care to avoid discoloration or staining.

- Don't wash anodized aluminum pans in the dishwasher — washing by hand in hot, sudsy water is best.
- Don't leave water soaking in aluminum utensils or store moist foods in aluminum containers because chemicals in some foods and water may cause pitting in the metal, odors, and bad flavors.

Remove stains or discoloration in aluminum pots by boiling a solution of 1 to 2 tablespoons cream of tartar or lemon juice to each quart of water for about 10 minutes.

To remove burned-on food, boil water in the pan until it loosens the crud. Then scour with a soap-filled steel wool pad if necessary.

## Dealing with non-stick finishes

Remove stubborn stains on non-stick finishes with either one of these two solutions:

- 1 cup water, 2 tablespoons baking soda, and 3 tablespoons oxygen bleach
- Or 3 tablespoons automatic dishwasher detergent and 1 cup water.

Put the solution in the pan and let it boil on the stove for 15 minutes. Wash the pan, rinse, and dry. Season the pan by wiping the inside lightly with cooking oil before using it again.

To avoid stains, use medium to low heat for cooking. Extremely high temperatures used continuously discolor the surface.

## Cleaning copper, cast iron, stainless steel, plastic, or glass pans

The most glamorous of pans, copper is an excellent heat conductor but can discolor when in contact with food. To prevent discoloration, practically all copper cookware is lined with stainless steel or a nonstick coating. Wash copper cookware in hot sudsy water and dry afterwards. Soak off burned food with a sudsy detergent solution.

To polish unlacquered copper, use a commercial cleaner or rub with a paste of 3 tablespoons lemon juice and 2 tablespoons salt. Rinse and dry thoroughly.

Use wooden or plastic utensils to prevent scratching the surface.

### Cast iron

I love cast iron cookware. The good news is that it heats evenly and is good for baking, browning, and frying. The bad news is that it must be kept properly seasoned or it rusts.

Some pans are pre-seasoned by the manufacturer. If yours isn't, scour the inside with a steel wool pad and soapy water. Rinse and wipe dry. Then wipe it with vegetable oil and set the pan in a warm oven (set on 250° F) for a couple of hours. Take it out of the oven and wipe off any excess oil.

Never wash cast iron cookware in an automatic dishwasher.

Wash by hand in warm, sudsy water, rinse, and hand dry immediately. You can also quickly dry it by setting the pan on a burner set on low for a couple of minutes until the moisture evaporates.

### Stainless steel, plastic, and glass

You may have cookware with stainless steel, plastic, and glass or ceramic finishes. The following tips will help you maintain them properly:

- ✔ **Stainless steel:** Stainless is a tough workhorse and can withstand years of wear. Wash by hand or in the dishwasher. Dry immediately afterwards to cut down on water spotting. Burn stains may be removed by using commercial stainless cleaner or rubbing with synthetic scouring pad using a paste of baking soda and water.

- ✔ **Plastic:** Check the manufacturer's instructions when you buy plastic cookware. Most are dishwasher safe, but some must be put on the top rack to keep them away from the heating element. To remove any stains, rub with a nylon scrub pad and a mixture of baking soda and water. Rinse and dry.

- ✔ **Glass and glass/ceramic:** This kind of cookware is popular because it conducts heat well and can go right from the oven to the table as a serving container. Many can go from the freezer to the oven; others are for rangetop or microwave use. Always read the owner's manual to check the limitations of your cookware. Clean in hot, sudsy water or in the dishwasher.

  To clean off burned-on residue on the inside or outside, soak the cookware overnight in a mixture of liquid dishwashing detergent and water. Scrub the next morning with a nylon net pad.

# Chapter 10

# Battling the Bathroom

- - - - - - - - - - - - - - - - - - - - - - - - - - - - - - - - - - - - - - - - - - -

### In This Chapter

▶ Cleaning a little bit every day

▶ Fighting mildew

▶ Doing the dreaded job: The toilet

▶ Cutting down on the clutter

- - - - - - - - - - - - - - - - - - - - - - - - - - - - - - - - - - - - - - - - - - -

*C*leaning the bathroom is one of those hated jobs — one that ranks right up there with cleaning the oven. Although manufacturers have managed to come up with a self-cleaning oven, they have yet to come up with anything close to a self-cleaning tub, shower, or toilet. To get the bathroom clean, you still have to bend and stretch and get out the cleanser, sponges, brushes, and scrubbers. It doesn't seem fair, but take heart. The ideas in this chapter help make cleaning the bathroom a little easier.

## A Daily Dose Will Do It

First, on your family chore list, make sure that each person in the family is assigned to clean up after his or her shower. By "clean up," I don't mean getting out the scrub brush — a quick rinse of the stall with the showerhead is all it takes, followed by a swipe with a squeegee or paper towel.

After showering is actually the optimum time to clean because the steam generated by the shower loosens any grime that's there.

Bath people aren't off the hook either. After a bath, quickly wipe off the bottom of the tub with a sponge and then rinse with spray from the shower.

To keep bathtub rings from forming, rub the walls of the tub with a nylon net ball or pad while the water is still draining.

Now, how hard is that? This bare minimum of cleaning keeps soap scum and hard-water deposits under control, saving a major, heavy-duty clean-up later after the scuzzy stuff has set.

Now, you can work on the area around the sink. Spray some cleaner in the sink and let it sit for a couple of minutes while you're drying your hair. Wet a paper towel and use it to pick up any stray hairs on the countertop. Then quickly wipe the cleanser out of the sink.

If the faucet has a few spots on it, shake some baking soda onto a dry cloth and rub it over the chrome. Fingerprints and water spots come right off. The benefit to using this method is that no rinsing or wiping clean is required.

Quickly remove spots from the mirror by wiping the spot with a damp tissue and buffing it with a dry one.

If you have time, wipe off the toilet seat and the top and back of the bowl under the seat and around the rim with a paper towel dampened with spray household cleaner. Take the toilet brush and scrub inside the bowl for a few seconds. Every couple of weeks put some disinfectant into the bowl, swish around, and flush. Pick up any dust or stray hairs on the floor with a dampened paper towel. Voilà! In less than five minutes, your bathroom is sparkling clean to the naked eye. (And I do mean naked!)

# Mildew Loves Your Bathroom

Those little dark spots that appear on tile and grout are not just dirt. They're spores of a living organism called mildew. Mildew floats around in the air and breeds in a damp, humid environment like your bathroom (or basement). Not only is it unappealing, but it can damage whatever the spores attach to.

## Keeping mildew at bay

Keep mildew at bay by reducing the humidity in your bathroom. Your best bet is to install a ceiling fan that is vented to the outside. If that's too complicated or expensive, run a portable fan for a few minutes after every bath or shower, which will provide enough ventilation to significantly reduce the humidity. *Warning:* Be sure to position the fan near the door and away from any water; don't let the fan get wet and don't touch it with wet hands. If you have a window in the bathroom, open it slightly when weather permits. Get the air flowing to dry up the humidity and get rid of mildew spores.

Make a point of drying off anything that you use for bathing as soon as possible. After you get out of the shower, pull back the curtain across the length of the tub so that air can get to the total surface and dry it without leaving any damp spots that breed mildew. If you have a shower enclosure, leave the shower door open slightly after you're finished to give steam a chance to escape.

Don't leave used towels in lumps on the floor. Make a family rule: Everyone hangs up his or her towel on a bar or over the shower rod. If you don't have enough hanging space, bring in a quilt rack for extra storage. Or install an over-the-door rack to hang towels to dry.

## Fighting the battle against mildew

Attack mildew as soon as you see it because it continues to grow if left unchecked. Mildew is sometimes tough to remove and requires strong cleaning solutions. Use a commercial mildew remover or some of the solutions we suggest below.

 When using any strong chemical cleaner, such as bleach or ammonia (especially in a confined area like the bathroom), be sure to ventilate the room well. Turn on a fan and open the door and windows. Be sure to wear protective eye covering (here's another use for those swimming goggles!). That may seem a little excessive, but the fumes are strong and can irritate eyes and nasal passages. Never mix bleach and ammonia. Rinse off completely after you apply either one and avoid using one right after the other.

 Be sure to wear rubber gloves when using any strong solution. And be careful of clothing, towels, and bath mats. Many bathroom cleaners contain bleach that can permanently stain fabric items, wall coverings, and countertops if spilled or splattered on them.

## Winning the mildew wars

Here's a plan of attack for getting rid of mildew in specific areas of your bathroom:

- **Tile:** Remove mildew spots from tile by wiping with a solution of ¼ cup bleach to 1 quart water. Before using bleach, make sure that no residue is left on the tile from any cleaning solutions that contain ammonia. Rinse the surface well after washing.

- **Grout:** Mildew seems to go straight for the grout in most bathrooms. You can spot it right away — black speckles seem to pop up like weeds. Clean the grout with a commercial mildew stain remover or wipe with the bleach and water mixture mentioned in the previous bullet point. Apply the solution with a cloth or sponge to avoid splattering the bleach on clothes or nearby fabric.

To get into the hard-to-reach spot between the wall and the tub, soak paper towels or cotton balls in the bleach and water solution and place against the grout. Leave in place for a couple of hours so that the bleach penetrates the grout, and then rinse well. Scrub lightly with a soft tooth-brush dipped in the bleach solution, if necessary. If you're more comfortable with a "green cleaner," try full strength vinegar or a baking soda and water paste.

✔ **Shower curtain:** If your shower curtain is mildew-ridden, take it outside and brush off all the dark stuff. Then throw it in the washer in warm water on the delicate cycle. Put in ½ cup detergent and ½ cup baking soda for the wash and 1 cup white vinegar in the rinse cycle to prevent further mildewing. Take the curtain out before the final spin cycle and hang it over a curtain rod to dry. If any mildew still exists, brush it off.

If mold on your shower curtain continues to be a problem, you may want to consider the guillotine method of mold removal. Cut off the bottom of the curtain, leaving enough so that the curtain just touches the top inside of the tub but avoids the side and bottom where mold collects.

✔ **Walls:** If your walls have just a small amount of mildew, wash them with a relatively mild solution of 1 part bleach to 5 parts water. Rinse well.

However, if the mildew is running rampant, the time has come to repaint the room. Before you repaint, though, you've got to kill off *all* the existing mildew. This takes a strong solution of 1 part bleach to 1 part water or a store-bought mildew-fighting solution. Use the solution all over the ceiling and walls. You must get rid of any mildew on any surface that you plan to paint. Wear protective eye covering and long-sleeved clothing and ventilate the area well. After killing the mildew, add a coat of shellac or stain-killing primer to keep the mildew from growing again in the same spots.

To help fight mildew in the future, choose paint that is mildew-resistant, or put an anti-mildew additive in any regular paint. Both are available at home centers and hardware stores.

# Deep Cleaning the Whole Bathroom

About once a week, you should give your bathroom a really good scrubbing. This section gives you tips on getting the whole room thoroughly clean, with special concentration on The Big Three: shower, tub, and toilet. These areas are the real victims of soap scum and water deposits, so they take a little more elbow grease than the rest of the room. If you clean them regularly, the task really isn't that bad.

## Shining shower enclosures

Nothing is worse than stepping into a dirty shower stall. You want to get clean, but you're surrounded by dirt. Washing yourself without touching the walls or the door is very difficult — and believe me, I've tried.

To deep clean a shower stall that has a heavy layer of soap scum:

1. **Turn on the shower for a few minutes at the hottest temperature to loosen the dirt.**

2. **Turn off the water and spray all surfaces with a heavy-duty cleaner or soap scum remover.**

    As an alternative, use a mixture of ½ cup vinegar, 1 cup ammonia, and ¼ cup baking soda in 1 gallon water.

    Ventilate the room and wear rubber gloves.

3. **Let the cleaner soak into the walls for a couple of minutes.**

4. **Use the showerhead to rinse the walls well.**

To clean out the shower door track, squirt it with an all-purpose cleaner and scrub it with a toothbrush or a rag wound around a screwdriver.

Pour some lemon oil on a rag and rub it into the metal frame and track to remove hard-water stains. My friend, Jane, likes to wipe the walls of her shower with a light coating of lemon oil. Not only does it smell nice, but it discourages future build-up of soap scum and mineral deposits. (Cover the bottom of the stall with a towel while you're applying the oil to prevent the oil from spilling on the floor and making it very slippery.)

Remove water spots from the glass door and give it extra sparkle by rubbing it with a mixture of clear vinegar and water. Dry with a soft cloth.

## Rub-a-dubbing the tub

Keep a spray bottle in the bath area that's filled with 2 teaspoons liquid dishwashing detergent and 1 teaspoon white vinegar in water. Spray this solution on the walls of the tub, let it sit for a couple of minutes, and then wipe it down.

I reserve a special toilet brush nearby for bathtub cleaning. (I store it in the bathroom under the sink.) The long handle keeps me from bending deep into the tub and the bristles are great for scrubbing bathtub rings.

Non-skid strips on the bottom of the tub can be tough to get clean. Sprinkle some mild cleanser or baking soda on a nylon scrubbing pad and scrub gently to remove any built-up dirt.

Even though your tub seems indestructible, it's not. Using harsh abrasives or steel wool can damage the finish.

If you have a fiberglass tub, be careful when cleaning because the surface can scratch easily. Each week, wipe the tub with a commercial fiberglass cleaning product or a nonabrasive cleaner, and then rinse well.

## Showering the shower curtains

You can wash most shower curtains in your washing machine. Read the care label for your curtain and follow the instructions.

Wash a pliable plastic curtain in cold water on the delicate cycle. Put ½ cup detergent and ½ cup baking soda in the machine along with a couple of large bath towels. The towels rub against the curtain during the cycle and scrub the dirt off. Add 1 cup vinegar to the rinse cycle to cut down on wrinkling. Remove the curtain immediately and hang it over the shower rod to dry.

If you have a stiff plastic curtain, wash it in the tub. Lay it flat in the tub, and pour over it a mixture of ¼ cup vinegar, ½ cup clear ammonia, ⅛ cup baking soda, and 2 quarts water. Open the door and windows to ventilate the bathroom well. Let the curtain soak for a few minutes to allow the cleaner to do the work. Then scrub the curtain with a sponge or nylon scouring pad, if necessary. Drain the tub and rinse the curtain with warm water. Add a few drops of mineral oil to the water to keep the curtain flexible.

## Cleaning the dreaded toilet

No one likes to talk or think about it, but we all have to do it. But if you clean the toilet often enough, stains don't have a chance to form and all you have to do is make a few wipes with a good cleaner.

You may think that you can avoid cleaning the toilet by getting one of those in-tank cleaners. I used to think that anything that changes the water to that lovely blue must be doing some good. They do sanitize the bowl and make you feel like you're living in a chemistry lab. But they don't eliminate the need for a good scrubbing now and then.

Be careful not to mix any chemicals (especially bleach and ammonia) or let two chemicals that could cause toxic fumes come into contact with each other. If you use an in-tank cleaner, don't put any other cleaner in the toilet until the in-tank cleaner is all used up and the water is totally clear. Clean the toilet bowl first, and then rinse and flush away any cleaner before using a cleaner on the outside of the toilet. Read the label on any cleaner because most cleaners are strong stuff. Always wear rubber gloves and be careful not to drip anything on the countertops or other surfaces.

To treat stains the easy way, pour ½ cup bleach into the toilet bowl. Let it soak for a couple of hours, scrub the toilet with a brush, and then flush. Be careful not to pour bleach into the toilet bowl until any cleaning substance containing ammonia has been flushed out.

Spray toilet bowl cleaner into the bowl and under the rim, swish around with a brush, and then flush. Spray the rim, seat, hinges, bottom, and outside of the tank with all-purpose cleaner. Wipe off with a paper towel and throw the paper away — in the wastebasket, not in the toilet. Paper towels can clog drains. Use a toothbrush, if necessary, to get into the crevices around the hinges and bottom of the tank.

## Cleaning countertops, faucets, and the rest of the room

Finish up the items in this list, and you're done! As we've said before, daily cleaning makes this deep cleaning a breeze.

- ✔ **Countertops:** Move everything to one side and spray with all-purpose cleaner, wipe with a paper towel or sponge, move everything to the other side, and then repeat the process.

- ✔ **Faucets:** Spray with all-purpose cleaner and buff with a dry cloth. Or use the paste of baking soda and water; rub it on, wipe it off, and rinse thoroughly.

- ✔ **Towel racks:** Give wooden towel racks a nice finish by periodically applying furniture polish with a soft cloth. Rub gently so that the polish can penetrate the wood. Clean chrome towel racks with a light-duty all-purpose cleaner and wipe dry.

- ✔ **Mirrors:** All fogged up? Turn on a hair dryer and move it back and forth in front of the mirror area for a few seconds. Your beautiful face will become visible almost instantly.

  If fogging is a problem, try running an inch of cold water into the tub before adding hot water. The fog should diminish. Or wipe the mirror with shaving cream.

Attack any smudges by dampening a paper towel or a wad of toilet paper with rubbing alcohol and wiping the area — no rinsing necessary. This not only leaves the mirror sparkling clean, but it also removes any sticky residue of hair spray or spots of toothpaste. (Many people have told me they use baby wipes to spot clean in the bathroom. Talk about quick — they are pre-moistened and you don't have to rinse.)

✔ **Soap dishes:** Take out the soap and rinse the dish with water. Keep soap from getting gummy by putting a small piece of nylon mesh (from a fruit or onion bag) under the soap in the dish.

✔ **Grout:** If you see that the grout between the wall and the tub or shower enclosure is cracking or separating from the wall, recaulk immediately. Water can seep behind the wall and cause damage.

If your countertop or wall grout is dirty, make a paste of baking soda and water and rub it into the grout with a sponge or toothbrush. Wipe off and rinse thoroughly. If you have a mildew problem, wash with a solution of 1 part bleach to 5 parts water.

✔ **Floors:** Move everything out of the bathroom and vacuum the floor. To get any stray hairs in corners, wipe with a damp paper towel. Then wash with a floor cleaner that is recommended for that surface. (See Chapter 7 for more information on cleaning floors.)

✔ **Bath rugs:** A cotton or synthetic rug with a woven backing can usually be machine washed and dried on a medium setting. Check the care label to see if it's washable. Wash rugs separately or with towels of a similar color because these rugs can throw off lots of lint. If your rug has a latex backing, wash in cold water and tumble dry on low.

# Stain Solvers

Most areas in the bathroom just need a quick wipe and they're clean. Sometimes mineral deposits or other stains can slow up the cleaning process. Here are some ways to solve those pesky problems:

✔ **Hard-water stains in the toilet:** Remove hard-water stains by pouring 2 cups vinegar or bleach into the toilet bowl. Let it soak for several hours or overnight. Swish out stains with a toilet brush. Clean any stains on white, vitreous china bowls by rubbing lightly with a wet pumice stone. Keep the stone wet while you're working on the stain. Don't use a pumice stone on colored, enamel, or plastic toilets.

✔ **Clogged showerheads:** Mineral deposits inside the showerhead can keep it from running properly. Remove the shower head, take it apart, and soak all its parts in vinegar for several hours. Scrub with an old toothbrush and clean the holes out with a toothpick or a metal skewer.

If you can't take the showerhead off, just slip a plastic bag filled with vinegar over it and fasten the bag with a rubber band. After several hours, remove the bag and clean off the deposits with a toothbrush and toothpick.

✔ **Rust on fixtures:** Use a commercial rust cleaner and follow the directions on the container.

✔ **Decals or appliqués on bathtubs:** Lift the edge of the decal, spray WD-40 or cooking oil under the surface, and let the oil soak into the adhesive for a couple of hours. Pry off the decal with a credit card and remove any remaining adhesive by rubbing it with more cooking oil or WD-40 and a nylon scrubber. (If you're using WD-40, do so in a ventilated area.)

✔ **Sluggish drains:** Pour ½ cup baking soda, ½ cup salt, and ¼ cup white vinegar into the drain and let it sit for 15 minutes. Pour 1 quart boiling water into the drain and then run tap water in the sink for one minute.

# Cut that Clutter

Depending on the number of bathrooms in your house (and who ever has enough?), you usually find stray stuff from every member of the family deposited there. Add to that the makeup, shaving gear, cleansers, and shampoo, and it's no wonder that you don't have enough room. Here are a few ways to find some extra space in this overcrowded area.

## Taking charge of the toiletries

Everyone's toiletries need not be spread all over the countertops. A little organization not only makes things neater, but also speeds up your morning routine, because you can find everything in one place.

Put all the toiletries and hair accessories for each person together in a basket or plastic bin. Include things such as hairbrushes, hairspray, makeup, hair dryers, toothbrushes, toothpaste, and shaving gear. Make one basket for every member of the family and store the baskets in the vanity or on a shelf.

## Shaping up the shower

Instead of covering the side of the tub or the bottom of the shower stall with a myriad of bottles, buy a shower caddy that hangs over the showerhead. Store shampoo, conditioner, sponges, scrubbers, and soaps there. And cut down on the number of bottles of shampoo: Each person doesn't need his or her own brand. Agree on one or two bottles that everyone in the family can use.

I transfer my shampoo and conditioner into small squeeze bottles that don't take up as much room in the shower. Because the tip is tiny, the shampoo squeezes out in smaller amounts, providing me with a double benefit: I save on space and don't use as much shampoo.

## Getting the clothes off the floor

In the best of all possible worlds, every family member takes his shower, picks up his stuff, and leaves the bathroom in the pristine condition in which he found it. But you know that rarely happens. Often, dirty clothes are left on the floor, right where they were dropped.

To save yourself from continual frustration, use a pretty covered basket or clothes hamper and designate it as the place for all dirty clothes. If you don't have room in the bathroom, store it in a nearby closet. This, at least, gets clothes up off the floor and one step closer to the laundry.

If you're in one of those worse possible worlds, you may need to plan a pick-up trip through the bathroom, confiscating anything you find on the floor and fining the perpetrator (money, time, possessions — be creative).

# Part III
# Home Laundry and Clothing Care

The 5th Wave    By Rich Tennant

"I think I found what's causing the holes in your laundry."

## In this part . . .

Clean house, clean person, I always say. They complement each other. In this part, you get the scoop on taking care of the clothes, fashion accessories, and household items that give you and your home style and personality. You'll get the facts on how to treat stains and pamper fabrics; the basics on how to iron and how to sew on a button or take up a hem. This part also gives you the answers to stuck zippers and other simple sewing tasks.

# Chapter 11

# Getting Clothes Ready for Cleaning

The secret to easy-care washing is knowing your fabrics and how to treat them. Most garments and other fabric items have care labels that tell you what the item is made of and how to care for it. These labels give you enormous help in cleaning your clothes. The care label tells you

✔ Exactly what type of cleaning method works best

✔ What wash-water temperatures to use

✔ How to dry and iron the item

✔ How *not* to treat the item

✔ What the fiber content is, which helps you determine how delicate the item is and how to treat a stain

Table 11-1 tells you at a glance how to deal with the most common fabrics.

| Table 11-1 | | Fabric Care | |
|---|---|---|---|
| *Fabric* | *How to Clean It* | *How to Dry It* | *Special Care* |
| Acetate | Dry clean. If label says washable, machine wash on gentle cycle in warm or cool water. | Air dry. | Iron while damp on cool setting. |
| Acrylic | Machine wash or hand wash in warm water according to label. | Dry on low or air fluff setting. | Turn garment inside out to avoid pilling. Sweaters: Pull into shape after washing and dry flat on a towel. |
| Corduroy | Can be cotton or cotton blend. Turn inside out to wash Hand or machine wash in warm water according to label. | Machine dry on warm setting. Remove while damp and line dry. Shake and smooth pile while drying. | Iron inside out. |
| Cotton | Wash in gentle cycle or by hand according- to care label. Use warm water for colorfast; cold water for bright colors that bleed. | Line dry or machine dry on low setting. Remove from dryer while damp. Remove cotton knits while damp and pull into shape. Dry flat on a towel. | Iron while damp on hot set. |
| Denim | Can be cotton or cotton blend. Machine wash inside out in water. Wash separately until color no longer bleeds. | Dry on low to avoid shrinkage. | Iron damp with hot iron. |
| Linen | Dry clean to keep finish crisp. Wash in gentle cycle in cold or warm water. Check for colorfastness. | Line or machine dry on low setting. Remove from dryer while damp. | Iron on wrong side; use hot iron on heavy linens; iron set on low for blends and light weights. |
| Nylon | Hand or machine wash on gentle cycle in warm water. Use all-purpose detergent. | Drip dry or machine dry on permanent press cycle. | If necessary iron on cool setting. |

| Fabric | How to Clean It | How to Dry It | Special Care |
|---|---|---|---|
| Polyester | Machine wash on warm setting with all-purpose detergent. | Drip dry or machine dry on low setting. | Do not wash with greasy items. Turn inside out to avoid pilling. Iron on warm setting. |
| Rayon | Can also be labeled as viscose. Dry clean to retain body. If label says washable, hand wash or machine wash in warm water with a mild detergent. | Machine dry on low setting. Remove while damp and pull into shape. | Do not twist or wring. Iron damp on warm setting. |
| Silk | Dry clean heavier weight or colored silk. If labeled washable, hand wash in cold water with mild or cold-water detergent. Rinse well. Test for colorfastness first. | Roll in towel to blot dry; then air dry. | Iron damp on cool setting. Do not bleach. |
| Spandex | Hand or machine wash in lukewarm water in gentle cycle. | Line dry or machine dry on low temperature. | Don't use bleach. Avoid overdrying. |
| Wool | Dry clean most items If labeled washable, hand wash in cool water and a cold-water detergent. Roll in towel and gently squeeze (not wring). | Dry flat on a towel. Do not machine dry. | Pull sweaters into shape. |

Many garments today are a combination of fibers that can sometimes throw you for a loop when you're trying to figure out how to treat them. A general rule is to clean items as though they were made only of the highest percentage fiber. For example, if a garment is 90 percent linen and 10 percent rayon, clean it like a linen garment. When you treat a stain, start with a stain-removal product safe for the most delicate fiber in the blend.

# Sorting and Checking Your Clothes

I found out really fast how important it is to sort clothes when one of my favorite white dresses turned a blotchy shade of gray in the wash. The culprit was a teeny little black sock that had made its way into the white wash load. A large wave of despair overwhelmed me. I really wished I could blame it on someone else, but alas, it was totally my fault. Luckily, I spotted the problem soon enough to be able to get the stain out. But from that day forward, I became a sorting maniac.

When sorting your laundry, you essentially match likes with likes — separating dark colors from light, sturdy wash from delicate fabrics, permanent press from cottons, and the like. When you sort your clothes well, you end up with a machine-load of items that require the same treatment. Sorting properly can reduce a lot of laundry problems.

You can sort your clothes in many different ways; use what works best for you. The following section provides some tips to help you sort :

## Separate but equal

Although you may love all your clothes equally, they don't necessarily mix well in the washer. A few minutes spent separating clothes ahead of time will prevent pulling out a load that seems dirtier than it was before you put it in.

- ✔ Separate white and light-colored clothes from dark ones. Even small amounts of dye in water can transfer to light-colored fabrics and ruin them.

- ✔ Separate any delicate fabrics, sheers, or items requiring a delicate cycle and low water temperature.

- ✔ Separate items that produce a lot of lint (chenille robes, towels, and sweatsuits, to name a few) from items that attract and show lint (dark fabrics, synthetics, and permanent press).

- ✔ Separate heavily soiled items, such as work clothes or items with grease stains, from lightly soiled items. Otherwise, light colors may pick up some of the soil and get a gray tinge to them.

- ✔ Separate any items that are marked "wash separately," which means that the color will run for the first few washings. To see whether the color is still bleeding, look at the suds in the wash water or put in a small piece of white cloth to see whether it absorbs any color.

Set up several small containers instead of one large hamper. This makes it easy to get family members to sort their own clothes. All they have to do is drop them into the appropriate container. Put a label on each container to show what type of clothes go inside — underwear, towels, shirts, lingerie, socks, whatever.

For example, set up one container for bleachable whites and throw things like white shirts, towels, and underwear in there. Set up another container for non-bleachable whites (assuming that your whites fit into only these two categories). Another container could hold light colors; a fourth, bright and dark colors; a fifth, delicate, hand wash, or wash-on-cool items. Just make sure that your method of sorting results in fabrics that require the same pretreatment, water temperature, wash and rinse cycle, use of bleaching agents, and so on.

## *An ounce of prevention*

After you've sorted your clothes, take time for some preventive maintenance that will help get them through the wash cycle intact without any surprising stains or masses of lint. Only the dirt should be gone. Here are some suggestions:

- Empty pockets and remove everything before placing clothes in the wash. If you've ever opened your washing machine to find that a pen leaked all over your clothes, a tissue disintegrated, or a key snagged a garment, you know how important this step is. Brush away any lint or crumbs.

- Close zippers and hooks to prevent snagging and to avoid any damage to the zipper. Take off any pins or ornaments.

- Tie sashes and strings and buckle belts to prevent tangling.

- Turn some garments inside out to prevent damage. I always turn the following inside out: sweaters to prevent pilling, printed T-shirts to protect the design, and jeans to stop fading.

- If you're washing a garment with a drawstring, tie the string together so that it won't disappear into the pocket while washing.

- Keep a small sewing kit (needle, thread, and scissors) near the washing machine. Laundry time is perfect for mending any rips, tears, loose buttons, or hems. The quick fix-up prevents them from getting worse in the wash.

- Put delicate items in a mesh laundry bag or a pillow case to protect them from being damaged.

- If you suffer from "lost sock syndrome," prevent losses while washing by keeping all the socks together in a pillowcase or mesh laundry bag. Use a rubber band or safety pins to keep the pillowcase closed.

If you spot any soil or dirt that needs special care when you check over your clothing, see the next section for help in pretreating your clothes before washing.

TIP

## How will my color run?

My experience has been that if you suspect something bad can happen, it probably will. So take precautions beforehand. Dark or bright-colored fabrics have a tendency to run, at least the first few times you wash them.

Do a quick cotton-swab test to see whether the color will run: Place the inner seam of the garment on a paper towel; then soak a cotton swab in water and press down firmly on the fabric. If no color comes off on the swab, the fabric is colorfast. If you see color on the swab, the color will probably run in the wash. Use care and hand wash the garment by itself in cold water several times until the color no longer runs.

## *Pretreating and soaking clothes*

Pretreat any dirty cuffs, collars, and any noticeable soil by rubbing on liquid detergent, prewash stain remover, or a paste of granular detergent and water.

If clothes are heavily soiled, soak them in a presoak solution or a detergent solution. Sort the clothes according to color before soaking. Then follow these steps:

1. **Mix the detergent or presoak with water in a sink or in a washer with a presoak cycle.**

2. **Follow the manufacturer's instructions for the length of time that you should soak an item — usually about 30 minutes.**

3. **Spin or wring out garments before starting to wash.**

Avoid presoaking fabrics like silk or wool. Soak elasticized clothes for only a few minutes.

# *Taking Care of Special Washing Problems*

Some items can pose problems when you're washing your regular load. Read the care labels first and follow the instructions carefully.

# Bedding

Many blankets are machine washable, if you take care to avoid shrinkage and stretching. Read the care label before you put any fabric in the wash. Some woolens, synthetics, and cotton blankets can be machine washed on the gentle cycle in cool water with mild detergent. Dry in the electric dryer on no heat or hang over two clotheslines to hold up the weight of the blanket. Don't dry synthetics or wool in the sunlight, which can cause shrinkage, discoloring, or an odor in wool. After they're dry, give them a few good shakes or put them in a dryer set on no heat to fluff them up.

You can wash most comforters; just make sure to follow the care label. Always check that all the stitching is intact so that the filling doesn't clump up when it's being washed. The big problem with washing comforters is fitting them in the machine. Don't stuff it in too much or try to wash more than one at a time. If your comforter doesn't fit in your washing machine, take it to a commercial laundry or the dry cleaner.

# Electric blankets

Read the manufacturer's instructions first. Dissolve detergent in the water temperature suggested by the label, and then put the blanket evenly in the machine. Rinse in cold water. Machine dry at medium temperature for about 10 minutes. Remove while damp. Line dry by laying it over a couple of clotheslines. Pull back into shape if necessary.

# Polyester and down (feather) pillows

Both can be machine washed: polyester in cold water, and down in warm water if the label says "washable." Balance the load by washing two pillows at a time or one pillow and a couple of bath towels. If you have a top-loading machine, push the pillows into the water until they become fully moistened. After a few minutes of washing, check the pillows and turn them over. Just like a lot of logs in the water, they tend to go back to the surface and float. Wash on a medium cycle for no longer than 8 minutes. Make sure to rinse thoroughly, at least two or three times.

Tumble dry on a low setting. Put a couple of tennis balls or a clean sneaker in the machine to help fluff down pillows. Stop the machine a few times and shake out the pillows to even out the damp spots. You can hang them on a line indoors or on a drying rack. Station a fan in front of the pillows to speed drying time. As you can imagine, pillows full of water take a long time to dry. But keep at it, because if they aren't thoroughly dry, there's a good chance that they may mildew.

## Foam and fiberfill pillows

Before you start machine washing foam pillows, place them in a mesh laundry bag or a pillow case pinned shut to prevent any foam from coming loose or tearing during washing. To dry, put the pillows in the machine on air fluff or low only. This is very important because if they're dried on a hot setting, the foam could catch fire. You can also air dry them with a fan blowing on them. After you take them out of the washer, wrap a couple of dry towels around them and squeeze as much water out of them as possible.

Machine wash fiberfill pillows in cold water. Balance the load by washing two pillows or one pillow and a couple of bath towels at a time. Machine dry on low heat. Machine wash down pillows separately with a mild detergent and warm water. Tumble dry on low setting with a couple of tennis balls or a clean sneaker to help fluff the down. Be sure to dry thoroughly (it can take a long time).

## Down jackets and comforters

Most down can be washed if the fabric that's covering it is washable. Of course, you should check the care label first. Wash down jackets and comforters separately from other items because they have an odor when wet that could transfer to other items in the wash. Stitch up any loose seams or tears before washing because those little feathers have a sneaky way of leaking through the smallest opening. Use the delicate cycle and mild detergent and avoid enzyme products. Rinse several times if necessary to remove any residue of soap.

Dry on delicate setting in the dryer. Put in clean tennis balls to prevent the down from clumping.

If you want to dry clean down-filled items, take it to an expert who specializes in cleaning them.

## Denim jeans

The color in denim jeans often runs the first few times you wash them. Machine wash them a couple of times in cold water with similarly colored items. Turn them inside out to prevent streaking or fading.

# Hand Washing Your Clothes

I hand wash a lot of clothes, sometimes because they're delicate and require special care, and other times because I don't want to wait to fill a washer load before I wear or use an item. Hand washing isn't really that labor intensive. It just requires a few seconds of care and a little longer time to get dry.

Hand washing requires the same kind of sorting and pretreatment as machine washing: Sort things by color and pretreat any soiled areas with liquid detergent.

Before you start, make sure that you don't have any rough fingernails or spots on your hands that could snag delicate garments, knits, or pantyhose. If necessary, wear rubber gloves.

To hand wash:

1. **Put your detergent or soap in a basin with either warm or cold water, depending on the care label instructions and the delicacy of the fabric.**

2. **Swish the garment gently through the suds a few times, but don't wring or twist it.**

3. **Soak the item for about 5 minutes. If not colorfast and the garment is bleeding dye, soak it for only a couple of minutes.**

4. **Gently squeeze out the detergent and then empty the basin and refill it with clean, cold water.**

   When I'm hand washing in the sink, I sometimes overdo it with the detergent, and the sink fills with gobs of soap suds that seem to take forever to go down the drain. A quick solution is to sprinkle salt on the suds, which dwindles them in seconds.

5. **Rinse out the garment thoroughly in clean, cold water until you have removed all the soap.**

   Keep rinsing until the water doesn't feel slippery and no suds appear when you push water through the clothes. Sometimes you need to rinse two or three times.

6. **Lay the item flat on a towel and roll the garment up to absorb moisture.**

7. **Hang the garment on a plastic hanger to dry or lay it flat on a drying frame or towel.**

   If you're drying the item outside, don't put it in direct sun.

   Gently pull knits and other stretchy synthetics back into their proper shape and dry them flat to avoid further stretching.

If you're hand washing a garment that isn't delicate and can stand up vigorous scrubbing, by all means scrub it. Sometimes especially dirty clothes will get clean only if they get individual attention. In that case:

1. **Fill the sink with as hot water as is suitable for the fabric. If the water is too hot for your hands, put on rubber gloves.**

2. **Scrub the article back and forth against itself or scrub with a tooth-brush, a soft brush, or even a clean white towel.**

3. **Keep dipping the article back into the soapy water and squeezing the soap through until all the dirt comes out.**

   You'll know that the dirt's out when the suds remain white.

4. **Rinse in clean, cold water several times until all the soap is gone.**

5. **Wring out the item until you've removed as much water as you can.**

   Roll in a towel to remove more water and cut down drying time.

If the fabric can stand it, put the garment in the dryer on warm or hot.

# Getting the Most from the Dry Cleaner

Using a dry cleaner is sometimes the safest way to clean clothes. Dry clean-ers have advanced solvents that can remove most stains. They can also preserve delicate fabrics and colors that can't survive laundering, and they can prevent knits from shrinking.

Most clothes can be dry cleaned, but be careful of any fabrics or finishes sealed with adhesives or vinyl, spandex, or rubber. Once again, always check the care label to see whether a garment can be safely dry cleaned.

When taking your clothes to the cleaners, use this wise advice to get the best results:

- ✔ **Take stained articles to the dry cleaner promptly after the items are soiled.** Don't put them back in the closet. You might forget about them, and the stains will become impossible to remove.

- ✔ **Discuss the stain with the cleaner.** Tell the dry cleaner what the stain is and whether you tried any homemade stain-removal techniques on it. If you spilled soft drinks, white wine, soda, or fruit juices on a garment, point them out. They need to be pretreated even if you can't see them. They often show up later as brown spots.

- ✔ **If one part of an outfit gets stained, clean the whole thing anyway.** Sometimes, the chemicals in dry cleaning can fade colors. If any change in color occurs, the whole garment will be the same color.

For the sake of your wallet and your clothing, don't dry clean your clothes every time you wear them. The chemicals are safe for your clothes, but are also very strong and can damage the fabric if used too often. Instead, hang up your clothes in an open space and let them air out. Brush off any loose dirt or dust with a soft brush.

# Chapter 12

# This Is the Way We Wash Our Clothes

· · · · · · · · · · · · · · · · · · · · · · · · · · · · · · · · · · · · · ·

## In This Chapter

▶ Selecting a detergent

▶ Loading the wash machine

▶ Removing stains

· · · · · · · · · · · · · · · · · · · · · · · · · · · · · · · · · · · · · ·

*W*hen I was growing up, I loved the laundry chute on the first floor of my house. I spent hours throwing things down the hole and even tried to climb inside it a few times. At first, I thought all you had to do to wash clothes was throw them down the chute. I was really shocked when I found out that was only the beginning.

With automatic washers and easy-care fabrics, doing the wash is much easier than it used to be — no more beating clothes against a washboard or the side of a rock. But laundry still takes up a sizable amount of housekeeping time. The sheer volume and never-ending amount of dirty clothes can get you down. Just when you finish doing one load, another starts piling up. But with the right products in hand and some basic stain and fabric knowledge, you can avoid clothing disasters and make doing your laundry much less of a chore.

In this chapter, I explain the basic steps to getting your clothes clean with a minimum of muss and fuss.

## Choosing Laundry Products

You can choose from a number of products to get your clothes clean. All you have to do is walk down the laundry aisle in a grocery store, and you're inundated by boxes and jugs that promise lots of things. What's in these containers, and which ones should you use for what?

# Tell-tale signs of hard water

A large percentage of households in the United States have to deal with hard water (excessive mineral content) and the problems that go with it. Minerals like calcium and magnesium leave a film on clothes that can make them appear yellow or gray. Not only is hard water bad for clothes washing, it can also build up scale in the plumbing system and hinder efficient operation of appliances like water heaters and dishwashers.

Some signals that you have hard water are:

- Clothes that look dull and dingy and feel stiff
- A ring around the bathtub that just won't go away
- Soaps that don't lather properly
- Glasses and dishes that spot often
- Chalky residue around drains and faucets
- Unpleasant taste in water

If you have any of these symptoms, check with your local water company. They'll be able to tell you the hardness level of your water, which is typically measured in grains per U.S. gallon (gpg). A reading from 1 to 3.5 gpg indicates slightly hard water; 9 or above puts you clearly in the hard-water class.

If the water in your area is hard, you'll benefit from using a water softener to soften the water and enable the detergent to clean properly. The following list describes the most commonly used water-softening agents:

**Prepackaged dry softeners:** These make water softer by taking out the calcium and magnesium ions present in hard water. You add them to the water along with detergent at the beginning of the cycle. *Non-precipitating softeners* inactivate the minerals that cause hardness, but they also contain phosphates. Precipitating softeners (non-phosphate) can leave a chalky film on clothes. Follow the package directions.

**Mechanical softeners:** If your water is really hard (over 10.6 gpg), a mechanical softener that's installed onto the water supply that removes the calcium and magnesium ions is probably more efficient. You can either purchase or rent this equipment.

**Borax:** An alternative to the packaged water softeners is borax. It works to break down the chemical salts in the water and boost the cleaning power of your detergent. Add about a cup of borax with your detergent at the start of the cycle.

# Soap or detergent: How hard is your water, and how hardy are your clothes?

The two basic substances you use to wash clothes are soap and detergent. Because detergents are the most commonly used products for washing clothes, I discuss them first. Detergents are synthetic cleaners with a wetting agent to break up and remove soil and "builders" that reduce water hardness and enhance cleaning efficiency.

Detergents are popular because they perform well in all levels of water hardness. Depending on the brand, detergents also can contain fabric softeners, oxygen bleach, enzymes that break down soils, whitening agents, and fragrances.

✔ Heavy-duty detergents are available in liquid or granular form for just about all washables, including heavily soiled items. They contain ingredients that help break down grease and oil and inactivate water hardness. Use the liquid form if you like to pretreat oily or greasy spots with detergent.

✔ Light-duty detergents in liquid or powder form are good for delicate washable fabrics, baby clothes, and lightly soiled items.

✔ Ultra detergents are more concentrated and come in liquid or granular form. The boxes are smaller and you use a smaller amount for each normal load— a great bonus if you live in an apartment and have limited storage space.

Although people use the term *soap* for practically every washing product, not every washing product is a soap. Soaps are basically made from the same ingredients that they have been for centuries — fats and oils (tallow or coconut) and is a commonly known soap product.

The drawback of soap is that it doesn't react well with the minerals in hard water and can leave a film that sticks to the clothes and the washer. In soft water, soaps are a good choice for lightly soiled items, delicate fabrics from silk to spandex, diapers, and baby clothes.

Don't use soap to wash flame-retardant children's sleepwear, because soap can reduce the flame-retardant properties.

# To whiten and brighten — chlorine or oxygen bleach

If you have time to lay your clothes out in the sunlight to whiten, you may want to forgo bleach. But the rest of us usually need some extra help to keep clothes white and bright, and that means bleach. Bleach whitens and gets rid of stains when used in conjunction with a detergent.

Remember, bleaches are strong stuff and, if used incorrectly, can permanently damage fabric. Never mix bleaches with other household chemicals or cleaning supplies, especially ammonia, rust removers, vinegars, and toilet bowl cleaners. The mixture can produce noxious fumes.

The two most common man-made bleaches (remember, the sun is a natural substance) are chlorine bleach and oxygen bleach.

### Using chlorine bleach

Chlorine bleach is an old standby. Who doesn't have childhood memories that associate the smell of chlorine with clean wash (or the swimming pool, but that's another matter)? Chlorine has always been the powerhouse bleach —

more effective than oxygen bleach on cottons, linens, and most synthetics. But it's also the most hazardous, and chlorine bleach can ruin some fabrics. A mistake made with bleach can be a mistake forever.

Here are some things to keep in mind when working with chlorine bleach:

✔ **Never pour bleach directly on fabric.** Always dilute it according to the instructions on the label. Used full strength, bleach can cause permanent spotting and harm the fabric.

✔ **Be very careful with the bleach bottle.** If you accidentally spill it on rugs, furniture, or clothing, there's a good chance that the stain will be permanent.

✔ **Be cautious of the amount you put in the wash.** Too much bleach can cause yellowing or weakening of the fibers in the cloth. Always check the manufacturer's recommendations for the proper amount.

✔ **Bleach on a schedule.** Bleaching too frequently can harm your clothes. Be conservative and use bleach every second or third load.

✔ **Don't use chlorine bleach on sheer or delicate fabrics on trim, or on fabrics with unstable dyes.**

✔ **Don't add chlorine bleach at the beginning of the wash cycle.** Put it in the machine about five minutes after the cycle has begun. This gives the machine plenty of time to fill up with water and thoroughly moisten all the clothes. To be extra safe, dilute the bleach in 1 quart water first.

✔ **Use chlorine bleach on washable whites and colorfast fabrics.** But always check the label first.

✔ **Don't use chlorine bleach on wool, silk, mohair, leather, spandex, or anything that's non-colorfast or flame-retardant.** Some permanent-press fabrics may yellow if you use chlorine bleach. Test first.

If you're in doubt about colorfastness, try this simple test to see whether the fabric is bleach-safe:

1. **Mix together 1 tablespoon of chlorine bleach and ¼ cup of water.**

2. **Dip a cotton swab in this solution and put a drop on a hidden area, such as a seam. Leave it on for 1 minute.**

3. **Blot with a paper towel and check for color change.**

If there's no color change, you can safely bleach the article. If the garment has any decorative trim, be sure to check that also. Rinse your test fabric thoroughly.

### Using all-fabric oxygen bleach

Less harsh than chlorine bleach, oxygen bleach comes in dry and liquid forms and can be used on most washable fabrics, including colored fabrics, washable silks and wools, and bleachable whites. It has a more gentle bleaching action to whiten whites that aren't safe for chlorine bleach. It brightens colored fabrics and does remove some stains. Check the instructions on the box to be sure.

If the care label on a fabric says "Do not bleach," *don't use any bleach,* not even oxygen bleach.

To test for colorfastness with oxygen bleach:

1. **Mix 1 teaspoon of dry or liquid oxygen bleach with 1 cup of hot water.**

2. **Dip a cotton swab into the solution and dab it on a hidden part of the garment.**

3. **Let the solution sit for several minutes and then check for a change in color.**

If the color doesn't change, it's okay to use oxygen bleach. Rinse out thoroughly.

Add all-fabric oxygen bleach to the wash water along with the detergent before you add the clothes. Let the machine fill slightly with water, add the bleach (swishing it around with a spoon to make sure that it's dissolved), and then add the clothes. Use as hot a water temperature as possible for the fabric because oxygen bleach is more effective at high water temperatures.

### Using other bleaching products

Occasionally, you have a laundry problem that requires the use of other bleaching products, such as color remover, hydrogen peroxide, or those familiar kitchen aids such as lemon juice and vinegar. The following list tells you when to use what:

- ✔ **Color remover:** Color remover does just what it says — removes the color from colored fabrics. As a laundry product, color remover is used primarily to get rid of dyes that have "bled" onto white garments in the wash, such as a white dress that was grayed by a sock. Be sure to follow the directions on the box and use it only on white garments. Rit and Carbona are two common product names of color removers.

- ✔ **Hydrogen peroxide:** Although usually kept in the bathroom, hydrogen peroxide has a gentle bleaching action that's safe for most fabrics. Because it's so mild, hydrogen peroxide is especially good for delicate fabrics. Mix a couple of tablespoons of hydrogen peroxide with a gallon of water and presoak delicate fabrics (except wool) for up to 30 minutes. Rinse thoroughly afterwards. (Do a color test first.)

✔ **Aids from the kitchen:** White vinegar, lemon juice, and the original bleaching agent, sunlight, are mild bleaches that can help fade a stain. Mix vinegar or lemon juice with equal parts water before applying it so that it won't damage the fabric. Rinse thoroughly after applying. Test first on a hidden area.

## Using bluing and other laundry aids

The following lists other helpful laundry aids you may need in the never-ending war against dinginess and dirt:

✔ **Bluing** is a product that has been around for years. It's used to renew whiteness in garments that are yellowing. It's not as popular today as it once was because many detergents already contain brighteners that make wash whiter. Dilute according to the instructions on the box and add either at the start of the wash or in the final rinse.

✔ **Enzyme presoaks** are used to soak out stains prior to washing and also to boost the cleaning power of detergents. They're especially effective on blood, protein, or food stains such as egg, milk, coffee, and baby food. They can also work on things like grass stains and fruit juice.

✔ **Prewash stain removers** come in several different forms — spray, liquids, sticks, and aerosols are used to treat heavily soiled areas like collars and cuffs or to treat spots and stains prior to washing.

  • Liquids work especially well on tough-to-get-off, oil-based stains on permanent-press fabrics and polyester fabrics. Liquids and sprays are squirted on the garments directly before washing.

  • The stick forms are convenient if you don't wash daily — good for those laundromat people — because you can apply it to a fresh stain and then wait up to a week to actually wash it.

✔ **Fabric softeners** reduce static cling (the stuff that makes your clothing stick to arms, legs, slips, hose, and other things), especially on nylon, polyester, and acrylic fabric. They also make fabrics feel soft and fluffy. Another bonus: Fabric softeners reduce wrinkling and thus cut ironing time.

  • Liquid softeners are added to the final rinse cycle. Never pour them directly on the fabric to avoid possible staining.

  • Dryer-added softeners — fiber sheets impregnated with softener — can be more convenient because you can just throw them into the dryer. As the dryer heats up, the softener transfers to the clothes. They aren't quite as effective in penetrating all the clothes as the liquid form is.

- Some detergents have built-in softeners, but they aren't as effective as the other forms. If your detergent already has a softener or bluing agent in it, don't use fabric softener.

- Don't pour fabric softener directly on clothes as staining can occur. If this happens, rub the area with bar soap and then wash again.

- Only use softeners occasionally, perhaps every third to fourth washing, to avoid the waxy buildup they can leave on clothing and towels.

✔ **Starches and sizings:** These products add body to limp clothing and increase soil resistance. Starches come in liquid and powder form and are best used for cotton and cotton-blend fabrics. Both are mixed with water and added to the rinse water according to the manufacturer's directions. Spray starch is an easy alternative if you want to add a quick finishing touch while ironing.

# And Now, You Wash

You may not like to do it, but it will really help if you are familiar with the manufacturer's instructions of your particular washer and the detergent you're using. Some have quirks that can affect the way you need to wash your clothes. For most machines, you can use the information provided in the sections that follow.

Measure the proper amount of detergent and turn on the machine for a few minutes to let some water run into it. Then add the detergent and any other additives you're putting in. Swish it around to dissolve it evenly throughout the water. Then add the clothes. Loading the washer this way is ideal because it allows the detergent to move evenly through the wash.

✔ Don't overload the washer. Lay garments in lightly to the top but not past the agitator. Clothes should be able to circulate freely throughout the machine.

✔ Avoid wrapping large items like sheets or towels around the agitator. Instead, put them on one side of the tub. If they become tangled, they won't wash properly and can also put stress on the gears of the machine.

✔ When you go to put stuff in the wash, separate the heavy items from lightweight ones. You want a balance of weights, but not all one thing or the other.

✔ Don't put in towels, rugs, or other linty items with dark or synthetic items that pick up lint. There's nothing more annoying than taking something out of the washer only to find that it's in worse condition than when it went in.

## Stain-proofing the washing machine

Keep the top of the washing machine clean. If you use the top to pretreat your laundry, make sure to clean it up afterwards. It's pretty hard not to spill soaps and detergents, stain removers, prewash sprays, and bleach onto the top of the machine. But these items can be corrosive and damaging to the surface if spilled and left moist.

Avoid using the top of the machine as a workplace. Not only can it damage the machine, but it can harm clothes if the spill isn't wiped up properly. If you inadvertently lay a blue shirt on a spot of bleach that's been spilled on the machine top, you've got a permanent stain. If you must use the top of the machine, lay a large plastic cutting board on top to protect it.

Be sure to wipe up any spills that get on the top of the door gasket, too.

Always check the care labels for water temperature and other washing recommendations (see Chapter 11); they provide the only safe way(s) to clean the particular item. The following are general guidelines for which water temperature to use when in doubt:

- ✔ **Hot water:** For heavily soiled items, white and colorfast clothes, and diapers (the cloth kind, of course)
- ✔ **Warm water:** Moderately soiled items, permanent press and wash and wear, washable knits and woolens, and noncolorfast items
- ✔ **Cold:** Lightly soiled clothes, dark or bright colors that can bleed, delicate or fragile fabrics, and items that might have a tendency to shrink

Even if you use hot or warm water for washing, you should use cold water for rinsing. Not only does it save energy and shrink your energy bill, but it also reduces wrinkling.

# Lessons for the Laundromat

It's hard enough doing the wash, but it's much more annoying to do it at a laundromat. Ask someone who's been doing it her whole life. Believe me, I know. Not only can it be a tedious task, but you have to contend with the extra stresses — will there be enough machines, do I have enough change, and how long will it take? Luckily, in the last few years, enterprising business people have tried to invent ways to make the laundromat a more pleasant experience. They've added bars, movies, videos, and coffeehouses. It can even be a great place to meet people. (I was always impressed with the stain-removing capabilities of one man that I used to meet at the laundromat. He introduced me to the positive aspects of enzyme detergent. If that's not a great pickup line, I don't know what is.)

Back to business, though. Use the following tips to get a better load of wash from the laundromat:

- ✔ **Round up your change.** Before you go to the laundromat, count your coins to be sure you have enough. Put them in a small bag or an empty film case. Make it a habit to take the change out of your wallet every day and save it in a jar just to do the wash. Even if the laundromat has a change machine, it's wise to come prepared just in case the machine is low on money. And bring more change than you think you'll need. Sometimes money gets lost in the machines or the dryers aren't working properly, and you end up using more coins than normal.

- ✔ **Lasso your supplies.** To save yourself the trouble of carrying a lot of large boxes and bottles to the laundromat, set up a kit of supplies in a basket or plastic carrying caddy to take with you. Premeasure the amount of detergent and fabric softener or bleach that you'll be using for the number of loads you're doing and put it in self-closing plastic sandwich bags or small food jars. Also put in some prewash stain spray, stain stick, and extra plastic bags to hold items that you can't put in the dryer.

- ✔ **Sort your clothes.** Sorting your clothes becomes even more important when you're using a laundromat. Because the machines usually have less settings, you can't customize the temperature and washing cycle like you can with a normal washer. Even if you have to spend more money and do smaller loads, the quality of the washing will be worth it in the long run.

- ✔ **Check the machines.** Before you put anything in the washer or the dryer, check to make sure that nothing is left over from the last load that could harm your wash. Look for stray pieces of paper, pens, crayons, or any other item that could cause stains. Consider bringing along an extra cloth to wipe out the machines if they look dirty.

- ✔ **Load lightly.** The biggest problem with getting your clothes clean in the laundromat is the tendency to overload the washer. It seems logical that the more you stuff in, the less money you'll have to spend. In reality, if you crowd too many clothes inside the washer, your clothes won't get clean. Because clothes can't circulate in the normal action, stains won't get properly removed. The result can be a gray or yellow tinge. Always put a mixture of large and small items together so the clothes can move around the tub.

- ✔ **Work with your dryer.** When you load clothes for the dryer, put light-weight items such as sheets and shirts and heavy items like jeans and towels together. You'll end up spending less money because all the clothes will dry at the same time.

Because you usually can't control the heat precisely, take out any items that you think could be susceptible to shrinkage (like knits and delicates) after the wash and air dry them at home.

Keep checking on your clothes and remove them as soon as they're dry. Overdrying causes wrinkling and wears clothes out.

# Removing Stains

There's nothing like the sinking feeling you get when you go to put on some clothes and find that they're stained. I guess I must be a pretty sloppy eater, because all my stains seem to appear in the same places — in the middle of the fronts of my shirts and on the tops of my thighs on pants.

I've always had pretty good success in treating stains, although several have eluded me. Luckily, most stains come out in the wash. But others can be a downright challenge to get rid of. Certain fabrics are more delicate or absorbent than others. Certain foods — spaghetti sauce, grape juice, curry powder, and mustard, to name a few — can permanently dye fabric.

You can use your laundry detergent very effectively as a stain remover by rubbing it on stains before you do the wash. And several commercial stain removers and sticks on the market today really work.

## Following basic guidelines

The problem with stain removal is that if you don't follow a few basic guidelines, you can actually make the stain worse than before you started. By using the wrong chemicals or temperature, you can make a stain permanent that might have been easily removed. Here are some guidelines for smart stain removal:

- ✔ **Treat the stain as soon as you can.** Many spots and spills are just lying on the surface of the fabric when they first happen and will be no problem if removed immediately. If they dry or sit for a few days, they'll be absorbed into the fibers and your chance of removing them will get dimmer and dimmer.

- ✔ **Remove as much of the spill as you can before applying any stain-removing product.** If you've got a mound of pudding, a blob of catsup, or a plop of tuna salad, use a dull knife or spoon to lift off any debris. This will prevent it from spreading and sinking into the fabric when you apply the stain remover.

✔ **Always read the care label of the garment before you apply any stain remover.** Different fabrics require different stain removers. And some fabrics can be damaged by something as innocuous as water.

✔ **Try to identify what the stain is before you start working on it.** Some stains can be permanently set if you use the wrong treatment. If you're in doubt, rinse or soak the fabric in cold water before laundering.

✔ **Always pretest for colorfastness with the stain remover before you apply it to the whole garment.** Put a drop of it on a seam or on the underside of the cuff. Rinse and let dry. If no color loss or fabric damage occurs, proceed with the treatment.

✔ **Blot, don't scrub.** Blotting absorbs the liquid that may still be sitting on top of the fabric. Scrubbing can force the stain into the material and spread it to other parts of the garment. Even worse, it can damage delicate or stretchy fabrics. Work from the outer edge of the stain toward the center, blotting as you go.

✔ **When you use bleach to remove a stain, treat the whole garment instead of a small spot.** This keeps the color even all over if any change should occur.

✔ **Always rinse or launder washable items to remove the residue left from the stain and the stain remover.** Then air dry the garment to make sure the stain is really gone. Some spots are hard to see when the fabric is wet. If you put them in a hot dryer, the stain can be set by the heat, making it impossible to remove.

✔ **Be careful not to spread the stain while you're treating it.** Center the side of the fabric with the stain over an absorbent cloth like a diaper or an old, clean, white towel. Keep turning the cloth or towel over to absorb the liquid as you apply the stain-removing liquid. This makes sure that the stain is driven into the towel and not further through the fabric. Check the towel frequently to see how well your stain remover is working — the more of the stain that comes out on the towel, the better off you are. Unless otherwise indicated, put only a few drops of stain-removal solution on the spot. Always use this method when treating candlewax, lipstick, or tar.

✔ **Be patient.** Sometimes you may have to apply the treatment two or three times before the stain comes off.

✔ **Stop ironing if you see a stain.** Heat often sets stains, making them impossible to remove.

✔ **Better safe than sorry.** Dry clean if you have any doubts whether a fabric will survive your own stain-removal treatments. The dry cleaners have solvents and special treatments that usually can get off any stain. Remember, once something is ruined, it often can't be replaced. And especially if an item is expensive or sentimental to you, it's worth the peace of mind to take it to the dry cleaner.

---

# Use duct tape on pollen

When I was in an antique store in France, I bumped into some flowers and got pollen stains all over my shirt. I was about to wipe them off with my hand when the owner told me, "No! No! Never rub. That will make them go deeper into the fibers of the shirt." She gave me some duct tape. I placed it directly on the stain and Voilà! The stain stuck to the tape and peeled right off without a trace.

---

Tables 12-1 through 12-4 provide lists of handy products (many you may have already) to keep on hand for getting rid of stains. Most are available at your local drugstore, hardware store, or home center.

| Table 12-1 | Things That Soak Up Stains |
|---|---|
| *Product* | *How to Use* |
| **Blotters:** (White paper towels, old (but clean) white terry cloth towels, soft white cotton cloths) | Place on top of the stain and press down; replace when soaked. |
| **Absorbers:** (Cornstarch, cornmeal, talcum powder, powdered starch) | Sprinkle over the spill while damp, leave it on until it absorbs the spill and has dried. Brush it off. Repeat treatment until everything is absorbed. Especially good for grease stains. |

| Table 12-2 | Things That Dissolve Stains |
|---|---|
| *Product* | *How to Use* |
| Enzyme presoak products: | Effective on protein stains like egg, blood, grass, dairy products, chocolate and body fluids. Follow package directions. |
| Detergents: | *Granules:* good on clay and ground-in dirt; *liquids* work well on food, greasy, and oily stains; use *liquid dishwashing detergent* as a mild treatment for delicate fabrics. Follow package directions. |
| Solvents: (Dry-cleaning fluids like Energine, Carbona, K2r) (most are flammable) | Follow package directions. |

| Product | How to Use |
|---|---|
| Acetone: (Flammable and poisonous.) | Can remove some glues, nail polish, and ballpoint pen stains. Test on any fabric first: It dissolves acetate and triacetate and can harm other fabrics. Follow package directions. |
| Household ammonia: | Dilute with water; follow package directions. Don't use on wool or silk. |
| Petroleum jelly: | Use as a solvent for greasy or oily stains, but then you must use a degreaser on the spot where the petroleum jelly was. |
| Glycerin: | An ingredient of many dry-cleaning solvents. Good for presoaking treatments to loosen stains. |

| Table 12-3 | Things That Remove Stains |
|---|---|
| Product | How to Use |
| Bleach: | Chlorine is good for white cotton and linen; oxygen is better for colors and permanent press. Follow package directions. |
| Hydrogen peroxide: | A very mild bleaching agent used to clean off blood, chocolate, or mustard. Usually mixed with water before applying to stain. |
| Lemon juice: | Use for mild bleaching. |
| White Vinegar: | Dilute with water before using on cotton and linen. |
| Alcohol: (Flammable.) | Always pretest. Denatured is best. Not for use on acetate, acrylic, rayon, or vinyl. |

| Table 12-4 | Things That Rinse Out Stains |
|---|---|
| Product | How to Use |
| Clean water: | Many stains, especially non-greasy ones, can be removed while fresh by flushing immediately with cold water or soaking for several hours in cold water. |
| Carbonated water: | A favorite for removing red wine and flushing out other spills. |

When dealing with any kind of household chemicals, you've got to take precautions. Here are some things to remember:

- **Never combine household chemicals unless specifically stated.** The combination of ammonia and chlorine bleach, for example, produces noxious fumes.

- **Most solvents such as dry-cleaning products, nail polish remover, and alcohol are flammable and emit dangerous vapors.** Use in a well-ventilated area and don't inhale them. Never use near any heating unit, a stove, or an open flame. Seal the bottle tightly when you're finished and store it in a cool place. Remember that after you've applied a dry-cleaning fluid to a fabric, you must rinse it out thoroughly before washing and remove all traces of the solvent before putting the garment in the dryer. Better yet, line dry the item.

- **If you've saturated any cleaning rags or towels with household chemicals, air them out and dry thoroughly outside.** Don't leave any saturated rags sitting in a pile or store them near the washing machine or dryer. Wash them out by hand thoroughly; don't put them in your washing machine or dryer. Dispose of them according to your local regulations.

## *Removing stains from washable fabrics*

Remember to always check the care label to see how to properly clean a garment. If the fabric says to dry clean, let the dry cleaner remove spots with dry-cleaning fluid. Always test for colorfastness on a hidden area before you start any stain treatment. What may be safe for some fibers will permanently stain others. If the garment is valuable or you have any doubt about how to clean it, be safe and take it to a dry cleaner.

Table 12-5 gives you tips for removing stains from *washable* fabrics.

| Table 12-5 | Removing Stains from Washable Fabrics |
|---|---|
| *Stain* | *How to Remove* |
| Alcohol | Treat as soon as possible so the spot doesn't dry. Sponge the stain with cool water and a few drops of liquid detergent. Rinse white fabrics in cold water with a few drops of vinegar. Rinse colored fabrics with a few drops of hydrogen peroxide. Wash as usual. Old stains: Try pretreating with an enzyme pretreat or detergent, or wash in hot water with bleach safe for the fabric. |

| Stain | How to Remove |
|---|---|
| Blood | Soak fresh stains in cold water. (Don't use hot; it can set the stain.) Saturate the stain with detergent or rub with a stain stick or laundry pretreat. Wash as usual. Dried stains: Soak in a solution of 1 quart warm water, ½ teaspoon detergent, and 1 tablespoon ammonia for cottons, polyester, rayons, and linens. Or soak in warm water with enzyme presoak or detergent. If the stain remains, rewash using bleach. Treat washable wool with 1 tablespoon hydrogen peroxide mixed in 1 quart water. |
| Candlewax | Harden with ice and scrape off with a dull knife. Put the stained area between several clean paper towels, and place a sheet of brown paper bag over the towel. Press with a warm iron. Replace towels as often as necessary to keep absorbing as much wax as possible. If any marks or stain remain, treat by placing the stain face down on clean towels and sponging with dry-cleaning fluid. Blot dry and then launder as usual. If the stain remains, rewash using a bleach that's safe for the fabric. |
| Chewing gum | Apply ice to the gum to harden. Scrape off the frozen residue with a dull knife. Sponge with dry-cleaning solvent. Rinse and launder. |
| Chocolate | Rinse the stain with cool water, and then soak in enzyme presoak solution for 30 minutes. Apply detergent to the stain. Wash. If the stain remains, sponge with dry-cleaning fluid, rinse, and launder. Or soak in enzyme presoak overnight and launder in the hottest water safe for fabric. Sponge washable wool with mild soapy warm water. |
| Crayon | The Crayola company recommends putting the stained spot face down on a few folded towels and spraying with WD-40; then let stand for several minutes. Turn the fabric over and spray the other side. Apply liquid dishwashing detergent to the stain. Keep replacing towels as they absorb the stain. Wash in hot water with detergent and chlorine or all-fabric bleach (if bleach is safe for the fabric) on the longest wash cycle of the machine. Rinse in warm water. |
| Coffee | First, sponge the stain with cool water to remove as much stain as possible. If safe for fabric, soak in all fabric bleach and warm water. Launder in warm water. If the stain-causing coffee contained cream, soak the stain in cool water and then sponge with dry-cleaning fluid. Rinse in cool water and then launder as usual. |

| Stain | How to Remove |
|-------|---------------|
| Cosmetics | Apply prewash stain remover, liquid detergent, or a paste of detergent and water until the stain is gone. Wash. If the stain remains, use enzyme detergent. |
| Dairy products | Pretreat with an enzyme presoak for at least 30 minutes or overnight for aged stains. Launder. If the stain persists, sponge on a mild solution of hydrogen peroxide and water for all fabrics but nylon. Or use chlorine bleach if it's safe for the fabric. If the stain remains, sponge with dry-cleaning solvent and then wash thoroughly. |
| Egg | Rinse in cold water. Soak for about 30 minutes in enzyme presoak and then wash. |
| Fruit juice/berries | *Note:* You must treat this stain while it's fresh. Soak in cool water for 30 minutes. If safe for the fabric, wash with chlorine bleach. Or soak the fabric in a mixture of 1 tablespoon hydrogen peroxide and 1 quart water. (Test for colorfastness.) Rinse and launder. Colored fabrics may be treated with oxygen bleach if it's safe for the fabric. |
| Grass | Rub enzyme presoak or detergent on the stain. Launder in the hottest water possible with bleach that's safe for the fabric. |
| Grease | Blot the residue or remove with a dull knife. Place the fabric face down on paper towels. Sponge dry-cleaning solvent on the back of the stain until it disappears. Change the towels as they absorb the stain. After the cleaning solvent is dry, rinse the garment and then pretreat with detergent or prewash stain remover. Launder in the hottest water that is safe for the fabric. |
| Ink | *Warning:* Ink can be tricky to remove. The problem begins with identifying exactly what kind of ink you're dealing with. A good bet is to call the company listed on the label and ask them their suggestions about stain removal. If there's no label, proceed cautiously. Some inks may be impossible to remove. Ballpoint pen stains: Dampen the area around the stain with denatured alcohol. Place the stain face down on some paper towels and apply denatured alcohol or dry-cleaning fluid to the back of the stain. Replace the towels as they absorb the stain. Repeat if the stain remains. Rinse and then launder. Other inks such as felt tip pens or liquid ink: To see if the stain will wash out, mark a similar piece of fabric with the ink, then try one of these methods: |

| Stain | How to Remove |
|-------|---------------|
|  | Pretreat with prewash stain remover and then launder. |
|  | Or flush the stain with cold water. Then soak in warm sudsy water with 1 to 4 tablespoons of household ammonia per quart of water. Rinse and then wash using bleach safe for the fabric or hydrogen peroxide and a few drops of water. |
|  | Or rub liquid household cleaner into the stain. Rinse. Repeat as many times as needed to remove the stain. Or try the ballpoint stain treatments. |
| Lipstick | Place the stain face down on paper towels. Sponge with dry-cleaning solvent or a prewash soil and stain remover. Replace the towels as they absorb the stain. Rinse off. Saturate the stain with detergent until any remaining marks are gone. Wash. |
| Mud | Let the stain dry; then brush off as much as you can. Then, soak in cool water. If it's a light stain, apply liquid detergent or a paste of detergent and water it; if it's heavy, pretreat with enzyme detergent. Launder. Use bleach that's safe for the fabric if the stain persists. |
| Mustard | Scrape off as much as possible without spreading the stain. Saturate liquid detergent or prewash enzyme presoak into the stain. Wash in fabric-safe bleach. For nonbleachable fabric, use hydrogen peroxide. Never use ammonia. |
| Latex paint | Carefully blot up the paint, and then rinse in warm water while the stain is still fresh. Saturate stain with detergent and then launder as usual. |
| Oil-based paint | Use the solvent listed on the label of the can as a paint thinner. If solvent is unavailable, scrape off as much paint as possible, and then sponge with turpentine until the stain disappears. Rinse thoroughly. Spray the stain with prewash stain remover and then launder. If paint has dried, soften with petroleum jelly and then treat as above. |
| Perspiration | Rub with prewash stain remover and then launder in detergent and warm water. If the stain has changed the color of the fabric, and sponge with ammonia for fresh stains, vinegar for old stains. (Pretest first.) Rinse with water and then launder. If the stain remains, wash with oxygen bleach. |

| Stain | How to Remove |
|---|---|
| Scorch marks | Deep scorches may be impossible to remove because the fabric has been permanently damaged. Wash using fabric-safe bleach. |
| Shoe polish | Use a spoon to scrape off any residue from the garment. Rinse the stain with dry-cleaning fluid or sponge on pre-wash stain remover. Rinse thoroughly, and then massage detergent into the dampened area. Wash using a bleach safe for the fabric. |
| Tomato sauce | Rinse in cool water. Soak in prewash stain remover for about 30 minutes. Launder. If the stain persists, soak in equal parts vinegar and water or sponge with a solution of 2 tablespoons ammonia to 1 cup water. Rinse and then launder. Use a bleach safe for the fabric if the stain remains. |
| Urine | Blot up the stain. Soak for a half an hour in enzyme pre-soak and liquid detergent solution. Rinse in cold water. Sponge any remaining stain with white vinegar. Rinse and wash in warm water. If odor persists, pet stores sell an enzyme product to decrease the smell. |
| Vomit | Sponge with water and a few drops of ammonia. Then soak in enzyme detergent and water. Rinse and then wash. |
| Wine, Red | Cover with table salt and massage gently into the spill. (If white wine is available, you can flush the stain with that.) Rinse in cool water for 15 minutes and then rub the area with prewash stain remover or liquid laundry detergent. Let sit for 15 minutes. Rinse and then launder using a bleach safe for the fabric. If the stain remains, rub with enzyme laundry detergent; then wash with bleach safe for the fabric. The dried stain may not come out, but you can try soaking in ammonia and water or white vinegar. Pretest to make sure that it's safe for the fabric. |
| Wine, White | Blot up the spill while fresh and rinse in cool water. Rub the stained area with a little liquid laundry detergent and a few drops of vinegar. Rinse and then launder. |

# Getting rid of unknown stains

Often, you don't know exactly what caused the stain; you just know it's there, an annoying reminder of a spill or drip. Although removing these stains is a challenge, it's often worth the time it takes to rescue a garment or other household item. Try to identify the cause of the stain.

You can usually treat grease stains in washable garments with a liquid or spray laundry pretreating product or dry-cleaning fluid.

For nongreasy stains, you can usually sponge or soak them out with water, liquid laundry detergent, and bleach.

If you can't remember whether it was the cheeseburger or the raspberry freeze that you dropped on your shirt, try this method:

- First, soak the stain in cold water for 20 minutes. Then apply detergent to the stain. Let sit for 30 minutes. Rinse; then wash in warm water and air dry.

- If the stain persists, soak in enzyme detergent or presoak overnight and then wash in the hottest water that is safe for the fabric. If that doesn't work, wash with a bleach that's safe for the fabric.

- Stain still there? Now get really serious by sponging it with dry-cleaning solvent and then applying liquid laundry detergent. Rinse and air dry.

If you think the stain is rust, apply a commercial rust remover. Also, remember that you can always try the dry cleaner.

# Chapter 13

# A Smooth Operation: Drying and Ironing

**D**rying and ironing are the finishing touches to your clothing care. If you do these two things correctly, you can reduce your workload and make your clothes look their best. But if you do them incorrectly, you shrink your clothes, your fabrics are ruined, and wrinkles are ironed in, instead of out. You may take drying and ironing for granted, because they are chores that you must do, day in and day out. If you put some special care into both chores, you can reduce the time you spend in the laundry room.

## Dryer Basics

Most dryers are relatively simple to operate. But a few precautions will help you have trouble-free operations. As with other appliances, make sure that you read owner's manual. Store it in a safe place so you can find it when you have any trouble. These hints will help you make the most of your dryer time:

▸ **Clean the lint screen.** Before you start any load, clean out the lint screen. The dryer is one of the biggest electricity hogs in the home, and it runs at half its normal efficiency if the lint screen is clogged. The drying time is longer and more electricity is used, so each load costs more to operate. In addition, a blocked lint screen can lead to overheating and fire. If the lint screen is bent or broken, be sure to replace it.

✔ **Get rid of sharp objects.** Check clothes before you place them in the dryer. Avoid putting anything sharp or pointed inside. If you prepared your clothing properly for washing (see Chapter 11), you removed any ballpoint pens or pins from the pockets of your clothes. (Otherwise, you really have a mess at this point, in which case, you should read the stain-removing section of Chapter 12.)

But other things on clothes can scratch the interior of the dryer: open zippers, clasps, and hooks. Double-check all the clothes as you transfer them from the washer, and close all open zippers and hooks. Just to be safe, turn anything inside out that could scratch the interior of the dryer.

✔ **Keep the drum spotless.** Look inside periodically to make sure that the drum is clean. Dyes can run off of noncolorfast clothing and clothing that is being washed for the first time. These dyes can leave stains inside the dryer. You must clean the dye off, or your next load of clothing may get some of those "mystery" stains that drive us crazy. After you remove all the clothes, spray some liquid household cleaner into a cloth and rub the stain with it. Let the cleaner sit for a minute or two and then wipe off the residue with a damp cloth. Put a few rags into the dryer and run it on air-only for about 15 or 20 minutes to eliminate any cleaner residue and make sure that all the stain is gone.

✔ **Inspect the vents.** A few times a year, check to make sure that the dryer is venting properly. An obstruction in the duct or an extra-long duct can restrict the flow of air and cause longer drying times.

  1. First, make sure the dryer is turned off.

  2. Look at the exhaust duct outside your house and remove any leaves, branches, or other debris.

  3. Inside, take the duct off the vent that links it to the outside and clean it out with a soft brush or the crevice tool of your vacuum cleaner.

Cleaning the vent is important not only for dryer efficiency but also for safety. Lint built up in the ducting system can start a fire.

For maximum airflow, keep the duct to less than 50 feet and make sure it is straight.

✔ **Check the door seal.** If you suspect that your dryer is not as hot as it should be, check to see whether it is losing heat.

Hold a piece of tissue paper in front of the door's edge while the dryer is on. If the paper is drawn toward the door, the seal isn't tight enough and needs to be replaced. Look in the manufacturer's manual to see how to replace the seal on your machine.

## Drying dangers

Some things are downright dangerous to put in the dryer. The following things are better off being dried on the clothesline:

- ✔ If clothing or rags have been saturated with or come in contact with paint, oil, gasoline, flammable liquids or solids, or dry cleaning solvent, keep them out of the dryer. These can be extremely flammable when exposed to heat. Wash these items by hand and dry them on a clothesline or drying rack instead.

- ✔ Never put rubber-coated items, laminated fabrics, vinyl, plastics, foam rubber, or garments that have a trim made from these items on a hot setting in the dryer. They can melt or ignite when exposed to high heat.

- ✔ Don't put fiberglass curtains or draperies in the dryer unless the label states that the item is machine washable and dryable. You'll embed glass fibers in the dryer that are virtually impossible to remove.

Avoid these additional no-no's to prevent drying difficulties:

- ✔ Don't put knitted woolens in the dryer (unless you don't mind having them come out several sizes smaller). Heat shrinks woolens.

- ✔ Don't worry about getting everything bone dry. Elastic bands in shorts, some socks, and bras can be slightly damp when you first remove them from the dryer, but they dry quickly. Drying clothes causes excess wear and wrinkling.

- ✔ Don't put anything in the dryer that still has a stain on it. If a stain doesn't come out in the wash, re-treat the stain and put the item back in the washer. If you dry it, the stain is set in by the dryer's heat, and chances of it ever coming out are slim.

- ✔ Don't put heavy, hard-to-dry items in the same load with lightweight clothes. Because drying times are different, the lightweight items will be dried properly but the heavier ones will still be damp.

## Drying with all brains and no brawn

If you follow these few simple guidelines, you won't have any surprises when you take clothes out of the dryer.

- ✔ Always check the care label on clothes, and check the recommendations in your dryer's appliance manual for fabrics before you put clothes in the dryer. Some delicate clothes can be ruined if you dry them on the wrong setting. And when that happens, you can't fix those mistakes.

✔ Remove clothes from the dryer as soon as the cycle is finished. If you leave clothes lying in a pile in the dryer, their accumulated weight will cause excessive wrinkling. Take them out and fold them or hang them up immediately after the cycle is finished.

Okay, you were too lazy to immediately take the clothes out of the dryer, and now they're all wrinkled. Don't despair. Just toss in a wet towel and reset the dryer. Check after 15 or 20 minutes to see if the wrinkles are gone.

✔ Always put permanent press and no-iron clothes through their proper cycle to minimize wrinkling, as these fabrics are designed to be run through a special dryer cycle. Remove them from the dryer as soon as they're dry.

✔ Don't overload the dryer. Fill it no more than about half full to leave room for clothes to tumble freely. Put only one washer load in the dryer at a time. This not only cuts down on wrinkling but also reduces the amount of time needed for clothes to dry.

✔ Make sure to shake out each piece of wash when you move it from the washer to the dryer. Often, items like sheets and pants get tangled around each other. If you don't separate them before putting them in the dryer, all the surfaces won't be exposed evenly to heat.

✔ Turn dark items inside out to cut down on lint accumulation. Avoid putting them in the dryer with items like light-colored towels or bath mats that usually shed like crazy. If you're drying large items like blankets, put a length of netting inside to catch the lint.

## Drying au natural

There was a day when every backyard had a line full of clothes gently drying in the breeze. Many people believe that air-dried clothes have a sweet smell and soft feel that can't be matched in the dryer. Even though most of us usually opt for the convenience of the dryer, certain situations dictate when air drying is the best choice. Always check the fabric label for care instructions, and if you have the slightest doubt about putting something in the dryer, hang it on a clothesline, a hanger, or a drying rack. Delicate lingerie, some cottons, linen fabrics, or large items that are too bulky for the dryer are usually good choices for air drying.

If you're using a clothesline outside, wipe down the clothesline with a damp cloth to make sure that it's clean and free of dirt and dust. Shake out and smooth down clothes to remove as many wrinkles as possible before you hang them up. With your hand, straighten and smooth out the seams. Hang clothes by the firmest part, such as the shoulder seams or the waistband. Take clothes off the line before they are completely dry to make ironing easier. Turn dark-colored items inside out to prevent fading from the sun.

## Drying in the bathroom

For many people, including myself, drying outside is not a workable option. Hanging a clothesline from the 10th floor of an apartment building is impossible. But I still like to air dry several items from each load of laundry. Many of my knit clothes have kept their color and sizing for years because I've saved them from the intense heat and tossing of the dryer. One particular outfit, a faux animal print, hung around long enough to return to fashion favor!

When you air dry on hangers, use padded hangers so that clothes don't get bumps in them. You don't have padded hangers, you say? Loop some old shoulder pads or pieces of foam rubber over the ends of a hanger and secure with safety pins or rubber bands.

Some items need to be dried on a flat surface to make sure that they don't get stretched out while drying. Roll up sweaters, knits, and other stretchy fabrics in towels to absorb the excess water. Then unroll each item carefully, reshape it, and lay it flat on a clean, fluffy towel or on one of those plastic-coated wire racks that fit over the tub. When one side is dry, turn the item over and dry the other.

Never position a hanger or drying rack near a heater or in the sun. The heat can cause an item to shrink or the color to fade.

## Using fabric softeners

You can choose from two basic kinds of fabric softeners. According to the Soap and Detergent Association, your particular clothing needs should determine which type you use.

- ✔ If you're plagued by static cling (usually associated with synthetic clothing), use dryer sheets. They work in the dryer, where the whole static cling problem starts.
- ✔ If you just need a general softening of your clothes, liquid fabric softener added to the rinse water in the machine is better.

Liquid softeners rinse through and permeate the entire load of wash. Dryer sheets only affect the areas that the sheet touches when it's tossed around.

Greasy stains can occur with liquid fabric softeners if you pour them directly on fabrics. To be extra safe, dilute the softener in a small amount of water before adding it to the washer, even if you put it in a rinse dispenser. If you get a stain from any fabric softener, rub the area with a bar of soap and rewash.

## Other uses for fabric softener sheets

Many people have devised other uses for both fresh and used softener sheets.

**Fresh dryer sheets** are often put in drawers, musty suitcases, cars, or kitchen trash cans to sweeten them. Smelly athletic shoes are deodorized when stuffed with the little sheets. Tape some sheets over the heating vents in any room where people are smoking to get rid of the cigarette smell. I've also heard of hikers tying them onto shoulder straps to keep mosquitoes away. I don't know about the bugs but, at least, the hikers smell sweet.

**Used dryer sheets** can be used to wipe off the dust from the TV, furniture, or mini blinds. The same properties that eliminate static cling in your clothes will help keep dust off your household objects. Try rubbing a used dryer sheet over fly-away hair to put it back in place. After you use sheets in the dryer, dust off the top of the washer and dryer with them. Or use them in place of a rag to polish your shoes or clean off eyeglasses. Save a few and substitute them as stuffing for small craft projects. Or use them to store threaded needles. After you pull the needle through the sheet, the thread won't get tangled.

# Ironing Basics

I may be one of the few people on this planet who really like to iron. I find something very satisfying about changing a limp, wrinkled pile of clothing into something smooth and perfectly pressed. You can watch TV, listen to the radio, or just daydream while you do this chore. What better way to start off the day than to put on a newly ironed outfit?

Okay, I hear you. You're not an idyllic ironer like me. You're not alone. In fact, one study by Black & Decker Household Products indicated that 60 percent of the population dislikes ironing and wants to get it done as quickly as possible. (My friend, Elaine, doesn't even own an iron.) If you take care of your iron and follow a few basic guidelines, you won't cringe at the thought of ironing. Ironing may just go a little easier, and your clothes will look much better.

## Taking care of your iron

Many of us have been ironing since childhood (or at least I have), so we tend to take the iron for granted. But it's an appliance that can give years of good service if you take care of it properly. And with the price of irons these days (some even hitting upwards of $150), getting as much use out of it as possible is a smart idea.

Make sure that you read the instruction booklet that comes with your iron and follow the directions for cleaning and maintaining it. Check regularly to make sure that the soleplate hasn't picked up any dirt. The last thing you want is to iron a new shirt only to find that your iron has deposited something on the front.

Unplug any iron before cleaning it, and clean it only when it is cold. If your iron has a non-stick soleplate, give it a quick wipe with a damp cloth every now and then. Metal soleplates should be cleaned with a mild detergent and water solution and wiped clean with a soft cloth. Never dip an iron into any cleaning solution. Always put the solution on a cloth and wipe the surface. Avoid the use of abrasive cleaners or scouring pads on either kind of iron — they can scratch the surface.

Sometimes, the use of spray starch leaves a sticky brown residue on the soleplate. To clean it off, mix baking soda and water into a paste, dip a damp cloth into it, and rub it gently on the surface. Clean it off with a dry cloth. If you still have residue, clean the iron with a paste of mild cleanser and water, and then wipe with a damp cloth. Flush out any remaining cleanser by turning on the iron and pressing the steam control button. Hold the iron over a cloth that can absorb any residue that drips out.

If you notice scratches on the surface of a metal soleplate that could snag a garment, rub the scratches very lightly with extra fine waterproof sandpaper, just until the surface feels smooth. Then wipe the soleplate with a cotton ball dipped in vinegar and water.

After you've finished ironing, empty the iron and store it in an upright position. If you store the iron flat, excess moisture can drip out of the steam holes. Not only does this make a mess, but it can also cause pitting on the soleplate.

## *Hot stuff: Better safe than sorry*

Because an iron is an appliance that heats up, it creates the potential for some accidents around the home. Make sure that you turn the iron controls to "off" when you stop using it, even if just for a minute or two, and leave the iron upright. When you're done ironing, unplug the iron, even if it has an automatic shut-off.

The water inside the steam tank stays hot for quite a while after the iron is turned off. If the iron tips over or if you tilt it while moving it, watch out for the remaining water in the reservoir, which can cause a burn if spilled on your skin.

Set up the ironing board near a socket so that the cord isn't stretched too far. You don't want anyone to trip over the cord and knock over the iron and the ironing board. Make sure to buy an ironing board that's sturdy on its feet and stands flat on the floor.

# Ironing how-to's (in case your mom didn't tell you)

This may seem too simple to be said, but I'm going to say it anyway: The proper way to iron is to move the iron back and forth over the length of the fabric. Don't iron in a circular motion. Go with the weave rather than against it to prevent stretching, especially on knit or synthetic fabrics.

## Pressing matters

Pressing is different from just plain ironing. To press properly, you move the iron up and down, lowering onto and lifting it up from the fabric rather than moving it back and forth. This up and down motion lets you smooth the fabric without any danger of stretching it. Naturally, pressing is the method of choice for delicate fabrics such as lace, wool, and napped, piled, or quilted textures. Place the fabric face down on a thick towel and press the wrong side of the fabric with a steam iron on the appropriate setting.

## Using a pressing cloth

A pressing cloth is a piece of fabric that's positioned between the fabric and the iron to protect the fabric from damage.

You can use any piece of lightweight soft cloth: a men's handkerchief, a piece of lightweight muslin, cheesecloth, or an old cotton sheet. Use a pressing cloth on any delicate or expensive fabric. It protects the fabric from many nasty things: scorching, excessive heat, dirt on the iron, and spotting caused by steam. "Better safe than sorry" is one of my favorite mottoes.

## Sequencing your ironing: Start low and aim high

If you're ironing several things at once, start by working on the items that need the lowest setting on the iron (usually anything synthetic or silk) and work your way up to the high-setting items (cotton and linen).

Because an iron heats up faster than it cools down, you save time by ironing similar items together, rather than waiting for the iron to switch temperatures up and down. A risk in not properly sequencing your ironing is that you may put a hot iron down on something that needs a cool iron and scorch the fabric.

If you're going to use the steam setting, allow the iron to heat up to the proper temperature to generate steam before you start. If you don't, the iron can drip water onto the fabric and possibly leave spots.

### Preventing shine

Dark fabrics, satin, silk, wool, linen, and crepe fabrics should be ironed on the wrong side of the fabric to prevent shine. If you already have some shiny patches caused by ironing, place a damp pressing cloth on top of the shiny surface and press. Repeat until the area is dry. Raise the nap of the fabric by gently moving a very soft brush (such as a baby's hairbrush) across the fabric.

### Preparing to iron

Even if your iron has the greatest steam in the world, clothes just seem to come out much crisper if they're damp when you start to iron. If you're going to iron right after you do the laundry, remove clothes from the dryer while they're a little damp. Because I rarely do that, I keep a spray bottle on the ironing board to give clothes a quick spritz of water before I start. Then I roll the clothes up for a couple of minutes to let the water soak in evenly.

Spray starch also gives clothes a nice finish, but it has a tendency to build up on the soleplate of the iron. To prevent this, spray the starch on the wrong side of the fabric and roll the clothes in a tubular shape to let it soak into the fabric.

An iron should not sizzle when it touches fabric. If the iron sizzles, the temperature is too hot.

### Reducing wrinkles

You can never totally eliminate wrinkles (from your clothes or your face!), but you can reduce the time required to get rid of them. Just follow these few logical tips before you even get close to the iron. Think of this list as an SPF for your clothes — So Perfectly Finished ironing!

- ✔ **Don't leave your clothes in a pile.** Hang up or fold your clothes when you take them out of the dryer, especially if they're still damp. (Hang them up when you take them off, too, if they can stand another wearing before being washed.) Any clothes left in a pile (in the dryer, in a clothes basket, or on top of the dryer) will be full of wrinkles when you start to iron. And if they dry in that state, the wrinkles will be even harder to iron out.

- ✔ **Don't overdry your clothes.** If you pull your clothes out of the dryer and you notice that they're full of wrinkles, it's probably because they were dried too long on too high a temperature. Throw them back into the dryer with a couple of damp towels and dry on medium heat for several minutes. The wrinkles should fall right out.

✔ **Don't crowd clothes.** A closet that's stuffed to the gills prevents you from finding things and is not good for your clothes. If you pull your clothes out of the closet in the morning and they seem unreasonably wrinkled, your closet is probably overcrowded. Instead of wrinkles falling out, they are mashed in. Go through the closet and eliminate things so that your clothes have room to breathe.

## Ironing know-how for novices

Start with the smallest parts of a garment, such as the cuffs or collar, and proceed to the larger ones. Move the garment away from you across the ironing board as you proceed. This prevents wrinkles in the parts you've already pressed.

### Ironing a shirt or blouse

This concept seems simple enough, but many people forget that if you iron in the correct order, you're less likely to get wrinkles while you're ironing. Follow these steps for the best results when ironing a shirt or blouse:

1. **Lay the shirt flat on the board and iron the underside of the collar first, working from the ends towards the center.**

   This prevents puckering.

2. **Iron the front side of the collar.**

3. **Iron the inside of the cuffs, flip them over, and iron the outside.**

4. **Slip the shoulder over the narrow edge of the board and iron towards the center; repeat on the other side.**

5. **Press the sleeves, working down from the top near the seam.**

6. **Iron the body of the shirt, starting on one side and continuing around to the other.**

Figure 13-1 illustrates this process.

After you finish the body of the shirt, go back and press the collar and any spots on the shirt that you may have missed or that have become wrinkled.

### Ironing pants

Follow these instructions to get a good pleat on your pants:

1. **If necessary, iron the insides of the pockets so that they lay flat.**

2. **Slip the waistband around the narrow part of the board and iron the top of the pants.**

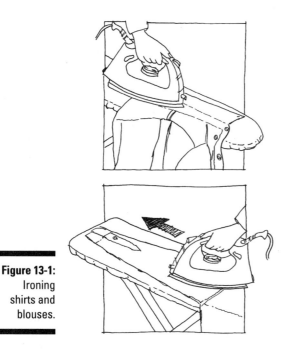

**Figure 13-1:**
Ironing
shirts and
blouses.

3. **Lay the pants flat on the ironing board with the legs on top of each other, match up the inseams, and flatten the sides of the legs together.**

4. **Fold back the leg on top and iron the one on the bottom; flip the pants over and repeat the process.**

5. **Put the legs together again, match up the inseams, and iron the outside of each leg, making a crease with the steam iron.**

## Handling buttons, pleats, and other problem areas

Poufs, pleats, buttons, and bows can cause problems while you're ironing. Conquer them all with these tips:

✔ **Delicate buttons** need to be covered to avoid nicking or scratching. Most irons have a built in button groove or channel just above the soleplate. This allows you to press around the button while it rides into the channel. For extra protection, you can hold the tip of a small spoon over the button and press the surrounding fabric.

If your buttons aren't special and you're in a hurry, turn the fabric over and iron the reverse side. Press lightly, and you won't damage the buttons.

✔ **Pleats** need to be ironed from the top to the bottom (see Figure 13-2). Hold the pleat down and iron the inside of the pleat first. Then iron over the outside. If you feel that you don't have enough hands to hold the pleat down and iron at the same time, clip some clothespins onto the ends of the pleats to hold them together. When you get near the bottom, unclip the pins. If you don't have any clothespins, insert some straight pins through both layers of the pleats and into the ironing board cover at the top and bottom. Just make sure that you don't iron over the pins. Remove them when you move to the next section.

✔ **Raised embroidery designs** can bunch up or pucker when ironing. Lay the fabric right-side down on top of a thick towel, and steam press with the appropriate setting for the fabric.

✔ **Seams,** especially on garments of a heavy fabric (such as wool), should be ironed on the inside first to flatten them. Then flip the garment over and iron the outside.

✔ **Sequined or beaded garments** should be ironed inside out on top of a plush towel. Use a pressing cloth and press with the iron on a gentle setting.

✔ **Shoulders of jackets or blouses** often bunch up and wrinkle near the seam when they're laid flat on the ironing board. Roll up a towel and push it up into the top of the sleeve near the shoulder seam. The towel provides a cushion so you can iron directly onto the seam and get a rounded edge.

✔ **Silk** is delicate and can be stained easily. Test the temperature of the iron on a hidden part of the garment first. Usually, a medium temperature iron is sufficient. To avoid any water spots or stains, set a steam iron on "no steam" or use a plain (non-steam) iron.

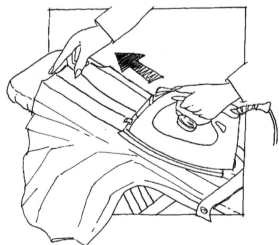

**Figure 13-2:**
Ironing
pleats.

- **Ties** with slight wrinkles can be touched up by covering them with a handkerchief or cheesecloth and pressing lightly with a steam iron. If you're really picky, you can cut a piece of cardboard to the shape of the tie and insert it inside to hold the tie's shape and keep the sides of the tie from pressing flat.

- **Velvet and corduroy** should be pressed inside out on top of a thick towel or on another piece of the same fabric. Use a light action and barely touch the back of the fabric.

- **Zippers** can sometimes pucker and refuse to lay flat. First, close the zipper and press the inside flaps. Then, open the zipper and press the surrounding fabric. Flip the fabric over to the right side and iron the outside fabric next to the opening. Don't let the iron touch the teeth of the zipper. If the zipper is plastic, it could melt them.

Iron tablecloths, draperies, and other large items at the widest end of the ironing board. Lay a plastic tablecloth or an old sheet on the floor beneath the ironing board so that the item doesn't gather dirt or dust as it hits the floor. Or you can position a couple of chairs or a card table next to the ironing board and drape the item over them as you go along.

## Steaming: A quick fix

If you're in a rush or you just can't stand to iron another thing, the shower method of wrinkle elimination just may be the ticket. It's a favorite of those who travel often.

Just turn on the shower to the highest heat, let it run for a few minutes, and then put your shirt (jacket, pants, skirt, or whatever) on a hanger or throw it over the pole. Let it hang for a few minutes, and the hot steam should relax the fibers in the item so that the wrinkles steam right out.

# Chapter 14

# A Stitch in Time: Repairing and Storing Your Clothes

*I*'m amazed at how much time and care most of us put into selecting, storing, and cleaning our clothes, but when a button needs sewing or a hem falls down, all activity stops. We stare blankly at the mishap, unable to pick up a needle and thread and make repairs. Either we let the item sit in our closet for a few weeks (dare I say months and years), or we run, dollar bills in hand, to the nearest tailor. I'm here to tell you that you can save time, as well as money, by making small repairs yourself. A button doesn't take more than five minutes to sew back on — much shorter than the time spent going to the tailor.

In this chapter, I set you up with a basic sewing kit and give you the pointers you need to make these simple repairs

## Creating a Sewing Kit

As with any other repair around the house, having the right tools makes taking care of your clothes easier. Obviously, a needle, thread, and scissors are essential, but creating a sewing kit filled with a few useful items — mentioned in the upcoming list — will help you get professional results with a minimum of time and effort. Store your sewing supplies in an old tool kit, fishing tackle box, or even a plastic shoe bag hung over a door. Keeping them together in one place eliminates the need to run all over the house to find them in a clothing emergency. Some people like to keep threaded needles and scissors in the bedroom or laundry room to make any needed repairs while getting dressed or washing clothes.

Here's a list of the necessities:

- ✔ Assorted needles — sharps can be used for most everyday sewing
- ✔ Tape measure
- ✔ Ruler (to measure fabric when it's on a flat surface)
- ✔ Box of straight pins

## Products that make repairs easier

These are some products that are not only fun to use but also make your repair jobs go just a little faster:

- ✔ **Seam ripper:** An instrument with a very small, sharp, pointed tip designed to slip under the stitches on a hem or seam to quickly rip them out. Because the tip is so tiny, you can slide it into small stitches where scissors won't fit. Be cautious when using it, however, because one slip can rip the fabric underneath as well as the thread. A seam ripper is one of my favorite items.

- ✔ **Knit picker:** Loop this into pulls in sweaters and other fabrics to restore the yarn to its proper place.

- ✔ **Liquid seam sealant:** A glue-like substance you can squeeze onto the edges of fabric or cording to make the fabric stop fraying. Give a shot of this to loose ends of fabric in the seam around zippers if they are sticking.

- ✔ **Iron-on patches:** Pieces of fabric in neutral colors that have fusible bonding on the back. If you have a rip in a pair of pants or a piece of fabric like a sheet or curtain, these patches can do the repair trick without a major sewing job. You cut the patches to fit, position them over the holes, and iron them on.

- ✔ **Velcro:** A specialized fabric used to close things up. I've always thought of Velcro brand fasteners as a miracle product — it fulfills that promise in sewing, too. It comes in many different shapes, sizes, degrees of stickiness, and thickness. In addition to strips, Velcro fasteners are available as little round discs that are a quick substitute for buttons or snaps or a sturdy closure when you don't want to or can't make a button-hole. You can use the tape for decorating products such as sink skirts or pillow covers.

Seam Ripper

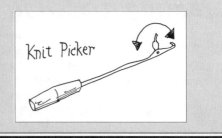
Knit Picker

Store pins by pushing them into a bar of soap. The soap helps lubricate the pin tips so they will slide easily into the fabric.

✔ Pair of small, sharp scissors

✔ Assorted colors of threads — black, white, brown, or any dark color to match your wardrobe, and transparent, monofilament thread to use when you don't have a color to match the garment

Tape down the ends of threads so the spool doesn't unwind in the kit.

✔ Buttons in black and white and different sizes

✔ Iron-on invisible tape for hems and repairs

✔ Iron-on patches

✔ Hooks, eyes, and snaps

✔ Safety pins

Hold safety pins together in a small box — breath mint or dental floss size — or slip them together on a large sized safety pin.

✔ Magnet to hold and pick up pins

# Simple Sewing for First-Timers

For day-to-day sewing and repairs, you need to master just a few sewing basics. If you can figure out how to use a cash machine or send e-mail, you can definitely sew on a button or take up a hem. But first, I need to cover a few preliminaries that come even before hems and buttons. These basics are worth repeating for those whose homemaking skills end with boiling water.

## Threading a needle

If you have trouble threading a needle, don't throw in the towel as far as simple mending projects are concerned. Everyone has days when the thread just doesn't want to go into the hole.

A few simple tricks can help ease the frustration:

✔ Always cut thread on a slight angle with sharp scissors. Never break it by hand. That just creates frayed ends that will not fit into the eye of the needle smoothly, no matter how many times you try.

✔ Hold the thread about one inch from its end between your index finger and thumb. Hold the needle with your other index finger and thumb. Aim the thread for the eye of the needle and push it through.

If you're having trouble locating the eye of the needle, hold a piece of white paper behind it before threading.

If you're having trouble getting the thread through the needle, draw the thread through a bar of soap or the stub of a candle. Or you can try spritzing it with a shot of hair spray. The methods act to stiffen the thread so you can easily get it through the eye of the needle.

✔ Push the thread through the eye of the needle until it extends about ½ inch beyond the opening; keep pulling until about a third of the length of thread is on the other side of the needle.

This gives you a good-sized piece of thread to hold on to while you're sewing. If you make it shorter, it's likely to pull back through the hole as you're sewing and you'll be forced to rethread. (Always an annoying task, even if you *can* see where the hole is.)

✔ Resist the urge to leave a really long tail of thread so you can make any repair without having to rethread the needle. Keep the length of thread to about a foot — otherwise the thread tends to get tangled.

If all else fails, use a needle threader, a very thin, looped piece of wire attached to a plastic or metal holder that helps in threading a needle (Figure 14-1 shows how it's done).

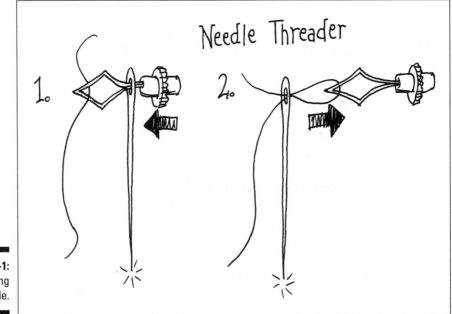

**Figure 14-1:**
Threading
the needle.

I never really needed one of these until I got to a "certain age," but if you can't see the eye of the needle anymore, or if needle-threading is something you never mastered, this little gadget is for you. You push the wire through the eye of a needle, loop the thread through that, pull the whole thing back through the eye, and you've threaded the needle. It's a simple concept, but, boy, does it do the job!

## Knotting the thread

After you get the thread through the eye of the needle in the length you need, you have to knot the end of the thread to anchor the stitches in the fabric. To do this, wind the end of the thread around the end of your index finger about three times. Then, carefully roll the circle of thread off your finger. Holding the needle with the thread in it in one hand, pull the circle down between your fingers until it forms a knot. Leave about ⅛ inch of thread under the knot and cut off the rest.

# Making Button Repairs

Buttons are the items you probably most need to repair. I don't know if you've noticed, but buttons today seem to be sewn on with about two lengths of thread, so they tend to fall off easily. Check your clothes every time you take them off to be sure that all the buttons are there. I really get annoyed when I'm in a rush to put on a shirt or dress and discover that a button is missing.

If you buy clothes that have extra buttons, store the extras together in a small glass jar so you can find them when necessary.

## Removing an old button

If you have to remove a button, first slide the teeth of a comb around the thread underneath the base of the button to protect the fabric from cuts. Then lift the button up slightly and cut through the threads with a razor blade or small scissors.

If you're throwing away an old shirt or dress, cut off any buttons and put them in your sewing kit. You can use them to make future repairs on other shirts.

## Sewing on a button

The secret of properly sewing on a button is to make sure that the button is securely attached yet still flexible. If sewn on too tight, the button won't lie flat against the fabric and can stretch the buttonhole when pulled through.

Buttons come in two varieties (see Figure 14-2). Most common are *sew-through buttons*. Sew-through buttons have two or four holes through which the button is sewn to the garment. You see them on almost all shirts. *Shank buttons* have a smooth top with small metal or fabric loops under the button through which they're sewn to the fabric.

**Figure 14-2:**
Buttons
come in
sew-
through
and shank
varieties.

Here are some tips for sewing on buttons:

✔ To sew on a four-holed button, first stitch through two of the holes several times and then knot the thread underneath the fabric. Sew on the other two holes separately. Why? If one side breaks, the other side will stay put until you have time to fix it.

✔ Give newly fixed buttons added protection against breakage by dabbing a little clear nail polish on the threads on top of the button. This prevents the threads from breaking and makes the button last longer. Threads around metal buttons really benefit from this treatment because the buttons have sharp edges that can wear away the thread after a time.

✔ If you find a broken thread on a button, tie a knot in it to keep the button from falling off until you have the time to sew the button back on.

✔ No thread? Look in the medicine cabinet. Dental floss is a great substitute for button thread. It's especially good for heavy duty garments like coats and jackets because dental floss is stronger than most threads.

### Using sew-through buttons

To keep sew-through buttons flexible, leave a short length of thread under the button so the button has room to move (this thread is called a *shank*). Maintaining this flexibility is essential for thick fabrics to keep buttons loose enough to fit through the buttonholes without stretching the hole and the fabric.

When sewing on a button, I like to double the thread so it's strong enough to resist breakage. To do this:

1. **Cut a length of thread approximately 2 feet long.**

2. **Pull half of the thread through the needle, let both ends hang down, and then tie both ends together in a knot as close as possible to the end.**

3. **Center the button where you want to sew it on the fabric and hold it there.**

4. **Starting from under the fabric, push the needle up through one hole of the button and draw the thread down into the other hole. Repeat six to eight times and knot it underneath.**

If you want to make a button with a shank (usually for thick fabrics, jackets, and coats), hold a match or toothpick over the button, and draw the thread over the match and down into the other hole on the button and through the fabric. Pulling the thread over the toothpick gives you the extra length of thread to make the shank. Repeat this about six to eight times.

To make the shank, pull the needle and thread up through the fabric but stop before you go through the button. Remove the toothpick, lift up the button, and wind the thread several times around the drawn threads between the button and the fabric. Then, push the needle through to the underside of the fabric and knot underneath. This process is illustrated in Figure 14-3.

### Using shank buttons

To sew on a shank button:

1. **Locate the spot where you want the button and pull the needle through the fabric from the underside.**

2. **Sew a couple of small stitches to mark the spot where the button will be and to form a base for your stitches.**

3. **Position the button over the stitches and stitch through the button loop and the fabric about four to five times.**

4. **When you feel that the button's attached firmly enough, insert the needle to the underside of the garment and knot.**

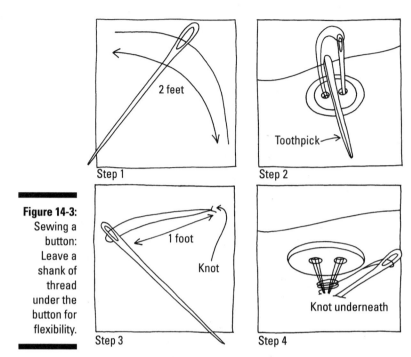

**Figure 14-3:**
Sewing a
button:
Leave a
shank of
thread
under the
button for
flexibility.

# Adjusting a Hem

I always hem my own clothes when needed. Hemming was one of the first things I learned when I started to sew. It doesn't take any particular sewing skills — you can even do it without a sewing machine if you don't have one. Once again, a few minutes work can save you money. In less than the time it takes to go to the tailor, stand to have the garment measured, and make a return trip to pick it up, you could have hemmed it yourself.

When you go to mark your new hem, make sure that you or the person who wears the garment (if you're hemming for a friend or family member) stands in front of a full length mirror so you can get a 360 degree picture. You want to be able to see the garment from the front, side, and back.

## Hemming a skirt

Put on the skirt and mark where you want the new hem to be. To get an even line, measure the skirt from the bottom up to the desired new hem length and mark with pins, chalk, or a soap sliver in a couple of places. Take off the skirt and mark evenly all around. Take out the old hem with scissors or a seam ripper and press flat. Allow about two inches for the depth of the new hem and mark all around so you'll know where to cut.

You can speed up the marking process by marking the desired hem depth on an index card and using that as a gauge. This will keep you from having to use a tape measure all around the hem.

Cut off the excess fabric and turn up the fabric along the marked hem line. Pin in place. Put the pins at right angles to the edge of the skirt so the hem lies flat when you're sewing it.

If you can't find any pins, you can hold the hem in place while you sew it with clothespins or paper clips.

Try on the skirt again and double check the length. I like to use the seam-binding tape because it makes a neater, more finished look and keeps the fabric threads in place. Sew on seam-binding tape or use iron-on hem tape available at sewing stores. If you don't want to use seam binding, turn the fabric under ¼ inch and press.

To sew the hem to the skirt, make a stitch in the hem tape on the inside and then another stitch on the front side of the fabric that you will be able to see from the outside. For the best-looking hems, make the stitches on the outside of the skirt as small as possible, so they are practically invisible from the outside.

Doing this isn't as hard as it sounds because the stitches on the inside hemming tape can be less delicate because no one sees them. To get started, take a stitch in the hem, and then make a tiny stitch through the front of the garment, picking up only one or two strands of the fabric on the outside. That way, you only see a tiny speck of thread from the outside. Bring the needle back into the seam binding about ¼ or ½ inch ahead of the last stitch. Repeat, moving back and forth between the seam binding and the outside. Look at another hem to see what I mean. Be careful not to pull the thread too tightly or the fabric will pucker. Continue stitching the same way all around the skirt. Knot the thread at the end.

## *Hemming pants*

Take out the old hem, unfold the pants hem, and iron it flat. Put on the pants with the shoes you normally wear with them and mark where you want the new hem to be. Fashion stylists say that pants should touch the top of the shoe in front and taper slightly longer in back. They should brush the shoe without wrinkling and dip down in back. Mark where the new hem will be with pins, tailor's chalk, or a sliver of soap. Take off the pants. Turn the pants legs inside out and pin up the hem where you've marked it. Use the existing hemline as a guide to gauge how deep the new hem should be. Do one leg and measure the second from the first. Put on the pants again to make sure they're the correct length. Then take them off and cut the fabric about two inches below the point where you want the hem to be. Turn under the raw edge at the bottom of the pant leg about ¾ of an inch, pinning as you go. Press with an iron. If the fabric is heavy, sew seam binding onto the edge to finish instead of turning it under.

Make a 1 ¼ inch hem by folding up the fabric, pinning and pressing into place. After you've pinned up the hem on pants, lay them flat on a table with the creases in the legs together to make sure that the hems are the same length and that they're even.

Try on the pants again to make sure the hem is in the right place. Sew into place by pushing the needle inside the hem fold and pushing it through to the front single layer of fabric. Catch a thread or two; then push the needle back into the fold about ¼ inch ahead and repeat the stitches.

Resist the urge to leave a long enough tail of thread so you can hem the whole pants leg without having to rethread the needle. I've tried this several times (being a basically lazy person), and it just results in tangled thread. Not only that, but if the hem comes down, the whole thing will unravel at once. If you use several short lengths, you'll only have to repair the loosened part.

## Letting down a hem

To make a garment longer, rip out the old hem and press to flatten the material. Mark the new hem, pin in place, and stitch in the same manner used for hemming a skirt (see the previous section, "Hemming a skirt," for details.)

If the crease from the old hemline still shows, try sponging the wrong side of fabric lightly with white vinegar, cover with a dry press cloth and press with a hot iron. (Be sure to test the vinegar on a hidden part of fabric first to make sure it doesn't discolor the fabric. If it does, try going over the mark with a damp pressing cloth.) If the crease still remains, cover it up creatively with ribbon or cording, depending on the style of the garment.

## No-sew fixes for drooping hems

If you're like most people, sooner or later a hem is going to come out, and you'll have to fix it when you just don't have the time or materials to do the job in the most perfect way. But don't panic — use these very quick fixes to solve the problem. Some you can actually leave in for several months (or maybe forever). Use any of these when a needle and thread are not available:

✔ **Duct tape**: What *isn't* this miracle tape good for? Especially effective with jeans and heavy fabrics, this can go through the wash several times and still stays in place. Cut the length of tape you need and tape the hem to the inside of the garment to hold it in place.

✔ **Fusible web bonding tape:** This is another one of those items that you'll find lots of uses for, and it's a quick and permanent way to repair a hem. Cut the tape to the length you need and lay between the hem and the garment. Press with an iron set on "wool" and steam. (Use a pressing cloth if the fabric is usually ironed on a lower setting.) You can leave the tape in place through washing and dry cleaning. The tape is available in different weights — be sure to use one that's appropriate to your fabric. A heavy one may show through on a lightweight fabric.

✔ **Safety pins:** Pinning hems in place is a logical choice, if you can find enough safety pins. Insert the pins in the same manner as if you were using a needle. Just pick up a couple of threads on the outside of the garment with the sharp end of the pin and snap it shut on the inside of the hem.

✔ **Double-sided mending tape:** Both sides of this tape are sticky to hold two pieces of fabric together. To use, leave the paper backing on one side of the tape and press the sticky side into place on the inside of the hem. Remove the remaining backing and fold the hem up to meet the tape. Smooth the hem into place by pressing the area gently with your fingers from the center out to the edge. You must remove the tape before washing, dry cleaning, or sewing.

✔ **Liquid seam sealant:** Be careful with this sealant — check to make sure it won't stain the fabric. Put a few drops on the edge of the hem and spread with your finger. Press the hem back into place and wipe off any excess glue with a damp cloth. Wait about 5 minutes to dry. It will last through washing but not dry cleaning.

# Quick Tricks for Minor Problems

These are the minor annoyances that happen day in and day out. Here's how to solve them fast and keep them from becoming major problems:

✔ **Loose drawstring:** If a drawstring comes out of a hood or a waistband, attach a safety pin to one end and use it to guide it through the tube. After it's in place, permanently attach the drawstring by sewing it to the garment with a couple of stitches in the middle.

✔ **Runs in stockings:** Dab some clear nail polish or a gluestick at the top and bottom of the run to stop it.

✔ **Sticking zipper:** Rub a little liquid dishwashing soap or wax over the teeth to coat it. Then, then move the zipper up and down to distribute it over the length of the zipper. This lubricates the teeth so the zipper moves freely in the future. Carefully wipe off any residue to make sure it doesn't get on fabric.

✔ **Zipper, broken teeth:** If the bottom of a zipper has broken or loose teeth, stitch a few threads over the area where the break has occurred. This will create a new bottom stop for the zipper. The whole thing will be slightly shorter, but it will still work.

✔ **Zipper, head broken off:** If the head comes off, cut off a few of the lowest teeth and push the zipper head back onto the track. Then, create a new base by sewing over the bottom of the zipper with strong thread where you've cut off the teeth so the zipper won't come off again.

✔ **Zipper pull comes off:** Slip a safety pin or paper clip through the hole as a substitute pull.

# Before you throw it away

If you have some garments that seem a little off kilter, don't stuff them in the back of your closet or throw them out. These few simple adjustments can make garments seem like new.

✔ **Change the size of shoulder pads:** The size of the shoulder pads can really date an item. Reducing the size or changing the shape can give a totally new look. Look for shoulder pads in the notions department of fabric stores. Save the old ones and use them to make a padded hanger. Attach them to the

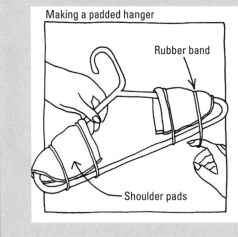

Making a padded hanger

Rubber band

Shoulder pads

ends of a hanger with safety pins or rubber bands to cushion against bumps and hold straps in place.

✔ **Shorten skirts:** Skirts or dresses can look dated from a hemline that's too long. Just shortening a dress or skirt as little as an inch or two can give them a new shape and proportion that may fit better with current styles.

✔ **Change the buttons:** Many jackets or blouses come with buttons that are just "make do." A change of buttons can make a garment look more casual or dressy or just give it a more custom look. Check the Yellow Pages for a button store in your area and look around the notion department of fabric and department stores. Flea markets and antique stores are also great places to find unique buttons.

✔ **Change the details:** Depending on the style of the garment, sewing on pieces of lace, cording, or fringe in the right places can give new zest to a tired piece of clothing. Look in fashion magazines to see what trims are in style this year.

✔ **Pills on a sweater**: Remove fuzz balls and tiny knots by gently rubbing with sandpaper, or cut them off of with a single-edge razor.

✔ **Remove lint:** Make your own lint remover by wrapping wide adhesive tape with the sticky side out around an empty toilet paper tube. Roll over the surface to pick up lint, stray threads, and hair. To get to a small area, wrap the tape around your finger with the sticky side out.

✔ **Mending a tear:** Minor tears can be fixed easily with iron-on adhesive patches. They come in different weights and colors so you can use them for anything from a shirt to a jacket. You can find them in fabric stores or in department stores where needles and threads are sold. Patches make it easy to mend any tear because all you have to do it cut the patch to fit, position it under the tip, and iron it on. Follow the manufacturer's instructions on the package. When you're ironing a patch onto a middleweight to heavyweight fabric, put a piece of aluminum foil on top of the ironing board and under the hole. The foil intensifies the heat and prevents the patch from sticking to the ironing board. For extra protection, make a couple of quick stitches across the edge of the tear before you put on the patch to hold it in place and prevent further stress.

✔ **Ripped seam:** On the inside of the seam, sew over the missing stitches. Sew about one inch beyond the opening on either side to strengthen the seam and stop it from ripping again. Knot at the end.

✔ **Loose snap:** Push a threaded needle through the underside of the fabric and the hole in the snap. Make five or six stitches through the hole and then knot.

# Storing Clothes

Although we often ignore them, the kind of hanger you use can keep your clothes looking good. Wooden hangers are best to hold heavy garments like suits and jackets and help them keep their pressed look. Because they're bigger and take up more space in your closet than regular hangers, they prevent you from stuffing too many things in the closet and overcrowding it, which causes wrinkles. Here are some tips to help store your clothes so they look good and are ready to wear when you need them:

✔ Hang skirts from their waistband on a clamp or clip hanger. Hang any delicate or sheer garment on a padded hanger to avoid marks on the shoulders. Avoid using metal hangers, which can stretch fabric and cause bumps.

✔ Don't store anything in dry cleaner bags. The plastic doesn't allow clothes to breathe. Cloth bags are a better solution.

✔ Avoid putting wool or silk in airtight containers. The fibers need room to breathe.

Always thoroughly clean garments before storing. Sugar stains such as wine, although not noticeable at first, can set and turn brown over time.

Never let mothballs touch clothing — put them in old socks or hosiery and hang them from the closet rod.

# Chapter 15

# Caring for Shoes and Other Accessories

● ● ● ● ● ● ● ● ● ● ● ● ● ● ● ● ● ● ● ● ● ● ● ● ● ● ● ● ● ● ● ● ● ● ● ● ● ● ● ● ● ● ● ● ●

### In This Chapter

▶ Maintaining the life of your shoes

▶ Keeping leather comfortable

▶ Handling gems and other jewelry with care

● ● ● ● ● ● ● ● ● ● ● ● ● ● ● ● ● ● ● ● ● ● ● ● ● ● ● ● ● ● ● ● ● ● ● ● ● ● ● ● ● ● ● ● ●

*A*ccessories are accents that can make or break your outfit. If the accessories look good, the outfit looks good. But accessories tend to be out of sight and out of mind until you need them. Try to make it a habit to inspect your accessories before you put them away, and make any necessary repairs at that time or close to it. Here's how to keep shoes, hose, jewelry, and other accessories in tip-top shape.

## Using Shoe Smarts

The best way to keep your shoes in good shape is to give them a good rest. Don't wear the same pair day after day — let them air out between each use. Feet can perspire as much as a cup of moisture a day, so shoes need a period to dry out and get back to normal shape.

If you have problems with perspiring feet, leather or canvas shoes are your best bet. They allow the feet to breathe. Check the label to make sure both the uppers and bottoms are leather. Avoid shoes made from vinyl or other man-made materials if you have foot perspiration problems.

To keep odors at bay, shake a little baking soda on the insides or stuff them with newspaper.

New shoes often have slippery bottoms. Rub the bottoms of the shoes with some fine sandpaper to prevent them from slipping.

## Drying wet shoes and boots

It happens to all of us at one time or another. You're caught in the rain, you step in a puddle, and your shoes get wet.

Most shoes can withstand a good soaking if you treat them with tender loving care afterwards. When you get home, take off your shoes and stuff them with newspaper to retain their shape. If the paper gets soaked, replace with dry newspaper. Shoes dry faster if air circulates around them so, if they're really wet, put them on a rack or hang them from a chair by hooking the heels on the rungs.

Never dry shoes near a radiator or heat source, which may cause the shoes to shrink and crack.

While the shoes are still slightly damp, rub them with saddle soap to keep them from stiffening after they're dry. Remove salt stains by rubbing with a cloth dipped in a vinegar and water solution. Water stains can be removed by rubbing with a soft toothbrush dipped in a soap and water mixture. First wipe off the stain and then go over the whole shoe with a very slightly damp-ened, soft cloth.

If your boots are wet, you can speed up the drying process by going over them with a hair dryer set on cool or a vacuum set to the exhaust setting. Boots dry better when they're standing up straight, so roll some newspaper into a tube and slip it inside.

Some boots leave marks on the tips of your socks or nylons from the dye in the leather when they get wet. I solved that problem by putting a couple pieces of tape in the toe area of the boot.

Weatherproof your boots and shoes against rain and snow by spraying the outsides and seams with silicone spray. Be sure to clean salt off boots by wiping with a cloth dipped in vinegar and water. Just like on your car, salt can do nasty things to leather.

## Lavishing shoes with care

After each wearing, wipe off leather shoes with a soft cloth and brush suede shoes. Wipe the inner linings with a cloth dampened in soapy water.

If you really want to be nice to your shoes, store them in cedar shoe trees, which absorb moisture and help maintain the shoes' shape. Put the shoe trees in immediately after wearing, while shoes are still warm and pliable.

Don't put shoes in plastic bags; they cling to the shoes and stop shoes from breathing. Wrap them in tissue paper and store them in shoe boxes or use cloth bags.

To recondition leather shoes, brush off any surface dirt. Then apply shoe cream with a soft cloth and rub into the shoe until everything is absorbed. If possible, leave the cream on overnight to let the leather thoroughly absorb it and recondition. Buff shoes with another soft, clean cloth or shoe brush. If you have laces on your shoes, remove them first to avoid coloring them.

If shoes are new, coat with wax polish before wearing to protect against harsh weather or rain.

When shoes get muddy, let them dry and then wipe off as much dirt as you can with a soft brush. Wipe with a damp cloth to remove all the dirt. Stuff the shoes with newspaper so shoes retain their shape; then let them dry.

You can remove most scuffs by rubbing the mark lightly with the side of an art gum eraser, found in most art supply stores.

Nonleather shoes deserve the same care as leather. Wipe them with a soft cloth to clean before storing them. If needed, use an all-purpose shoe cleaner like Lincoln E-Z Cleaner. Wipe the shoes with shoe cream periodically to keep them soft and pliable.

### Perking up patent leather

For a quick shine and to prevent cracks, dab a small amount of petroleum jelly on a cloth and rub into the shoe. Wipe off with a dry cloth.

To clean patent leather, spray glass cleaner on a soft cloth and wipe off the dirt. If shoes have cracks, massage them with leather conditioner and buff with a soft, dry cloth.

Don't store patent leather shoes in a cold attic or basement; cold temperatures can cause them to crack.

### De-spotting your blue suede shoes

For day-to-day cleaning, wipe off surface dirt from suede shoes by brushing them with a special nylon or rubber suede brush or by rubbing with a terry cloth towel.

To deep clean, pour some suede shampoo on a damp sponge or cloth and lightly rub all over the shoe.

Remove rain spots and bring up the nap by rubbing the shoes gently with an emery board. If the nap has flattened, hold the shoe about 5 inches over a kettle with steam coming out and brush the leather in one direction.

### Keeping canvas shoes fresh

Before you wear new canvas shoes, such as tennis shoes, for the first time, spray with fabric protector or spray starch to help them resist scuffs and stains.

Clean canvas shoes by applying a light coating of carpet shampoo and rubbing it in thoroughly with a toothbrush. Let dry and then brush off. Or shampoo with an all-purpose shoe cleaner following the directions on the bottle. Scrub the rubber soles with a toothbrush dipped in a mild soap and water solution.

Remove grass stains from white shoes by wiping the stain with a cotton ball dipped in nail polish remover.

To clean shoestrings or laces, remove them and put them in a 16-ounce jar with a tablespoon of liquid laundry detergent and a ½ teaspoon of all-fabric bleach. Shake and let sit for a few minutes. Then rinse well.

If ends of laces become frayed, dip them in nail polish and shape to a point with your fingers or tweezers. After the laces are thoroughly dry, they'll have a hard point just like new.

Stinky sneakers can be a real problem. To make them smell sweet (or at least wearable) sprinkle baking soda on the insides and shake to distribute it all over. Or stuff the shoes with wadded up newspaper and let sit for about 24 hours to absorb the odor.

### Removing grease from fabric shoes

If you get a grease spot on nonwashable fabric shoes, sprinkle cornstarch on the spot to absorb the grease. Let it sit for several minutes and then brush the starch away. The grease should leave with it.

# Treating Gloves Kindly

Oh, how many of us mistreat our gloves! Don't leave them crumpled up in coat pockets. After each use, shake them out, stretch them back into shape and store them flat. If your gloves have a care label, follow the instructions on that.

Believe it or not, you can wash *unlined* leather gloves. Put on the gloves, dip them into some warm water, and rub on a little mild soap, such as Murphy's Oil Soap. Keep gently rubbing them together as if you were washing your hands. Empty the wash water and replace it with warm, clean water. Thoroughly rinse the gloves and your hands. Take them out of the water and gently remove them from the water and your hands, and wrap the gloves in a soft towel to remove the excess water. Flatten them out and stretch them back into the proper shape; then lay them flat on a towel to dry.

Never put wet gloves near a heat source; they could shrink.

Lined leather gloves should be professionally cleaned.

# Freezing Pantyhose

Pantyhose in the freezer? Sounds ridiculous, but to prevent runs, many people swear by wetting pantyhose, placing them in a plastic bag and freezing them. After they've frozen, remove the bag and dry off the hose.

If your hands are like mine and feel like the back of an armadillo, you can cause runs just by putting on your pantyhose. Wear a pair of cotton gloves when putting on or taking off your hose or rub moisture cream all over your hands to soften any rough or chapped spots that can cause a snag.

Wash pantyhose by hand with a mild detergent. After you wash them, roll them in a clean, dry towel to remove excess moisture and then hang them dry. Never wring them.

If you want to wash your hose in the washing machine, put them in a mesh bag on the delicate cycle with warm or cool water, never hot.

# Caring for Leather

Although leather is a sturdy material, you must be careful to keep it away from water and food spills. If leather gets wet, allow it to air dry. Don't expose it to direct heat. Protect the collars of leather coats and jackets from perspiration by wearing a scarf. If you have a leather or suede garment cleaned, bring in all the parts at once in case a color change occurs. Using spot cleaners on leather can sometimes change the color or leave a sticky feel.

Leather and suede clothing can have many different types of finishes. That's why trying to clean them yourself can be a problem. You can clean off small spots on a grain leather by wiping with a damp cloth. Dry off with a soft rag. (Always test in a hidden area first. You don't want to end up with an isolated clean spot on a jacket with a well-worn patina.) If the jacket is dirty all over, get it professionally cleaned.

If you've spilled something greasy on your leather coat, sprinkle cornstarch or Fuller's Earth on the spot and let sit for a couple of hours. Brush off the cornstarch thoroughly with a dry sponge or brush, as it can discolor the garment if left on. The cornstarch acts as an absorbent to soak up the grease. If any part of the stain remains, take it to a professional.

Treat suede garments with care. If a spill occurs, blot it up with a clean, dry cloth and then air dry. Bring up the nap by rubbing lightly with a dry sponge or soft suede brush. Take to a professional if spot remains.

To clean leather luggage, wipe off scuff marks with an art gum eraser. Clean by wiping with a damp cloth and saddle soap. Let sit for 30 minutes. Rub off well with a soft cloth and then buff with a clean cloth.

Take care of leather handbags and briefcases just as you would any other fine leather. Don't use colored polishes. A purse or briefcase often gets rubbed against your coat or legs, and the color can come off on your clothing and create even bigger problems.

Fake leather or vinyl purses and briefcases can be wiped off with a damp cloth.

# Cleaning Jewelry: Precious and Precious-to-You

Jewelry is more than just pieces of metal and stone. Not only does it dress up a simple outfit, but it often carries poignant memories of a special person who gave it to you or a special occasion when you wore it. That's why you should treat it as tenderly as you can.

Put your jewelry in a covered or contained space to protect it and enable you to find it when you want it. The containers that people have used to store jewelry stretch the limits of the imagination: Fishing tackle boxes, empty egg cartons, ice cube trays (for earrings), velvet covered frames, plastic shoe bags, and utensil trays can all be used.

If you've got a lot of small pieces, choose something that has several compartments. Don't just throw jewelry into one large container. Some stones can scratch on another and leave permanent marks. If you have valuable jewelry, line the container with a soft fabric like velvet. Fasten the clasps of necklaces and bracelets so they won't wind around each other and become tangled. Take off your jewelry before gardening, housework, or other active sports. Check for loose stones periodically by gently tapping the item and listening for a rattling sound. If you have a necklace or earrings with different gems (diamonds and pearls, for example), the Jewelry Information Center in New

York recommends that you use the cleaning method for the softest, most delicate gem. And be sure to wash your jewelry in a plastic bowl or pan to avoid losing any down the drain.

TIP

Add a piece of chalk to your jewelry box to prevent costume jewelry from tarnishing.

TIP

To untangle a knot in a necklace, lay the chain on a piece of wax paper and put a drop of salad oil on top. Carefully insert two straight pins into the center of the knots, and gently pull it apart until the chain loosens up. Wash in a solution of warm water and a mild soap to remove the oil residue. Rinse well.

WARNING!

When getting dressed, always put on makeup, hairspray, or perfume before you put on your jewelry. The chemicals in them can damage the finish.

## Caring for diamonds, emeralds, and other gems

To care for your diamonds, lay necklaces flat to avoid the stones scratching each other. Store them in a lined box. Clean diamonds by placing them in a solution of warm water and a couple drops of alcohol, ammonia, or an ammonia-based household cleaner. (Make sure that ammonia is safe to use on the other metals or gems that are in the piece.) Let them soak for several minutes. Lightly brush the front and back of the ring or earring with a soft toothbrush to get rid of any dirt embedded in the mounting. Rinse, drain, and very gently wipe dry with a soft cloth. Fred Ward, in his book *Gem Care* (published by Access Publishers Network), says that the easiest way to clean diamonds is to soak them in vodka for a few minutes, rub them with a soft toothbrush, and rinse in warm water.

Rubies, sapphires, and garnets are hard stones that hold up well. Don't let them rub together when storing them as they can scratch. Emeralds are more delicate. Avoid any alcohol or strong chemicals when cleaning them. Use mild, soapy (nondetergent) water and a soft brush.

## Caring for gold and platinum

To clean gold and platinum jewelry, soak them for several minutes in a solution of warm water mixed with alcohol or a mild soap. Don't use ammonia as it can discolor the jewelry. Rinse in clean warm water and place it on on a terry cloth towel or soft absorbent cloth and pat dry. Don't wear gold or platinum chains, earrings, or bracelets in a swimming pool; chlorine can damage the finish.

# Caring for pearls

Pearls are more delicate than other jewelry because they are so porous. Wipe them gently after each use with a soft, damp cloth or a leather chamois cloth. When storing pearls, use a cloth or velvet bag; plastic can dry them out Periodically, gently wash your pearls with a soft cloth and a mixture of luke-warm water and mild soap suds. Don't use anything abrasive like a toothbrush to clean them off. Rinse and pat dry with a clean cloth or lay on a towel to dry.

Don't pull or stretch newly strung pearls. Be patient, they will stretch out slightly as they are worn. Check the strands carefully when you put them on and have them restrung when necessary so you won't have to deal with any loss due to breakage.

Never douse pearls with water; take them off when you bathe or swim.

# Caring for Sterling silver

To tell if you have good silver, look for the Sterling mark stamped onto the piece. Silverplate is a layer of silver bonded onto a base metal and should be cleaned the same way as silver.

Use a paste polish to clean silver, advises Diana Sheil of The Silver Information Center. Rub it on gently with a soft cloth like a T-shirt. Be sparing with the polish; two thin coats are better than one thick, heavy coating. Rinse well with warm or hot water and dry thoroughly with a terry cloth towel. You don't have to spend a lot on polish, the grocery store brand works just fine. Or use a polishing cloth such as Connoisseur's Jewelry Wipes. You just wipe the jewelry with the cloth and even the most heavy tarnish comes off.

If you're cleaning an intricate design, don't clean off all the tarnish in the crevices of the design. Tarnish gives it detailing and highlights the design. Avoid using one of the jewelry "dips," where you dip the piece into a solution. They take off all the tarnish.

For a quick touch-up (don't do this regularly) when you don't want to run for the polish, rub a bit of regular toothpaste (not gel) on the silver and rinse off with hot water, according to Diana Sheil.

The best way to store silver is to put it in a tarnish-resistant bag made of chemically treated flannel cloth. If you didn't get one when you purchased the silver, you can buy them at a store that sells silver. Or wrap it thoroughly in acid-free paper and store in a plastic bag.

For more information on the care and buying of silver, go to The Silver Information Center's Web site at www.silverinfo.com.

# Part IV
# Home Troubleshooting

The 5th Wave                    By Rich Tennant

"Each Spring we put out the human pest-strips. They're relatively inexpensive and keep the salespeople from getting in the house."

# In this part . . .

Okay, no matter how organized and clean you make your home, accidents happen, and things will go wrong. This part helps you solve some of the minor household problems that can drive you crazy. Squeaky doors and stairs? Loose screws? Find the solutions here. I also tell you how to make those unwanted guests — ants, spiders, fleas, and other pests — get out and stay out.

# Chapter 16

# Tool Tips for the All-Thumbed

- - - - - - - - - - - - - - - - - - - - - - - - - - - - - - - - - - - - - - - - -

## In This Chapter

▶ Creating a basic tool box

▶ Using common tools

- - - - - - - - - - - - - - - - - - - - - - - - - - - - - - - - - - - - - - - - -

Go into any hardware store, and you'll be confronted with a myriad of tools for every task. What do you really need? That depends on the number and kind of home repairs you're going to do. How much should you spend on tools? Buy good quality but don't go crazy. It pays to select top quality tools but getting something expensive may be a waste if you only intend to nail a few pictures to the wall or screw in a dresser knob. Pick up the tools and inspect them. Make sure they're comfortable, sturdy, and easy to hold. Ask for advice at your local hardware store, talk to your tool-handy friends, or look on the Internet. Then pay as much as your budget will allow.

In this chapter, I help you put together a basic tool kit, provide some short-cuts, and present tips for becoming comfortable with a variety of tools so you won't feel helpless (or fund-less) when problems arise.

## Quick-Fixers

Whether or not you can handle a hammer, these four all-stars of the quick-fix scene will get you through many common household situations with ease:

- ✔ **Blue tack:** This reusable adhesive can hold lightweight pictures, posters, or decorations on walls without making a hole.

- ✔ **Duct tape:** (Remember Tom Hanks used it to get back to Earth in the movie *Apollo 13.*) Fix a leaking hose, repair pipe, — the variety of repairs is endless.

- ✔ **Glue gun and glue sticks**: The tools of choice for decorators and home fixers — they dry super fast, and you can glue tons of stuff, from fabric to wood.

- ✔ **Staple gun and staples:** Basically, a very powerful stapler with a grip-and-lever handle. It works faster than nailing to attach carpeting to stairs, fabric to a headboard, or plastic sheeting to a window.

Once you get used to these quick-fixers, you may never want to reach for a real tool again. Glue gun fanatics insist that everything should be glued instead of nailed, and staple gun people are the same way. Experiment and you'll find plenty of uses.

# Basic Tools

For heavy-duty fixes, however, you need to keep a few tools on hand. Here are some basic tools that I find useful for every home dweller:

- **Adjustable wrench:** Get an 8-inch size to handle most small- to medium-sized nuts and bolts. Before buying, try adjusting the jaws to make sure they open and close smoothly.

- **Assorted nails and screws:** Just the sort of things empty jelly jars were meant to hold.

- **Claw hammer (13 or 16 ounces):** I find the smaller one easier to hold and use, but test it for yourself. Wood, steel, and fiberglass handles are available. I prefer fiberglass, because it's light and strong.

- **Crosscut saw:** Handy for cutting anything from plywood to paneling.

- **Files (wood and metal)**

- **3/8-inch variable speed reversible drill:** Uses bits to drill holes and insert or remove screws. You can get plug-in or cordless models. If yours is cordless, remember to keep the batteries charged. If you've ever had to put together any "easy-to-assemble" bookcases or furniture with a hand screwdriver, you'll appreciate the magic of the powered model.

- **Heavy duty extension cord**

- **Plunger:** It's not a versatile tool but a real lifesaver when you need it.

- **Putty knife:** Get two: a 1-inch-wide one for filling cracks and holes and a 3-inch-wide one for larger openings.

- **Safety goggles:** Use when the repair involves hammering, splintering, or even painting overhead. Protect your eyes; they're the only ones you've got.

- **Sandpaper (fine to coarse grade)**

- **Screwdrivers:** The two basic types of screwdrivers are slotted and Phillips head. The *slotted screwdriver* has a single straight edge. The *Phillips screwdriver* has multiple edges in the form of a cross. Each type of screwdriver fits into its corresponding type of screws: single slot and Phillips. In general, you should have three different sizes of each type — large, small, and in-between. Be sure they have comfortable grips.

- ✔ **Slip-joint pliers:** A wide variety of jaw sizes on this tool enables you to grip anything, including nails, nuts and bolts, and pipes. You may want some needlenose pliers for gripping something in a tight spot, such as a small nail head that you can't get a claw around to remove.

- ✔ **Tape measure:** A 25-foot retractable model with a metal tape and a thumb lock does the trick.

- ✔ **Utility knife or single edge razor blades**

Other great items to have:

- ✔ **Carpenter's level:** If you hang lots of shelves or pictures, a level can really help you get them straight.

- ✔ **Fishing line (clear):** Great for hanging things such as pictures and curtains.

- ✔ **Saber saw or jigsaw:** A power tool with a short, thin blade that moves up and down; easy to handle for small cuts around the house.

- ✔ **Steel wool:** You'll need this for many tasks such as fine buffing or removing dried paint. Have a few different grades, from #1, #2, to #0000.

- ✔ **Wire cutters:** Most needlenose pliers have a wire cutter for smaller gauged wires.

You may find some other tools that meet your needs. That's okay. Just add them. The idea is to have the right tool available when you need it, if you're likely to need it routinely. For specialized tasks such as stripping floors, renting the tool you need may be more cost- and space-effective.

Keep your tools in a box that is substantial, but not too heavy to lift when full of tools. Make sure the latch is sturdy. The Black & Decker company makes a toolbox that doubles as a vise and a work surface. If your space is limited, a toolbox that serves double duty can be a real find.

# Shortcut Tips for Stand-in Tools

My father, an engineer, always told me to have the right tool for the right job. If you've ever tried to tighten a screw with a butter knife, you know how important the right tool can be. But, hey, lots of times you either don't have a screwdriver or can't find it, so a knife (or metal nail file) will have to do.

Here are some fast, in-a-pinch tips for when the tool you need is not the tool at hand:

- ✔ **When you're missing a clamp:** Need to clamp two boards together to glue or drill a hole? Use masking tape to hold them tight. Wrap it several times around the item.

✔ **When you're missing a file:** Use an emery board. A neighbor's child once brought over his dead handheld video game for me to fix. He had new batteries in it, but still no go. I opened up the battery compartment and noticed a little corrosion on the terminals from the old dead batteries and filed it off. Like magic, it worked. Just don't ask me how to win the game.

✔ **When you're missing a carpenter's level:** Fill a soda or olive oil bottle about half full with water. Lay the bottle on its side on a shelf and look to see if the line of liquid is level in the bottle.

✔ **When you need a sandpaper block:** If you need to sand something, you'll realize how important a sandpaper block is. In a pinch you can use a slightly damp (to keep it flexible — not wet), thick sponge. Wrap the sandpaper around it and it will easily bend over curvy surfaces.

✔ **When you need a turn of the screw:** Can't remember which way to turn the screwdriver? Remember, left is loose, right is tight.

✔ **When you need a tape measure:** Measure your thumb, hand span, or length of your foot to mark off a distance.

✔ **When you need a tool belt:** Every carpenter has one, but you can just as well use a kitchen apron with pockets. Remember carpenter jeans? That little loop on the side is for holding a hammer.

# *Emergency Preparedness*

Even if you're not going to do a lot of home repairs, you need to know the location of the controls for the different systems in your home. At some point you'll need to turn these systems on or off, or direct a repair person to them. Here are the most common system locations:

✔ **Water valves:** Practically everywhere water is used, you'll find a valve to turn it off. You'll find one located near the toilet, under the sink, near the dishwasher, and above the water heater.

✔ **Fuses and circuit breakers:** Fuses or circuit breakers for the electricity are on the main service panel in your home. (Most modern apartments have some circuit breaker somewhere in the apartment.) Put labels on the circuit breakers so you know which room or appliances they control.

✔ **Gas supply valves:** Each gas appliance has its own shutoff valve. Before anything happens, make yourself familiar with all the shutoff points. If you don't know where they are, call your utility company or ask your home repair person or a handy neighbor. (Remember, if you smell a strong odor of gas, open doors and windows, leave the house, and call the gas company.)

# Personal Safety Dos and Don'ts

Safety first!

There's no point repairing a household item and then needing to repair yourself or a family member as a result. Remembering what to do and what not to do are first steps to maintaining personal safety.

Never allow children to play with your tools or be in the area where you are working. Kids are especially fascinated with power tools and you should be instructed never to touch them. Purchase a separate set of play tools for them to use.

## Safety dos

When performing household repairs, remember the following safety tips:

- ✔ Use the tool to perform the task for which it was intended. For example, if you need to pound something in, use a hammer, not a wrench or a staple gun.

- ✔ Wear safety goggles. Even if what you're doing seems like a harmless job, screws can fall or pieces of wood can become airborne and land in unwelcome places.

- ✔ Always read the instructions that come with all power tools. Save the instructions in the tool box for future reference.

- ✔ Draw tools such as knives or saws away from you rather than toward you to avoid accidentally slicing yourself. Also, always stand to the side as you work.

- ✔ Ask for help. Don't be afraid to get assistance when lifting or handling heavy loads.

- ✔ When using a screwdriver or hammer, always keep your free hand away from the point where the tool meets the head of the screw or nail.

Always start with a gentle tap or two to set the nail; then remove your hand. If you have problems holding a small screw or nail, keep it steady with the teeth of a comb, a large bobby pin, a blob of clay, or needlenose pliers.

- ✔ If you feel awkward handling a certain tool or climbing a ladder, follow your instincts and don't use it.

## Safety don'ts

When it comes to safety, these don'ts are major no-no's:

- Never, never work on any internal wiring in your house. Always call a licensed electrician. You could void your house insurance and violate local statutes.

- Don't work on any electrical appliance without pulling the plug first.

- Don't work on even minor plumbing fixes like replacing faucet washers without turning off the water supply first. Most houses have valves underneath each of the sinks.

- Don't try to do your own roofing. Ask friends or neighbors for references from reputable contractors.

- Don't tear down anything substantial, such as a wall, without consulting an expert beforehand.

- Don't try to fix things that are still under warranty, such as appliances. You could void the warranty.

- Don't lift power tools by their cords.

Of course, having the world's greatest set of tools won't do you much good if you don't have some basic idea of how to use them. The following section contains techniques for getting the most from your basic tools.

# Basic Techniques: Hammering, Sawing, Drilling, and Stuff

How do you get to play the violin at Carnegie Hall? Practice, practice, practice. That rule applies to home repairs as well as music. And, even if you don't know a wrench from a wing nut, the more fixes you do around the house, the more comfortable you'll feel doing them. Read this section and do a dry run with your tools before you're actually confronted with a mini-emergency or a project that needs to be done pronto. Practice will give you the confidence to tackle things you never thought you were capable of.

## Using a hammer

For most household hammering jobs, I prefer a small 13-ounce hammer, which is easier for my hand to grip and hold.

# Finishing nails

If you're nailing furniture or shelves and you want to end up with a smooth surface, use finishing nails. They have very small, tapered heads that have a slight indentation on top. This indentation is for a nail set.

A *nail set* is used to drive the head of the finishing nail below the surface of the wood. It fits in the little indentation and then you hammer down on it. You can also use another nail to do this, but that takes a little practice.

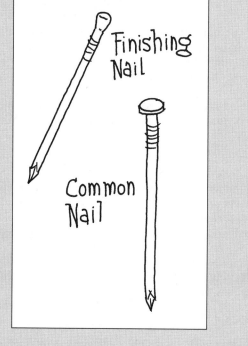

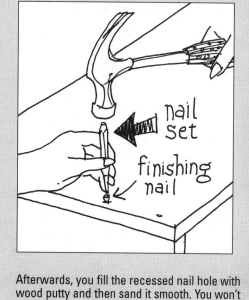

Afterwards, you fill the recessed nail hole with wood putty and then sand it smooth. You won't see all those nasty nail tops and everyone will be amazed at your skill.

When hammering, always start the nail with a few gentle taps. Grasping the hammer toward the end of its handle, drive the nail in, keeping your wrist straight and the face of the hammer square to the nail head. Always stop just before the head of the nail reaches the surface and then tap it down firmly. Doing this will help prevent hammer gouges in the surface.

If you bend a nail while hammering it in, tap it back to level, if possible. If you need to remove the nail, pull it off with the claw part of the hammer (that's the back of the hammer with those nasty-looking metal points).

If hammering on wood or any soft surface such as a plaster wall, put a piece of heavy cardboard beneath the nail to prevent damaging the surface as you pry the nail out.

If you have a hard time holding a small nail, cut a slit through the edge of a piece of cardboard and hold the nail in the slit. You can also hold the nail in place with tweezers, a comb, or needlenose pliers.

## Using a saw

I can hardly look at a saw without it conjuring up memories of some obscure horror movie where a person comes to an unpleasant end. Many of us dread using a saw, but it's really quite simple and safe, if you follow a few basic rules. I found sawing kind of tricky until I really got into the rhythm of it.

Before you start to saw, make sure to hold the piece of wood you're going to saw firmly in place. If this is difficult to do with your free hand, use a clamp to hold it down.

### First, mark your spot

Before cutting anything, measure the length of what you want to cut and then measure it again, just to make sure your measurements are correct. (All good carpenters live by the saying: "Measure twice, cut once.") Mark where you want to cut with a thin pencil line. If you really want to get fancy, you can etch the line with a heavy needle to eliminate any telltale pencil marks.

Always cut on the outside of any measurement line you draw. If you don't, the cut will be short the width of your saw blade — $\frac{1}{16}$ of an inch.

### Make your cut

To begin cutting with a hand saw, start with a few light backward strokes This creates a path for the saw so you can easily stay on track when you start cutting. Cut with smooth, even strokes following your measuring line. When you get down to the bottom, always support the end you're cutting with your free hand to prevent the end from splitting off.

When using an electric jigsaw or saber saw, always let the blade do the work for you. Don't force it. Rest the soleplate on the edge of the wood where your cut starts, then gently squeeze the saw's trigger. Let the blade stop first before removing it from the cut or laying it down. If you feel the wood isn't cutting smoothly, it's probably time to change the blades. Be sure to unplug the saw first before changing blades or performing any other maintenance.

## Using a drill

You've never really known a sense of power until you get a power drill in your hands. With a flick of a finger, you can permanently alter the state of wood, metal, or cement and practically everything else in your path.

Becoming familiar with your drill starts you on your road to many successful home repairs. Before you use a drill, you have to insert the proper *bit* into it; the bit is a screwlike shaft used to drill into surfaces. You can purchase sets with a variety of drill bits.

Some drill models have a *chuck* at the tip of the drill, which holds the drill bit in place, and a *key* to open and close the chuck when you want to remove a bit or insert a new one. A keyless chuck is also available on many drills. After inserting and securing the drill bit, hold the drill with two hands to keep it steady when the bit goes into a surface. If you wobble, you can break the bit. Always hold the drill straight to the surface you're working on, rather than at an angle.

If you're drilling through a piece of wood, always place another piece of scrap wood beneath it to drill into. This will do two things: Prevent you from drilling into your work surface and prevent the wood from splitting on the underside where the drill comes through.

## Using a screwdriver

Using a screwdriver is relatively simple, but you must remember to never *strip* a screw. Not a burlesque term, stripping a screw means that you've removed the cross-like slots on the top of a Phillips head screw or the slots in a standard screw. This usually happens because you used the wrong size screwdriver for the screw you're trying to insert. As a result, the metal eats into the screw's slots and "strips" them away, so that when you turn the screwdriver, there's no slots in the screw for it to grab on to.

You can also mess up a screw by trying to tighten or insert the screw too quickly, or by not holding your screwdriver firmly in the screw's slot. This can easily happen when using a cordless or power screwdriver. If the screw does start to strip, remove it while you still can and replace it with a new screw.

To avoid stripping a screw, always remember the screw-driving motto: Right is tight, left is loose. In other words, turn the screwdriver to your right to tighten a screw, to your left to loosen it.

When selecting the size screwdriver to use, remember that if the tip of the screwdriver is too narrow, it can damage the screw head and make the screw hard to remove. If it's too large, the tip won't fit in the slot and you won't be able to get a tight grip.

# Got a loose screw?

To prevent wood from splitting when screwing in a screw, drill a small *pilot hole* to insert the screw into. Always select a bit about ¼ smaller than the screw you're using.

If a screw loosens in its hole or if you drill the hole too large, you can correct the problem by inserting a wooden matchstick or toothpick in the hole. Break the stick off at the top and try reinserting the screw. If the screw is still loose, add another matchstick and try again.

### Getting a screw in

Some screwdrivers have a magnetized end that hold onto screws when you place them in the hole. You can also use tweezers or a bobby pin. Better yet, placing a piece of chewing gum or putty on the end of your screwdriver will help hold it in place.

If a screw is tough to get in, make it easier by drilling a small hole (called a *pilot hole*) for the screw. The hole should be slightly smaller than the screw to give the screw head something to catch onto.

You can also rub a little soap or candle wax on the threads to help ease the screw in. But remember, soap can act as a bond or glue, so don't use it if you plan on removing the screw anytime soon.

If you're using a hand-held screwdriver, remember that the longer the screwdriver blade, the more turning power you'll have.

If you have a problem holding onto the handle, cover it with a rubber bike handlebar grip or put on a pair of rubber gloves.

### Getting a screw out

If you're trying to remove an old screw, clear any debris out of its slot first. The screw may have been painted over, for instance. Scrape out the paint with a utility knife before you start, or tap the screwdriver gently through the slot with a hammer to clear it. Then, remove the screw, always turning to the left.

If a rusted screw is stuck, spritz it with a little lubricant spray, such as WD-40, or put the screwdriver in the screw head and tap the end of the screwdriver with a hammer while trying to turn the screw.

## Using the plunger

A plunger — humanity's original environmentally safe, low-tech machine — is your first line of offense against clogged toilets and drains. You can help your plunger along by rubbing a little petroleum jelly around the lip of the suction cup, which will increase its suction substantially. (Wipe it off after each use.)

Remember, never use a plunger if you've already poured some sort of chemical drain cleaner down your drain or toilet. These cleaners are extremely caustic and poisonous, and you will be plumbing and splashing away in a dangerous pool.

To use a plunger on your drain or toilet, first plug up the overflow hole with a rag. Then hold the plunger over the clogged drain and move it up and down rapidly 10 to 20 times. On the last stroke, lift up the plunger to see if the drain is unclogged. If still clogged, repeat the process. If still clogged after three or four tries, you probably need to call a plumber.

## Using sticky stuff like glue

Manufacturers are constantly coming up with newer and better adhesives. Always consult your local hardware and home store folks to see if they have any new gooey-sticky-magical products available. Even as I write, some chemical engineer somewhere is brewing something even stickier than maple syrup or honey.

When using any glue, always read the instructions carefully to see how long the glue takes to harden (setup time) and for any ventilation restrictions. Some adhesives can be extremely flammable and toxic to breathe. (A friend's parents once tried to install a linoleum backsplash in their kitchen, which involved putting lots of adhesive on the wall to attach the linoleum. The fumes were ignited by the pilot light on the stove and a fire started.) Remember, as with gasoline, the fumes ignite quickly, not the liquid.

Store glues in cool, dry places and always recap them rightly to prevent them from drying or spilling out.

To keep the cap from getting stuck to the top of the tube, coat the inside threads with petroleum jelly.

After you've applied the glue, always be prepared to wipe off any excess with a damp cloth (for wood) or whatever else will do the job. Never allow any spills to set and dry, making them difficult and sometimes impossible to remove. Some glues have a solvent that will allow you to loosen their bond. Get one when you buy the glue in case of accident.

You can find a great number of fairly versatile glues. But no "universal" adhesive exists that is perfect for every surface. Always find the best adhesive for the particular materials and task — see Table 16-1 for some ideas.

| Table 16-1 | Which Adhesive for Which Task? |
| --- | --- |
| *Task* | *Adhesive to Use* |
| Household (ceramics, some metals, and more) | Check label instructions, usually the most general type |
| Metal | Usually a two-part epoxy resin adhesive; check with the store for the type of metal to be glued |
| Wood (Interior) | Carpenter's glue for most tasks |
| Wood (Exterior) | Waterproof powdered synthetic-resin, usually a two-part mixture applied separately to two pieces being glued |

For some tasks, you may want to use an electric glue gun, which melts a *glue stick*. You have a choice of glue sticks for different surfaces. When you press the glue gun trigger, it pushes a plunger or grip down on the glue stick, which then pushes the stick through a heated chamber, forcing the melted glue out of the nozzle. The glue sets while cooling — it's HOT, so be careful. You can also find low-temperature glue guns that set more quickly; these are used often for craft work. Glue guns work best for fast fixes that don't require the smooth, patient touch that most adhesives need. For example, a pad of felt might come loose from the bottom of a lamp. Fix it fast with a bead of hot glue. I've even used it for an emergency repair on the sole of a shoe!

Another great product comes in the form of a puttylike, reusable, adhesive substance marketed under various brand names such as FUN-TAK. Not suitable for heavy objects, it's great for keeping pictures straight on a wall or for holding lightweight pictures or posters. Just put a little ball of it on the bottom back corner of a frame and press it into place. To remove it from the wall, roll it gently off the surface.

Test any product of this type on an inconspicuous spot first to make sure it doesn't stain after you remove it.

# Chapter 17

# Quick Fix-Ups around Your Home

· · · · · · · · · · · · · · · · · · · · · · · · · · · · · · · · · · · · · · · · · ·

### In This Chapter

▶ Fixing doors and floors and furniture

▶ Hanging pictures, shelves, and other stuff

▶ Making wall repairs

▶ Unscrewing a broken bulb and other odds and ends

· · · · · · · · · · · · · · · · · · · · · · · · · · · · · · · · · · · · · · · · · ·

*E*ven if you feel that you're all thumbs, every now and then something in your home will stick, break, or flood with no repair person in sight, and you'll need to try and fix it yourself. Relax, you can do it. With a few simple household tools (see Chapter 16), you can conquer most minor repairs. You don't need to arm yourself with a blowtorch and sledgehammer to unstick a door (unless it's the door to that bank vault where you keep all that money you saved by doing your own repairs).

In this chapter, I give you tips to help you perform some of the most common household repairs. Even if you don't always want to fix it yourself, knowing what's involved will keep you from getting taken by incompetent help.

## Solving Door Problems

Everyone has a sticking door, a squeaky door, or rattling door parts at one time or another. In this section, I explain how to keep your doors opening smoothly and soundlessly.

### Unsticking doors

First find out where the door is sticking. Look over the door carefully to check for any worn areas on the paint or finish. If you can't see anything, slip a piece of carbon paper on the top or bottom of the door frame and close the door on it to see where it rubs. If you don't have any carbon paper, use blackboard chalk to mark the areas.

If the door is tight on the hinge side, check to see if too much dried paint is preventing easy opening action. If so, strip or sand off some of the paint and then repaint it. If the door rubs on the floor, the problem may be loosening hinges. Check the hinge screws to make sure they're all tight. If they're loose, try replacing screws with ones that are about 1½ times longer for a firmer hold. If that doesn't do the trick, hold a piece of coarse sandpaper beneath the door and move the door over it until it swings freely. If the door is tight on the jamb side, try coating the edge of the door with paraffin or a candle wax.

Always fix a sticking door in cool, dry weather. Warmth and humidity swells wood, so your problem may be the weather, not the door.

## Dealing with squeaks and rattles and slams

You can more easily fix a squeaky door than a squeaky shoe, and for a lot less money. To ease the squeak, simply lubricate the hinge and the hinge pin with a little household oil like WD40 or petroleum jelly to ease the squeak.

Though a necessity in every haunted house, a rattling doorknob in a house without spirits can be just plain annoying. Fix the rattle simply by tightening the tiny set screw in the front that holds the knob to its spindle, the metal shaft that runs through the door to hold both knobs in place. If that doesn't work, remove the doorknob and look at the spindle. If the spindle is bent, you'll have to replace it.

If a sliding door rattles, check the bottom door channels, or guides, and replace them if they're worn or missing. If not, try lubricating the channels with a graphite or silicone spray. Don't use oil; it will accumulate dirt.

Occasionally, you hear door slams for no apparent reason. If you have kids, your kids may be the cause of the problem. But if your kids are good and the door is not (or if you have no kids and your house isn't haunted), cut a few tabs of weather stripping or foamy self-stick tape and apply it to the top and bottom of the doorstop molding to cushion the slam.

## Fixing Floors and Stairs

If you have carpeting, wood, or linoleum flooring installed in your house, reserving extra yardage or setting aside sections of it for repairs is always a good practice. I'm not talking about bedroom-sized portions, more like linen closet-sized.

In the following sections, I explain how to deal with various types of floor problems.

## Replacing wood parquet tiles

If a section of your wood parquet floor is damaged, remove it with a 1-inch chisel and hammer, starting in the center of the tile to be replaced. Don't worry about breaking the tongue and groove (a lip and a slot to which it interlocks), which connects each tile to the next.

Chisel a hole in the center of the tile by pounding on the end of a chisel with a hammer (see Figure 17-1). Then slide the chisel underneath, moving it to the outer edges of the tile to break up the glue. Take off the tile and scrape away any mastic (resin or varnish) on the floor. Level off the floor by rubbing it lightly with sandpaper. Vacuum up the excess and remove any dust.

Check to make sure the new tile will fit in with the old ones. Use a keyhole saw to remove the tongue (the protruding edge) from one side of the new tile, as shown in Figure 17-2.

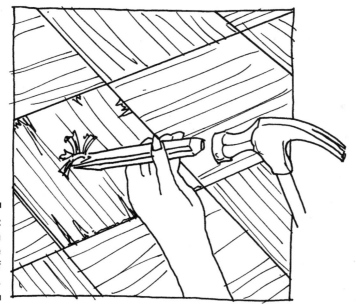

**Figure 17-1:**
Chiseling a hole in the center of the tile.

Brush on new adhesive underneath the section and apply wood glue to the sides. Replace the tile, being extra careful to fit the new grooves into the tongues of the old tiles. Wipe off excess glue and allow the tile to set 24 hours.

**Figure 17-2:**
Removing
the tongue.

## Replacing vinyl tiles

Remove old vinyl tile by placing a towel over the tile and going over it with an iron set on low to loosen the adhesive (see Figure 17-3).

**Figure 17-3:**
Loosen the
adhesive
with a low
iron.

Use a putty knife to carefully pry up the tile without damaging those surrounding. Check to see if the new tile fits. (If necessary, adjust the new tile to fit by sanding its edges with a fine-grade sandpaper.) Vacuum the area to remove any dirt or debris; then apply new adhesive to the subfloor, as shown in Figure 17-4.

Put the new tile in place and wipe off any excess adhesive. Use a rolling pin on the tile to press it into place. (Cover the pin with plastic wrap to make sure no glue gets on the rolling pin.) Weigh down the tile with books or bricks for at least 8 hours. Figure 17-5 illustrates this process.

If you have a vinyl tile that's pulling away from the floor and curling up around the edges, place a towel over the tile and hold an iron on it long enough to soften the adhesive underneath. Lift up the tile and apply fresh adhesive to the curled area. Weigh down the tile with books or a brick until the adhesive dries.

**Figure 17-4:**
Apply new
adhesive to
the subfloor.

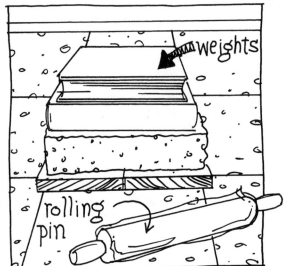

**Figure 17-5:**
Replacing
vinyl tiles.

# Replacing ceramic tiles

Replacing a cracked or worn ceramic tile may seems a little stressful, but it's not really that hard. Just make sure that you wear safety glasses. Use a cold chisel and hammer. (A cold chisel is very similar to a wood chisel, but its heavier steel is designed for cracking out masonry and old pipes.) Start at the center of the tile and crack it out to the grout. Remove the tile and the grout around it. Vacuum out remaining pieces thoroughly. Use a paint scraper and sandpaper to get up any remaining glue. Remove any other debris. Apply tile adhesive and place in the new tile, centering it in the opening. Let set overnight. Follow tile grout instructions on package to fill the area around the new tile.

# Fixing squeaky floors and stairs

Squeaky floors may be caused by loose boards. Find the *joists* (supporting beams) that the flooring boards are attached to by locating the existing nail heads. Hammer 1 ¼ inch finishing nails or brads (another type of nail) through the flooring into the joists to stop the squeaks. Always try to fix a squeaky floor before installing any carpet. If a squeaky floor develops, lift up the carpet to hammer in the brads.

For a quick fix, try a lubricant like graphite. Sand some graphite from a pencil and work it into the cracks. A little talcum powder may also work. Wipe off the excess.

(**Downstairs neighbor tip:** If you can't get rid of squeaky floors, install carpeting with a pad.)

Hey, squeaky stairs are even more creepy than squeaky floors. Try blowing a little graphite into the seam where the stair meets the riser to lubricate it. If that doesn't take care of it, carefully remove the molding — called the *shoe molding* — where the stair meets the riser. Pry the two slightly apart and squeeze some wood glue or resin adhesive into the space. Wipe off the excess. Replace the molding and allow the glue to set before using the steps.

## Fixing carpet problems

For immovable surface stains like glue spills or minor cigarette burns, try using a razor to gently shave the stain off the carpet surface.

If that doesn't do the trick, use that spare piece of carpeting you saved as a replacement. (If you don't have one or can't find it, cut away a small piece of carpet from a hidden area such as inside a closet or under a piece of furniture that's never moved.)

Here's how to repair small stains using double-face-faced carpeting tape (available at home centers or carpet stores), heavy-duty fabric glue, and a utility knife:

1. **Cut pieces of scrap carpeting slightly larger than the damaged spot. To keep your cuts straight, use a metal ruler to guide the utility knife.**

2. **Cut out the damaged area, using the cut piece of scrap carpeting as a template. Be careful not to cut through the pad.**

3. **Remove the damaged piece and put the new patch in place to make sure it fits. Carefully trim it with scissors, if necessary. Then remove the patch.**

4. **Put double-sided tape around the edges of the hole. Lightly apply fabric glue around the edges of the patch. Lay the patch on the tape and press firmly in place to secure. Fluff up the fibers to make it match the surrounding area.**

If the patch is large, use a kitchen bowl as a stencil and cut around the stain with a utility knife. Then, use the same repair procedure described for small repairs. (I know this works because I once spilled a gallon of black paint on an unnamed friend's carpeting and repaired it before they got home using this same method. They never knew what happened!)

# Furniture Fixes

Dressers, drawers, and side tables don't just hold our socks, T-shirts, and tea cups. They're also the proud holders of those little annoyances like tippy legs, sticky drawers, and loose handles. But don't fret, for every problem, there's a solution.

## Fixing sticky drawers

To repair a sticking drawer, first remove the drawer and check to see if anything has come loose on the drawer or internally in the cabinet. Sometimes, you need to re-glue a loose side or tap the drawer back together with a hammer. Usually, it's the runners or *drawer channel glides* (internal supports that hold the drawer on both sides) that cause the problem (see Figure 17-6). Rub the sides of the glides with a bar of soap or a piece of wax. Move the drawer back and forth in the cabinet to distribute the soap. If that doesn't work, try inserting two or three flat head thumbtacks toward the front on each drawer channel glide. They should do the trick.

**Figure 17-6:** Getting the channel glides back on track.

Humidity can also swell a wood drawer. Try putting the drawer in an oven set on low for several minutes or outside in the warm sun for a couple of hours. Then put the drawer back in to see if it slides smoothly. If it does, apply a coat of wood preservative to the unfinished wood to stop it from swelling again.

## Ironing out dents

When you started your new exercise routine, did you accidentally bump a dresser with those shiny new barbells? If you did, try ironing the dent away. Put your iron on a medium steam setting. Dampen several layers of clean cotton fabric, put them on the blemish, and let the iron sizzle away until it stops talking back. Repeat applications if necessary, checking the surface after each one.

## Tightening chair rungs

Fixing loose chair rungs is always something that everyone puts off until Uncle Harry collapses the chair one Thanksgiving. Don't wait. As soon as the chair starts to wobble, find the source. Usually, a rung is beginning to work loose, which means that the glue is old and needs to be replaced. Work the rung loose all the way if you can. If that's not possible, dab around it with a cotton swab and a little warm vinegar to loosen the glue. Then pull out the rung.

To remove glue inside a round mortise, wrap sandpaper around the end of a dowel or wooden spoon and insert it into hole. Or use your utility knife to scrape off all the old glue; be careful to take off just the glue, not the wood.

After you've scraped away all the glue, slip the rung into the hole. If it fits snugly, coat it with glue and insert it in the socket. You don't want a loose fit. If the rung still appears loose, wrap some thread around the end before you coat it with glue to make a tight fit. To hold it together while it's drying, wrap some twine around the two legs just below the rung and tie loosely. Then insert a couple of pencils into the twine and twist to tighten. You may want to wrap a soft, thick cloth around each leg first to prevent the rope from biting into the wood.

A broken chair rung can be fixed by gluing it with wood glue and then wrapping it tight with masking tape. And, of course, wipe off any excess glue before taping it. After it sets, remove the tape.

## Dealing with loose knobs

If knobs on furniture wiggle, a screw is usually loose somewhere. Find it and tighten it. If the knob is broken, you need to purchase a replacement, which is sometimes hard to match with what you already have. Instead, why not give your furniture a whole new look with ceramic, metal, or wood knobs? Many decorative ones are available today at home centers. Just make sure that they fit in the old hole.

## No winning against warping

*Warping* (curvature of a normally straight piece of wood) usually is caused by moisture getting into unfinished wood. Warping is a tough problem. You may want to try a cabinet shop or take some artistic license and consider the piece a distressed antique.

## Topping tippy legs

The easiest way to deal with an uneven table or chair leg is to call a waiter over to put a folded napkin under it. Oops! You're at home, so I guess the waiter's out (though you can still fold something under the short leg to even it out).

The good-looking and long-lasting way to fix the problem follows: First, move the item to make sure that the floor isn't crooked.

If your floor is fine, you need to find out which leg is off and place pieces of cardboard or a wooden *shim* (a thin, usually tapered object used to fill in spaces) under it until the wobbling stops. If it's less than $\frac{1}{16}$ inch, you may be able to sand down the other legs to the level of the shimmed one. If it's more, mark the other legs with a pencil and trim off with a hacksaw.

# Wall Works

Walls are another area that take a beating and call for frequent intervention. The following sections describe ways to manage the most common problems.

## Sealing small holes

Did you decide to rearrange those photos on your wall? Those photos do look better by the door, but now you have all those little holes in the wall where the photos used to be. What to do? Apply some ready-mix spackle. You can purchase a small container of it at a home center store.

To fix the hole, first brush away any loose material or cracked edges. Moistening the area with a damp sponge sometimes helps, but check the instructions on your spackle first. Then use your finger or a putty knife to apply the spackle into the hole (see Figure 17-7).

**Figure 17-7:**
Fixing a
hole.

Let it dry and then sand it smooth with a fine grade sandpaper. After you finish, reseal the spackle tube tightly because it dries out quickly.

If you want a fast fix-up for a tiny hole, try using a dab of white tooth paste or typewriter correction fluid.

## Securing screws that pull out

Screws often lose their grip in wood when the hole becomes too large to hold the threads. You can try several solutions to fix this:

- ✔ The first and simplest is to insert one or more glue-coated wooden matchsticks, wood-shavings, toothpicks, or even golf tees into the hole. Snap them off level and then try reinserting the screw (see Figure 17-8).
- ✔ You can also fill the hole with wood putty. Let dry. Then, reinsert the screw.
- ✔ Finally, try inserting a slightly larger screw in the hole.

## Repairing ripped wallcovering

If a piece of wallcovering gets ripped or torn, always try to repair what's there first. You may be able to simply rub the back of the tear with some latex adhesive and smooth it into place.

**Figure 17-8:**
Filling in for
screws.

If you can't repair the tear with what remains, you'll have to patch it. Ideally, when you wallpaper you should save any remnants left over from a roll, which you can later use for repairs. If no remnants are available, remove some wallcovering from an inconspicuous area — behind a dresser, for instance — to make a patch. You can also try to purchase a new roll. To make the patch:

1. **Cut a piece of covering to match the pattern, making sure it is slightly larger than the damaged area.**

2. **Hold the piece against the wall, lightly taping it into place if necessary.**

3. **Then cut through both layers of the covering with a sharp utility knife.**

   If possible, follow any vertical or horizontal lines in your pattern, which will help hide the cut edges.

4. **Remove the damaged area and fit the new patch in place, securing it with adhesive.**

Depending on where the damage is, this might be the perfect time and place to hang a picture over the damaged spot.

# Removing paint splatters

Remove paint stains and splatters as quickly as possible; don't let them dry. Use the proper solvent for the type of paint.

- ✔ Most latex and acrylic paints can be removed with water.
- ✔ Cellulose paints should be treated with cellulose thinners.
- ✔ Oil-based paints should be sponged with paint thinner in a well-ventilated room.

If small drops of paint have spilled onto carpeting and dried on, try using a sharp utility knife or single-edged razor blade to shave them off.

# Hanging things on the wall

Hanging pictures is one project that practically everyone has to cope with at one time or another. Whether it's your children's artwork or an old painting of your ancestors, you need to consider the weight and size of the item you're dealing with and the kind of wall you're hanging it on.

Put your item on the bathroom scale to get an exact weight and use a tape measure to find out exact dimensions. Take these measurements with you to the hardware store.

You can choose from many different types of hangers and hooks available for practically every hanging situation. The instructions on the back of the package will tell you which one to choose.

Overcompensate slightly when buying supporting hardware for an object. If the frame actually weighs 20 pounds, buy a hook that will support 70 to 80 pounds. Overcompensating gives you the peace of mind that your precious object won't fall off the wall.

### Getting it straight

Finding the right place to make a hole in the wall for the hook can be hard. To make it easier, cut a piece of paper exactly the same size as the frame. Put the paper on the back of the frame and pull up the wire in its center until it forms a "V" shape. Mark that point on the paper. Use this pattern to decide where you want to hang the picture on the wall. When you've picked the perfect place, poke a hole through the point on the paper and mark where you want to hang it on the wall. When you hang the picture, it will be at exactly the level you want.

Another easy method is to hold the picture by the wire and decide where you want it. Lightly wet your fingertip and press it on the wall where the nail should go. The fingerprint will stay wet long enough for you to use it as a mark on the wall.

### Keeping it still

If your pictures won't hang straight, wrap the wire with masking tape on either side of the center where you hang the hook to stop the wire from sliding. Another remedy is to hang it with two hooks. Keep a picture from moving by putting a couple loops of masking tape with the sticky side out or FUN-TAK on the bottom two corners of the frame. If the tape or tacky stuff sticks to the wall when you take down the picture, use a gentle rolling motion to remove it.

### Finding the stud

Very heavy items are best nailed into the *studs,* the vertical supports in the wall, for additional support. Studs are usually 16 inches apart but in some new construction can be as much as 24 inches apart. Most of the time, studs are wood, but some modern high rise apartments have steel. If you're going to be doing a lot of hanging, you might want to buy a *stud finder,* an electronic device that signals when it passes over a stud.

Other ways of finding a stud are to knock lightly on the wall with your fist or a hammer in a horizontal direction. The wall will sound hollow until you reach the more solid tones of the stud. Or check the baseboards for nail heads that are usually driven into the studs.

### Knowing your wall

Most walls in homes today are composed of plasterboard, drywall, or wood paneling nailed to studs. Because a cavity is created between the walls, they sound hollow when you knock on them. If you start nailing and the nail goes in easily, you've hit a hollow spot between the studs. If the nail goes in easily and then meets some slight resistance, you've probably hit a stud. If you meet more resistance, stop and inspect where you're nailing.

Don't force a drill or hammer into anything. It could be a pipe or something else that shouldn't be messed with.

### Hanging lightweight items

To hang an item that weighs 10 pounds or less, you can use prepackaged picture hooks and nails or the adhesive hangers on plaster and drywall. For something a little heavier, two hooks nailed at about two-thirds the width of the frame will give it extra support and prevent it from shifting.

To prevent damage to the wall surface, you may want to use a fastener called an *anchor,* which helps prevent chipping and is especially helpful in plaster and cement walls (see Figure 17-9).

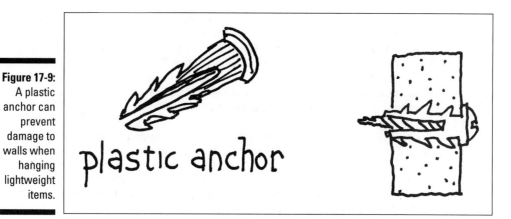

**Figure 17-9:**
A plastic anchor can prevent damage to walls when hanging lightweight items.

You drill a hole slightly smaller than the anchor (see the recommended drill size on the package). Then hammer the anchor into the wall. When you insert the screw, it opens up the anchor, hooking it into the wall for a more secure grip.

### Hanging medium to heavyweight items

To hang objects that weigh 20 pounds or more in hollow walls, consider using toggle bolts or expansion bolts, usually called *molly bolts* (see Figure 17-10).

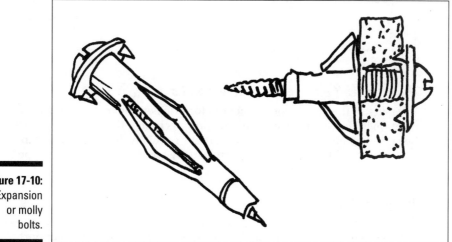

**Figure 17-10:**
Expansion or molly bolts.

Expansion bolts, or molly bolts, are a combination anchor and toggle bolt. They open up, securing the housing inside the wall and gripping it. They won't fall off when you remove the screw, so you can change what you're hanging. They come in a variety of wall widths. To use, drill a hole for the bolt to fit, put the molly inside, and turn the screw until it flattens against the wall. If you're hanging something weighing 30 pounds or more, use at least two fasteners to distribute the weight more evenly.

*Toggle bolts* have spider-like legs that open and snug up to the inside of the wall. Their disadvantage is that when you remove the bolt, the toggle drops off inside the wall. To use, you drill a hole big enough for the bolt to fit into. Then you take off the screw and put it through the hanger on your frame or shelf. Reattach the toggle and push the toggle assembly back into the wall and tighten the screw (see Figure 17-11).

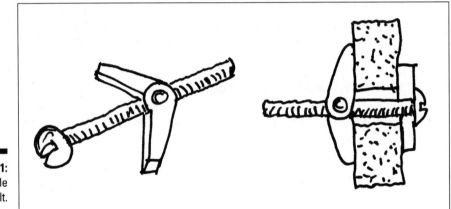

**Figure 17-11:**
A toggle bolt.

### Hanging stuff on brick or concrete walls

You can use the same type of anchors for brick or concrete walls that we mention in the previous section. The process is slightly more complicated because you need a bit for your drill that's specially designed to drill into masonry walls. Drilling into concrete usually takes more time, but if you're patient, you can make it.

### Hanging shelving

One of the most common forms of shelving uses slotted metal shelf supports. If the shelves are going to hold heavy items, such as books, the supports should be attached to studs in the wall. See the section "Finding the stud" for how to find the studs in the wall.

To put up metal shelf supports:

1. **Attach the top of the first support loosely to the wall.**

2. **Check for vertical straightness with a level (see Figure 17-12) or plumb line.**

   A *plumb line* is basically a string with a weight on the end that makes it hang straight. You should hold the top of the string where the first support is attached to the wall and then let rest of the string with the weight hang down. The place it touches at the bottom is the perfect vertical measurement.

**Figure 17-12:**
Finding
plumb.

3. **Mark the position for the bottom screw.**

4. **Have someone hold the second support in position with brackets and a shelf attached.**

5. **Use a level on the top to check for horizontal straightness (see Figure 17-13).**

6. **Mark the screw positions on the second support and attach to wall studs.**

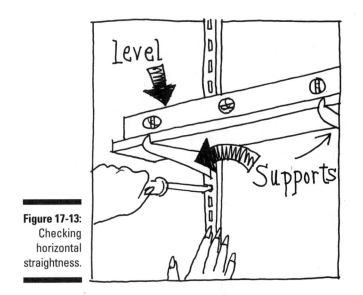

**Figure 17-13:**
Checking
horizontal
straightness.

As a general rule, shelves will sag (bend downward in the middle) with weight and age. To prevent this, avoid placing shelf supports more than 30 inches apart — 24 inches is ideal.

# A word about wood

Suppose that you're going to make your own shelves or bookcase. These three tips are fresh from the lumber yard:

✔ Measure what you'll need and have the lumber yard pre-cut it to your specifications for a small cost.

✔ To save yourself from some back-breaking lifting, check to see if the lumber yard will deliver the wood to your home. Delivery is often free if you buy a certain amount — and it's much easier than loading all that lumber into your car.

Just to make things a little more tricky, lumber is not the actual size that it's labeled. For example, a 2x4 isn't actually 2 inches by 4 inches. Here are some common lumber sizes and their actual measurements:

1 x 2 (actually ¾ inch x 1 ½ inch)

1 x 8 (actually ¾ inch x 7¼ inches)

1 x 10 (actually ¾ inch x 9¼ inches)

2 x 4 (actually 1½ inches x 3¼ inches)

Keep this in mind when you're premeasuring.

# Miscellaneous Household Fix-Ups

Some home fix-ups just don't fit into any category, but that doesn't mean that they aren't performed day in and day out. Here are common ones that I've done several times in my own home.

## Glue together china and glassware (or turn it into art)

I love cheap, or should I say inexpensive, wine glasses — I never feel bad when they break. Let's face it, stemmed glasses seem designed to tip over: all that liquid high off the table, supported by one thin, little stem. If you have really fine china or glass, use it. Don't just let it sit in a cabinet somewhere because you're afraid it will get broken. Enjoy its beauty. But if it does get broken, you should really contact a professional, depending on its dollar or sentimental value, for the best repair.

You can repair minor cracks and chips with a good household cement. Broken handles or knobs that get a lot of stress and strain will probably require a stronger bond, such as epoxy. Remember, if you repair it, the object will never be as strong as it once was.

Not that I'm a butterfingers or anything, but I have broken a few plates and bowls in my day. To avoid frantic piecing and gluing the pieces of my accidents back together, I've come up with a unique solution. I make mosaics out of them. Save all the pieces and crack up the rest of the now not-treasured object into workable chips and bits and use it to tile a frame or a lamp. Recycle your accidents.

## Unscrew a broken light bulb

Before you do any repair or maintenance on a lamp — or anything electrical, for that matter — always unplug the item first.

Often, if a glass bulb is rusty or has been in a lamp a long time, it sticks when you go to unscrew it, causing it to break. It's scary when it happens, but it's a simple problem to remedy.

Cut a potato in half and jam it onto the light bulb base stuck in its socket. Then, using the potato as your grip, unscrew the bulb. Before replacing the bulb, make sure you wipe off any moisture the potato may have left in the socket.

If the potato doesn't work, you can also use needlenose pliers to firmly grip one edge of the metal base and slowly turn it out.

## Revive a vacuum cleaner

I have actually retrieved two vacuum cleaners from the garbage in my apartment building — two practically new vacuum cleaners that people thought were broken.

If you have a hose-type vacuum cleaner, remember that pieces of debris can get stuck in the hose. When that happens, some folks think that their vacuum no longer works, so they toss it. Don't make that mistake: Always check the hose first. Remove it from the vacuum and take off any attachments. Stretch it out and try to look through it. If there's no light at the end of that tunnel, then you probably have a traffic jam in there. You can use a broom handle or a bent hanger to dislodge anything inside.

## Stop and think

Check out the basics before reaching for the hammer or calling a repair person. Is the item plugged in all the way? Is it turned on? Is the tape rewound? Is the power on? Are openings blocked? Don't just think the answer (though you need to think through what the problem might be). Know the answer. Check it out. Then you won't make your repair bigger than it needs to be, or need to fix something that wasn't broken before you tried to fix it.

# Chapter 18

# Preventing Indoor Pests

• • • • • • • • • • • • • • • • • • • • • • • • • • • • • • • • • • • • • • • • • • • • • •

## In This Chapter

▶ Eliminating avenues for pest entry

▶ Dealing with ants, fleas, flies, moths, roaches, and other common kitchen pests

• • • • • • • • • • • • • • • • • • • • • • • • • • • • • • • • • • • • • • • • • • • • • •

*N*othing is creepier than spotting an army of pests marching across the floor. They're invading your territory, and they haven't even received an invitation (at least, not one you know about). If you see one bug, ya gotta know that there's more than one around. They're entering your house from some hidden place, and they're up to no good.

Remember that the best offense is a good defense. Mount your defensive strategy immediately:

- ✔ **Lock out bugs.** Screens should be everywhere — not just on the windows, but covering any opening such as the chimney, vents, and shower and bath drains. Check periodically to make sure the screens have no rips or tears to allow pests inside.

  Inspect the outside of the house for any cracks or crevices where varmints can enter. Look for openings around the telephone, cable, and electrical wires that enter the house.

- ✔ **Cut down on bugs' liquid refreshments.** Pipes, faucets, toilets, bathtubs, and washing machines provide much-needed drink for any thirsty critter. Check under sinks in the bathroom and kitchen, and check the laundry area for dripping pipes and faucets or for standing water. Look for condensation on pipes and for leaks around the toilet area.

  Regularly pull out and empty the drip pan under the refrigerator.

  Don't let water collect and sit for several days in the saucers under your plants.

- ✔ **Stop feeding them.** Don't ever leave food sitting around unprotected. Store any food supplies — such as sugar, cereal, or coffee — in kitchen cupboards tightly sealed in glass or plastic containers.

> Wash dishes after each meal. If you want to leave a pot or pan soaking in the sink, fill it with soapy water and wash it before you go to bed.

> Clean out the pet bowl after Fido or Fluffy is finished. Even better, serve dog or cat food on paper plates and throw them away afterwards.

> Make sure your garbage can is covered with a tight-fitting lid.

If bugs do invade your home (and they're incredibly resourceful critters), then you need to go on the offensive. Human beings have used a multitude of toxic chemicals as they wage war against pests. Although many pests have been killed, even more have proved resistant to even the strongest insecticides. Meanwhile, the earth's natural resources and our own bodies are constantly being exposed to their chemical effects, risking a healthy future. For yourself and your environment, when you see or suspect pests, try the following nontoxic bug beaters first. Some of these products will be on the shelves right in your kitchen; you'll find others in your neighborhood garden center.

✔ **Soap:** Simple soap will act to kill or drown bugs within your home, and you get the added benefit of cleaning up in the process. Mix together 1 tablespoon of liquid dishwashing soap in a quart of water. Spray it on the bugs or set it around in saucers. When the bugs search for water, they lap up the soap and it's curtains! Because this soapy solution is so mild, you may need to reapply it every few days to maintain its effectiveness until the bugs leave.

✔ **Diatomaceous earth:** Diatomaceous (dye-at-oh-MAY-shuss) earth is a horticultural-grade mineral dust, available in garden centers, that kills insects without affecting animals, birds, or people. Mix this mineral dust with water and spray it on plants, or sprinkle it around a garden as a bug barrier. Wear a mask and goggles when you apply the mixture to prevent the dust from getting in your mouth, eyes, or nasal passages.

✔ **Pyrethrum:** This pesticide, made from the blossoms of dried pyrethrum plants (a daisy-like type of chrysanthemum), is an effective insecticide against many bugs, from roaches to termites to white flies. It works fast and is not harmful to humans.

In the following sections, I give advice for eliminating specific pests, from roaches to rats. I hope you won't need these tips, but another battle mantra is to know your enemy. Consider the following sections an introduction.

## Combating Common Kitchen Bugs

It makes sense that bugs would love to join us snacking in the kitchen. Many of them love to eat the grains and dried foods that we store on the shelves where they live: flour, grains, beans, spaghetti, nuts, and so on.

## Apartment dwellers unite!

If you live in an apartment, remember that you are not alone. You have to coordinate your pest war with everyone else in the building, especially those living near you. It doesn't do much good if you get rid of the bugs in your apartment if they crawl in the next day from your neighbor's place. Get together with your neighbors to agree on a method of pest control. Try to convince others to use non-toxic methods first.

If your building has a common laundry room, check to make sure the pipes are dry. Keep the garbage area clean and make sure that pick-up is frequent. If anyone has pets, establish policies about picking up and disposing of their droppings. Meet with the landlord to make sure the property is kept clean and pest control methods are in place.

Two of the most commonly seen kitchen bugs are:

- ✔ **Meal moths:** Meal moths like to hang out in dried foods, soup, flours, crackers, chocolate, and pet food. You can sometimes see them flying around at night. You can tell they've been in the food because they leave little threads that clump together with the food on the sides of the package.

- ✔ **Flour beetles:** These bugs are also very common. They eat the same varieties as the meal moths — grains, flour, dried beans, and so on. They lay eggs that become covered with flour and stick on the side of the container.

Some classic methods of repelling these prolific bugs include sprinkling bay leaves in the storage containers or spreading them on kitchen shelves, a favorite of meticulous housekeepers for years. (Bay leaves also keep roaches at bay.)

Another kitchen spice — black pepper — not only repels, but also kills the bugs. You can sprinkle it on shelves, but you might want to think twice about sprinkling it in your grains or flour unless you're a dyed-in-the-wool pepper lover.

To get rid of any bug that might be in flour or grains when you bring them home from the store, put the whole bag in the freezer. Leave it there anywhere from three days to one week. The cold temperature kills off the bugs. If you've got a bad bug problem, consider storing all your grains and flours in closed containers in the refrigerator. Most flour companies recommend this bug-safe method.

Inspect all boxes and bags of food when you bring them home from the store. Look for holes in the bag or clumps that cling to the side. Throw out or return any that have bugs. To be extra cautious, transfer the bug-free food to metal, glass, or heavy plastic containers with tight-fitting lids, preferably with a rubber seal.

If you do find bugs on your shelves, remove whatever food they're in and throw it out. Check everything else around it to make sure the bugs haven't moved on to their next course in the box next door. Remove any infested food and wash the area with a heavy-duty household cleaner.

## *Attacking ants*

One thing ants don't like is a clean kitchen. Keep your kitchen clean, and the ants will be put off. Minimally, do these three basic tasks:

- ✔ Always wash the dishes after meals and wipe off counters.
- ✔ Clean off jars that contain sticky or oily substances that drip — such as honey, corn syrup, or maple syrup.
- ✔ Sponge down the counter with a cloth soaked in vinegar or spray the surfaces with citrus oil and water — both smells that ants don't like.

Use any of these three methods to keep ants out of the house:

- ✔ Plant peppermint at the entrances or crush mint leaves and sprinkle them around the door.
- ✔ Place coffee grounds around the doors and windows where they enter.
- ✔ Follow the ants back to where they entered the home and make a solid line about ¼ inch wide with cayenne pepper, turmeric, powdered charcoal, and powdered cleanser containing chlorine bleach. They won't want to cross the barrier.

If you develop a problem with ants indoors, spritz the ants with a household cleaning product such as window cleaner or household spray like Formula 409. Or use a mixture of 1 teaspoon liquid dishwashing soap and water in a spray bottle. While you're spritzing, clean up everything around the ant. If you spot some tiny cracks, cover them with petroleum jelly temporarily. When you have more time, permanently caulk wherever the ants enter — usually windowsills, baseboards, and thresholds.

Ants outdoors are usually not a problem — they clean up dead things. But if ants are invading your garbage can, plant peppermint or tansy around it to deter them from terrorizing your trash. If that's not possible, crush some dried mint and sprinkle it around the can.

If ants are in outdoor places where you don't want them to be, spray the ants with the same soap mixture you used indoors.

To keep ants at bay while you're having a picnic, place each leg of the table in a bowl of water. Ants don't want to swim over it.

If you need to destroy the ants' nest, pour boiling water down the hole or squirt soapy water into it.

## Fighting fleas

Fleas can make the lives of both you and your pet miserable. Not only do they ride in on your animal's fur, but they can jump off and hide in the furniture and carpet. Fleas love the warm humid temperatures of late summer and fall, so the problem escalates at that time of year. If your pet is starting to scratch a lot, check him for fleas by looking beneath the fur to see if any tiny black dots appear on the skin. If you can't see them but are still concerned, take your pet outside and have it stand on some damp, light-colored paper. Comb through the fur with a fine-toothed, metal comb. If your pet has fleas, tiny black dots show up on the comb; when you shake the dots onto the paper, they turn red. Comb your pet often to pick up fleas and eggs on its fur. Then dip the comb in a mixture of rubbing alcohol and water to kill the fleas.

The best way to keep fleas off your pet is constant grooming and cleaning. Bathe your pet often and give it a good, thorough shampoo with a mild soap. Rub the soap all over the animal's body, literally from head to tail. Let the shampoo sit on the skin for about five minutes, and it will drown the fleas. Always groom your pet outdoors if you think it has fleas to keep them from infesting the house.

Many pet shampoos made specifically to fight fleas are available that contain herbal repellents such as oil of citronella, eucalyptus, or pyrethrum. Or you can add orange oil to the pet's regular shampoo. Although these substances are nontoxic, you should use them with caution. Consult your veterinarian.

You can make your own flea-repelling potion with simple ingredients you have around the house. Cut up three lemons and put them in a bowl with 3 cups of boiling water. Let it steep overnight and sponge this mixture over your pet's skin. The fleas should die immediately.

Or you can make your own flea trap by placing a small cushion on the floor and topping it with a heating pad set on low heat. Cover that with a piece of flannel with some diatomaceous earth (mineral dust available in garden centers) or boric acid sprinkled on top. When the fleas jump on the flannel to get warm, they meet their demise. Keep dogs and children away from this magic pillow.

Even though you clean your pet, you could still have fleas lingering around the house. Vacuum all carpets, upholstered furniture, and floors every few days to keep down the fleas. Throw away the vacuum bag afterwards to avoid reintroducing fleas when you vacuum next.

If you have a real problem, you may need to sprinkle your carpet with a flea-treating borate powder. Check with your pet supply store for specific brands. Rub the powder evenly into the carpet and then vacuum, following the instructions on the box. To avoid breathing in the powder, wear a dust mask and goggles while you apply this mixture.

## Buzzing off the lowly fly

Who hasn't been driven crazy by a fly buzzing around? Flies seem to appear in the most unlikely places and at the most inopportune times. I can never figure out how a fly can get inside a 10th floor apartment building in the middle of winter.

Even though you may think "It's only a fly," you need to eliminate flies as soon as possible because they carry lots of germs with them. Many diseases, from hepatitis to cholera, have been attributed to the fly.

Be on the attack when you see flies. Hit them with a fly swatter or a rolled up piece of paper or magazine.

 If you can't catch the fly, spray it a little hair spray, spray starch, or rubbing alcohol to stun them and slow down their buzzing enough for you to land a punch. Another sneaky way to outwit flies is to shut all the doors and close the drapes. Make the house dark but leave a slight opening so that some light comes through. The fly will fly towards the light and you can swat it.

Some natural repellents are quite good for warding off flies:

- ✔ Put sweet clover from your front yard in little bags of netting (you can buy the fabric in a fabric or camping store) and hang above doorways in your house.

- ✔ Make a potpourri from bay leaves, cloves, eucalyptus leaves, and clover blossoms. Crush slightly to release the scent and hang in netting bags.

- ✔ Outside of the house, a few basil or tansy plants around the doorways will keep them away.

Avoid using pest strips or aerosol pesticides, which emit toxic vapors that can get into your lungs.

This won't come as any surprise to you, but flies like garbage and food. So keep the fly population down with good cleaning habits.

✔ Don't leave food out on the kitchen counters.

    If you like to leave fruit out at room temperature to ripen, check it often and remove any that's getting soft. To fight off an attack of fruit flies, place a cup or bowl with sweet wine or liqueur in it near the fruit. The flies will dive into the alcohol and die happy.

✔ Hose down garbage cans after they're empty, dry them thoroughly, and sprinkle the bottoms with dry soap. Always keep the lids on and repair or replace them if they get any cracks or holes.

✔ Separate your wet and dry garbage if possible. Wrap anything that's soggy with several layers of newspaper.

✔ Rinse out bottles and cans that you're saving for recycling.

✔ After your pet finishes eating, remove the food and wash out the bowl. Pets and flies seem to be companions for life.

## Managing mice and rats

Once again, good sanitation habits help keep mice and rats away.

✔ Get sturdy metal garbage cans — rodents can eat through plastic. Cover them with tight-fitting lids and use a stand at least a foot high that keeps them upright off the ground.

✔ Don't leave pet food dishes filled up outside.

✔ Inside the house, keep any food on the shelves in glass or metal containers if you have a rodent problem. Nothing should be left on the counters.

✔ Keep closets, basements, attics, and garages clean. Eliminate any stacks of magazines or newspapers that rodents can use to hang out in and build their nests.

To keep mice and rats from entering your house, seal up any openings. Make a thorough search around utility cables, basement windows, cracks in masonry, and dryer vents. Cover up any holes with caulking, steel wool, metal, and cement. Put metal barriers on the bottom of doors if the doors don't fit tightly. Mice can get in tiny openings as small as ¼ inch wide. If you suspect you have a mouse problem but haven't seen one of the little rodents yet, don't be surprised. They're very adept at hiding. You can tell they're around by the droppings, gnawed wood, or smudge marks along the walls where they usually run.

To get rid of mice, you have to set traps near their nests.

- ✔ To find the nest, sprinkle some talcum powder on the floor where you've seen signs of them scampering about. When the mice step in the powder, they leave tracks on their way back to the nest.

- ✔ Position the traps along walls where the mice usually run and put the baited end next to the wall. Try to locate the area where mice are most active and put several traps near it, spaced no more than six feet apart.

You can choose from two basic types of traps: glue boards and wooden traps.

- ✔ *Glue boards* have gluelike paper that rodents stick to when they run on it. Entice the animals to step on the board by placing some food in the middle of the trap. The problem with glue boards is that the animal will be alive when you catch it. If you have the stomach for it, you can "dispose" of the animal by drowning it in water or hitting it with a stick, or you can try releasing it outside. Never touch a rodent with your fingers; wear disposable gloves or pick them up with tongs or pieces of wood.

- ✔ *Old-fashioned wooden traps* are the most familiar. You can bait them with a variety of things, including pieces of cheese, bacon, dried fruit, or a spoonful of peanut butter sprinkled with cornmeal. Change the bait frequently so it looks fresh and appealing.

Be careful to keep these traps out of the range of young children. They could be injured if the trap snaps their fingers or if they eat the bait. Avoid using poison. Not only can the poison mistakenly be eaten by children, but if the mice ingest it, they may die slowly in the walls of the house, leaving an unpleasant smell afterwards.

## Conquering clothes moths and carpet beetles

You can usually see the telltale signs of moths or carpet beetles when you take your clothes out of storage for the season. After moths have chomped on your clothing, you can see holes with jagged edges; the mark of carpet beetles is little round shapes. Both pests feast on hair, lint, wool, fur, and various other fabrics. Although most people blame clothes damage on moths, carpet beetles can damage your wardrobe in addition to attacking upholstery, curtains, and carpets.

Cedar closets have long been used to repel moths. Of course, most of us don't have the luxury of a cedar-lined closet. However, you can buy cedar planks and paneling at home centers to install on the walls of an existing closet. Cedar coat hangers and chips or small hanging balls of cedar have some repelling qualities, but they aren't as effective as lining the whole closet.

 Another moth control method is to tie a few bay leaves together and hang them from the closet rod. Or make herbal sachets by wrapping a combination of lavender, mint, cloves, eucalyptus, or black pepper in a square of loose fabric or netting. Experiment to see what scent you like best. Just remember to squeeze the herbs from time to time to release the scent.

The best defense against moths and carpet beetles is to keep your closet and everything in it perfectly clean. Before you store clothing, make sure that it's newly washed or dry cleaned. If you can, air out clothes that haven't been worn for a while by taking them out of the closet and giving them a good shake before hanging them out in the sun on a clothes line.

 If you're an apartment dweller, like me, or don't have a clothesline, put the clothes in a dryer on air fluff for a few minutes. Afterwards, if you're going to store them for a long time, place the clothes in sealed containers. Throw in a few bay leaves or some bars of soap to keep insects away.

Vacuum closets regularly to remove hair, lint, or insects. To protect against insect infestation, don't carpet your closets. Not only can the carpet be hard to keep clean, but it provides a nice, cozy environment in which moths and carpet beetles can dine.

## Mothballs

Although mothballs do kill moths, they must be used in a totally sealed area to be effective. Most of us don't have a closet or storage area that will stay locked up tight, without other family members going in to check on something from time to time. In addition, because mothballs emit toxic vapors that are noxious to breathe and deposit a bad odor that's hard to remove from clothing, they should be your choice of last resort.

If you have some clothes that smell of mothballs, put the clothes in a large plastic bag with a couple of fabric softener sheets and let sit for three or four days. Or put them in the dryer with some fabric softener sheets for about 20 minutes on air-fluff setting.

If the closet smells of mothballs, place kitty litter in a nylon stocking and hang it in the closet. Or open a small can of fresh coffee grounds and leave it in the closet until the smell disappears.

When you see signs of infestation, remove everything from the closet. Check for damage and throw away anything that's been attacked. Dry clean or wash the rest of your clothes. Recheck regularly, because you can easily miss some of the insects themselves or their eggs.

## Getting rid of roaches

The roach problem is one of the most common and most repulsive for home-owners. Roaches are especially prevalent in older houses and apartment buildings.

You may hate to hear this, but roaches are a lot like us. They just want food, warmth, and water. And they spend their time inside your home looking for it. Prevent them from getting it and they might just go somewhere else (such as your neighbor's house).

If you suspect that you may have a roach problem — but aren't sure where they're coming from — you need to find out where the little critters are hiding. Roaches are like vampires; they hate the light of day. Outsmart them by turning off the lights and shining a flashlight on the areas where you think they might be lurking. You'll see them go scattering about.

Less adventurous roach seekers can put out those roach motels with the sticky stuff on them. When the bugs step on them, their feet get stuck and they can't move. Put the roach motels around the baseboards and walls in the kitchen, bathroom, and any other place you think roaches might hang out. Check the motels frequently and keep track of how many get caught in the trap. You'll be able to see which areas of your home need more serious help.

Even though they're never welcomed with open arms, roaches love the warmth of the human home. They love to hang out in narrow cracks and crevices and like to have a snug hiding place such as stacks of newspapers. Because roaches aren't usually invited to sit by the fireplace with us, they have to search for their own cozy hangouts. Refrigerators, stoves, hot water heaters, and dryers are some of their favorites.

Periodically, give appliances a thorough check by pulling them out and clean-ing the area behind and underneath. If you see signs of roaches, vacuum up droppings from the floor and wash the area thoroughly with a strong house-hold cleanser. Throw away the vacuum cleaner bag afterwards.

The best thing to use to get rid of roaches is boric acid. It's very effective, and it's better for the environment than more toxic pesticides because it doesn't evaporate into the air and isn't absorbed through the skin. Be sure to get the kind that's rated 99 percent pure acid, which is more effective than other kinds.

You still have to be cautious, however, because boric acid can be toxic if ingested. Always keep it out of the reach of small children and pets. When you apply it to infested areas, don't let it get on your skin or breathe it in. Put on a mask and gloves, and wear a long-sleeved shirt and long pants to avoid exposing any skin.

To apply, sprinkle, spray or use it as bait directly on surfaces where roaches live so they'll scamper through it. Here's how:

- ✔ **Sprinkling boric acid around:** When you sprinkle it around, the roaches walk in it and ingest it when they clean themselves. Put it along the edges of baseboards, in corners, and under appliances. Spread the acid around evenly where they gather — just dumping it in blobs won't be effective because they will figure out how to travel around it. Use a bulb duster or turkey baster to gently blow it into small crevices, baseboards, and under walls and sinks.

- ✔ **Spraying boric acid:** Mix a very light solution of 1 teaspoon boric acid to 1 quart water and shake well. Spray it in the crevices, baseboards, or dark corners where roaches lurk. Reapply as necessary. Be careful not to spray it where kids or pets can get into it.

- ✔ **Making a bait:** If you'd rather make up a yummy bait that the roaches will eat, mix together ½ cup borax (another form of boric acid), ¼ cup flour, ¼ cup cornmeal, ⅛ cup powdered sugar. Sprinkle the mixture onto plastic lids or paper plates and let it sit for about 10 days. Repeat if roaches are still around. Be sure you place this mixture in areas where children or pets can't get to it because it is poisonous if eaten.

For a natural repellent, spread around some crushed bay leaves on kitchen shelves and under the sink.

Cockroaches also hate the smell of garlic. Some people like to cut up garlic cloves and sprinkle them around drawers and baseboards. As long as the odor lasts, the roaches will stay away. However, in a couple of weeks, you'll have to put out fresh garlic slices again. Although I like the smell of garlic, many people feel that living with the smell of garlic is worse than living with the cockroaches.

Commercial bait traps, such as Combat, are also effective and very safe because they are self-contained. They may be good to use if small children and pets are running around the house.

## Sinking the silverfish

Silverfish (those tiny, almost translucent worm-like things that may scurry about your bathroom) love areas with high humidity and usually move at night, eating the glue in book bindings and wallpaper and the paste on stamps, to name a few favorites. Like moths, they also like to snack on dirty or starched clothing.

Control silverfish, first of all, by ventilating your house well and reducing humidity with a dehumidifier, especially in moist areas like the bathroom and the basement.

If you find silverfish in books, clear off the shelves and vacuum both the books and the shelves. Dust shelves, cracks, and crevices with boric acit, diatomaceous earth, or epsom salts. If you're putting books away for long-term storage, lock them up and sprinkle some boric acid around the container to keep silverfish out. With all these treatments, avoid areas that are accessible to animals or young children and wear goggles and a mask while applying. A safer but less effective alternative would be to sprinkle the shelves with cloves.

 Make a silverfish trap by wrapping a glass jar with strips of masking tape from top to bottom. This creates a rough surface for the bugs to climb on. Mix a little flour and sugar and put it in the bottom of the jar. Place the trap near the area where you've found silverfish. The bugs will be attracted to the food and climb in, but won't be able to climb out. Check the trap each day. If you trap any silverfish, clean them out and replace the food.

## Keeping spiders in check

After I read the book *Charlotte's Web,* I always considered spiders to be my friends. In fact, they are, because spiders help keep other pests under control. Most spiders are harmless, just not too pleasant to look at.

If you see spider webs in your house, brush them away with a broom covered with an old T-shirt. If any spiders fall down, crush them with your foot. Keep the whole house clean by frequently vacuuming their hiding places, which are along baseboards and mouldings and inside closets, and you'll probably never see a spider.

Keep the outside of the house clean, too. Trim bushes and trees so the branches aren't hanging over the house. Don't let leaves pile up near the house and under shrubs and trees. Inspect the gutters frequently and remove any leaves that have accumulated.

To keep spiders from entering the house, soak a few cotton balls in rubbing alcohol and put them where you think the spiders are coming into the house. For even more protection, soak a cloth in rubbing alcohol and wipe the inside and outside of the windows with it.

# Part V
# Home Health and Safety

The 5th Wave    By Rich Tennant

"I'm not sure what's causing that smell in the house unless...wait a minute. Is this dang thing leakin' again?!"

## In this part . . .

*B*eing safe in your own home is always a major concern. In this part, I provide some simple and common-sense tips to make your house more secure while you're at home or away. In addition, I help you child-proof your home and maintain a healthy indoor environment for everyone, minimizing allergies and illnesses. You find out how to deal with pollutants, combat allergies, and dispose of toxic substances. I also take you through your foodlist and provide a checklist how long food stays fresh on the shelf and in the fridge. You need more than one way to outwit the germs in your home.

# Chapter 19

# Evading Space Invaders: Home Security and Safety

- - - - - - - - - - - - - - - - - - - - - - - - - - - - - - - - - - - - - - - -

## In This Chapter

▶ Locking up your home

▶ Protecting it while you're on vacation

▶ Preventing fires and household accidents

- - - - - - - - - - - - - - - - - - - - - - - - - - - - - - - - - - - - - - - -

*S*tarting off a chapter on home security with a camping anecdote may sound strange, but here it goes anyway. Once, when I was camping in New Mexico with a friend, we noticed a woman across from us putting her husband's pants on a clothesline to dry while she sat in one of their chairs to read. After a couple of days, we became friendly with this neighbor and realized that, in fact, she had no husband — she was alone. She told us she always hung up the pants and put out several chairs as a protective deception. To me this story demonstrates how important common sense and thinking ahead are to home security, whether at home or at a campsite.

Few things are as intrusive as having your home burglarized. Talk to anyone who has been a victim of a robbery, and they will tell you not only of their stolen property but also of the violation to their peace of mind. Although nothing in life comes with a 100 percent guarantee, you can improve security and discourage intruders in many ways.

## Love Thy Neighbor

The most effective security system around is to know your neighbors. Statistics show a drop in the crime rate when neighbors bond together to watch out for each other. The U.S. Department of Justice studied communities with neighborhood crime watch programs and, without a doubt, use of the programs all led to a decided drop in property crime rates.

Starting a neighborhood crime watch program can be as simple as introducing yourself to your neighbors. Or you can contact your local police department to get more information on the subject. Essentially, you gather together some neighbors who are interested in watching over each other's homes. Perhaps your local law enforcement will send a representative to discuss house and neighborhood security with your group. To start your version of a neighborhood watch you should:

- ✔ Introduce yourself to your neighbors and let them get to know you.
- ✔ Know each other's routines.
- ✔ Exchange pertinent phone numbers and emergency strategies.

If the neighborhood you moved into or live in already has such a group, block club, or organization, be sure to get involved and join in — the cost will be minimal for the security gained.

## Lighten Up

Good lighting can make you look good and your house look bad to burglars. Because most lighting is unattractive to burglars, use it as a deterrent to intimidate intruders. Besides acting as a safety device, lighting can also create a stagelike setting that burglars will be wary of performing on.

Be aware of your setting. Use lighting that's both protective and considerate of your neighbors. Illuminate as large an area as possible with the lowest level of lights. A dark rural setting may require a higher level than a closely spaced urban one. Don't shine floodlights into a neighbor's bedroom. Use two lights around your front door, if possible, so if one burns out, one still remains to light the way. Here's how to use lighting to make your home more safe:

- ✔ Install infrared detectors to your existing lighting, front steps, path, or floodlights so they light up when someone passes by them. They come on only when needed so you save energy and fool intruders into thinking they've been spotted.
- ✔ Use a time clock device to activate your outdoor lights. But don't forget to adjust it for Daylight Savings Time.
- ✔ Have your address well lit so emergency crews or the police can find your house quickly.
- ✔ Put timers on indoor lights and appliances. But be sure to program timing that mirrors your normal habits. You may want to have a kitchen light that turns on at 6:30 a.m. and off at 9 a.m. or a bedroom light that turns on at 7:00 p.m. and off at 10:00 p.m. Vary the timers' schedule periodically so it will appear realistic if someone is observing your home.

# Landscape Your Yard for Security

Another line of defense against robbers is to keep your yard landscaped in such a way that anyone lurking around your house could easily be seen from the street. Anything that provides a hiding place is a boon to a burglar. It may be time to take out the clippers and make your home more secure.

✔ Keep your hedges and shrubs well trimmed. Don't give intruders a place to hide beneath windows and doors.

✔ Check any trees in the yard. Trim any branches that are near windows or the side of the house so they don't offer a burglar an opportunity to climb inside.

✔ If you have a large yard or patio, install low lighting around the perimeter to light up large empty areas.

Although not strictly yard advice, when working outside the house for any reason, be sure to put away any ladders or anything that someone could use to climb inside the house or garage. And always lock the garage and any doors leading into the house, even when you're nearby. A number of folks have been surprised to find that burglars had waltzed in through unlocked doors while the owners had been working in their yards. See the following section, "Making Windows and Doors Safe," for more ways to protect yourself from such trespassing.

# Making Windows and Doors Safe

Unless you're Santa Claus, the easiest exits and entrances to a house are through the windows and doors. You may find it hard to believe, but many robberies are conducted by walking through unlocked doors. So be sure to double-check that you locked up tight when you are in the house or when you leave.

Walk around your house and think like a burglar. Test every entrance for easy entry. Many local law enforcement agencies offer free security checks on your home. You may be amazed at what they can tell you. Taking the time to do these simple steps can save you a bundle. Use the tips in the following sections to make sure your doors and windows are protecting you as they should.

## Using doors defensively

Doors are your first line of defense Here are some things you can do to make them even more secure:

✔ Every outside entrance door should have a dead bolt lock in addition to its doorknob lock (see Figure 19-1). A dead bolt is installed separate from the door knob lock; when its key is turned to the lock position, a strong metal bolt slides at least an inch into a metal box called a strike plate on the frame of the door. A rim mount lock is like a vertical dead bolt and mounts on the interior door frame. It's easy to install, but you should use screws that go halfway through the door.

**Figure 19-1:**
Every out-
side
entrance
should have
a dead-bolt
to guard it.

✔ If an elderly or disabled person lives in the house, make sure the door knob is easy to grasp. If the knob is slippery for the person to hold, wrap the knob with some tape or replace it with a lever type handle. Otherwise, you risk not having the door closed completely, if at all.

✔ Outside doors should be solid core and at least 1 ¾ inches thick. Avoid hollow-core doors; these are hollow inside and can be easily kicked in.

✔ Your entrance and exit doors should open in, not out, so that the hinges are on the inside and can't be removed. If your door swings out, put in metal door pins that mount into the side of a door and go into a hole in the door frame as the door closes. This prevents someone from removing the hinge pins and lifting out the door.

✔ Install a wide-angle peephole so you can get a good view of anyone in the door area. If someone in the house is restricted to a wheelchair, install a peephole at the proper height for them.

✔ If anyone knocks or rings the doorbell, don't automatically open the door to look outside and see who's there. If you think you're protected by a door chain, think again. Door chains can usually be kicked open.

✔ Check your patio or sliding doors and install a security bar and sturdy lock. You can also purchase a bar with special lights and an alarm.

✔ Garage door? Keep it locked. If you have an electric door opener, unplug it during vacations and install a padlock when you go away.

✔ Always have your key in hand when you go to open the door. Don't stand at the doorstep fumbling through your briefcase or purse. If you have a problem locating your key, put it on an odd-sized or colorful key holder so you'll be able to locate it in the dark if necessary. You might want to consider buying a keychain with a small battery-operated light.

## Securing the windows

Though windows offer easy access to would-be burglars, you can take the following precautions to secure them:

✔ If your home has windows near or on a door, install grilles to prevent a thief from reaching in to open a door. Use nonremovable screws for attaching the grille.

✔ Make a daily or weekly check to see if windows are secure. Double-check and lock them before you leave the house.

✔ You can secure double-hung windows with 20-penny nail bolt locks by drilling a hole through the top of the bottom window into the bottom of the top window and then inserting the 20-penny nail (see Figure 19-2). To open the window, you remove the nail.

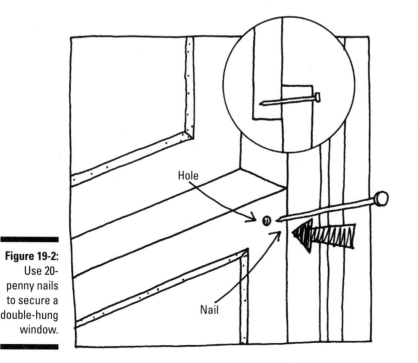

**Figure 19-2:**
Use 20-penny nails to secure a double-hung window.

Hole

Nail

✔ Install key sash locks, which are attached at the bottom of the upper sash and keep the bottom sash from moving. Check local restrictions on these first and store the keys away from the windows.

✔ Check and secure any basement windows with screws, locks, or metal bars.

# Taking a Vacation

When you're away, not only will the mice play, but so will the cat burglars. The trick is not to oversecure your house by shutting all the blinds and curtains. Remember, you want it to appear as if someone is at home. And, of course, whether on vacation or not, always try to store valuables out of sight.

Here are some easy ideas to safeguard your home while you're away:

✔ Have a neighbor pick up your mail and newspapers or cancel delivery until you return. Give them the phone number of your vacation destination in case they need to contact you.

✔ Give someone a key to check on, and take any deliveries into, the house.

✔ Use timers on all your lights and appliances and vary their schedules. Keep one on a radio or television but don't turn up the volume too loud.

✔ Set the answering machine to pick up after one ring if you can, or turn down the phone ringer so a thief can't hear the ringing if it's going unanswered.

✔ Don't leave phone messages on your machine that announce your vacation plans to the world.

✔ If you're going away for several weeks, have someone maintain your lawn or shovel the snow.

✔ Ask a neighbor to park in your driveway, which makes it look like someone is home.

✔ If you park at the airport, don't leave any papers in the car that have your address on them.

# Selecting Security Systems

Today, you can choose from many home security systems. If you decide you need one, choose a system that fits your lifestyle and budget and make sure it has a money-back guarantee, in case it doesn't fit your needs. Always ask whether a contract is available to provide future maintenance for the system.

Your options include two basic types of systems with endless variations in between.

✔ The first is a local system: A sensory device sends a signal to a system of lights and siren bells that are usually loud enough to frighten away any intruder.

✔ The second type of system also sets off a house alarm, but sends a signal to an alarm company and/or police department as well, alerting them to a break-in.

Here are a few important things to keep in mind when you're selecting a home security system:

✔ Make sure the system fits your needs. If you're alone, putting an alarm on every door is no problem, but in a family full of kids rattling every door, you could have some difficulty with false alarms or with leaving the alarm unset to allow access to those rooms, which negates the good an alarm can do.

✔ Many systems are sensitive to light, motion, or heat, which means even a draft or a pet strolling through your living room could set it off. If you frequently have guests or have little children running about, you may want to look into something else.

✔ Make sure your system and the controls can't be seen through the window. A knowledgeable burglar could disconnect wires or other control mechanisms if he sees what kind of system you have.

✔ Let burglars know that you have protection. Sometimes just an alarm sticker on the window is enough to keep them away.

Before you purchase an alarm system, check with the company and the police department for their policy on false alarms. Most companies typically will charge you for false alarms after an initial grace period. Because of the large number of false alarms, police in several communities will not respond after three or four mistaken alarms. You'll have to work with everyone in the family to avoid unnecessarily setting off the alarm.

# Making Your Apartment Secure

The bad news about apartment security is that most landlords don't want to spend any extra money to install up-to-date security devices. The good news is that apartments are generally safer because it's harder to get inside the building and into each apartment.

When you're searching for an apartment, look for one that has a security system in place. Check to see whether the door has a peephole and a deadbolt lock. Make sure the entrances, exits, and garage look secure and are well-lit.

After you've selected an apartment building or complex, here are some things you can do to make your apartment more secure:

- ✔ Put an alarm on your door. You can get one with a delay that will give you enough time to get in the door without it going off.

- ✔ Put up an extra security bar on the inside if you feel that the regular lock isn't secure enough. Good ones to look for are the Fox Double-Bar Lock, a door-mounted cylinder that moves two steel bars into the door jambs. If you can't drill holes, the Fox Lock device is a piece of pipe that fits around the door knob on one end and grips the floor with a rubber shoe on the other. You can open the door while it's in place.

- ✔ Don't allow strangers to enter the building. If someone says they are visiting a tenant or delivering a package, tell them to wait in the lobby while you go to your apartment and call the tenants.

- ✔ If any areas of the building aren't well lit or are often empty, don't linger there. If the laundry room is in the basement or an out-of-the-way place, bring a friend or go on the weekend when it's busy.

- ✔ When you enter the building, have your key out and ready to unlock the door. Don't stand out in front or in the lobby reading your mail or searching for your keys.

- ✔ If you have windows on the ground floor or next to a fire escape, put up bars or a grate to prevent intruders.

- ✔ A friend of mine had what I considered a low-tech security device in his apartment. He put plants and bottles on the window sill and upper sash of the bottom window. If someone tried to open the window, the "alarm" of the breaking glass and pots would alert him that someone was trying to break in.

- ✔ Get to know your neighbors. They can alert you or call the police if they see anything strange.

See the following section for tips on what to do in the event that your security measures fail and you're victimized by a burglar.

# Common-Sense Dos and Don'ts when Security's Breached

No super duper security system or titanium bolt on your door can make up for leaving your door unlocked. The best defense is usually common sense. Here are a few do's and don'ts:

# Dos

Do the following to prepare for or follow up on a break-in:

- Do have an escape plan in case you hear an intruder. Get out of the house quickly and call the police from a neighbor's place.

- Do mark all your valuables. Contact your local law enforcement — they may be able to loan you an electric engraving pen and you can get recommendations from them about what items to mark and which identification numbers to use. This will not only help to recover your property, but will aid in later prosecution of the burglar.

- Do make a written inventory of all your possessions along with pictures of the valuable items. Or make a videotape of your possessions, describing each item and what it's worth. Keep these in a safe place like a safety deposit box.

- Do call the police immediately if you discover your house has been broken into or robbed.

- Do have a phone by your bed with a quick dial programmed for the police department.

- Do have home insurance if you have a lot of valuables. Check with a reputable company or agent for the proper amount of protection.

- Do secure your home, but don't oversecure it. In case of a fire, make sure that it's easy to get out of the house. Everyone in the house should be aware of escape routes and the locations of keys for locks or bars over doors and windows.

- Do have separate car and house keys.

# Don'ts

You may think of doing the following don'ts:

- Don't purchase a dog just for guard dog purposes. A loud bark is a great low-tech security device, but the main reason to have a dog is companionship, which carries a lot of responsibilities. If you just need something guarding your house, you can buy an alarm.

- Don't leave valuables like computers and video equipment where they can easily be seen.

- Don't confront a burglar. And don't tip-toe around if you hear an intruder. Let them know you're there by shouting that you're calling the police. If you're alone, pretend there are other family members that you are alerting.

✔ Don't put your name on the mailbox. Just list the house number. And avoid listing your full name in the phone book. List yourself by the last name or with an initial.

✔ Don't let anyone in your house whom you don't know and aren't expecting; always ask for proper identification. Don't be intimidated. If you feel unsafe, you probably are. Go with your gut. Offer to call up the office to check on their identity. Or tell them they will have to come back at a later time; then arrange to have a friend there with you.

✔ Don't go in your house if you come home to an opened door and things are amiss. Go to a neighbor's house and call the police.

✔ Don't include your address in classified ads. If strangers come to your house to buy something, have friends there.

✔ Make sure that, if your local newspaper writes up a special family vacation or other event the story appears in print "after" the event. Funerals are especially vulnerable periods because you have to publicize them before the event. If possible, don't include your address in the announcement and have a friend stay at your house while you're at the funeral home or cemetery.

✔ Don't make your address impossible to see with small numbers. Address numbers should be at least 6 inches high, readable, and facing the street so that emergency crews can find your place quickly if needed.

# Teaching Your Kids to Be Safe

Most kids are so open and unsuspecting that you need to teach them how to react with strangers and anyone coming to the house, especially when you aren't there.

Have a family meeting and tell them what you think is proper behavior. Most kids have a tendency to tell everything about themselves and their family. Explain to them that they shouldn't give out any vital information to strangers. For example, when they answer the telephone, instruct them to tell the caller that "My mother can't come to the phone right now," rather than "My mother's at work and won't be home for hours."

Make sure you teach your children how to dial 911 in case of an emergency. Always leave a list of emergency numbers by the phone, as well as your street address written down. It's amazing how many people forget their addresses in an emergency! Or make it easy for your kids to call by getting a programmable phone so they only have to learn to punch in simple numbers. If you have baby-sitters, give them the list of emergency numbers and a number where you can always be reached. (Your home address and phone number written out prominently is good for sitters, too.)

# Avoiding Home Safety Hazards

Keeping safe from hazards inside the home is as important as protecting yourself and your family from outside intruders. The following safety tips will help prevent fires and other disasters:

✔ Always keep a fire extinguisher handy.

✔ Make sure extension cords are in good condition and aren't worn or damaged. If the cord feels hot while you're using it, unplug and discard it. If an outlet or switch is hot to the touch, do not turn it on. Call an electrician to check it.

✔ Dry your hands before using or plugging and unplugging an appliance. Stay away from water when using an electrical tool.

✔ If an electrical appliance falls into the tub, sink, or pool, don't reach into the water to get it, even if it is turned off. Unplug it first. It can electrocute anyone who touches the water or who is in the water. Have an electrician install ground fault circuit interrupters in any outlet in a wet or damp environment, like the kitchen, bathroom, basement, or garage. GFCIs shut off power if they sense a short in the circuit from an appliance or tool, preventing electric shock when a plugged-in appliance falls in water.

✔ Don't remove the grounding prong on a three-prong plug. If you only have two pronged outlets in your house, get an adapter with a ground tab.

✔ Unplug small appliances when you're not using them and when you go away on vacation. Never use an extension cord for major appliances or for heat-producing appliances such as a portable heater or iron. Always unplug appliances before repairing them.

## A word about Internet security

As you read this, the Internet is expanding and growing. Much of that growth is nourishing and increasing the depth and knowledge of our world, but some of it can be intrusive to your security and the privacy of all you own.

Recently I was able to obtain, via the Internet, directions from my mother's house to my brother's home in the same city. This seemed incredible to me and really great at first; but on further thought, it led to endless speculation about what else others, who are complete strangers, might find out about me, my friends, and my family. It's wise to be aware of the amount of information that can now be transmitted to others without your knowledge.

- ✔ Make sure any appliance you buy is listed by the Underwriters Laboratories (UL) or design-certified by the American Gas Association Laboratories (AGA), a blue star seal on the rating plate for gas models.

- ✔ Do not pour water on a grease fire. Pour baking soda on it or use your fire extinguisher. If the fire is in a pot, put a lid on the pan to smother the fire and turn off the flame underneath.

- ✔ Put out a fire in a trash can by covering it with a lid or a cookie sheet or a large pan.

- ✔ If a fire starts in the oven or broiler, close the door, and turn off the oven. Keep your face away from the oven door. Don't take the food out until you're sure the flames are out. Same goes for fires in microwave ovens.

# Chapter 20

# Childproofing Your Home

. . . . . . . . . . . . . . . . . . . . . . . . . . . . . . . . . . . . . . . . . . . .

## In This Chapter

▶ Putting together a first-aid kit

▶ Keeping kids safe in your home

▶ Choosing safe baby furniture

▶ Teaching kids about safety

. . . . . . . . . . . . . . . . . . . . . . . . . . . . . . . . . . . . . . . . . . . .

*T*he home is a veritable minefield for young children. You can't let down your guard and assume that nothing dangerous will happen. Of course, you can buy locks and covers to install, and you can find secret storage places in which to keep hazardous items from curious hands, but nothing takes the place of diligent parental supervision. I offer loads of helpful suggestions in this chapter, but the best way to deal with the arrival of a new member of the family is to give your house a thorough once-over and be constantly on the alert for situations that could harm your child.

## Coping with Kids

In this chapter, I give some general and many specific tips, but these tips can't cover every situation in your home.

To get an accurate feeling for what needs to be done, crawl around your house on your hands and knees. (You can lock the door and close the blinds before starting this, if you want to.) Look at the room from a child's perspective. You'll see things that you take for granted: plugs, cords, sharp corners, holes to stick little fingers in, and so on. Look at them with the sense of new discovery that a child has. You'll get an idea of what needs to be covered up or hidden.

But remember: Nothing is absolutely childproof. Even with all the right equipment and precautions, you still must supervise your children and their friends carefully at all times. Safety begins with the ideas in the sections that follow.

## Be prepared for any emergency

Write down any phone numbers that you might need in an emergency and post them near every phone in the house. Include your child's doctor, the number of the hospital emergency room, the poison control center, the pharmacy (hopefully one that's open 24 hours), and the police station. If you have a phone that you can program these numbers into, do so.

Keep a first-aid kit in the house and make sure that your list of emergency phone numbers is in it. The last thing you want to do is search desperately for phone numbers in an emergency. Make sure that all family members (even children) know what the kit looks like and where it's stored. Mark a big white cross on the box so that any child or adult, even a neighbor, can find it if necessary. Just make sure the family understands that the kit is to be saved for emergencies only and not to rifle through it and pull out bandages or scissors for day-to-day problems or projects. When you hire a babysitter, show her the location of the first-aid supplies and emergency phone numbers. And don't forget to give her a phone number where you can be reached.

## Anticipate what's going to happen

I'm constantly amazed at the small spaces kids can get into, the locks they can dismantle, the furniture they can move, the disgusting things they choose to put in their mouths, and the number of boxes they can pile up to reach almost anything. Let your guard down, and you'll find that the one

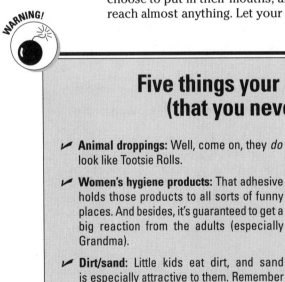

**WARNING!**

## Five things your child will get into (that you never dreamed of)

- **Animal droppings:** Well, come on, they *do* look like Tootsie Rolls.

- **Women's hygiene products:** That adhesive holds those products to all sorts of funny places. And besides, it's guaranteed to get a big reaction from the adults (especially Grandma).

- **Dirt/sand:** Little kids eat dirt, and sand is especially attractive to them. Remember this when planning meals: This is the beginning of their aversion to healthy and/or home-cooked food. Sand is a tough competitor.

- **Toilets:** "Looks like a pool, sounds like a pool, so it must be a pool. Wonder if the kitty can swim in it. How do *I* get in it? Can I make Mom's glasses go bye-bye in it?"

- **Litter boxes:** "Are the big caterpillars in that house alive? They must be sick — they're not moving. I'll go make them all better."

thing you swore they would never do is the one thing they find the most fascinating. Every door and drawer can be locked up tight, yet kids seem to have the uncanny ability to find the one door that you couldn't close off or the one minuscule pin that was left on the floor. Notice what your child's developmental stage is now. Think ahead and plan for what items your child can reach or dismantle in the future. Never assume that anything is safe.

## Decorate with kids in mind

When you're decorating your home, consider more than whether the kids will trash the white sofa or stain the rug. Think about their safety. Some furnishings and surfaces are more child-friendly than others. Planning for that before buying furnishings not only prevents stains, but it prevents accidents as well.

For example, soon after kids start walking, they also start running and jumping in the house. So prepare for it:

- Add rugs with a nonskid backing to prevent toddlers from sliding and falling.

- Remove furniture that has glass tops or sharp corners from rooms where your family hangs out.

- When arranging furniture, keep chairs, tables, and sofas away from windows. Kids can climb on these items while reaching and possibly falling out of windows.

- Avoid long curtains and eliminate long pull cords for blinds or draperies — kids can trip on all these things.

These are just a few items that can be dangerous in your home. As your baby grows and you talk to other parents about their experiences, you'll get a better idea of what's child-friendly and what's not.

## Teach kids simple safety precautions

As soon as possible, educate your children about potential dangers around the home. Warn them about poisonous products and show them the symbol for poison. Insist that they stop and ask permission before eating anything. This will prevent them from eating nonfood items like toys or dirt and cut down on food problems in the future.

# Put together a first-aid kit

You can buy basic first-aid kits in the pharmacy section of most stores. These kits are probably good enough for the majority of situations. If you'd like to make up your own, or if you just want to compare the quality of the one you're purchasing, use this list as a guideline for what should be in every family first aid kit:

- Sterile adhesive bandages in various (about 10 per kit)
- Five or six 4-inch sterile gauze pads
- One to two cloth triangular bandages
- One 3-inch sterile roller bandage
- An assortment of butterfly bandages
- One roll of 1-inch medical adhesive tape
- Sterilized needle for removing splinters
- Antiseptic
- Syrup of ipecac (not to be used unless instructed to do so by your pediatrician or poison control center; check expiration date periodically)
- One or two pairs of latex gloves (check for allergies before using)

## Include medications

Keep the following nonprescription medicines in your first-aid kit:

- **A nonaspirin pain reliever** is best for kids in most situations and when you're not sure what's wrong. Remember that children's medication is a different strength than adult medication, and the medicines are usually available in liquid form. You don't want to give a child any adult strength medicine. Ask your pediatrician what dosage you should give your child for his or her size and weight. If you like, put this item in the first-aid kit, but be sure to periodically check the expiration date and throw it out when it's expired.

- **Anti-diarrhea medication** is good to have in your first-aid kit, but call your pediatrician before using it.

- **An electrolyte replacement drink for kids,** such as Pedialyte, is another worthwhile addition to your first-aid kit. Again, however, if you feel that your child is ill enough to need this supplement, you should check with the pediatrician.

### Add other useful items

Other good additions to the first-aid kit include:

- ✔ Tweezers
- ✔ Five or six 2-inch sterile gauze pads
- ✔ One 2-inch sterile roller bandage
- ✔ Tongue blades
- ✔ A few plastic self-closure plastic bags (invaluable for making ice packs).
- ✔ A rubber bulb syringe for suctioning out an infant's nose and mouth if your child vomits and begin to gag on it or if your baby gets a cold.

Also include a family-oriented medical book with a home emergency section, such as *Family Medicine For Dummies* (published by IDG Books Worldwide, Inc.). Such a book can provide some guidance on things like how to tell the difference between a sprain and a broken bone, as well as other helpful information in an emergency or when you're just stuck for what to do.

When in doubt, always at least *call* the pediatrician's office. Someone is available to answer questions even in off-hours. If you're confronted with an injury that you think is life threatening, call 911 or take the child to the nearest emergency room.

# Childproofing Your Home — Room by Room

Each room presents its own set of problems. Use this section as a general guide to eliminate dangers, but stay alert. It's hard to foresee what seemingly harmless thing can become a problem.

## Keeping the kitchen safe

The kitchen is one of the most dangerous rooms in the house for kids (and I'm not talking about your cooking!). For starters, you can find high temperatures, fire, sharp objects, chemicals, and heavy pots and pans. Take some safety precautions, or you'll have a recipe for disaster:

- ✔ **Lock up everything in the kitchen.** From the cleaning supplies to the trash, to the spices, to all your electrical appliances — lock everything away from kids. Don't forget the silverware, knives, matches, and plastic bags. Any number of accidents can happen here: poisonings, bleeding injuries, burns, and suffocation. Sooner or later ( sooner if you have more than one child), even the best parent will be momentarily distracted. The difference between a serious accident and an annoyance could be the fact everything is locked up tight. Put childproof locks on all kitchen cabinets and drawers (see Figure 20-1).

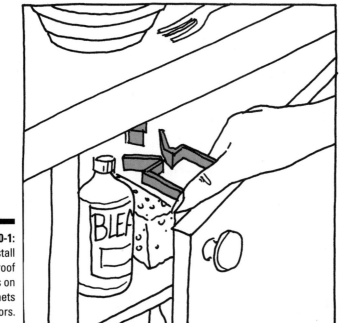

**Figure 20-1:**
Install childproof latches on cabinets and doors.

✔ **Use the stove's back burners and keep pot handles turned towards the back of the stove**. Those wonderful smells coming from the stove are irresistible to kids and can prompt them to grab for the handle instead of complimenting you on your culinary achievement. If you're shopping for a stove, get one with controls at the back of the console instead of the front so that little hands can't reach them.

Cautious parents often remove the control knobs from stoves and keep them in a nearby jar when the stove is not in use.

✔ **Don't use a tablecloth on your kitchen table.** Kids can easily pull down hot foods or liquids.

✔ **Store cleaning products and soaps in high cabinets and keep the cabinets locked.** Containers for household chemicals often have labels with colored lettering and artwork that make them very attractive to young eyes. Most kids are up for drinking anything, especially something that's colored blue or green. If a child swallows any household chemical, call the poison control center or the hospital immediately.

✔ **Use safety straps to prevent your kids from falling or climbing out of high chairs, swings, and strollers.** Even if they're all strapped in, don't feel that it's any substitute for parental supervision. Never leave them alone. You can't rely on the straps to hold every kid in. Some kids have an almost magical ability to slither their way out of a restraint that might give Houdini a problem.

✔ **Give up cookie jars until the kids are older.** Storing a treasure like cookies in full sight gives kids even more motivation to climb on top of countertops and stoves. Keep snacks and cookies out of sight and out of mind.

✔ **Get switchplate locks to stop any unwanted use of the garbage disposal or other appliances.** These locks are too difficult for most kids to manipulate because they require a double movement of holding down a tab while turning on the switch.

✔ **Unplug electric appliances when not in use.** Even better, put them away in a locked cabinet, if possible.

## *Barring accidents in the bathroom*

Next to the kitchen, the bathroom presents the most dangers in the home. The toilet, medicines, cleaners, and the threat of drowning make this room a real target for accidents. And because parents often store bath toys in or near the tub, children can be lulled into the feeling that this is another play area. Use the following tips to help keep the bathroom safe:

✔ **Keep young children from unsupervised use of the bathroom by devising a way to lock the door from the outside.** You can use plastic sliding door handles that have to be squeezed together to operate the handle. Simple hook and eye closures installed high up on the bathroom door are another simple solution. Older children and adults in the family can reach it, but a young child won't be able to.

✔ **Buy only medications and household cleaners in containers that have childproof caps.** I know that they're annoying, but they can keep a child from downing a whole bottle of aspirin or floor cleaner.

✔ **Keep makeup, deodorant, and shampoos out of children's reach.** These items seem innocuous and aren't harmful to adults, but they can be hazardous to kids. A baby can have an adverse reaction if he drinks or swallows them.

✔ **Scour your bathroom for scissors, tweezers, and razors that can cause cuts or scratches if picked up and played with.** Your best bet is to put these away in cabinets and drawers that have locks on them. Some people find it easier to keep these locked in a nearby closet when children are young. Do whatever you find most convenient.

✔ **Before you bathe your child, put a few drops of water on your wrist to check the temperature.** Wrists are more sensitive to hot water than fingers are, and testing for what can be too hot for a baby's skin is a good idea.

Consider lowering the temperature on the water heater thermostat to 120 degrees to avoid burns from excessively hot water.

✔ **Never leave your child alone in the tub or near the toilet.** A child can drink what's inside or fall inside and drown. A small amount of water is all it takes. Many parents put a locking lid on the toilet or install Velcro strips to keep it shut while the child is still a toddler.

## Being safe in bedrooms

Children spend time a lot of time in bedrooms, both theirs and yours. And although the bedroom seems less hazardous than other rooms, lots of accidents still happen here. When you're babyproofing the room, just think, if children can put it in their mouths, they will.

✔ **Keep your purse or makeup bag off the floor or chairs.** These are irresistible temptations for your child who sees you playing with what's inside and wants to join in the fun.

✔ **Don't lay your baby down to sleep on your bed.** The child can roll off or suffocate in any soft comforters or pillows.

✔ **Keep all cribs in good working condition without any loose hardware, missing bars, or spindles.** The slats should be no more than 2 ⅜ inches apart. Measure any old or borrowed cribs to make sure that bars aren't spaced too far apart. The danger: Babies risk being strangled or suffocated if they are trapped between broken crib parts or bars that are too wide. Make sure that the crib has a firm, flat mattress and no soft bedding underneath. Don't put extra cushions or large soft toys in the crib. The baby can roll over on them and suffocate.

Lower the crib mattress when your baby learns to sit up and stand. That keeps you child from vaulting out of the crib when he or she learns how to reach the top.

✔ **Never put a crib near a window.** Window treatments and their cords are dangerous for children. Babies soon learn to play with the cords and can wind cords around their necks or try to eat the plastic doohickey on the bottom. Cut cords short and tie them up out of reach.

# Bringing safety to basements and garages

Make this a family rule: Kids aren't allowed in the basement or garage without parental or adult supervision. The potential for accidents abounds here, starting with tools, nails, and paint on up to water heaters, furnaces, and irons. Put a lock or a hook and eye on the top of the door so that little ones can't get in. And then follow these guidelines for adding safety to your basement or garage:

✔ If you store anything flammable or poisonous, such as oil, gasoline, or fertilizer, lock these items in a sturdy metal cabinet. Never leave liquids standing around in buckets that kids can drink from or fall into.

✔ Store lawn and garden equipment or power tools in a metal cabinet. Hang shovels and rakes on a rack high off the floor so kids won't step on them and knock them over.

✔ Don't stack sports equipment or lean bats, hockey sticks, or pogo sticks against the walls.

✔ If you store recyclables in the garage, put them in a sturdy container with a locking lid.

✔ If your automatic garage door opener has a motion sensor, check to make sure that it registers at near-ground level so that it can detect whether children are running through a lowering door. Check also to make sure that your door stops when it hits something.

✔ Teach kids that the car is a dangerous vehicle. Don't allow them to sit alone in the car and pretend to drive or play games. And don't let them have access to the trunk; be vigilant when your trunk is open to make sure your children stay away from it. You don't want to give them the impression that the car is another play area. Teach them that, when the car is running, they either enter the car or get out of the garage.

Regularly give your garage and basement a general clean up to examine and get rid of some of the stuff that's stored there. Both rooms tend to be a dumping ground for items that are frequently forgotten. Take the doors off things like old refrigerators and other items you're discarding. You can bet that, if it's at all hazardous, some child will get into it sooner or later if you aren't careful.

# Maintaining safe hallways, entrances, and exits

Stairs and doors pose the biggest threats in hallways and entrance ways, addition to the need for clearly marked and maintained exits in case of fire. Take these few small steps to insure the safety of these areas:

✔ **Don't skimp on smoke detectors**. Put one on each floor near the bedrooms and the kitchen. If you have gas appliances (stove, furnace, or fireplace), install carbon monoxide detectors nearby. Be diligent about changing the batteries. Check them at least twice a year.

✔ **Install safety gates at both the top and bottom of stairways (see Figure 20-2).** Gates stop kids from crawling either up or down. Even with these precautions, nothing replaces diligent adult supervision. My sister said that her son routinely found a way to climb to the top of a supposedly unscalable gate by dragging over a footstool or chair to boost himself up. (See "Buying Childproof Products," later in the chapter, for information about buying baby gates.) Make sure all older children and adults can open the gates in case of fire. Have a fire drill at least once a year.

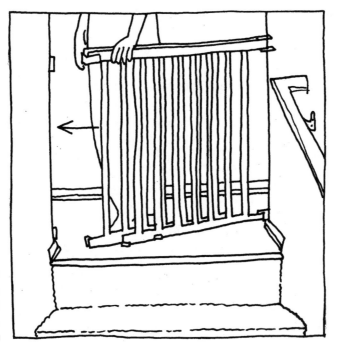

**Figure 20-2:**
Install gates
on stairs.

✔ **Choose childproof covers for faceplates around wall outlets that slide up over the slots of sockets when they aren't in use.** Plug-in outlet protectors are popular, but they can be pried loose by determined children and then swallowed or chewed.

# Living safely in the living room

Decluttering your decorating style is a good idea if you have children. Kids can get at anything and everything. *Object d'art* is *object d'play with* in kid language. Make your living room safe with these tips:

✔ **Move anything that is potentially dangerous to a high shelf or a cabinet.** This includes vases, knickknacks, pictures, computers, and cigarette lighters. Also, go through accessible drawers and remove anything sharp (such as knitting needles, pencils, or scissors). When you come in from outside, don't drop your purse or grocery bags on the floor. Take them to the kitchen, put away the groceries, and store your purse or briefcase in a place that's inaccessible to children.

✔ **Babyproof your furniture.** Floor and desk lamps can be pushed over or pulled down by the cord. Move desk lamps from low tables and relocate floor lamps behind heavy pieces of furniture.

  • Tape cords securely to the floor, wall, or under furniture. Even better are wall- or ceiling-mounted fixtures.

  • Put cushioned corner protectors on sharp edges of coffee and end tables.

  • Lock trunks or horizontal cabinets for safety. Kids can crawl inside or lift the lids and shut them on hands or heads. Buy slow-closing hinge locks that prevent the lids from slamming down.

✔ **Declutter tabletops.** By the time you reason with a two-year-old that he shouldn't pick up Aunt Norma's cut glass candy dish, the dish may be history. Remove doilies or tablecloths from the tops of tables. Anything that's stored on top, including heavy vases, glass objects, and breakable collectibles, can be pulled off in an instant. These items can either break or fall on top of your baby. If you have any books or magazines that you don't want shredded, put them in a childproof area.

✔ **Keep the TV set inside a locked cabinet or entertainment center.** At the very least, put the VCR up high so that little fingers can't get stuck inside. And if you ever want to find the remote control again, store it up high also.

✔ **Move houseplants out of reach.** Houseplants are messy if they're knocked down, and falling pots and plants can seriously harm a baby. Even if the plants themselves aren't poisonous, they can upset a baby's stomach if ingested.

✔ **Make sure that throw rugs have a rubber backing or pad.** You don't want the kids to slip as they are running through the house. If necessary, attach the rug to the floor with double-faced carpet tape. Make sure that all carpeting is solidly attached to the floor with nails and that all nails are flush with the floor.

## Doing the safety thing for doors and windows

Doors and windows provide easy access to accidents. Take these precautions to insure your child's safety:

- ✔ **Close and lock all windows at your child's level to prevent him or her from falling out.** Screens are made to keep bugs out, not to keep children in.

  If you want ventilation, open the tops of double hung windows. For extra protection, install security screens or guards — they are required by law in some areas. At the very least, move furniture away from windows so children can't climb up.

- ✔ **Discourage kids from playing around windows.** Don't put any furniture or playthings near them. Don't give your kids a bad example by leaning out the windows or hanging things from them.

- ✔ **Be careful of any doors that have spring-loaded mechanisms.** You might consider removing them or dismantling the mechanism while kids are young so that these doors don't slam shut onto a child. The problem: You want to see through a doorway, but you also want to keep the kids out. The solution: Put up a lockable half door.

## Yanking hazards from the yard

Be watchful. Supervise children at all times, even in the most benign situations. Don't leave kids alone in the house or the yard. Put a lock on the gate not only so kids can't get in, but also so they can't get out. Children act first and think second. You don't want to see them running madly down the street, chasing after something that interests them — your neighbor's pit bull, for example. Here are a few hints for accident-proofing your yard:

- ✔ **Keep playground equipment in tip-top shape.** Remove anything that could cut or scrape tender skin (your kid's or your own). Sand down rough edges, remove splinters, and cover dangerous hardware such as open S-hooks or protruding bolt ends with capped or acorn nuts. Cover the ends of hollow tubing with plastic caps. Not only can tiny fingers get caught inside, but also insects such as bees and wasps love to nest there. Check to make sure that openings in ladders and guardrails are less than 3 ⅜ inches or more than 9 inches to eliminate the danger of kids' getting their arms, legs, or heads stuck.

✔ **Pad your playground area well.** Whether they're jumping off swings or climbing on monkey bars, kids will fall on the ground. The Consumer Product Safety Commission recommends putting 12 inches of wood chips, bark, sand, mulch, or mats of safety-tested rubber to cushion falls beneath all equipment in public playgrounds. The padding should extend at least 6 feet in all directions from the play equipment and should be twice the height of the bar that holds the swings.

✔ **Be savvy about swings.** Give yourself a treat! Get on the swing yourself and do a test run every month or so during the summer. Make sure that ropes and chains are secure. Look for any sharp edges or open hooks. If you've got an old-fashioned swing hanging from a tree limb, check the ropes for wear and tear. A good safety precaution is to thread the rope through some old sections of garden hose and position the hoses where the rope passes over the tree limb. Any cement holding the legs of a swingset in place should be below ground level and covered by several inches of wood chips or other material.

✔ **Avoid using pesticides or chemicals on the lawn or on plants near where kids play.** Practically every kid eats a handful of grass now and then. And even if your kids don't eat grass, traces of those chemicals can be tracked onto the carpet in the house on the soles of their shoes. If you've got a baby who is crawling around on the carpet and putting things in his mouth, this can be a real danger.

Get kids in the habit of removing their shoes when they come in from playing. Put a basket by the door to keep the shoes neat and tidy. This keeps the carpet clean and prevents the carpet from absorbing any chemicals from the outside.

✔ **You can't really childproof a pool — you must watch everyone in the pool constantly.** Even a few seconds of distraction can lead to tragedy. Install a fence around the pool and always lock up the pool area. You may be required by law to do this. Check your local code requirements.

- Make sure that kids always wear child-sized lifejackets and don't allow them to run in the pool area.

- Install textured concrete or slip-proof material in the pool area. (Concrete can be hard on kid's feet, so if your kids' feet are getting sore, let them wear water shoes.)

- Unless the pool is deep enough, make sure that kids jump into the pool feet first only.

- Keep rescue equipment handy by the side of the pool; take CPR training and have your teenagers take CPR training as well.

During the nonswimming months of the year, cover the pool with a sturdy cover that supports at least 30 pounds of weight per square foot. Fasten the edges securely so that no gaps are visible.

# Buying Childproof Products

Buying baby equipment is always fun. But it can also be confusing. If you are purchasing baby items for the first time, you may not be sure of what to look for. Because so many products are available to choose from, making the right decision can be daunting.

Although most things manufactured today are safe, some can pose hazards if certain safety factors aren't checked out. Before you buy any equipment, look for the seal of the JPMA (Juvenile Product Manufacturers Association). JPMA offers certification programs for high chairs, strollers, walkers, gates/enclosures, and full-size cribs. The seal assures you that that the products meet the latest consumer-safety specifications.

In addition, check to make sure that the item hasn't been recalled. A list of recalled items is available from the Consumer Product Safety Commission at 800-638-2772 or its Web site `www.cpsc.gov`.

When you decide on a product, check for anything obviously unsafe — protruding or loose hardware and any parts that can scratch, cut skin, or come off in your baby's mouth. Remember: no matter how childproof and sturdy the product is, nothing beats diligent supervision by you, the parent.

## Keeping cribs safe

Cribs manufactured today are very safe and must adhere to mandatory safety standards. Nevertheless, cribs are still associated with more accidents than any other piece of furniture in the nursery. When you go shopping for a crib, look for the JMPA seal of approval.

- ✔ Examine all joints to be sure that they're tight and that spindles and slats are firmly in place.

- ✔ Check for loose hardware and tighten up screws. Babies spend lots of time here, so they're likely to find loose screws and get them out, or worse, swallow them.

- ✔ Avoid cribs with sharp or high protrusions on the corner posts or on the end panels or with cutouts on the end panels.

When your child is able to stand, set the mattress at its lowest point and take out the bumper pads or toys that they can use as a stepping stool to climb out of the crib. Change to a youth bed when the child is 33 inches tall.

If your crib has casters, place them in cups if you have older children around. This will prevent a nursery version of the Indy 500 powered by the siblings.

Be sure to do a thorough once-over of your crib before turning it over to baby number two or three. If cribs aren't used for a while, you may need to get out the screwdriver and tighten up a few things to bring it up to snuff.

Never leave your baby alone in the crib when the sides are lowered. Pull them up and lock them in place after you put the baby inside. Another thing you may not think about: Don't dress your baby in loose-fitting T-shirts, shirts with drawstrings, or necklaces. Clothing parts can get caught on the hardware or posts of the crib and cause an accident.

Avoid draping diaper bags or toys on the ends of the crib where the baby can get tangled up. Keep those hanging crib toys only until the baby starts to push up on her hands and knees. After that, remove such toys from the crib to prevent problems.

---

## Buying or using hand-me-downs

If you have a baby coming, buying a new crib is best. Hand-me-downs or tag-sale purchases (especially cribs made before the 1973 safety standards) can have dangerous flaws in construction that have been corrected in later models. Look carefully at these things before you purchase or use an old model:

✔ Take along a tape measure and check for these important measurements: The dropside should be at least 9 inches above the mattress at its highest setting. The raised side should be at least 26 inches above the mattress support at its lowest setting. Slats should be firmly in place and not more than 2 ⅜ inches apart. The top edge of the four posts should be even with the top of the crib's end panels.

✔ Firmly shake the crib from all sides and look for loose legs and screws and solid construction. Make sure that the lock on the dropside is secure and doesn't open easily.

✔ Put your fingers between the mattress and the sides. If you can fit two fingers in the space, the mattress is too small. Put the mattress to its lowest point. Make sure that the end panels are below the mattress support and that no gap exists between the two where a child's hands or head can get caught.

✔ Check the paint for signs of peeling or chips. Cribs made before 1970 may be coated with a finish that contains lead.

## Buying a safe stroller

When you're shopping for a stroller, check out each model thoroughly by setting it up, unfolding it, and locking it in place. This should be easy to do, but some of them require an engineer to set up and lock — as you'll soon find out. You don't want to be trying to drag a stroller out of the trunk and set it up while your toddler is running amok in the parking lot. You need something that's simple and quick. Make sure the stroller you choose has a locking mechanism that keeps the stroller open after you unfold it and set it up. Hold the handlebars; they should be at a comfortable height, about waist level.

Try steering the stroller with one hand. A good stroller moves in a straight line without veering to either side and resists tipping backwards when you press down lightly on the handles. The weight of the stroller can be an important factor, especially after a long day of pushing. A lighter model will be easier to navigate, which is especially important for the many times you're trying to carry a screaming child while pushing an empty stroller. A stroller with a long, wide wheelbase and a low mounted seat, secured deep within the frame, resists backward tipping and more easily negotiates curbs and sidewalk irregularities.

## Choosing a safe high chair

Padded plastic high chairs are more comfortable and easier to keep clean than wooden ones. A large tray with a wide rim that can be handled with one hand is best. (Guess where your other hand is!)

A wide chair base will make the high chair more stable and less apt to tip over. (Of course, you've got to keep an eye on your child at all times and never let them stand up in the seat.) Fasten the seat belt, pull on it, and make sure that the latch is secure.

If you're using a hand-me-down chair, double-check that the chair has no tiny or sharp parts that could scratch or cut or come off easily. Make sure that the paint or chrome is in good condition without any peeling or rusty spots.

## Investing in an infant swing

According to many mothers, an infant swing can be their lifesaver — the perfect solution to calming a fussy baby who doesn't like to be put down. If you're buying a new infant swing, get a battery-operated model — a real plus because it prevents continuous cranking that often wakes the baby when he or she is asleep. Look for strong restraining straps that keep the child secure in place and a seat with strong stitching and heavy-duty snaps. Check for legs that are mounted on a wide, sturdy base to resist tipping. Again, keep a watchful eye on the baby and other siblings when the baby is in the swing.

## Getting a baby gate

Buy a hardware-mounted baby gate that has a swinging door. Such gates are more reliable than pressure-mounted models that can come off the wall if pushed hard enough.

Avoid using the old-fashioned accordion-type gate because kids' fingers and other body parts can get stuck in them.

Before you buy a gate, measure the width of the door where the gate will go and determine the height you need protected. Mount the gate with no more than one or two inches of clearance between the floor and the bottom of the gate. If your gate has vertical slats, check to make sure that the spacing is less than 2 ⅜ inches. Again, you must supervise your children around the gate. Little kids don't know that they aren't supposed to climb over the gate — in fact, a gate looks like a challenge. Keep large toys and stools away from the gate; kids can use them to climb up and over the gate.

# Babysitting for Friends or Family

If you thought you were home-free because your kids are grown or you're blissfully single, don't relax too much. Next week, your sister may call and ask you to baby-sit with the kids for a few days so she can take the first vacation she's had in four years.

Don't panic. You may not have time to make your house totally baby-safe but you can take some quick precautions to make your baby-sitting worry-free.

---

## Never-never land

The following is a list of never-do's. Never — not once, not ever — do the following things:

- ✔ Never leave a child alone in the bathtub.

- ✔ Never leave your child alone on any elevated surface.

- ✔ Never put your newborn to sleep on his stomach.

- ✔ Never take a nap or leave the house with young children unattended and free to wander.

- ✔ Never let a young child ride in a car without a child safety seat.

- ✔ Never let an older child ride in the car without a seat belt.

- ✔ Never let your child ride a bike or roller skate without a helmet.

- ✔ Never keep a loaded, unsecured gun in the house. Always hide guns where children can't get at them and, if possible, keep the firearm and the ammunition stored separately when you're not home.

Be sure the child's parents or guardians tell you how to reach them in an emergency and give you a list of emergency numbers: the child's doctor, the hospital, a friendly neighbor, police and fire department. You should be informed about any medicines the child is taking and any allergies and illnesses. Have the parents fill out a release form giving you the authority to have the child treated in case of medical emergency. This form is available from their doctor's office.

## Hiring a baby-sitter

Even though you may feel desperate when trying to find a baby-sitter, be sure to invest some time and effort in looking for the right one. Ask friends and relatives for recommendations. When you start interviewing, always ask for references and then be sure to call them and ask how the sitter got along with the children.

Ask the sitter very specific questions about how he or she would handle certain problems like a sore throat or a cut finger or what she would do

if the child can't fall asleep. Ask what kind of games she likes to play with the kids. Invite him over for a couple of hours to see how he gets along with your children.

If the sitter seems young, assess whether he or she is mature enough to handle stressful situations and make rational decisions. If you have the slightest doubts about the person, keep looking. A parent's instincts are usually right.

# Chapter 21

# The Things That Pollute Your Home

*I*f you're coughing, wheezing, or otherwise feeling low, it may not be that nasty flu bug that's going around. It may be home sweet home! Unfortunately, in this day and age, many things inside and outside the home affect your health and well-being. You've probably all heard the horror stories of people leaving their homes in the middle of the night due to some unknown chemical lurking between or within the walls. Even if the pollutants that may be in your home aren't life threatening, they can still cause discomfort and distress.

If you suspect something is wrong with the air in your home, take a good look around — with your eyes and with your nose. Have you noticed any strange but definitely unidentifiable odors? Do you have condensation on windows and walls or mold and mildew on walls and furnishings? Is your house well-ventilated? Or does the air seem stale and stuffy?

Has anyone in your home had a change in his or her health patterns lately? Certain symptoms may be indicative that something at home is the problem. Watch out for persistent flu-like symptoms that start with the heating season, asthma attacks, and frequent respiratory or bronchitis infections in children. Have you noticed any health reactions after remodeling, weatherizing, using new furniture, or moving into a new home? Do you get an adverse physical reaction after using household products?

**The ultimate question:** Do you feel healthier when you aren't at home?

The preceding questions highlight some of the more common symptoms, but by no means all. The type of symptoms that show up depend on the intensity and type of pollutant, the length of exposure, and the physical makeup of the individual. Some people react strongly right away, and others respond only after a long exposure. The elderly and children usually are more susceptible than others.

# Indoor Chemical Pollution — It's Serious Stuff

Problems with indoor air pollution continue to mount because our homes are sealed up more tightly than ever before. For example, modern homes have central air conditioning, heating, and windows that don't open and shut. These features are good for energy efficiency but may be bad for your health.

In addition, because more and more furniture, appliances, and cleaning products are made with potentially toxic ingredients, the air indoors can sometimes be more polluted than the air outdoors. The following sections outline some of the most serious causes of indoor air pollution and what to do about them.

## Formaldehyde (pressed wood products)

Formaldehyde is a colorless gas (which may or may not have an odor) that many household products release into the air. Particleboard is a major source, but formaldehyde is also found in many of the things that we use to furnish or decorate our homes, such as permanent press fabrics, insulation, carpeting, interior plywood, veneered or laminated furniture and cabinets, cosmetics, and paints. The combustion byproducts from all types of stoves — kerosene, coal, wood, and gas — also emit formaldehyde. Homes built during the 1970s often used urea-formaldehyde foam insulation to preserve energy. Mobile homes often have high levels of formaldehyde.

Some people are more susceptible and will react to concentrations that don't seem to bother most other people. Intense fumes from formaldehyde are very irritating and can cause watery eyes; burning sensations in eyes, nose, and throat; wheezing; coughing; fatigue; skin rashes; loss of coordination; and nausea. Extremely large concentrations can cause asthma, liver and kidney damage, and central nervous system failure. Reactions have been noted in some people who live in houses that are closed up, in new homes that have large concentrations of plywood, or in houses with new kitchen cabinets or lots of new furniture.

### How to detect it

Testing is the only way to know for sure if your home has high levels of formaldehyde, because it doesn't always have a detectable odor. You should be able to find firms that test for formaldehyde by checking for "environmental testing firms" in your local Yellow Pages, contacting your local health department, or contacting the Consumer Product Safety Commission at 301-492-6800. Keep in mind, though, that the testing can be expensive, possibly costing several hundred dollars so it's impractical unless someone is experiencing symptoms.

### *What you can do about it*

Lowering the level of formaldehyde in your house depends in part on what the source of contamination is.

- ✔ If the cause is furniture, simply remove the offending pieces.

- ✔ If the cause is formaldehyde insulation, close up the routes where the gas enters your home. Look at cracks around electrical outlets, baseboards, floors, walls, and ceilings.

- ✔ If kitchen cabinets are the problem, a plastic laminate countertop will stop some contamination. Because formaldehyde cannot penetrate plastic laminate, covering the top surface of the cabinets with a good countertop will do some good.

Formaldehyde is at least partly blocked by coatings, so applying varnishes and special sealants to all exposed edges and surfaces — such as the undersides of countertops, cabinet interiors, and drawers — will give some protection. Because high humidity and high temperatures increase the release of formaldehyde fumes, keep the temperature at a moderate level and control humidity through air conditioning or dehumidifiers. Increase ventilation by opening doors and windows and running exhaust fans. Time is also on your side; after a year formaldehyde levels in new products drop by half.

When remodeling or beginning new construction, do some research and pick low-formaldehyde materials. For any work inside, use exterior-grade plywood products, which emit less formaldehyde.

## *Carbon monoxide: a stealthy killer*

Carbon monoxide is a colorless, oderless gas produced by incomplete burning of fuel. Blocked-up flues or chimneys can prevent the venting of exhaust to the outside. A cracked or rusted heat exchanger on a fuel-burning furnace can allow combustion gases into your living areas. Fuel-burning space heaters, ovens, ranges, or grills operated in the home without adequate ventilation may produce carbon monoxide. Other sources are car exhaust from an attached garage; wood or gas burning stoves; damaged chimneys; airtight homes; or backdrafting of furnace or fireplace gases.

Carbon monoxide replaces oxygen in the blood and starves the brain and other parts of the body of oxygen. At high enough levels, exposure can be fatal. Determining if carbon monoxide is causing symptoms at less than fatal levels is difficult because the symptoms can mimic the flu or an allergy. Weakness, muscle aches, irregular heartbeat, a sense of stuffiness in the home, nausea and vomiting, headache and sleepiness, or fatigue can be caused by low levels. High doses can cause paralysis, coma, or even death.

## Plants that purify the air

Plants have always been good for our indoor environment, not only because they look so beautiful, but also because they absorb carbon dioxide and give off oxygen. Studies have also found that they freshen the air by absorbing toxic organic pollutants, such as benzene and formaldehyde, around the home. The peace lily, English ivy, Boston fern, and chrysanthemum are good all-around pollution fighters.

### *How to detect it*

Install carbon monoxide detectors in the areas of your home that have fuel-burning devices. You can choose from several different detector models on the market today. They all sound an alarm when levels become dangerous; some give you a digital readout of exactly what the carbon monoxide level is in your home. Always make sure that the batteries are working in these devices; change them when you change the batteries in your smoke detectors.

### *What you can do about it*

Your most important defense: Keep all combustion equipment well maintained and safety inspected:

- ✔ Start by checking the color of the gas flames on your stove: a properly functioning stove has a blue flame. A yellow-tipped flame indicates that a gas range is not burning properly and should be adjusted.

- ✔ Install an exhaust hood, which is vented to the outside, above the gas range and turn it on whenever you cook.

- ✔ Vent gas dryers to the outside. Avoid devices that route the hot air exhaust from the dryer back into the room.

If you have a fireplace, be sure to keep it in good shape. Have it inspected and cleared of debris every fall before heating season begins. Check the flues and chimneys for cracks, disconnected flue pipes, soot around openings in your furnace or boiler, soot or creosote buildup, exhaust odors, and broken pieces of masonry. Make sure that each combustion device has a separate flue. Inspect chimney caps after heavy snows or ice storms to make sure the grill hasn't become covered with ice or snow, preventing the exhaust of gases. Open the flue when using gas or wood burning fireplaces. Experts recommend that you never use unvented combustion appliances, such as kerosene heaters and lamps, indoors.

You may think that this warning doesn't need to be given, but people do this more often than you think: Never barbecue in the house or garage! Exercise safety with the car — make sure that the garage door is open when the car is running; never allow a car to sit and idle in the garage.

# Asbestos: a lung destroyer

If your home was built before 1978, asbestos may be present in several places. It was used in the adhesive and backing beneath linoleum floor, sheetrock, roofing and siding materials, tile floors, insulation, acoustic ceilings, decorative plaster, pipe and heat duct wrapping, door gaskets, boiler wraps, and even appliances manufactured before 1986. After that date, the government recognized the danger, and any product containing asbestos had to contain a warning label.

Asbestos is generally not a problem if it's intact, in good condition, and not losing fibers from crumbling and breaking. Pulling up old linoleum, ripped insulation around pipes, and weathered or chipped exterior siding can release tiny asbestos fibers into the air, which you can breathe into your lungs. If you inhale them continuously, the fibers become embedded in the lungs and can cause cancer after 15 to 30 years of exposure.

### How to detect it

Your state health agency or local EPA office can direct you to inspectors who determine asbestos levels and contractors who can safely remove products that contain asbestos. You can also check the Yellow Pages for agencies.

### What you can do about it

If you're sure that asbestos-containing materials in your home are intact and not breaking up or emitting dust, leave them alone. Don't try to remove any material containing asbestos; don't saw or drill into it. If you suspect you have asbestos flooring, the best solution is to cover it up with another flooring.

# Lead: an old invader

Lead is a metallic substance that is common in housing constructed before 1978, when it was banned from paint. The most common sources are lead paint and lead in the water supply. If you live in a home near major paths of traffic, the soil may be contaminated from long-term use of leaded gas. If the exterior of your home is painted with lead paint, it could chip off and contaminate the soil around the house.

Lead paint that is intact and in good condition may not pose an immediate hazard. When the paint starts to peel, chip, or flake, or you disturb it during painting or remodeling, it can become a health hazard. The lead may even disperse as a dust that can be breathed in or fall fall on toys, furniture, carpeting, or other areas of the house and contaminate them.

Other sources of lead in homes is through lead pipes or lead solder in water piping. Brass and bronze faucets sometimes contain lead that may leach into the water.

Small children, unborn babies, and the elderly are most vulnerable to lead poisoning. In children, lead exposure can result in brain damage, lowered IQ's, and reading and learning problems. In both children and adults, lead can cause high blood pressure, anemia, and kidney and reproductive disorders. All children up to age six should be tested for lead in their blood. Your local public health department can give you information about lead testing for children.

### How to detect it

To figure out whether your home has significant concentrations of lead, you can try the do-it-yourself route or hire a professional.

Do-it-yourself kits are available at some home and building centers, ceramic supply stores, and paint stores. You chip off a piece of paint, right down to the underlayment — and either send it to a lab or use the kit to measure the level yourself. The problem is that these kits are not very sensitive, and you may have difficulty getting accurate readings on surfaces with multiple layers of paint.

The most accurate, and more expensive, way to evaluate your home is to have a professional detection service conduct an assessment. You can contact your local board of health for information on local testing agencies.

If you suspect lead paint on the exterior of your home, the state agricultural extension service office can direct you to agencies that test the surrounding soil. Water testing may be necessary if you suspect contamination of your water supply. Check to see if your city offers free or low-cost testing. The local Environmental Protection Agency can give you more information. Any of these evaluations can help you determine if lead is present in your home and if the presence poses a health hazard.

### What you can do about it

On the simple side, you can control the exposure to lead in your home through frequent damp mopping to control lead dust, which is especially important if your house or apartment building was built before 1980. Pick up loose paint chips with masking or duct tape. (Vacuuming can cause the dust to be blown around the house.) Wash children's hands, faces, pacifiers, and toys.

Don't disturb the paint in any way, such as by using heat guns or blow-torches, or by sanding, scraping, or sandblasting the paint. Painted surfaces should only be covered by wallpaper, paneling, or new lead-free paint. Lead-paint removal should only be done by qualified professionals. Children should always be removed from the home until post-removal testing determines that the home is safe.

You must treat lead from drinking water with a distiller or reverse osmosis water purification system — or consider drinking bottled water instead.

# Radon: a recent threat

Radon is a naturally occurring, radioactive gas that comes from decaying uranium in the soil and rock beneath and around the foundation of homes. It also comes from ground water wells and some building materials. Odorless and colorless, radon gets into buildings through cracks and openings in the foundation and floors, crawl spaces, floor drains, concrete block basement walls, and well water.

If you suspect radon, don't allow anyone to live or sleep in the basement, which is where you'll find the highest contamination levels. Just remember that your forced air heating and air conditioning systems spread the radon throughout the house. Once trapped inside a closed-up home, radon can escalate to dangerous levels. Exposure to high levels of radon for a lengthy period of time can cause lung cancer.

### How to detect it

First, consult your local EPA office to check whether the area you live in is known to have high radon levels. If large amounts of your home have exposed brick, stone, or concrete, you should test your home regardless. You can get an alpha track detector kit for home testing and send the completed test to a lab for analysis. These long-term (taking at least one month) kits are considered the most accurate. The cost of about $20 to $25 per kit includes postage and test results from the lab where you mail the kit. You can also get short-term — and less accurate — carbon-detector radon kits that take from 2 to 7 days and cost $10 to $20.

### What you can do about it

Begin by caulking cracks in the basement concrete and masonry and sealing floors and walls with latex paint. Sometimes you can keep your basement windows open and install fans to circulate fresh air from outside. Cover exposed soil (such as in a crawl space) with concrete or a sealed polymeric vapor barrier.

It's wise to ban anyone from smoking in the house because it doubles your risk of dying from lung cancer if exposed to radon. Try ventilating the house more — open lots of windows and keep the vents in the crawl space open.

You must retest for radon after trying these home "fix-up" techniques. If they are not successful, you can have a qualified contractor set up a venting system that keeps the radon in check and removes it.

# Electromagnetic radiation

Electrical current passing through home wiring, electrical appliances, and high-voltage power lines gives off electromagnetic radiation. Not all forms of electromagnetic radiation are considered problematic — only the high-frequency waves. Low-frequency wavelengths, such as visible light and radio and television waves, aren't considered dangerous.

At this time, studies done on electromagnetic fields (EMF) have been conflicting: some link EMF to certain types of cancer, others say no definite link exists. Some people feel it is prudent to be on the safe side regarding electromagnetic radiation exposure until all the research comes in.

Your home has many sources of EMF: The rule to remember is that the closer you are to the source, the higher the EMF level. Some devices that generate high levels are electric blankets, electric alarm clocks, electrically heated water beds, electric power saws, electric can openers, hair dryers, electric shavers, mixers, microwave ovens, loop-style electric heating cables, electrical panels, and vacuum cleaners.

Some problems that have a possible link to EMFs are childhood leukemia, various types of cancer in adults, Alzheimer's disease, and miscarriages. More vague symptoms of exposure include loss of balance, uneasiness, mental confusion, and hearing unusual noises.

## How to detect it

To get an accurate reading of your home or office's exposure to EMF, you can use one of a few available scientific reading devices. One is a small meter that you carry or wear to record magnetic field exposures automatically. It measures the field every 24 seconds for a 24-hour period.

If you are concerned about EMFs generated by nearby high voltage, electric power lines, transformers, and substations, contact your local electric utility for assistance. They will usually come to your home and measure the EMF level generated by their equipment. You can also rent equipment to measure levels in your home.

### *What you can do about it*

You can avoid exposure to EMFs in three main ways.

- First, increase the distance between yourself and the source of EMFs. For example, place your electronic alarm clock away from your head and body so you are not exposed to the EMFs from it all night. Turn off your computer when you aren't using it.

- Avoid unnecessary proximity to high EMF sources; don't let children play directly under power lines or on top of power transformers for underground lines.

- Reduce time spent in the electromagnetic field; turn off electric appliances when you are not using them.

## *Information resources*

For more information about indoor pollutants, contact these agencies:

- Environmental Protection Agency Information Resources, 202-260-5922, for information on how to test for and handle asbestos, formaldehyde, lead, radon, carbon monoxide, and other household toxins; their Web site is www.epa.gov/.

- EPA-Indoor Air Quality Information Hotline, 800-438-4318.

- Toxic Substances Control Act Assistance Information Service Hotline, 202-554-1404.

- American Council of Independent Laboratories, 202-887-5872, for a list of laboratories that test for lead, radon, and other contaminants around the house.

- National Lead Information Center, 800-532-3394. An EPA-sponsored number that provides printed material about lead poisoning and how to prevent it. Also provides a listing of state and local agencies with more information.

- National Safety Council, 800-621-7615, or their Web site at www.nsc.org.

- Safe Drinking Water Hot Line, 800-426-4791. Gives information about contaminant detection in drinking water.

- U.S. Environmental Protection Agency Radon Hotline, 800-SOS-RADON.

# Using Household Products Safely

Several products around the house can pollute the air and create a hazard. The problem products are those containing volatile organic compounds, which are organic solvents that evaporate easily into the air. Some may be flammable, other have fumes that cause drowsiness, headaches, and more serious problems in high dosages. Some of the problem ingredients that you may see listed on labels are petroleum distillates (found in furniture polish and spot removers), minerals spirits, chlorinated solvents, carbon tetrachloride, methylene chloride (found in paint strippers, degreasers, and waxes), trichloroethane (found in drain cleaners and spot removers), toluene, and formaldehyde. Be sure to read labels of any household product carefully so you know what its ingredients are and how to properly use it.

A number of other household products can also be a hazardous if used improperly. Be careful with ammonia (deadly if mixed with chlorine), carpet shampoo, glues, liquid spot removers, paints, varnishes, drain cleaners, pesticides, mothballs, and toilet and oven cleaners. Their fumes can harm nasal passages when breathed. Obviously, they should never be swallowed.

Protect yourself: Wear rubber gloves, a mask over your mouth, and goggles to protect your eyes. Always make sure the room you're working in is well-ventilated. Do anything you can to get the air flowing: Open all the windows and doors. Bring in a fan if necessary. After working with any of these substances, thoroughly clean off any surface that they touched — floor, countertops, or furniture.

## Get that air flowing

If too little air enters a home, any substances polluting the home can accumulate and rise to levels that can cause physical discomfort and possibly health problems. Because many homes today are built specifically to be airtight, they may have higher levels of pollutants than older homes. And because many areas of the country have weather that requires windows and doors to be shut throughout much of the year, even homes that might be considered "leaky" may have problems from the lack of outdoor air entering the home. Some signs that your home may not have enough ventilation are:

- Condensation on windows or walls
- Smelly or stuffy air
- Dirty heating and air conditioning equipment
- Storage areas where books, shoes, or other items often become moldy

Don't ever mix any of these household chemical products together, and avoid using one right after the other. Traces of one chemical may be left that might not mix with the next chemical you use. Federal regulations require that manufacturers indicate the toxicity of a product on the box. Look for the words *warning, danger, poison, flammable, volatile, caustic,* and *corrosive.*

In the garage, you may have such items as brake and transmission fluid, antifreeze, oil, gasoline, window washer fluid, and battery acid. Keep them away from heat. Always store them off the floor, preferably in a locked cabinet, especially if you have young children.

# Why Are You Sneezing?

Aside from the really serious stuff discussed previously in this chapter, lots of other things in your house can make you cough, sneeze, and feel generally awful. Most of them are common, everyday annoyances that you don't even give a second thought. The following sections discuss some of the allergens that plague thousands of people each and every day.

## Mold and mildew: A spreading concern

One of the things that attracted you to your latest house was the lovely wallpaper in the bathrooms. Unfortunately, when you moved in, you discovered that the pattern was caused by mold. What to do?

### Understanding the enemy

Mold — a fungus — thrives in places that are damp, under ventilated, dark, and warm. It grows on organic materials such as paper, textiles, grease, dirt, and soap scum. You can find it in all sorts of places: crawl spaces, bathrooms, humidifiers, refrigerator drip pans, foam rubber furnishings, books, your future Olympian's sweaty running shoes, and many other places. In order to stage a successful war against mold, you need to remove any existing contamination and prevent further outcrops. Some suggest that if you have mold in your yard, you should keep windows closed to prevent outside spores from drifting into your home and establishing new colonies.

### Getting rid of the enemy

To thoroughly get rid of this fungus requires repair and prevention. You need to check your home for leaks and damp spots that could harbor mold. Bathrooms, stuffy closets, basements, and kitchens are particular trouble spots. Seal all walls, patch cracks, and take care of leaky plumbing. If an area is dry, you won't have mold. Use a dehumidifier in trouble spots, such as basements. Make sure the drain tubes for dehumidifiers and refrigerators are working properly and clean the units regularly with a disinfectant such as chlorine bleach. Keep humidity levels at less than 50 percent.

Increase air circulation to keep excess humidity down throughout the house. Remove as much moisture as possible at the point of production. Install and use ventilation fans in baths, kitchens, and laundry areas or anywhere else where you use a lot of water. Make sure that the fans are vented to the outside of the house, not into the attic. Get in the habit of turning on the fan over the stove every time you cook, not just when you are burning dinner. Clothes dryers need to be vented to the outside of the house (preferably with flexible metal tubing). A whole-house fan increases ventilation as well.

Mildew is common in closets. Remove all old clothing, boxes, and books that are no longer used or needed and may be harboring mold spores and preventing good air circulation. Clean any existing mold and thoroughly dust the items. Leave a low-wattage bulb burning (if it presents no safety hazard) or use a desiccant (moisture removing chemical) such as activated charcoal.

Books can harbor a lot of dust and mold. Dust and wipe books and shelves often and throw out any old or mildewed books. Often, books that have been stored in a basement or attic have a damp feel to them. Take steps to solve this problem before it develops into mold. Sprinkle some talcum powder on the pages. Let the powder sit for several hours, then wipe it off. The talcum powder will absorb some of the moisture. Put a few pieces of activated charcoal in a bowl and store it in the bookcase to help prevent future problems.

Foam rubber furniture, along with upholstery and rugs, is prone to developing mildew. Ideally, you should vacuum furniture on a weekly basis to help prevent problems. If you see mildew on furniture, wipe it off carefully so the spores don't become airborne. Wash with warm water and a small amount of mild dishwashing detergent, then rinse and wipe dry. If mildew remains, wipe it with rubbing alcohol (after testing in a hidden area first), then wash and wipe dry. It's important to dry wet fabric quickly and not allow anything to be damp for too long. Likewise, carpeting must be dried after shampooing to discourage new growth.

If you see white furry deposits or black spots on siding, tile roofs, brick stucco, or patios, it's time to do some heavy cleaning. Put on a face mask and goggles and brush off the deposits with a stiff brush (outdoors, if possible). Use a commercial mildew remover or try a mixture of ¾ cup liquid bleach with a gallon of water. Wet the surface with the bleach solution for 5 to 15 minutes. Don't put the solution on any surface if you're in the direct sun. The heat of the sun will make the solution dry off too quickly and its effectiveness will be lost. Be sure to rinse thoroughly with clean water. Bleach can corrode aluminum window frames or unpainted gutters. Never use this mixture on unpainted wood.

## *Dogs and cats: Man's (and woman's) best friends?*

He may be your best friend but one you can't stand to get near. Unfortunately, animal dander and saliva are two of the most common allergens. Short of getting rid of little kitty or old Fido, you can take action to reduce the level of allergens in the house:

- ✔ Groom your pet frequently to reduce dander. While you're brushing your pet, spray an antistatic spray, such as Static Guard, on the grooming tools to keep hairs from sticking to you or the furniture and carpeting. Brush your pet outside or in the garage, if possible.

- ✔ Designate some rooms of the house as "off limits" for your pet. Don't let animals get on top of the furniture or sleep on the bed. They can unknowingly leave dander behind that can cause reactions.

- ✔ If you're buying a new pet, choose an animal with characteristics that are less likely to irritate your allergies. Choose a nonshedding dog, such as a poodle, rather than one that will constantly shed fur onto the furniture. Some breeds and genders are less allergic than others.

- ✔ Be diligent about removing pet hairs from furniture or other furnishings. Quickly get hairs off furniture by wiping with a damp sponge or a piece of masking tape wrapped around your finger.

## *Dust mites: There's more in your bed than you think*

Don't ever get into a conversation about dust mites with someone close to bedtime. Even though you can't see, hear, smell, or feel them, they (and their droppings) seem to be everywhere, wreaking havoc with your allergies. People throw out really scary statistics that can turn anyone's restful sleep into something out of a horror movie. How about "a queen size bed can contain over a million dust mites" or "one tenth of the weight of a five-year-old pillow is dust mites and their waste particles?" It's enough to give you insomnia. Anyone for tree house living?

Dust mites are so small that you can't see them with your naked eye. But they are almost guaranteed to be in your home, no matter how clean it is. More people are allergic to dust mites (specifically their feces) than any other substance in their home. They are found in carpeting, mattresses, stuffed toys, upholstered furniture, and pillows. Mites thrive in humid climates, so they're more prevalent during the dog days of summer — August and September — and are at their lowest in January. Your bed and bedding is their breeding ground — it's moist and hot. Although you probably can't get rid of them, you can try a few things to keep them in check.

### Blocking off the bedroom

Wash off all bedding in the hot water possible every week (at least 130 degrees). If you can't wash your comforter weekly, try buying allergen proof covers for it. You can also buy allergen-proof coverings for the mattress, box springs, and pillows. Periodically vacuum the mattress and box spring. And don't forget to wash off any stuffed toys and animals that you keep on the bed that could contain dust mites.

### Cleaning up

Vacuum religiously. This will get them up and away from one of their breeding grounds. If you're really allergic, don't use a conventional vacuum that vents dust out the exhaust hatch, which results in tossing them back into the air again. Best to use a central vacuum system or one that has a special high efficiency particulate air (HEPA) filter. If you don't have either, at least put on a dust mask while vacuuming. Use a silicone treated cloth when dusting so the dust isn't dispersed into the air. If you are really allergic, you may want to switch from carpeting to wood floors.

## All cotton ain't all that natural

All cotton doesn't always mean all natural or non-toxic. Because of conventional American farming practices, cotton production uses tremendous quantities of pesticides, herbicides, and other toxic agricultural chemicals. Inevitably, some residues from these chemicals get on the cotton fibers. In addition, permanent press chemicals (which can be formaldehyde-based resins), synthetic dyes, stain-resistant treatments, and other compounds are often added to cotton fibers during the milling process. As a result, all cotton fabrics can be laden with chemicals. For more information, contact the U.S. Consumer Product Safety Commission at 1-800-638-CPSP (1-800-638-2777).

# Chapter 22

# How Safe Is Your Food?

*H*ere in the United States, we're incredibly lucky to have a wide variety of fresh foods available at all times. All you have to do is stroll through the aisles of any grocery store to see the abundance of fresh meat, veggies, and cheeses from all over the world. And yet the food supply still has problems. Foods are harvested, caught, or picked sometimes days or weeks before they arrive at the store. Every now and then, there's a snag in the system: Trucks break down, coolers don't work, food gets misplaced. Because of these some-times-uncontrollable circumstances, you have to be even more careful about selecting and maintaining food that is safe and ready to eat. You don't have any control over what's happened to the food before you buy it, but you can handle it more carefully once it goes into your shopping cart and into your home.

## Buying Fresh Food

Even though most of us would say that we care about getting the best food, we often tear through the grocery store, grabbing things off the shelves and throwing them into a cart without paying much attention to what we're taking. Shopping has become more a race against time than a careful selection process for the freshest food. What you choose to buy and how you transport it home are the first steps to food safety.

First, make sure that foods that are supposed to be refrigerated at home are also refrigerated well in the store. Always touch the packages of dairy products, meat, and fish to make sure that they're cold. Don't buy these products if they feel lukewarm or if the package has any holes or tears in it. Frozen foods should feel rock solid, not mushy. Eggs should also be kept cool in the refrigerated section. Before you buy, open the carton and check each one to make sure they aren't cracked or leaking and sticking to the carton.

Meats, poultry, fish, and dairy products should all have "sell by" dates displayed prominently on the package. Some eggs also have dates on the carton. A "sell-by" date tells the store how long it should display the product for sale. Look for these dates and avoid any for which the expiration date has passed. Some products also have "use by" dates, or include such dates instead of "sell by" dates. These dates tell you the useful life of the product so you'll know how long you can safely store it.

Inspect canned foods, too. Dents on the seam or rim, cracks, or bulging lids are indications that the food inside may be unsafe to eat.

Plan your food purchases in the grocery store so that foods won't get too warm or leak before you leave the store. Buy canned, dry foods like flour, sugar, coffee, and vegetables first. Pick up frozen foods, poultry, meat, seafood, and hot, prepared deli foods right before you go to the checkout. If it's hot outside, keep an ice chest in the car to store foods that need to be refrigerated, especially if you're going to make other stops on the way home. Even short stops in hot weather, just to run into a store for a few minutes, can cause food to warm to dangerous levels if it's left sitting in a hot car.

# Handling and Preparing Food

Unfortunately, much of the meat, fish, poultry, and some dairy products that you buy contain contaminants that can cause illnesses if you aren't careful when handling it. Luckily, good clean habits solve most of your food safety problems.

### Washing your hands

You can never be too clean.

Always wash your hands thoroughly, before and after you prepare food, for at least 20 seconds with warm water and soap. If you're interrupted while preparing food, wash your hands before you stop to do something else. This prevents you from spreading any bacteria onto any other surface you may happen to touch, like the cabinet doors, the countertop, or knife handles.

Wear disposable gloves or plastic sandwich bags while cutting up chicken or mixing meat loaf, so that all you have to do is remove them to answer the phone or go to the front door.

# Keeping your equipment clean

When you finish preparing food, thoroughly wash everything that comes in contact with meat, fish, poultry, or eggs, including cutting boards, sponges, knives, countertops, and any plates that have held raw meat.

Launder towels or dishcloths that have touched such bacteria-carrying foods in the washing machine in the hottest water possible with 1 cup chlorine bleach. Wash sponges in the dishwasher if you have one and then disinfect them by putting them in the microwave until they're dry, usually about one to six minutes, depending on the size of your microwave.

Use separate cutting boards for cutting raw meats and chopping fresh vegetables or preparing a salad. Even the slightest bit of juice from raw poultry, meat, or seafood leaking onto any food that won't be cooked can be a problem. Separate cooked and raw foods when you're preparing them. If you only have one cutting board, wash and disinfect it thoroughly before using it with different foods.

# Thawing food safely

Don't thaw frozen meat, poultry, or seafood at room temperature. It may feel cold to the touch, but bacteria can still multiply. Choose one of these three easy and safe methods:

- **Defrost in the refrigerator.** Always set the meat on a plate to prevent juices from leaking onto other foods.
- **Defrost in the microwave according to the instruction manual.** Cook the food immediately after defrosting.
- **Defrost in a plastic bag in a pan filled with cold water.** Change water every 30 minutes.

# Cooking it right!

Health experts suggest that you thoroughly cook meat, poultry, and fish as well as dishes with eggs to kill harmful bacteria. Use a quick-read meat thermometer to give an accurate reading. Place the thermometer at the thickest portion of the meat away from the bone. Always roast meat in an oven set to at least 325 degrees. Long, slow cooking in an oven below that temperature may encourage bacterial growth. Avoid interrupted cooking: Don't cook food partially ahead of time, store it, then finish grilling or roasting it later. Follow these temperature guidelines from the USDA for determining when food is thoroughly cooked:

✔ Cook ground meat to 160° F.

✔ Cook ground poultry to 165° F.

✔ Cook beef, veal, lamb steaks, roast, and chops to 145° F.

✔ Cook fresh pork to 160° F.

✔ Cook whole poultry to 180° F. for dark meat and 170° F. for white.

Examine the meat carefully after it's done: Meat or poultry less than 2 inches thick should have clear juices and no pink in the center; fish should flake with a fork, and eggs should be firm.

Refrigerate meat while it's marinating. If you plan to use the marinade as a sauce later, boil it first to kill any bacteria. Don't use the same brush to baste raw and fully cooked meats.

Never forget that two hours is the maximum limit for any prepared or cut food to be left at room temperature — one hour in warm weather. After that, toss the food out.

# Refrigerating and Freezing Foods

Foods purchased refrigerated need to be in a cold refrigerator at 40° F. or less. The cold doesn't actually kill bacteria, but it slows down their development.

Checking the temperature in your refrigerator is easy: Buy an appliance thermometer at a kitchen equipment or hardware store and place it on one of the middle shelves. Keep testing and adjusting the temperature in your refrigerator until it's at the proper temperature. You may have to readjust the temperature during the summer or winter if the room becomes excessively hot or cold.

Refrigerators all have different areas that are colder than others (on mine, the coldest area is on the top shelf at the back). Look at your appliance manual or check with an appliance thermometer to see where your cold spots are. Store the more perishable foods, such as fish, poultry, and cheese, in these cold spots. You can safely leave raw meat, poultry, or fish in its store wrapping as long as the wrapping has no rips or tears. Put the wrapped meat on a plate to catch any drips. Quickly wipe down any stains from dripped or spilled food.

Store milk in the coldest part of the refrigerator, not the door, where the temperature fluctuates because the door opens and closes. Ditto for eggs, which you should leave in their cartons, rather than stored in the little indented egg-keepers in the door.

All leftovers, including vegetables, should be refrigerated within two hours and eaten or frozen in no more than three days. Cool down hot food fast by dividing it up into small portions in shallow containers. Date the container so you can tell at a glance how long it's been on the shelf. Keep leftovers towards the front so they don't get lost. Every week, go through the refrigerator to remove any food that may be spoiled.

## Facing freezer facts

The optimum temperature for the freezer is 0° F. Food stored at that temperature is generally safe. Wrap foods well with heavy freezer wrap, ziptop plastic freezer bags, or rigid plastic containers with tight fitting lids. Cool off hot foods before putting them in the freezer to avoid raising the freezer temperature. Date and label packages with the food name, date frozen, and portion size. If foods have been frozen for a long period, check the quality after defrosting. Some frozen foods may have an off or bad odor and should be thrown away. Other foods may not look so good, but are still edible.

As far as safety goes, you can freeze the following items (but you probably won't want to eat them when they thaw out):

- Mayonnaise (it separates)
- Lettuce, tomatoes, radishes (turns mushy)
- Soft cheeses (becomes crumbly)
- Cooked egg white or eggs in shell
- Yogurt (separates)
- Cottage cheese (separates)
- Custard and cream pies (get watery)
- Potatoes (mushy if raw, tough if cooked)

Table 22-1 presents guidelines for how long some common foods can be stored safely in the refrigerator or freezer.

| Table 22-1 | Timelines for Refrigerated and Frozen Foods | |
|---|---|---|
| **Beverages** | **Refrigerated** | **Frozen** |
| Fruit beverages | 3 weeks unopened | 8–12 months |
| Juice in cartons, punch | 7–10 days opened | 8–12 months |

*(continued)*

### Table 22-1 *(continued)*

| Dairy Products | Refrigerated | Frozen |
|---|---|---|
| Butter | 1–3 months | 6–9 months |
| Cheese, hard (Cheddar, Swiss) | 3 mos. Unopened; 2–3 weeks opened | 6 months |
| Cheese, soft (Brie, Bel Paese) | 1 week | 6 months |
| Cream cheese | 2 weeks | Do not freeze |
| **Dairy Products** | **Refrigerated** | **Frozen** |
| Cream, whipping, ultrapasteurized | 1 month | Do not freeze |
| Egg substitutes, unopened | 10 days | Do not freeze |
| Egg substitutes, opened | 3 days | Do not freeze |
| Eggs, in shell | 3–5 weeks | Do not freeze |
| Eggs, raw whites | 2–4 days | 12 months |
| Eggs, raw yokes | 2–4 days | Doesn't freeze well |
| **Deli Foods** | **Refrigerated** | **Frozen** |
| Entrees, hot or cold | 3–4 days | 2–3 months |
| Store-sliced lunch meats | 3–5 days | 1–2 months |
| **Fish** | **Refrigerated** | **Frozen** |
| Lean fish (cod, flounder, haddock, sole, etc.) | 1–2 days | 6 months |
| Fatty fish (bluefish, mackerel, salmon, etc.) | 1–2 days | 2–3 months |
| Shellfish (shrimp, scallops, crayfish, squid, etc.) | 1–2 days | 3–6 months |
| Cooked fish | 3–4 days | 4–6 months |
| **Meat and Poultry, Fresh** | **Refrigerated** | **Frozen** |
| Beef, Lamb, Pork or Veal chops, steak, roasts | 3–5 days | 4–12 months |

| Meat and Poultry, Fresh | Refrigerated | Frozen |
|---|---|---|
| Chicken or turkey, whole | 1–2 days | 12 months |
| Chicken or turkey parts | 1–2 days | 9 months |
| Cooked meat and chicken | 3–4 days | Meat: 2–3 months; Poultry: 4–6 months |
| Ground meat | 1–2 days | 4–6 months |
| **Meat and Poultry, Processed** | **Refrigerated** | **Frozen** |
| Bacon | 7 days | 1 month |
| Ham, canned ("keep refrigerated" label) | 6–9 months | Do not freeze cans |
| Ham, cooked, slices or half | 3–4 days | 1–2 months |
| Hot dogs, packaged | 2 weeks | 1–2 months |
| Hot dogs, opened | 1 week | 1–2 months |
| Lunch meats, packaged | 2 weeks | 1–2 months |
| Lunch meats, opened | 3–5 days | 1–2 months |
| Sausage, raw, bulk-type (not in patties or links) | 1–2 days | 1–2 months |
| Sausage, smoked links, patties | 7 days | 1–2 months |
| Sausage, hard, dry (pepperoni) | 2–3 weeks | 1–2 months |

Source: Food Marketing Institute

# Keeping produce perfect

Most raw fruits can be left out for a short time on the countertop in a bowl or a basket. Once the fruit ripens or is cut, however, you need to refrigerate it to prevent rot and mold (that's assuming you don't eat it as soon as it's ripe, of course). Most raw vegetables need to be refrigerated, but potatoes and onions are best stored at cool room temperature between 55 and 60°

Fahrenheit, away from the light. Oddly enough, don't put potatoes and onions together in the same box or basket because their natural gases interact and cause the potatoes to rot more quickly.

I had an aunt who stored her potatoes (and sometimes onions) in the legs of old clean pantyhose, as shown in Figure 22-1. She claimed they lasted longer this way because the nylon allowed more air to circulate around them. She dropped them one by one into a cut-off leg and tied a knot between each one to separate them, then hung the whole thing from a hook in the cellar.

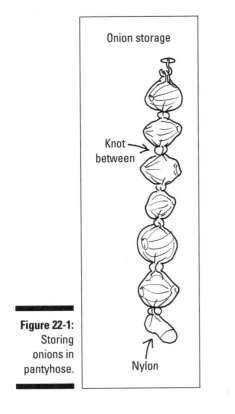

**Figure 22-1:**
Storing
onions in
pantyhose.

Table 22-2 presents guidelines for the maximum amount of time to safely store fresh produce.

| Table 22-2 | Timelines for Keeping Fresh Produce | | |
|---|---|---|---|
| *Fruits* | *Shelf Life* | *Refrigerator* | *Freezer* |
| Apples | 1–2 days | 3 weeks | Cooked, 8 months |
| Bananas | Until ripe | 2 days (skin blackens) | Whole, peeled, 1 month |

| Fruits | Shelf Life | Refrigerator | Freezer |
|---|---|---|---|
| Citrus fruits | 10 days | 1–2 weeks | Do not freeze |
| Grapes | 1 day | 1 week | Whole, 1 month |
| Peaches, nectarines | Until ripe | 3–4 days | Sliced, lemon juice & sugar added, 2 months |
| Pears, plums | 3–5 days | 3–4 days | Do not freeze |
| **Vegetables** | **Shelf Life** | **Raw, Refrigerated** | **Blanched or Cooked and Frozen** |
| Asparagus | None | 3–4 days | 8 months |
| Beans, green or waxed | None | 3–4 days | 8 months |
| Cabbage | None | 1–2 weeks | 10–12 months |
| Carrots, parsnips | None | 2 weeks | 10–12 months |
| Cucumber | None | 4–5 days | Do not freeze |
| Garlic, ginger root | 2 days | 1–2 weeks | 1 month |
| Lettuce (iceberg) | None | 1–2 weeks | Do not freeze |
| Lettuce (leaf) | None | 3–7 days | Do not freeze |
| Spinach | None | 1–2 days | 10–12 months |
| Tomato | Until ripe | 2–3 days | 2 months |

Source: Food Marketing Institute

# Handling take-out foods

We're now a nation of take-out foods, from the salad bar to the deli counter to the hot dog stand. Most take-out foods are eaten right on the spot, but often we buy it early in the day to eat for dinner later. Just remember that these foods are perishable; although they're cooked, they can cause illness when not handled carefully. Keep cold foods cold by placing them in the refrigerator.

Any food that's already hot when you pick it up should be eaten within two hours. To keep it safely, put it in a 200° oven so that its internal temperature registers 140° Fahrenheit on a meat thermometer.

## Dealing with a power outage

If the refrigerator goes on the blink or if the power goes out, what should you do? First, check the cause of the trouble. It could be a blown fuse or an accidental disconnection, and you may be able to restore operation easily yourself. Without power, the food in the fridge will stay cool for about four to six hours. Food in a full freezer will stay frozen for about two days with the door shut.

If the power isn't going to come back on before then, try to move the food to a freezer or refrigerator that's still functioning — possibly at a neighbor's house or a nearby school. If you can't move the food, get some blocks of dry ice to put on top of packaged food. Be sure to handle the dry ice carefully according to instructions from the ice store

If you aren't going to eat the take-out food within two hours, break the food up into small amounts and store them covered in shallow containers in the refrigerator. Two hours is the limit that any perishable food should be left at room temperature. After that, throw it out.

# Providing the Perfect Pantry

The shelf life of any food is determined by many factors before you even pick it up in the store. The timelines given in Table 22-3 are general guidelines to follow — some foods will last longer and some less than the times suggested. Follow storage instructions on the label, if any.

| Table 22-3 | How to Care for Packaged Foods | | |
|---|---|---|---|
| *Type of Food* | *Unopened, on Shelf* | *Opened, in Refrigerator* | *Opened, on Pantry Shelf* |
| Baking powder | 6 months | N/A | 3 months |
| Baking soda | 18 months | N/A | 6 months |
| Barbecue sauce, bottled | 12 months | 4 months | 1 month |
| Biscuit or pancake mix | 15 months | N/A | Use by date on package |
| Flour, white | 6–12 months | N/A | 6–8 months |
| Flour, whole wheat | 1 month | 6–8 months | N/A |

| Type of Food | Unopened, on Shelf | Opened, in Refrigerator | Opened, on Pantry Shelf |
|---|---|---|---|
| Beans (dried), lentils, split peas | 12 months | N/A | 12 months |
| Canned goods, low acid (meat, poultry, fish, gravy, stew, soups, beans, carrots, corn, pasta, peas, potatoes, spinach) | 2–5 years | 3–4 days | N/A |
| Canned goods, high acid (juices, fruit, pickles, sauerkraut, tomato soup, foods in vinegar-based sauce) | 12–18 months | 5–7 days | N/A |
| Catsup, tomato; cocktail sauce; chili sauce | 12 months | 6 months | N/A |
| Cereal, ready to eat | 6–12 months | N/A | 3 months |
| Coffee, beans in nonvacuum bag | 1–3 weeks | 3–4 months, frozen | N/A |
| Coffee, ground, canned | 2 years | 2 weeks | N/A |
| Crackers | 8 months | Frozen or refrigerated, 3–4 months | 1 month |
| Gravy, jarred and canned | 2–5 years | 1–2 days | N/A |
| Herbs, dried | 1–2 years | N/A | Stored in cool, dark place, 1 year |
| Jams, jellies, preserves | 12 months | 6 months | N/A |
| Juice boxes | 4–6 months | 8–12 days | N/A |
| Mayonnaise, commercial | 2–3 months | 2 months | N/A |
| Milk, canned evaporated | 12 months | 4–5 days | N/A |

*(continued)*

### Table 22-3 *(continued)*

| Type of Food | Unopened, on Shelf | Opened, in Refrigerator | Opened, on Pantry Shelf |
|---|---|---|---|
| Mustard | 12 months | 1 year | N/A |
| Oils olive or vegetable | 6 months | 4 months | 4–6 months |
| Nuts, jars or canned | 12 months | 4–6 months (frozen, 9–12 months) | N/A |
| Pasta, dry, eggless | 2 years | N/A | 1 year |
| Pasta, dry egg noodles | 2 years | NA | 1–2 months |
| Rice, white or wild | 2 years | 6 months | 1 year |
| Rice, brown | 1 year | 6 months | 1 year |
| Salad dressing, commercial, bottled | 10–12 months | 3 months | N/A |
| Salsa, picante and taco sauces | 12 months | 1 month | N/A |
| Shortening, solid | 8 months | N/A | 3 months |
| Spices, whole and ground | 2–4 years | N/A | included in total |
| Spices, paprika, red pepper, chili powder | 2 years | Store in refrigerator | N/A |
| Tea, bags | 18 months | N/A | 12 months |
| Tea, loose | 2 years | N/A | 6–12 months |

*Source: Food Marketing Institute*     *N/A = not applicable*

Most packaged foods stay fresh and safe for a relatively long time unless the container is damaged. To keep foods fresh-tasting and safe from bugs after you've opened them, it's best to transfer the foods to a glass or plastic container with a tight-fitting lid. Label the jar with any information you'll need: the type of food, the date you put it in the container, and any necessary cooking instructions.

If you're tired of making labels, just cut off the package label and tape it to the jar or slip it in under the lid.

## Storing canned food

I think most of us feel that food in cans and jars can be stored till the first family buys a condo on the moon. It keeps for a long time, but not forever. (Refer to Table 22-3.) Any packaged or canned food should be stored at a moderate, dry temperature, away from the heat of the kitchen range, the oven, refrigerator, freezer exhaust, and furnace. Extremely high temperatures can shorten the food's shelf life or reduce its quality and can actually damage the food. When you're stocking the shelves, pull the older cans to the front and put the new cans from the store in the back.

Cans or jars that contain spoiled food often have dented seams, bulges, cracks, or leaks, and lids that are bulging or dented. Go through your pantry periodically. If you find any can or jar that looks damaged, don't taste it — throw it out. Canned food can be contaminated with *botulism,* which causes serious illness if consumed.

After you eat any canned food, store the leftovers in a covered container in the refrigerator and eat them within a couple of days. Keeping leftover food in its can is not unsafe, but the food can develop a bitter taste.

Read the instructions on all your food labels. And refer to Table 22-3 for information on how you should care for your packaged foods.

## Storing bakery items

Bakery items prepared with custard, meat, or vegetables, whipped cream, and eggs must be refrigerated. Breads not containing these ingredients can be kept on the shelf, but if you spot any mold forming on the surface, throw them away. Table 22-4 presents timelines for safely storing baked goods.

| Table 22-4 | Timelines for Storing Bakery Items | | |
|---|---|---|---|
| *Type of Food* | *Shelf Life* | *Refrigerator* | *Freezer* |
| Bread, commercial | 2–4 days | 7–14 days | 3 months |
| Bread, flat (tortillas, pita) | 2–4 days | 4–7 days | 4 months |

*(continued)*

**Table 22-4 (continued)**

| Type of Food | Unopened, on Shelf | Opened, in Refrigerator | Opened, on Pantry Shelf |
|---|---|---|---|
| Cakes, angel food, sponge | 1–2 days | 7 days | 2 months |
| Cakes, chocolate | 1–2 days | 7 days | 4 months |
| Doughnuts, glazed, cake | 1–2 days | 7 days | 1 month |
| Doughnuts, cream-filled | None | 3–4 days | Do not freeze |
| Muffins | 1–2 days | 7 days | 2 months |
| Pies, cream | None | 3–4 days | Do not freeze |
| Pies, fruit | 1–2 days | 7 days | 8 months |
| Pies, pumpkin | 2 hours | 3–4 days | 1–2 months |

*Source: Food Marketing Institute*

For more information about safe handling, preparation, and storage of food, the following sources have a wealth of information:

✔ USDA's Meat and Poultry Hotline: 1-800-535-4555; 10:00 a.m. to 4:00 p.m. Eastern time, Monday through Friday; recorded messages available 24 hours a day.

✔ FDA's Food Information and Seafood Hotline;1-800-332-4010; recorded message and fax service available 24 hours a day.

✔ Partnership for Food Safety Education Web Site at www.fightbac.org.

# Part VI
# The Part of Tens

The 5th Wave    By Rich Tennant

"They're relatively quiet and they keep food scraps from accumulating on the countertop."

## In this part . . .

*H*ere's a special Dummies treat for you — tens of tips and tricks that make managing your household tasks quicker and safer. Find ten things you can do around your home in ten minutes each, ten things that can accomplish a great cleanup if you've got only ten minutes total to do it in, ten aids for folks in wheelchairs or who have arthritis or other physical ailments, and the biggest ten of all — ten tips for hiring help. Even people who love to clean can use a break once in a while. Indulge yourself, and have fun with your home.

# Chapter 23

# Ten Things You Can Do in Ten Minutes

You may not have an entire afternoon to straighten the closet or clean up the garage, but everyone has at least ten minutes at some point when they can get *something* done.

Looking at your chores as little bursts of energy rather than as hopeless hours of drudgery will help you get more done in less time. The chores in this chapter are some you can do while talking on the phone, waiting for a repair person, or watching TV — painless enough, when you know they're going to end soon.

## Clean Out a Junk Drawer

You may think that this takes more than 10 minutes, but if you stay focused, you can do it in the ten-minute time limit. This is a good task to do while talking on the phone.

Put a box on a counter or desktop next to the drawer to hold things that need to be moved. Then dump everything out of the drawer onto the counter or desktop and ruthlessly go through the stuff. Throw away any old batteries, no-name keys, dried up glue, and other unneeded junk. Anything that belongs elsewhere, put in the box.

After you're finished, you will still have a junk drawer, just one with a lot less junk. When you have another free ten minutes, put the stuff in the box back where it belongs.

# Update Your Address Book

Times change and so do people. I bet you'll find that about 10 percent of the numbers in your address book are obsolete. Go through and cross out any numbers that no longer exist; if they're on a rolodex, remove the cards or correct them. Take another ten minutes, another time, if you've got a large list.

# Clean the Front of the Refrigerator

Since the invention of the magnet, most refrigerators have become repositories for everything from children's artwork to schedules to favorite photos. Remove everything that's been there more than a couple months and either throw it away or file it in the household file. Then wash down the door and replace the items you need.

# Straighten Your Desk

Nothing makes me feel more chaotic than a messy desk. Straightening it up shouldn't take longer than ten minutes if you have your folder and file system set up. See Chapter 2 for more details.

Fast decisions are *de rigeur* when straightening your desk: Pick the item up, file it, or throw it away. Put anything else that belongs on your desk in neat little piles on top or in the appropriate drawers. (Invest in pencil holders and other desktop organizers if you're overloaded with stuff.) This may be as close as you get to feeling like a CEO (Chief Executive Officer, in case you've never aspired to that height).

# Change the Sheets

I hate to change the sheets. Maybe it's because it's hard to get to the side of my bed or because the sheets don't fit. But if you change sheets fast, it's over before you know it — just like a shot at the doctor's office. The trick is to attack the bed the way professional maids do a million times a day in hotels: Complete one side of the bed and then the other.

1. **Put on the bottom sheet and tuck it in on one side. (I like to start on the right.)**

2. **Add the top sheet and the blanket together. Starting at the top, tuck in both, working along the right side from the top to the bottom of the bed.**

3. At the foot of the bed, lift up the mattress and push the sheet under it at the end of the bed. Make a 45-degree-angled corner on the side with the blanket and sheet together and tuck it in on the right side.

4. Go to the other side, pull the sheet and the blanket taut, and repeat what you did on the first side.

# Hand Wash Some Clothes

You can preserve delicates and lingerie if you hand wash them often, and sometimes you need one thing cleaned in a hurry.

Hand washing is no chore at all if you do a little at a time. See Chapter 11 for information on how to hand wash your clothes.

# Clean Out Your Purse or Briefcase

Talk about black holes. You can quickly clean these out with the "dump and purge" method. Sit at a large table or on the floor with a wastebasket nearby. Pour out everything that's inside so you can see it all at once. Throw away all those crumpled-up receipts, sticky notes to yourself, dried up pens, gum wrappers, and other trash. Try to group all the categories of things together: pens, wallet and checkbook, comb and makeup, organizer, and so on. If you don't have any pockets inside, consider storing each category in zip-top plastic bags to keep everything separate. Just be prepared for weird comments when people see your purse filled with plastic bags.

# Straighten Out the Medicine Cabinet

This should be easy and fast. Look at the expiration dates of all your medicines and throw them out if they're outdated. Get rid of rusty razor blades, makeup more than six months old, dried-up perfume, used-up lipstick . . . you know the drill. Wipe off the shelves with a damp paper towel. Put plastic lids under the shaving cream or any other metal container to prevent rust rings in the future.

# Reduce Your Junk Mail

Send a postcard to the Direct Marketing Association and ask to have your name taken off all lists. On the card, include your name and address exactly as it appears on all your mailing labels. If you receive mail addressed to two or more different names or addresses, include this information as well. Send to Mail Preference Service, P.O. Box 9008, Farmington, NY 11735-9008.

# Sweep or Vacuum One Room

A clean sweep or fresh vacuuming works wonders for a room, and if you do it regularly, you can do it quickly. Nothing makes a room look cleaner faster. See Chapter 7 for more about caring for floors.

# Chapter 24

# The Best Ten Minute-By-Minute Cleanups

- - - - - - - - - - - - - - - - - - - - - - - - - - - - - - - - - - - - - - - - - - - - - - - - - -

## In This Chapter

▶ Swift solutions for tidying up the kitchen and bath

▶ Quick ways to hide and sort clutter

▶ Fast fixes for freshening the air

- - - - - - - - - - - - - - - - - - - - - - - - - - - - - - - - - - - - - - - - - - - - - - - - - -

The house is a mess, but who cares? You deserve a break and you're just about to settle down in your favorite chair when the phone rings. You hesitate, should you answer it? Will it be another annoying telemarketer, or someone offering you a million dollars. At the last possible moment, you jump up and get it. It's Aunt Bessie, your mom's sister. Her train got delayed so she's going to drop in and isn't it great, she's only a half a mile away. "Great," you mumble out loud. Inside you're cursing: I knew I shouldn't have answered it! Don't panic, you don't have time to clean what really needs cleaning, but you can fix up things so no one will notice the grime. If you can't get to all of these, pick and choose the ones you think are most important. Here's the plan:

✔ **Shut the doors:** What they don't see won't hurt them, right? People don't have to see everything. Focus your cleaning on the few critical rooms your guests will go to (probably the bathroom and the living room) and shut out the rest. Close the doors to anything unsightly — a messy cabinet, unmade beds, the basement, and so on. You can clean these later or just choose to leave them that way.

✔ **Get rid of the clutter:** Grab a big basket or a shopping bag. Go around quickly and pick up everything that's on the floor or out of place and throw it in the basket. Hide the basket where no one will see it. This one move will improve things 100 percent.

✔ **Make perfect piles:** Stack the magazines, books, and newspapers that are left in nice, neat piles. Make sure you put your classy magazines on top of the piles. If things are orderly, people may think they're decorating accessories. After all, some photographers I know use stacked books for coffee tables.

- ✔ **Freshen the bathroom:** Take a damp paper towel and give the counter, the sink, and the toilet a quick swipe. Pick up any towels on the floor and fold them (if they're clean) or put them in the clutter basket (if they're dirty) to be dealt with later. Hang up a couple of pretty guest towels (that you save just for unexpected guests) on the towel bar. Rinse out the soap dish and put in a fresh bar of soap.

- ✔ **Neaten the kitchen:** Remove any dirty plates, glasses, utensils, and platters from the countertops and stuff them in the dishwasher. My sister likes to stuff everything in a cold oven — you just have to remember to remove them before turning on the oven the next time. Or pile them neatly in the sink if the dishwasher is full or if you aren't lucky enough to have one. Get rid of any dirty kitchen towels or mitts and replace them with clean ones. Wipe off the countertop with a damp sponge.

- ✔ **Dust off anything big:** Dust on small things is easy to ignore. On something large, it can be a screaming indicator that dusting is not your favorite household chore. I'm always amazed when I'm home during the day how much daylight makes the dust stand out. You can even see it floating in the air! Check the piano, the large mirror in the hall, your black leather sofa, the TV screen, and if you spot those little particles of dirt, wipe them off quickly with a slightly damp cloth.

- ✔ **Make something sparkle:** Most people notice shiny objects — whether it's a diamond ring, a silver candlestick, or a brass trophy. Spend a couple seconds polishing the brass frame on top of the TV, the silver bowl on the coffee table, or the chrome faucet. Some sparkle gives your guests the impression that your whole house is thoroughly clean. A quick wipe with a soft, lint-free cloth will probably do the trick.

- ✔ **Clean off the floor:** Look around the floor and use your handheld vacuum to pick up any obvious dustballs or pieces of dirt. Double check around the legs of sofas tables and chairs — dust seems to accumulate there. Shake out the mat by the front door.

- ✔ **Polish the telephone:** Telephone? Yes, telephone. Peg Bracken in *The I Hate To Housekeep Book* insists that the telephone is one of the most important things to clean before guests arrive. It's often dirty, but we're used to the grime. And yet, guests get a real close-up-and-personal look when they make a call (as they often do). Take a second to wipe off the handpiece and buttons with a cloth slightly dampened with household cleaner.

- ✔ **Light a scented candle:** For guests, and for myself, I often light a scented candle. It makes a room inviting and cozy in an instant. But even better, the aroma can also mask any offending garbage odor, cooking smells, or just stale air. I love the scent of evergreen, but vanilla or cinnamon is nice too. If lighting candles during the day is not your thing, give the rooms a last minute shot of fragrant room deodorizer. Or do something really simple; open the window and let in some fresh air.

# Chapter 25

# Ten Tips for Hiring Help

*T*his chapter provides not only guidelines that will help you choose the right help, but also tips for creating a good relationship after you've hired them.

## Don't Feel Guilty about Hiring Help

You're too busy, you hate to clean, your family is a bunch of slobs, you haven't washed the walls in ten years, you want to support the economy — all good reasons to hire a cleaning service. When you realize you need help, go for it. Don't be haunted by the old adage: You should clean up your own messes. The guilt will go away fast when you recognize how much easier and more comfortable your life will be with a clean home.

## Decide What Kind of Service You Need

You can choose from many types of cleaning services. If you have one big job you want done, such as carpets, windows, floors, or upholstery, call a company that specializes in those services and has the latest equipment and products to do your cleaning in the most efficient manner. It should be able to handle any problem that arises.

If you need someone to help with general housecleaning, check into a cleaning service or hire a freelance housecleaner. Most cleaning services will tackle everything from washing walls to room-by-room cleaning and have a large staff so they can replace your person when sick. A freelancer may prefer to do just light-duty cleaning but also may be more willing to run errands, do your laundry, or shop for groceries. Decide what is best for you.

# Interview the Candidates

Before you even begin your quest, don't forget to ask friends and neighbors for references and suggestions. Their experiences and suggestions, including names and phone numbers, may save you a heap of time.

It goes without saying that you should interview any worker who will be coming into your home on a regular basis. I like to talk to people face-to-face because I feel that gut reactions go a long way. But if you don't want strangers coming to your home before you know who they are, interview over the phone.

What should you ask the candidates? Before hiring any housecleaner, discuss exactly what *you* want them to do. Some may routinely wash the floor, dust the furniture, or scrub down the stove but won't wash the walls or windows unless asked. Don't assume they'll do everything you want them to do. Ask up front if they have any restrictions or things they won't do.

Find out answers to the following:

- ✔ What exactly does their fee cover? For example, do they charge for a minimum number of hours?

- ✔ Ask about what happens during their vacations, and who will come if they are sick. If you are interviewing freelance housekeepers, establish up front who (if anyone) will replace them when they are sick. The substitute may not be acceptable, or you may be uncomfortable allowing an unfamiliar person into your home.

- ✔ Find out how long they've been in business and what kind of training they offer their employees.

- ✔ Ask for a complete list of names of people who will be coming to clean.

# Get References

Always get references, whether you're hiring a freelancer or a service. Ask for at least two or three names and call them. Don't be satisfied with just a letter of reference that could be written by anyone. Ask the person supplying the reference specific questions so you'll know that he or she is a bona fide employer who has actually hired the person in question. If you're considering a service, call the Better Business Bureau to find out if any complaints have been filed against the company's name.

# Get Proof of Bonding and Liability

Things happen, as the saying goes. And if you're going to have a cleaning service in your home, you're wise to be prepared for any mishap. The Maids International, Inc., a nationwide cleaning service, recommends that you see written proof of bonding and liability insurance. (Bonding means that the service has registered money up front to insure payment of any theft claims; liability insurance covers breakage on items in the home and injury to the homeowner.) Make sure the company is *third-party fidelity* or *third-party employee dishonesty* bonded, which protects the maid service and the homeowner against theft from the employee. Ask to see the company's Certificate of Insurance that lists the limits for bonding (usually around $25,000) and liability insurance. Look for a current date and the signature, name, address, and phone number of the insurance agent. You can call the agent to verify that the company's certificate is authentic.

# Find Out What Cleaning Products and Tools They Use

Discuss who supplies the cleaning products and what equipment the cleaners use. Some cleaning services like to bring their own brands and even their own mops and vacuums. Ask to see a list of what they use. This list could be a real issue in a house where family members are allergic to certain products or if the agency routinely uses strong or toxic products to clean areas where kids or pets play. If you have certain brands you prefer that they use, specify the brands ahead of time and stock up before they arrive.

# Establish a Routine

Make a definitive list of what you need done on each visit. You may want the home cleaners to vacuum the rug, dust the shelves, clean out the bathroom, and straighten out the kitchen. Don't assume that they will know what needs to be done without anyone telling them.

Write the chores down in the order of importance so you won't be disappointed if what you considered the big job was left undone. Also note any changes in the weekly routine. If you washed the kitchen floor before they came and you need the basement stairs cleaned instead, put a big star next to "Clean the stairs" on your list (or whatever other indication you agree on for a change) and let them know they don't need to wash the kitchen floor.

# Show How You Want It Done

If you have any special ways you want things done, show the person before he or she starts. You may dust the furniture with a special cloth, wash your dark clothes in cold water, or fold a complete sheet set together. Do a complete run-through with the person and write down anything needed for future reference. You can't expect everyone to have the same cleaning habits that you have, and this pre-planning will save both of you frustration.

# Clean Before They Come

I know you hate to hear this, but it's really more efficient to spend a few minutes picking up clutter before the cleaning crew comes. You're paying them to clean, and that's tough to do if too much stuff is in the way. Remove stray shoes, newspapers, and magazines from the floor you want them to vacuum. Hang up the clothes covering the furniture you want them to polish. One incentive: If the house cleaners put your stuff away, you may never find it.

# Don't Dodge Uncle Sam

If you pay a housekeeper or maid $1,100 a year or more, the law says you must pay Social Security and other taxes for that person. Most professional cleaning services withhold taxes for their employees, but you should check to make sure before you hire them. If the person is a freelancer, you may be required to pay Social Security taxes and state employment taxes for them. Your accountant should be able to advise you on what you owe. Or call the Internal Revenue Service or go to their Web site at www.ustreas.gov and look for the Household Employers Tax Guide. Also contact your state tax agency to see what state or local taxes you need to pay.

# Chapter 26

# Ten (Or so) Tips for the Physically Challenged

● ● ● ● ● ● ● ● ● ● ● ● ● ● ● ● ● ● ● ● ● ● ● ● ● ● ● ● ● ● ● ● ● ● ● ● ● ● ● ● ● ● ● ● ● ●

### In This Chapter

▶ Making floors and stairs safe

▶ Creating a safe environment in kitchens and bathrooms

▶ Locating financial assistance for remodeling and specialized equipment

● ● ● ● ● ● ● ● ● ● ● ● ● ● ● ● ● ● ● ● ● ● ● ● ● ● ● ● ● ● ● ● ● ● ● ● ● ● ● ● ● ● ● ● ● ●

*M*aking your home safer for the physically challenged is easy — if you know what to look out for. Here are some basic safety and convenience tips to make your home much more accessible for the elderly, wheelchair-confined, and others with special needs:

✔ **Make floors safe:** Remove all throw rugs, if possible, in the home. They make falling too easy and can get caught in walkers and canes. Secure any door mats to the floor surface with double-sided carpet tape, tacks, or staples. If you have wood floors, avoid using any wax or polish that will leave the floor slippery and always wear shoes or slippers with treads in them.

✔ **Batten down the bathroom:** The bathroom is one of the easiest places to slip and fall. You should have at least two grab bars to lean on while climbing in and out of a slippery bath. Mount them securely to shower or tub walls. Bars should support at least 250 pounds and be well anchored into wall studs. Before installing, check with your local govement for building code recommendations.

Nonslip adhesive strips or a rubber mat on the floor of the tub or shower also help prevent falls.

A tub seat is another help for getting in and out of the bath. Portable or permanently installed, it enables you to sit in the bathtub and take a bath or shower without dealing with raising and lowering yourself onto the floor of the tub.

Consider whether any the following suggestions would work for you:

- Low-hanging mirrors that can be used by a seated person

- Soap caddie hung over the shower head to hold shampoo and other toiletries at an easy-to-reach level

- Long-handled bath sponges or scrubber, and liquid soap

- Good lighting around the sink for those with poor eyesight

  You may also find it helpful to install a raised toilet seat and/or handrails around the lavatory.

✔ **Prevent falls on stairs:** Put handrails along both sides of steps, inside and outside the home, to help maintain balance and give support whether you're going up or down. Don't make the rail too wide: You should be able to grasp it firmly with your thumb and fingers. If you want carpeted stairs, make it low pile carpet and firmly attach it at the edges and bottom. Check its condition regularly and repair any loose or worn spots that could cause falls. If your stairs aren't carpeted, put down nonskid tape in a bright color or rubber stair treads near the edge of each riser. Don't use throw rugs at the bottom of stairs and avoid storing things in bags or boxes on the stairs. Be careful when you're wearing shoes that are easy to slip in. If you have trouble climbing the stairs, relocate your bedroom and living space onto the same level.

✔ **Make entrances and exits easy:** A ramp is often recommended to help people in wheelchairs enter the home or go from level to level. But before you install it, consider the needs of the person who will be using it. Bifocal wearers often have trouble estimating the correct distance or incline of a ramp. If the ramp is wood, make sure it's covered with a non-skid deck paint. For a couple of steps or a short distance, portable ramps are available.

At the very least, keep the sidewalks or walkways well maintained. Remove toys, garden equipment, and other clutter from the surface. Shovel off snow and spread sand on iced-up sidewalks. The outside should be well lit to prevent falls and offer security.

✔ **Store frequently used items low:** Keeping things accessible is even more important for people who may be confined to a wheelchair or have difficulty balancing and reaching. In the kitchen, store things in the base cabinets if you're confined to a wheelchair. Or put items on rolling carts that can be moved out of the way when not in use. Get a long handled *grabber* to retrieve items on higher shelves. In a pinch, use barbecue or fireplace tongs if you can grip them tightly. Lazy susan turntables inside deep cabinets and on deep shelves can move things closer to your reach.

In the bedroom, put in a second, lower, closet bar for short items like shirts, and skirts to make it easier for someone who has a problem reaching (it also doubles the closet space).

✔ **Replace the faucets and doorknobs:** Installing a lever-type door handle makes it easy for everyone to open a door, whether you're a person with arthritis or carrying a heavy bag. The door can be opened with an elbow or knee if your arms are full. For temporary help, wind some rubber bands around the largest part of the knob to make it easier to grasp. Or get padded doorknob covers, which are available in hardware stores. In the kitchen and bathroom, single lever faucets let you control water temperature and volume with a hand or elbow. If you have separate controls for hot and cold water, wrist blades are available from many plumbing supply and hardware stores. They are wide, wing-type handles that can be easily pushed with the heel of a hand or arm.

✔ **Light your house well:** Good lighting in all areas of the house will help you to avoid falls and avoid frustration. People with failing vision due to illness or age need more light. For simple starters, use higher watt bulbs (check to make sure that they're safe for the fixtures) or put out more lamps. Install compact fluorescent bulbs under kitchen cabinets or inside closets. Make sure that stairs are well lit with switches at easily accessible heights — 44 to 48 inches is good for kids, people with hands full, and those in a wheelchair. Replace standard toggle light switches with rocker switches that are easier to flip on with the palm of your hand or elbow. Hook up lamps and fixtures to light-sensitive controls so that they turn on automatically when it gets dark.

✔ **Lower water temperature:** Lower the hot water thermostat to 120°F or less to cut down the chance of scalding in the bath or kitchen. Even better, put in an antiscald temperature control that keeps the water temperature from exceeding an established limit.

✔ **Get a grip:** Simple household chores can present problems if you have arthritis or can't grasp things tightly. For opening cans, get an electric can opener or one of those hand-held, wedge-shaped openers for screw-on lids. If you have a hard time holding onto household tools like brooms and shovels, pad the handle with foam pipe insulation (available at the hardware store). It's slit on one side so you can just slip it over the handle. Use rubber bands or duct tape to keep it in place. Just wearing rubber gloves can help when you're trying to grasp a slippery item or open a jar top. Sprinkle some cornstarch inside the gloves so they'll be easy to remove. Put items such as shampoo and ketchup in small squeeze bottles, which eliminates heavy containers to lift and tops to unscrew. Put long cords on shades or draperies to make them easier to pull up and down (if you don't have any young children in the house).

✔ **Make your kitchen user-friendly:** If you have knobs on your cabinets, change to large D-shaped handles on cabinet doors that are easier to grip. If possible, create several work surface heights so food preparation can be done standing or sitting. If you can't rearrange countertops, put in a table so you can sit down while preparing food. Or lay a cutting board across a pulled-out drawer for a lower work area. A wheeled cart with a butcher block top can provide another solid work surface and make it easy to move food or appliances from place to place.

Another energy saver: Put a bowl on the countertop to hold vegetable peels and other garbage while you're cooking. It will save you from bending down until you're finished.

For people in a wheelchair, empty out a bottom cabinet under the sink or cooktop so they'll have room for their knees when they pull up to work. Make sure that the controls on the stove are clearly marked so that people with vision impairments can see whether the heat is on or off. Cooktops with controls at the front are easier for people in wheelchairs to use.

If you need to remodel your home to make it more accessible or you need to purchase specialized equipment, there's money out there to help you. You may have to do some detective work and get a little aggressive, but there are many places to turn.

Start by checking with your local or state housing authority. They can tell you about the availability of loans or grants in your area for structural changes. Other sources of information might be state finance agencies, building inspection departments, community development departments, and even private organizations. It pays to be persistent and keep asking questions if you hit a dead end. Lots of sources are available but may require some research.

These three organizations are good places to start in your search for a loan:

- ✔ **The Farmers Home Administration (FmHA).** They give loans for home remodeling and repair in rural areas as well as grants to low income homeowners over 62.

- ✔ **The U.S. Department of Housing and Urban Development (HUD).** They provide a variety of loans for neighborhood improvement. Check with your local government or neighborhood HUD office to see if you qualify.

- ✔ **The Veterans Administration (VA).** If you're a veteran, check to see if you qualify for a low interest loan to make your home more accessible.

# Index

# Discover Dummies™ Online!

The *Dummies* Web Site is your fun and friendly online resource for the latest information about *...For Dummies*® books on all your favorite topics. From cars to computers, wine to Windows, and investing to the Internet, we've got a shelf full of *...For Dummies* books waiting for you!

## Ten Fun and Useful Things You Can Do at www.dummies.com

1. Register this book and win!
2. Find and buy the *...For Dummies* books you want online.
3. Get ten great *Dummies Tips*™ every week.
4. Chat with your favorite *...For Dummies* authors.
5. Subscribe free to *The Dummies Dispatch*™ newsletter.
6. Enter our sweepstakes and win cool stuff.
7. Send a free cartoon postcard to a friend.
8. Download free software.
9. Sample a book before you buy.
10. Talk to us. Make comments, ask questions, and get answers!

Jump online to these ten
fun and useful things at
**http://www.dummies.com/10useful**

**WWW.DUMMIES.COM**

For other technology titles from IDG Books Worldwide, go to
**www.idgbooks.com**

Not online yet? It's easy to get started with *The Internet For Dummies*®, 5th Edition, or *Dummies 101*®: *The Internet For Windows*® *98*, available at local retailers everywhere.

**IDG
BOOKS
WORLDWIDE**

Find other *...For Dummies* books on these topics:
Business • Careers • Databases • Food & Beverages • Games • Gardening • Graphics • Hardware
Health & Fitness • Internet and the World Wide Web • Networking • Office Suites
Operating Systems • Personal Finance • Pets • Programming • Recreation • Sports
Spreadsheets • Teacher Resources • Test Prep • Word Processing

# IDG BOOKS WORLDWIDE
# BOOK REGISTRATION

**Register This Book and Win!**

## We want to hear from you!

Visit **http://my2cents.dummies.com** to register this book and tell us how you liked it!

- ✔ Get entered in our monthly prize giveaway.

- ✔ Give us feedback about this book — tell us what you like best, what you like least, or maybe what you'd like to ask the author and us to change!

- ✔ Let us know any other *...For Dummies*® topics that interest you.

Your feedback helps us determine what books to publish, tells us what coverage to add as we revise our books, and lets us know whether we're meeting your needs as a *...For Dummies* reader. You're our most valuable resource, and what you have to say is important to us!

Not on the Web yet? It's easy to get started with *Dummies 101*®*: The Internet For Windows*® *98* or *The Internet For Dummies*,® 5th Edition, at local retailers everywhere.

Or let us know what you think by sending us a letter at the following address:

*...For Dummies* Book Registration
Dummies Press
7260 Shadeland Station, Suite 100
Indianapolis, IN 46256-3917
Fax 317-596-5498

™
...FOR DUMMIES

BESTSELLING
BOOK SERIES